HERODOTUS, *HISTORIES*, BOOK V

OKLAHOMA SERIES IN CLASSICAL CULTURE

HERODOTUS, *HISTORIES,* BOOK V

TEXT, COMMENTARY, AND VOCABULARY

Philip S. Peek

UNIVERSITY OF OKLAHOMA PRESS : NORMAN

Publication of the book is made possible through
the generosity of Edith Kinney Gaylord.

The original source of Herodotus's Greek text is as follows:
Hérodote, *Herodoti historiae. Recognovit brevique adnotatione critica instruxit Carolus Hude* (Oxonii: E typogr. Clarendoniano, 1908).

Library of Congress Cataloging in Publication Control Number: 2017060304

Library of Congress Cataloging-in-Publication Data

Names: Peek, Philip S., author. | Herodotus. History. Book 5. 2018.
Title: Herodotus, Histories, book V : text, commentary, and vocabulary / Philip S. Peek.
Other titles: Oklahoma series in classical culture ; v. 56.
Description: Norman : University of Oklahoma Press, 2018. | Series: Oklahoma series in classical culture ; volume 56 | "The original source of Herodotus's Greek text is as follows: Hérodote, Herodoti historiae. Recognovit brevique adnotatione critica instruxit Carolus Hude (Oxonii: E typogr. Clarendoniano, 1908)."—T.P. verso. | Includes bibliographical references and index. | Translated from the Greek, with parallel text in English and Greek.
Identifiers: LCCN 2017060304 | ISBN 9780806161037 (pbk. : alk. paper)
Subjects: LCSH: Herodotus. History. Book 5.
Classification: LCC D58.H473 P445 2018 | DDC 938/.03—dc23
LC record available at https://lccn.loc.gov/2017060304

Herodotus, Histories, *Book V: Text, Commentary, and Vocabulary* is Volume 56 in the Oklahoma Series in Classical Culture.

The paper in this book meets the guidelines for permanence and durability of the Committee on Production Guidelines for Book Longevity of the Council on Library Resources, Inc. ∞

⌁ CONTENTS

vii Preface

3 Introduction
32 Map: Selected Places from *Histories*, Book V

35 **TEXT AND COMMENTARY**

151 Appendix A: Case and Function Chart
156 Appendix B: Infinitives
158 Appendix C: The Subjunctive and Optative Moods in Summary
163 Appendix D: Parsing Terms
166 Appendix E: Top 500 Ancient Greek Words

189 Glossary
265 Index

∼ PREFACE

Substantially revised, this book began as the collaboration between my former student Andrew McCaffrey and me. It has been partly funded by the Center for Undergraduate Research and Scholarship (CURS) and by a Building Strength grant of Bowling Green State University, the first awarded in the summer of 2012, the second in the fall of 2017.

Andrew McCaffrey graduated from Bowling Green State University in 2013. He has earned his MA in Latin from the University of Michigan and is currently attending law school at the same institution. He thanks CURS for providing him the opportunity to contribute to this endeavor.

Since 1995 I have taught classics at Bowling Green State University and remain passionate about helping students learn to read ancient Greek. I hope this commentary assists them. I thank Geoffrey Steadman for his texts with running vocabulary, which have helped my students advance their reading skills; James Keenan for all he has been and done; and my ancient Greek students, in particular Bradley Corfman and Jordan Kilpatrick, who have helped me formulate the strategies used in this text. For their help in improving this text I thank the anonymous readers, Chris Baron, James Keenan, James Pfundstein, and Andy Schocket. Finally, I thank my wife, Elaine, and children, Zach, Brandon, and Madeline, for their support, encouragement, and helpful suggestions.

In creating the grammatical parsing and vocabulary, I have been careful
to keep each page error free. Given the many data points in this project, it is
inevitable that I have made mistakes. For these mistakes and any confusion
they cause, I offer my apologies and encourage you to send corrections to
me at peekps@bgsu.edu.

Beginning students of ancient Greek and of Latin learn a pick-and-choose
method of translating: find the subject and the verb and then put the rest of
the pieces of the sentence together as if building an item out of Legos. This
text encourages you to take each word in the order it comes and to strive
to read the language instead of picking and choosing its parts. If adopting
this method inspires you to read, then the text will have proved its worth.

HERODOTUS, *HISTORIES*, BOOK V

∼ INTRODUCTION

NOTE TO STUDENTS

This book owes its existence to my passion for reading ancient Greek and teaching others to do the same. Both give me great pleasure. My goal is for you to develop the skills that make the process of reading this ancient language as natural for you as reading English. In considering authors for you to further your study of ancient Greek, I have chosen Herodotus, one of the most readable of the great writers of Greek prose, because he is a natural storyteller and because his subject matter has wide appeal. Though you may pick up Herodotus and begin reading at any point in any book, Book V offers a narrative filled with insight into Greek and Persian customs, rivalry, and intrigue.

HERODOTUS AND BOOK V

Hailing from Halikarnassos, a cosmopolitan port town on the border between the Greeks and the Persians, Herodotus spans much of the fifth century, living from 484 to 425 B.C.E. In 490 (just before his birth) and again in 480 (just after it), the biggest and most successful empire the world had seen clashed with the fiercely independent city-states of Herodotus's own people. This surprisingly unsuccessful attack on the Greeks by the rich and powerful Persians may have been an impulse behind his life's work, the

Histories or *Researches*. Most biographical information about him is gleaned from this magnum opus, which takes as its subject the great accomplishments of the Greeks and the barbarians and, in addition to other things, the reasons why they warred with one another.[1] In writing it, Herodotus traveled throughout the Mediterranean and the surrounding lands, interviewing sources and looking over data. His compilation of this information became his *Histories,* regarded as the first history of the Western world.

Though parts of these *Histories* read as though Herodotus is a carnival barker, calling his audience to view the strange and incredible world of flying snakes, fish-eating horses, and gold-digging ants, underlying even these fantastic accounts lies a reasonable and rational mind, seeking to present what it has gone to great lengths to discover. Owing in part to these sideshow attractions, Herodotus's reputation, from his own day until now, has seen a variety of judgments. Known as both "the father of lies" and "the father of history," Herodotus is shown by modern historiography and archaeology to be systematic and consistently rational.[2]

As a whole, his work covers eighty-two years—from 560 to 478 B.C.E.—with references going as far back as the first eight gods to exist and as far forward as 430 B.C.E. In Book V he focuses on the Persians: their expansion into Thrakia and Makedonia and their conflict with the Greeks of Ionia. The Persian Megabazos marches through Thrakia into Makedonia, defeating various tribes along the way. In the midst of this Persian expansion, the Ionian Aristagores seeks help from Sparta and from Athens in his bid to have the Ionians revolt.

Within this overarching narrative, Herodotus names over 350 people and places, covering Asia, Africa, and Europe. His narrative begins at an uncertain past time and ends with Aristagores' death in about 497–96. Herodotus has a discursive style, often beginning a tale, offering the relevant

---

1. The *Suda*, a tenth-century Byzantine encyclopedia, notes that Herodotus was of a prominent family and that he went into exile on Samos because of the tyrant Lygdamis. The *Suda* further states that he helped expel Lygdamis and then later voluntarily went to Thurii owing to unpopularity with the people, and that he died there or at Pella.

2. Hornblower (2013, 31) notes that onomastics show Herodotus to have conducted careful research into the Ionian revolt and that epigraphical evidence indicate that he is impressively accurate.

backstory, and then resuming where he left off. His sentences are similarly structured, stating a subject, interrupting with ancillary information, and then completing the thought. In the upcoming section, I mimic a bit his start, pause, and restart style.

In Book V Herodotus lists the customs of the Thrakians, offers insight into the mindset of the Spartans, and records political intrigue at Athens concerning Hippias, Hipparkhos, Kleisthenes, and Isagores. Greek deception gets the better of the Persians. Aristagores brings great destruction on his fellow Ionians. Herodotus leads his audience down the royal road to Sousa and beyond. He presents the origins of the alphabet and the burgeoning of democracy at Athens, freed from tyranny and ruled through ἰσηγορία ("political equality"). Through this great range of topics, Herodotus provides the context needed for understanding the how and why of the upcoming battles of Marathon, Thermopylai, Artemision, Salamis, Plataia, and Mykale, all narrated in Books VIII and IX, the last two of his great work.

HERODOTUS AND HIS MANY READERS

In the preceding section I gave you a glimpse at what is to come in Book V. In what follows I offer you a general introduction to Herodotus and his work. In offering it I make no claim to originality. Rather my aim is accuracy in describing Herodotus and his work. I hope that as you read Book V you will find yourself agreeing with some parts of what I write below and disagreeing with others. I warmly solicit corrections and suggestions for improvement.

In considering the twenty-five hundred years of commentary that Herodotus's work has spawned, it is clear that his readers love to debate and question everything. Herodotus is called religious, skeptical, and a mixture of both.[3] He is a liar, scrupulously accurate, and again some mixture of the

---

3. Asheri et al. (2011, 42) often and understandably steer a middle ground: there is much that is gray in Herodotus's presentation of subjects and acts. Though Herodotus recognizes corruption and political expedience at work in religion, nonetheless a central thesis of his work is the role of the divine in human affairs. For a clear statement of the existence of the gods' influence in human affairs, see Book IX, chapter 100 of Herodotus's work. I will refer to Herodotus's work parenthetically by noting the book, chapter, and, where applicable, line number. For example, (II.14.3) refers to book 2, chapter 14, line 3.

two.[4] For example, of the times in the *Histories* when Herodotus claims direct autopsy (what he has witnessed with his own eyes), some scholars take him at his word, others partly so, and still others barely believe him.[5] For every word Herodotus has written, scholars have written over one thousand. While disagreement is to be seen ultimately in a good light, reading such polarized viewpoints may make you feel like Sisyphos struggling with his rock.

Though divided on many points, scholars credit Herodotus with the invention, in the West, of the genre of history.[6] At work at about the same time as him were Kharon, Hekataios, Skylax, and Xanthos, all helping to create, in varying degrees, this new genre. History, as it was being defined, differs from its predecessor, epic poetry, because it is written in prose and is concerned with recording the truth of what occurred.[7] As Thoukydides (1.22) rightly notes, getting at the truth is difficult even for eyewitnesses owing both to imperfections of memory and to the distortions of bias, both implicit and explicit. In our world with all its advantages, the historical genre remains a subjective one.

In creating this genre, Herodotus focuses on the eighty-two years from 560 to 478 B.C.E. Outside of this frame he refers back to the origins of the first eight gods and forward to events of the Peloponnesian War (431–404 B.C.E.). In crafting his narrative, he makes use of a variety of source material, records events he does and does not believe, and passes judgment where he deems it appropriate. He takes pains to establish the truth of what occurred. Where this is not possible, he still preserves what his sources relate. As he worked, he made mistakes and he got things right.

---

4. Asheri et al. (2011, 22, 56) credit Herodotus with the invention of a new literary genre that accepts creative license where the paradigmatic is of greater consequence than what actually happened. Writing in the century after Herodotus, Aristotle (*Art of Poetry*, 1451b1) makes the opposite point, arguing that poetry, with its focus on general truths, is superior to histories like that of Herodotus, where the focus is on specific facts. Fehling (1989) accuses Herodotus of creative reportage. Romm (2003, viii) writes that "many layers of imaginative material have been added, including speeches and dialogues, omens and portents, folktales and myths." Waddell (1998, 5) finds in him good faith and veracity. I accept a fallible author trying his best to be accurate.

5. Asheri et al. 2011, 6.

6. Asheri et al. (2011, 7–14) and Scott (2005, 9–14) consider the invention of the genre as well as how Herodotus's work came to take the form it currently has.

7. By Aristotle's day history was an established genre (*Art of Poetry*, 1451b1). Herodotus notes that Homer knew that the Trojans did not really have possession of Helen but that he disregarded this fact because it did not suit the requirements of the epic genre (II.116).

When reading his *Histories*, you may be struck by how familiar Herodotus's world appears. From then to now, there is much overlap; there are also
differences. One difference crucial for understanding Herodotus and his
world is the notion that the gods punish wrongdoing and excessive good
fortune.[8] They may chasten the malefactor or one of his relatives, though
innocent and born generations later.[9] Despite being god-loved, Kroisos suffers
for a murder committed some 150 years earlier by his relative Gyges.[10] The
tyrant of Samos, Polykrates, suffers an undeserved death owing to the great
good fortune he has enjoyed throughout his life (III.125). The same good
fortune undoes Kyros (I.214). Pheretime, the wife of Battus III, king of the
Kyrenaians, is killed by the gods for her excessive vengeance (IV.205). The
Spartans suffer for killing Persian heralds (VII.134–37). The Persian Mardo-
nios pays for the murder of the Spartan Leonidas (IX.64). Understanding
such a worldview is essential to understanding Herodotus's belief system.[11]

Fundamental for Herodotus is that the gods exist and cause events to
happen to humans.[12] Though they may punish excessive success, they do not
make innocent mortals do unjust acts.[13] Mortals themselves are accountable

---

8. Thus human prosperity never remains constant: τὴν ἀνθρωπηίην ὧν ἐπιστάμενος
εὐδαιμονίην οὐδαμὰ ἐν τὠυτῷ μένουσαν, ἐπιμνήσομαι ἀμφοτέρων ὁμοίως "knowing
that mortals' prosperity never remains constant, I will mention both together" (I.5.4).

9. Kroisos suffers for his great good fortune (I.34) and for Gyges' wrongdoing (I.91). Though
not without his redeeming qualities, Xerxes is guilty of arrogant pride (VII.24). For a
good discussion on Xerxes' faults and virtues, see Bowie (2007, 10–11). For a full expression of the idea of the divine, see Solon's fragment 13 in M. L. West, trans. (1994), *Greek
Lyric Poetry* (Oxford: Oxford University Press).

10. Asheri et al. think the meeting between Solon and Kroisos is made up for didactic purposes (2011, 34).

11. A contrary view is held by Romm, who writes that "even in matters as deeply personal
as religion, however, it is difficult to say with certainty what Herodotus believed or what
view his text expresses" (Romm 2003, xvii). Though I suggest that Herodotus's faith is
essential to understanding his *Histories,* he does not see a divine hand meddling in all
things. For a discussion on Herodotus's religious views that discusses this very point, see
Scott 2005, 31–32.

12. Bowie argues of the work that "insistent parallelisms are to show that things are not
random but divinely ordered" (2007, 14). Scott cautions against seeing things in the text
that are not there (2005, 25). Both have their points.

13. Asheri et al. argue that the gods are not driven by moral principles but also note that they
can be wise and just (2011, 39). Like mortals the gods are fallible, jealous, unpredictable,
as well as noble and concerned with just thoughts and actions. For their concern with
justice, see II.120.

for their actions.[14] Through prophecy, dreams, and portents, the gods may attempt to dissuade mortals from treading a given path (III.124–25). Conversely, they may encourage them to do wrong when they think mortals should know better: the gods will punish those who merely ask about handing over a suppliant to the enemy to be killed (I.159).[15] A wrong done must be righted through appeasing the offended deity (I.167). Death and suffering brought on by excess and injustice is thus a main theme of his work, as is the gods' hand in influencing events. Herodotus expends so much effort in arguing for the existence of the gods and their influence that perhaps he is reacting to the gainsayers of his day and speaking generally to his contemporary skeptics.[16]

A second difference between then and now is that for the Greeks and for most barbarians the most noble of pursuits was warfare. They despised business and crafts (II.167). Fighting for a just cause or not, males won praise with their bravery.[17] Fighting imparted prestige, and for the Greeks fighting to maintain freedom from oppression gave even more. Though they may

---

14. The Skythians are punished for plundering the temple of Aphrodite (I.105). Kleomenes is punished for his treatment of Demaratos (VI.84). The Persians are killed for profaning Poseidon's sanctuary (VIII.129).

15. Rather than Aristodikos's understanding of how the gods work, Asheri et al. see skepticism and irreverence at work (2011, 42). The Pythia tells the Parians that the gods, through the priestess Timo, were attempting to start Miltiades down a path with a bad ending (VI.135).

16. Since the time of Thales (624–546 B.C.E.), Anaximander (610–546 B.C.E.), and Anaximenes (585–528 B.C.E.), Greek culture has seen a divide between a mathematical and scientific explanation for why things happen and a mythic one. For example, myth says that earthquakes occur because of Poseidon. Thales reasoned that they occur because the earth floats on water. Practitioners of science do not necessarily reject the gods' existence—gods may still be credited with the creation of the earth—but they do seek alternative explanations. Xenophanes (570–475 B.C.E.) argued against the depiction of the gods as recorded by Hesiod and Homer and against the idea that they are fallible and jealous. He posited that they or the one god is unlike mortals in form and in thought. Protagoras (490–420 B.C.E.), an agnostic or atheist, argued that the existence of the gods has no bearing on mortal life and that all values are relative. The Athenians may have expelled him from their city and burnt his works in the market place (Diogenes Laertius 9.51–52; Cicero, *On the Nature of the Gods*, 1.23.6). Anaxagoras (510–428 B.C.E.) correctly explained eclipses and declared the sun to be a stone and not a god. The Athenians brought him to court and had him exiled on charges of impiety and pro-Persian sympathies.

17. The Lydians do not fight like cowards (I.80.6); the Medes are courageous and in the cause of freedom cast off slavery (I.95.2); Phanes is admired for his good judgment and bravery (III.4); the Skythians are admired for their martial prowess (IV.46); the Khians refuse to

have good qualities, may suffer undeservedly, and may do good things, tyrants are nonetheless by definition agents of enslavement and oppression.[18] No amount of do-goodism can counterbalance the injustice of this office, and brave Greek males fight to overthrow tyrants. At the same time, fighting when sure to lose was considered foolhardy (IV.93). Herodotus, the Greeks, and the majority of the cultures Herodotus encountered put warfare and bravery ahead of all else.

In history, as in other fields, researchers view their subjects from biased perspectives.[19] The two differences mentioned above form a part of the bias that informs Herodotus as he examines his world. His search is a broad one, directed at why the Greeks and barbarians fought but also generally at other things: birth, chronology, colonies, customs, deeds, flora and fauna, food, funeral practices, genealogy, geography, great works, marriage, origins, religion, sex. His curiosity and interest in the bizarre prompted English historian Edward Gibbon, best known for his *History of the Decline and Fall of the Roman Empire,* to comment that "Herodotus sometimes writes for children and sometimes for philosophers."[20] Gibbon's observation notwithstanding, in researching his wide variety of topics, Herodotus concerns himself with getting things correct.[21] At times he cannot, and so he simply records what he is told. At other times he wavers, offering variant accounts

---

behave like cowards (VI.15); Boges is praised for his bravery and loyalty to the Persians, choosing to fight the Athenians to the death rather than to flee. In the end he kills all the females and children who survived, throws the precious metals into the river, and kills himself (VII.107). The Persians fight with bravery against the better armed and trained Greeks (IX.62). On the flip side, Histiaios's flight to escape death is described as cowardly (VI.28).

18. Scott argues that Herodotus was neither for nor against democracy but "disliked oppression and approved of fair government of whatever complexion, even, perhaps, that of a tyrant" (2005, 28).

19. For an example of a different history that could have been written, see Plutarch's *On the Malice of Herodotus.* Of course, interpreters of history are subject to the same caveats. For a concise account of subjectivity in analyzing Herodotus, see Scott 2005, 36–37. For myself, I do not propose that my conclusions are the only ones or even the best ones. I can only hope that other readers of Herodotus see him through eyes similar to my own.

20. Edward Gibbon (1776–1789), *The Decline and Fall of the Roman Empire,* ch. 24, fn. 52.

21. For Herodotus's concern for justice and honesty, see II.177. For Herodotus as a conscientious researcher, see Scott 2005, 26, though he restricts this comment to the later books, including Book VI.

and leaving it up to his reader to decide. When he thinks himself able, he passes judgment. Of course, taken as a whole, the *Histories* themselves ultimately offer Herodotus's point of view of how the world works, from the origin of the first eight gods down to the Peloponnesian War.

In Herodotus's research, autopsy reigns supreme. For things he has seen, such as the camel, he speaks authoritatively, though in the case of their legs wrongly (III.103): they do not have four knees. A single "autopsic" source carries weight, and multiple sources who can confirm having seen the same thing are even better. This methodology endows him with an accuracy that archaeology often confirms. It also leads him to mistakes. For Herodotus the world is a messy place, with uneven contours, jealous gods, and corrupt priests—everyone should be able to observe this. As such, it cannot be that, as if drawn by a compass, the earth is a round sphere with Ocean surrounding its lands.[22] Likewise, because of Herodotus's belief that Greece is the center of the world, it cannot be that the sun appeared over the Phoinikians' right instead of their left when they rounded Africa, as they claim to have done (IV.42). He rejects the existence of the Eridanos River and the Kassiterides Islands (probably the British Isles), mainly because no one has provided an eyewitness account (III.115.2). He accepts without question griffins, polygenic rabbits, and black semen ejaculated by Ethiopians and Indians. Despite these mistakes, Herodotus can also be correctly skeptical. Though there is an autopsic source, he rejects the existence of one-eyed men called Arimaspians (III.116.2) on the basis of logic: how can they in all other respects be just like the rest of mankind but in this one characteristic differ so greatly?

In addition to autopsy, Herodotus consults a variety of sources.[23] Written sources of the historical genre he finds lacking.[24] Had he not, he surely would

---

22. Anaximander may have been the first to draw up such a map. See https://en.wikipedia. org/wiki/Anaximander.

23. Hekataios, a contemporary of Herodotus, is believed to be the source for parts of Book II on the Egyptians. Herodotus mentions a painting (IV.88) and cites an inscription for the battle of Thermopylai (VII.228). Herodotus references the writers Aeschylus, Archilochus, Hesiod, Homer, Phrynikhos, Pindar, and Solon and quotes prophecies throughout.

24. These written sources include the "histories" of Kharon, Hekataios, Skylax, and Xanthos. Of these he criticizes Hekataios; he may or may not have read the others. In antiquity he was accused of plagiarism: Pollio wrote a work called Περὶ τῆς Ἡροδότου κλοπῆς (*On the plagiarism of Herodotus*); Porphyry says he copied material for Book 2 from Hekataios (FGRH 1 T22, F324a). For more on the early historians, see Lionel Pearson (1939), *Early Ionian Historians* (Oxford: Clarendon Press).

have given them their due.[25] In large part he depends on oral sources that, when not wholly invented, come from eyewitness accounts.[26] Eyewitness accounts of events, even if triangulated and then written up, remain fallible, mostly because of imperfect memory and partiality. On such accounts history, then and now, though assisted by the invention of video and the smartphone, often relies. This is not to suggest that history cannot get things correct. Rather, humans' fallibility and subjectivity make accuracy a difficult achievement.

Herodotus is aware of history's pitfalls and of humans' ability to make things up.[27] In our world we too are aware of these tendencies. We preserve and pass on much of the past through our culture's collective memory and stories. As such, we tend to remember the past in ways that suit our present.[28] Since Herodotus depends largely on oral history for composing his work, one may think that he gives it a greater degree of reliability than some modern scholars or historians would. Though it may be true, this conclusion is an assumption.

There is evidence that argues against it. The *Histories* contain many examples indicating that its author regularly performed his due diligence. As a member of a culture that accepted lying and deception from both its gods and fellows, Herodotus is duly skeptical, casting doubt on the validity of sources, be they oral or written. In his work's events duplicity plays a central role. Nonetheless the notion that he is too accepting of the validity

25. Asheri et al. write that Herodotus and Thoukydides preferred oral sources without reflection (2011, 16, 18). Though authoritative, this statement lacks substance. Both have chosen to write; this choice suggests a recognition that to them written history has advantages over oral. If the two show a bias for oral history, it is to be explained more by the inadequacy of the written works available to them than to their preference for the oral.

26. Scott supposes family traditions, family histories, man-in-the-street tales, and eyewitnesses (2005, 14–21).

27. On using sources that are themselves concerned with getting things correct, see I.95. It is not so much that Herodotus displays a protohistorical phase of critical thought (Asheri et al. 2011, 23). The literature of his predecessors and contemporaries shows a culture as critically minded as ours. Rather, it is that his intellectual abilities are only as good as the evidence available at the time allows it to be.

28. For entrée into the world of orality and literacy, see Jack Goody and Ian Watt (1963), "The Consequences of Literacy," *Comparative Studies in Society and History* 5, no. 3: 304–45. For remembering the past as suits our present, see Andy Schocket (2015), *Fighting Over the Founders: How We Remember the American Revolution* (New York: NYU Press).

of his oral sources persists.[29] This contention is based to a significant degree on the prevalence in his work of origin stories, the folktale, and the court story.[30] All three display repeating features. The patterning in these tales casts doubt on their validity.[31]

Though aware of the unreliability of his oral sources, Herodotus does fail to be skeptical where circumstances suggest he should be. In saying this I accept that Herodotus is attempting to present to his audience the truth of what happened in the past.[32] The reasons for his failure, then, are difficult to determine. One explanation is that Herodotus, like all historians, is fallible, subject to a variety of factors that skew how he processes events. Just as in science a Newtonian view results in one set of equations and an Einsteinian view in another, so in history a given way of looking at and explaining events necessitates a finite number of conclusions and explanations. Herodotus's worldview constrains his analysis. And so arriving at an accurate understanding of why Herodotus wrote what he did requires looking as carefully as possible through his eyes.

---

29. The argument is that an oral culture is necessarily more willing to believe what they are told (Fontenrose 1978, 128; and Scott 2005, 14). There are reasons to believe that in the final tally they may be more astute at deciphering deception than their more literate counterparts. Be this as it may, the queen of the Massagetai (I.205) and the king of the Ethiopians (III.20–22) both display a perspicuity that argues for the illiterate being less gullible than our modern scholars think them to be. For Herodotus's own attitude toward naïve stories of the Greeks, see II.45.

30. Folk-type narratives take a variety of forms. One of these is that of the industrious maiden (V.12), presented in this way so as to capture a husband. Nikolaos of Damascus, writing some 450 years after Herodotus but using primary sources older than Herodotus, tells a similar tale of Alyattes of Lydia and an industrious Thrakian female. The question of the historicity of this tale type and of tale types and narrative forms in general is one that is not easy to answer. It is true that many narratives fit certain tale types and yet they still may be in essence historically accurate. It is also true that a tale type, by its convenience and because it explains such a variety of things, tends to persist whether it has historicity or not. Also of merit are tale types that most certainly are without any historicity but manage, by other factors, to achieve a validity that transcends their true falsehood. And so it may be argued both of the historian Herodotus and of any tale teller that historical truth is a difficult beast, untamable, of many a form, and irresistible.

31. Hornblower (2013, 32) cautions against arguing that the presence of the folkloric renders the whole unhistoric.

32. Asheri et al. find him, in a positive way, more concerned with paradigmatic truth than with what actually happened (2011, 56).

One constraint is Herodotus's belief of the role of the divine in influencing human affairs.[33] Prophecy is one way the divine exerts itself.[34] Nonetheless it is argued that prophecy, in the *Histories,* is nothing more than a literary construct whose function is foreshadowing.[35] But, for Herodotus, the prophetic is fundamental to the way his universe works. Yes, prophecy may be false and, yes, oracles may be bribed. But ultimately true oracles provide valid predictions and warnings.[36] Ignore them and suffer.

Similar to the divine is the wise adviser, also considered a literary construct. In folktale formula the wise adviser advocates against a particular path and suggests the calamities that inevitably follow. Not strictly divine like prophecy, tragic warners have a real presence in the discussion of most any decision offering risk.[37] Because they are predictive, warners serve a role similar to that of prophecy. Closely aligned with the divine, they are fundamental to Herodotus's worldview. Their divine connection explains why Herodotus is too accepting of their repeated presence in the stories he tells. It also explains Herodotus's failure to be skeptical of their accurate prediction of whatever calamities ensue.[38]

For Herodotus the divine is as self-evident as is the sun's rising and setting. It plays a role in choosing leaders and in affecting the outcome of

---

33. The gods are ultimately responsible for the rain, and if they wish they could destroy the Greeks by bringing on a drought (II.13.3).

34. In I.210, Herodotus notes that the gods attempt to warn Kyros of his impending death and of Dareios's ascent to the throne. At IV.79, the gods warn Skyles of a bad end if he goes through with the initiation into the cult of Dionysus. In VI.27, the gods warn the Khians of an upcoming military defeat. The gods warn the Greeks of upcoming disasters (VI.98). There is a portent that Xerxes will not defeat the Greeks (VII.57). There are prophecies that the Greeks will defeat the Persians (IX.43).

35. Asheri et al. write that oracles, dreams, portents, and prophecies are literary means used to prepare the reader for an impending catastrophe and its moral (2011, 41).

36. At VIII.77, Herodotus states his acceptance of the validity of oracles and prophecies, and at IX.65 he states his view that Demeter keeps the Persians out of her sanctuary because earlier they had burned her inner sanctuary.

37. In the popular culture of our world, Friday's pundits and predictors become Monday's accurate warners.

38. Back writing is a distinct possibility. Back writing can be a deliberate fabrication, an acceptable form of foreshadowing in a new genre that allows for creative license, or a consequence of the way the historian sees the world, as argued here. For a different perspective, see Bowie 2007, 9.

wars. Kandaules is punished and loses his power because he transgresses norms. The gods smile on the conspirators' defeat of the Magi (III.76) and the whinnying of Dareios's horse (III.86). Marked for kingship before he is born, Kyros escapes the death commanded by his grandfather Astyages (I.107–113), is raised by cowherds (I.114–116), and eventually comes to power as king (I.124–130). With the help of the gods, the Athenians drive off the Persians (VII.139). The gods send a storm to destroy some of the Persian fleet so that it is more equal to that of its Greek foes (VIII.13). Herodotus records for his audience the hands of the gods at work in mortal affairs. A consequence of accepting the role of the divine in human affairs is that the chronologically impossible becomes possible. And so the Greeks at Mykale can be informed on the same day of the victory of the Greeks at Plataia, thus giving them a boost in morale and influencing once again a battle's outcome (IX.100). The conclusion of all this is that his acceptance of the miraculous in events helps explain why so many readers find incredible what Herodotus seems too ready to accept.[39]

Though aware that the Greek religious system is far from perfect, Herodotus is respectful of the sacred. The Greeks do not perform intercourse in sanctuaries. Other cultures do, reasoning that if it is permissible for animals to fornicate in sanctuaries, it is for people to too. Herodotus finds this rationale disagreeable (II.64). To act disrespectfully is incomprehensible. He remains silent on divine matters that are to be kept unspoken (II.171). Killing with no justification is unholy (III.120). Desecrating an enemy's corpse is most ungodly (IX.78). And so when Kambyses, king of a culture also respectful of religion, mocks the customary and sacred, he must be mad, otherwise he would not have done so (III.38). Though reverence does not explain why Herodotus may have preferred a negative source about Kambyses over a more positive one, Herodotus's emphasis on being respectful of religion helps explain why his portrait of Kambyses is more negative than it perhaps should be.[40]

---

39. Thus Herodotus may have never thought to concern himself with the chronological difficulties presented in the sending of the man with the shaven head (V.35). Scott attributes his acceptance of the story to an oral culture's lack of interest in precise chronology (2005, 64–65). For a discussion of measuring in Herodotus, see Rubincam 2008.
40. His portrait of Kambyses is biased by his sources (Scott 2005, 6).

Herodotus also sees a connection between a culture's resiliency and its geography and prosperity. Rugged, barren land gives birth to tough and resilient people.[41] Too much good stuff and luxury result in weakness. The impoverished Persians defeat the wealthy Lydians (I.71). The poor and tough Massagetai defeat the now wealthy Persians (I.207–216), as do the poor and tough Greeks in the final books of the history. As the wheel of history turns, similar features in a country's people produce similar results. Plenty produces a contentment that can be bested and that more readily accepts another's sovereignty. The divine, reverence for it, geography, and prosperity all are essential aspects of the way Herodotus views his world.

In attempting to see things through Herodotus's eyes, we are attempting to uncover the story truth of his history. In doing so a fundamental principle is that our author is not deliberately deceptive in presenting the facts of his work. When it comes to Herodotus's numbers, such a principle seems to waver if not completely fall away. We can agree that, human nature being what it is, inflating numbers occurs too often. Even so the numbers in Herodotus appear way too exaggerated (VII.184).[42] But this observation is at odds with the care Herodotus takes in making these hyperinflated calculations. The two are irreconcilable. Nonetheless it may be noted that the care Herodotus takes in making them suggests that he believes in their accuracy; beyond this not much more may be said.[43]

Likewise, Herodotus believes in the accuracy of his speeches and takes care in researching and representing them (II.123). In Herodotean as in Thoukydidean studies, scholars view speeches as the creative license of the author.[44] This creative-license argument contradicts what both historians say. In his section on methods, Thoukydides states his approach: some he

---

41. Redfield's discussion of this phenomenon as a result of Herodotus's need for symmetry is overstated. See James Redfield (1985), "Herodotus the Tourist Author," *Classical Philology* 80, no. 2: 97–118.

42. For a discussion of numbers, see Rubincam 2008.

43. Asheri et al. think Herodotus purposely inflates numbers for literary and didactic purposes (2011, 44–45).

44. Asheri et al. think the invention an accepted part of the new genre (2011, 22). They also think the same of the consultation of oracles and seers, counsels, and debates (41). Flower and Marincola think that Herodotus most likely invented speeches and motivations (2002, 8, 22).

heard and others he got from sources. He notes that his lack of an eidetic memory forced him to write the speeches himself, sticking as closely as possible to both what was actually said as well as to what is typically said on each occasion he writes of.[45] Herodotus, it seems, worked similarly. Recognizing that none of his contemporaries will believe the Persian debate on the best form of government, Herodotus invites the inevitable polemics, happily vouching for the debate's actual occurrence.[46] Accepting that they cannot transcribe speeches word for word, both historians nonetheless say that they have attempted to record what was said as precisely as possible.

Herodotus's presentation of events vouches for his having researched the motivations of his subjects.[47] Upon realizing that Polykrates' good fortune will meet with a bad ending, Amasis breaks off his alliance with him. There could have been several reasons for this, including the ancient belief that bad luck, like a disease, was catching. Herodotus, however, states that Amasis does so in order to save himself from excessive grief when he learns of Polykrates' inevitable suffering (III.43).[48] Having agreed to assist exiled Samians in their quest to return home, the Spartans give a desire for vengeance as their reason for lending aid. The Samians, however, say the Spartans help so as to repay a favor (III.47). Herodotus leaves the question open. Herodotus gives two different motivations for Oroites' murder of Polykrates, again leaving it up to the reader to decide. Herodotus then asserts that part of Oroites' motivation was to prevent Polykrates from establishing a maritime empire (III.122). Herodotus notes that Histiaios lied to the Ionians about the intentions of Dareios, when he says that Dareios intended to uproot and to settle the Ionians in Phoinikia and vice versa. Dareios had no such plans (VI.3). Should his research not offer a motivation

---

45. Imagine that no copy of the Gettysburg Address exists but that the historian is able to consult oral accounts and eyewitness testimony. Though the text is not obtainable, some sense of the overall meaning Lincoln conveyed is.

46. Contemporaries of his and mine, Bowie (2007, 19) for one, disbelieve its occurrence.

47. At VIII.22, Herodotus notes what he thinks were the two reasons for Themistokles' inciting the Ionians against the Persians. At VIII.30, he writes of an inference for a motivation. He guesses at Eurybiades' motivations at VIII.63.

48. Strassler argues that it was Polykrates and not Amasis who broke off the alliance because he had decided to ally with Kambyses so as to protect Samos against Persia's growing strength (2007, 226).

behind an act, Herodotus may offer his own explanation (III.146). In each of these instances we encounter an historian intent on determining the truth of what happened as well as the underlying why. His why embraces ambiguity and accepts complexity.

There are often many reasons behind why events occur. Historians may focus on the big causative factors or on smaller ones. Though he is not unaware of the big causative factors and does name them, Herodotus often sees the ridiculous and petty meddling in affairs. Kroisos suffers because of Kandaules' need to prove to Gyges his wife's beauty (I.7–14). Kambyses attacks Egypt because of a personal grudge (III.1). The theft of a bowl may have influenced Samian and Spartan relations (III.47). Samos is destroyed because of the spite of Maiandrios and owing to a chance encounter between Syloson and Dareios (III.139 and III.146). Dareios attacks the Skythians to punish them for an earlier invasion (IV.1). Chance and Aristagores' debt and fear cause the Ionian revolt (V.35). The Ionian revolt, in turn, leads to the Greeks' burning of Sardis and to the eventual Persian invasion of Greece (V.101). Kleisthenes makes historic reforms at Athens out of contempt for the Ionians (V.69). History's meaning lies in the divine and inevitable as well as in chance and in grudges, envy, jealousy, madness, devotion, and loyalty.

In the above I have argued that much that is found wanting in Herodotus is due to the nature of how he saw his world. If we had a Herodotus perfect in our own eyes, then we would have a history unlike the one we possess. Our imperfect Herodotus displays a curious and capacious intellect that excels at engaging his audience as he presents his research. Throughout, Herodotus maintains the intent behind the thesis of his *Histories,* writing to ensure that

> μήτε ἔργα μεγάλα τε καὶ θωμαστά, τὰ μὲν Ἕλλησι τὰ δὲ βαρβάροισι
> ἀποδεχθέντα, ἀκλεᾶ γένηται
> "the deeds great and marvelous, done by Greeks and barbarians, not
> become forgotten."

Though scholars will continue to debate the merits of Herodotus as a historian, his curiosity and intellect ensure that he will continue to be read.

USING THE TEXT

Running Vocabulary

When beginning to read Greek or Latin, you will spend much time in your Greek-English dictionary, looking up the roughly 80 percent of words that do not occur with regularity. For example, of the 2,230 words in Book V of Herodotus's *Histories,* 1,815 occur ten times or fewer, a staggering 81 percent of the total. Of this 81 percent, 82 percent occur three times or fewer. I need hardly say that while reading Herodotus, you will be spending a lot of time flipping pages of your dictionary or clicking buttons online. This book seeks to ease this burden, enabling you to spend less time looking up words and more time learning to read and enjoying Herodotus's story telling.

I offer two tools to this end: a running vocabulary that corresponds to each page of the text, and a generalized list of the principal parts of verbs. Both are available on the publisher's website, www.oupress.com. Print it out for reference as you read. The running vocabulary glosses all words that are not included in the top five hundred most common ancient Greek words. At book's end there is a glossary that contains these top five hundred and the vocabulary in the PDF. It is a good idea to memorize the five hundred most commonly occurring words and to have an active working knowledge of the way verbs form their principal parts.

After the Greek text you will find grammatical and contextual notes that give narratological, historical, and cultural information. Rather than translating a syntactically complex passage, I direct you to the answer by parsing the essential parts. Rather than identifying strange forms, I have given the corresponding Attic counterparts. Endings typically contracted in Attic are left uncontracted in Herodotus's Ionic dialect—ποιέῃ instead of ποιῇ, for example. Since uncontracted forms are readily identified, I have not noted the Attic contracted forms.

Although this book frees up time you would otherwise spend digging up words, I have taken care to offer you a range of meanings, where possible, so that you must put thought into choosing the meaning that best fits the context and so that you are exposed to the various meanings many words possess. Any textual difficulties you encounter can often be cleared up by simply perusing vocabulary entries. You are advised to consult both the notes and the vocabulary entries carefully. You will find that the notes are repetitive, typically not referring you back to a previous one. My hope is that repetition will facilitate language acquisition and that the time you save from not flipping back and forth will enable you to focus on the passage at hand.

Parsing and Narratology

In the grammatical notes, the parsing—an analysis of the role each word in a sentence plays—is intended to be comprehensive. Though experts will be able to predict where you will struggle with particularly challenging passages, they will not be able to predict all the difficulties you will encounter. Thus, the comprehensive parsing is intended as an answer key to consult when you are struggling. An effective strategy is for you to consult this key only after making several attempts at resolving the difficulty on your own.

Narratological comments that indicate changing points of view are also intended to be comprehensive. All that Herodotus writes he does not necessarily believe. For example, he simply offers a large section of Book II on the Egyptians in accordance with what his sources have told him. He includes primary character text (speeches), which offer the point of view of the speaker and not necessarily that of our historian. For example, Aristagores, when trying to persuade Artaphrenes to go to war, crafts his speech to make it as persuasive as possible to his audience (V.31). Herodotus, however, knows that much of what he says is false.

Herodotus also offers secondary character text. In it an author indirectly hands over narration to a secondary character. This character now focalizes the words you read. Indirect statement is one tip that a handoff has occurred. Secondary character text is where textual analysis gets tricky. What content belongs to the author and what to the character is often unclear. There are instances when Herodotus will pass judgment and offer his opinion on things. Most often, however, he creates an uncertain narrative that combines his story with that of his subjects. His subjects are typically unreliable: they speak so as to achieve their ends. When Herodotus's narrative and that of his subjects align, then it can be said that his subjects' account reflects his own view of things. When the two diverge, their account is not one that Herodotus would approve. Teasing apart which narrative belongs to whom is often difficult. And so when Herodotus writes that Dareios "happened to see," we know that now the event is being presented from Dareios's perspective, one that Herodotus may or may not agree with. Although it is not always clear through whose eyes we are looking, it is important, when reading Herodotus, to discern the perspective that currently dominates. He has woven a variety of perspectives into his work. Being aware of the various threads and their colors will enable you to understand the complexity he has created. The result is a rich narrative, full of uncertainty and complexity. To assist this awareness, I have attempted in each paragraph to note when Herodotus has handed narration over to a secondary character.

Appendices A through D

Appendices A, B, C, and D contain resources for developing your translation and reading skills. Appendix A is a case and function chart. This chart provides the functions for the five cases in as pared down a form as possible. When stymied by the case of a noun or pronoun, you are encouraged to consult the chart to assist in understanding the syntax. Typically, you will be able to narrow down the choices to a couple of possibilities. Once the choices are narrowed, you should soon arrive at the correct understanding. In making the chart, I have offered, for example, as few genitive labels as can comprehensively explain the various functions of the case. Explaining more with less is the guiding philosophy. For the full treatment, you may consult Smyth's venerable *Greek Grammar* (2014).

Just as more-with-less is the principle guiding my presentation of the cases, so is the same philosophy used in explaining the infinitive (appendix B) and the subjunctive and optative moods (appendix C). Underlying each of these moods is the notion either of hypothesis or of an occurrence, subsequent to the time of the main verb, that may or may not happen. And so in presenting the subjunctive, for example, I do not offer the typical note that states, "subjunctive in a purpose clause in primary sequence." It is not that making this identification is without importance. Rather it is to press you to think beyond this identification to the underlying "why" behind the mood's use. Thus, a typical note in the commentary reads, "subjunctive because the mood refers to an event in the unknowable future." Appendix D contains a glossary of terms in the event that you wish to review the parsing terms used in the text.

Tips on Translating

Upon sitting down to translate, remember that a person fluent in ancient Greek would not be translating. With this in mind take each word as it comes, establish expectations for it, adapt these expectations as the meaning of the sentence unfolds, and let word order help guide you to an accurate understanding of the sentence. Repeat this process each time that you translate and your reading and comprehension skills will improve consistently.

Prepositions are always followed by a noun object in the genitive, dative, or accusative case. If one does not, then consider whether anastrophe, where the object comes first, has occurred (less common) or whether some words have intervened between the preposition and its object: πρὸς τὸ κήρυγμα ("due to the proclamation") versus πρὸς **ὧν δὴ τοῦτο** τὸ κήρυγμα ("due **in fact to this** proclamation"). If neither of these is the case, the preposition is probably not a preposition at all and is rather being used adverbially, and you will have to adjust your thinking accordingly. Adverbs typically come right before or after what they modify. Coordinating conjunctions join two things in parallel. Subordinating conjunctions, relative pronouns, and interrogatives initiate clauses and must be translated first. As in English, interjections ("drat," for example) express some emotion and stand on their own, separate from the rest of the sentence's meaning. Subjects typically come first, direct and indirect objects next, and verbs last.

When stuck in understanding a given word's meaning and function, be systematic in getting unstuck. Make sure you have identified the word correctly. If it is a noun or pronoun, consult the case and function chart (appendix A) to determine, by process of elimination, what function best fits the context. If it is an adjective or participle, determine what noun is being modified or supply the appropriate noun from the gender and number of the ending or from context. If it is an infinitive, consult the infinitives in summary (appendix B) to determine how it functions. If it is a finite verb, be sure to obtain the correct subject from the verb's ending. For adverbs, conjunctions, interjections, and prepositions, a simple refresher on the functions of these parts of speech should prove sufficient in getting you unstuck. If unable to understand a given sentence's meaning, try to determine the main thought, gotten from the subject and the main verb.

Once you establish the main thought, you will more easily understand the meaning of the words in the rest of the sentence.

Create expectations based on word order: words that are to be translated together are typically found together. And so expect words to form sense units that logically cohere to one another. When considering markers for when a word group or sense unit starts or stops, look to verbs and participles. For example, in the sentence Καμβύσης ὁ Κύρου ἐπὶ δὴ τὴν πόλιν ἐστράτευεν, ἄγων ("Kambyses, the son of Kyros, marched against the city, bringing"), the finite verb ἐστράτευεν marks the end of a word group, and the participle ἄγων marks the beginning of the next. Noticing that verbal markers are often stop or go signs will facilitate reading comprehension.

Similar to the verbal markers are subordinating conjunctions, relative and interrogative pronouns, and interrogative adverbs. These words mark the beginning of a new clause, and you should translate them first. Just as in the English sentence "he thinks that it is time to go," "he thinks" and "that it is time to go" form two discrete units, no single part of which can be moved into the other, so in ancient Greek you will find similar groupings of words that are discrete. "ἐπείρετο ὅ τι τε σιτέεται ὁ βασιλεύς" has two discrete parts: "ἐπείρετο" and "ὅ τι τε σιτέεται ὁ βασιλεύς." As in the English example, each part forms its own unit. There is an exception. At times the subject of a finite verb in a dependent clause is placed before the conjunction: for example, in οἱ Ἀθηναῖοι ἐπεὶ ἦλθον ("when the Athenians came"). Typically, however, subordinating conjunctions, relative and interrogative pronouns, and interrogative adverbs mark the start of a sense unit. Most often you are to bring no words that precede beyond the barrier they initiate.

Be aware of the following. In addition to ὑπό, Herodotus uses a variety of prepositions to express agency. ὑπό, ἐκ, and πρός are the most common. A direct object tends not to be repeated after it has been stated once. In the sentence "seeing **her**, we hugged **her** and put **her** in the car," ancient Greek will state the "her" once and leave the other instances understood. At times prepositions are used just as they would be found in English: ἐπ' ἔτεα πέντε translates as "for five years," and the preposition ἐπί, typically not present in extent of time expressions, functions just like the English "for." In a relative clause the antecedent is sometimes omitted: βουλόμενος ποιῆσαι **τὰ** δὴ καὶ ἐποίησε = βουλόμενος ποιῆσαι **ταῦτα ἃ** δὴ καὶ ἐποίησε ("wishing to do what things he did"). And so τά serves as the object of both ποιῆσαι and ἐποίησε. It is also common for the relative pronoun to be attracted into the case of the antecedent, whether it is present or missing: δεύτερα δὲ τούτων, τῶν ὁ μούναρχος ποιέει, οὐδέν ἰσονομίη ποιέει = δεύτερα δὲ τούτων, ἃ ὁ μούναρχος ποιέει, οὐδέν ἰσονομίη ποιέει ("secondly equality of rule does none of the things which monarchy does"). Attraction does not always occur. Note the following example: δεῖ ποιεῖν τῶν ἂν ἐπιθυμῶμεν = δεῖ ποιεῖν ταῦτα ὧν ἂν ἐπιθυμῶμεν. In this example, the relative pronoun takes its case based on the verb in its own clause. At times the antecedent remains within the relative clause, for example, εἶδεν ἐν ᾗ οἰκῶ χώρᾳ ("he saw in which country I dwell") instead of εἶδεν χώραν ἐν ᾗ οἰκῶ. It may seem like a lot to keep all of the above in mind. As is the case in many pursuits, the act of doing uncomplicates the complex. Applying a methodology that is consistent and critical in its approach will facilitate your language acquisition and enjoyment.

Once you have translated a sentence correctly, reread it a few times until you get a feel for how the structure of the sentence works. Repeat this process each time you finish a sentence. Though difficult to do when new to a language, in so much as you can, do not write down your translation. Rather read and reread, memorizing the meaning along the way. Do this for each sentence and you will find yourself well on your way to reading, not translating, Greek.

Frequencies and Expectations

As you read, develop expectations based on the following frequencies.[49] Since it has only one function, the vocative is straightforward and is often set off by commas. Its function is direct address 100 percent of the time. If a noun or pronoun is nominative, its function is almost always as a subject. If it is not the subject, it is a predicate nominative or it is in apposition to another nominative noun. If a word is in the genitive case, it will be translated in conjunction with another noun or pronoun in the sentence about 65 percent of the time, and the preposition "of" will be supplied. A good rule of thumb is to translate the genitive with the noun it is closest to (the rule of proximity), unless there is good reason not to. Of this 65 percent, the

---

49. I have obtained these frequencies by parsing the odd pages of Book V. In parsing, I did not count the objects of prepositions.

genitive of possession is most common (31 percent), followed by the partitive genitive (18 percent), and then the genitive of dependence (16 percent). The next two most common categories are the genitive absolute construction (12 percent) and the genitive as an object of a verb (11 percent). These five categories represent roughly 88 percent of the total instances. The remaining 12 percent are the comparative genitive (3 percent), the genitive translated in conjunction with an adjective or adverb (2 percent), the genitive of separation (2 percent), the genitive in apposition with another noun (2 percent), the predicate genitive (1 percent), the genitive of value (1 percent), and the genitive of time (1 percent). Although these are rough approximations, use them to help you create expectations for word relationships and word groups.

For the dative, the top five categories comprise 92.5 percent of the functions: indirect object (30 percent), object of the prefix or root of a verb (21 percent), means or instrument (17 percent), dative translated with an adjective, adverb, or noun (12.3 percent), and possession (12.2 percent). In each the dative is translated differently. For the dative used with an indirect object, the dative noun or pronoun is indirectly involved in the verb's action, and the reader should supply "to" or "for." For the object of a prefix or the verb itself, translate the dative in accordance with the specific meaning of the prefix or verb. For datives of means or instrument, supply "by" or "with." For translating the dative with an adjective, adverb, or noun, the meaning of the adjective, adverb, or noun is of central importance: for example, φίλος αὐτῷ ("friendly to him") and ἔχθιστος αὐτῇ ("most hostile to her"). For possession, the key is to make sure that the dative possesses the correct noun or pronoun. The dative in apposition (2 percent), the dative of agent (2 percent), the dative of degree of difference (1.5 percent), the dative of accompaniment (0.5 percent), the dative of respect (0.5 percent), the dative of time (0.5 percent), and the dative of place where (0.5 percent) make up the remaining 7.5 percent. As with the frequencies for the genitive, consider these percentages, though rough, when creating expectations for what function a specific dative noun or pronoun has.

The counted instances for the accusative are over double the counted functions for the genitive and dative: 388 for the genitive, 294 for the dative, and 725 for the accusative. The least common uses of the accusative are the accusative absolute (0.1 percent), accusative of duration of time and extent of space (2 percent), the accusative in apposition to another noun (4.5 percent), the accusative predicate (5 percent), the accusative of respect (5.1 percent), and the accusative subject of an infinitive or participle (11.3 percent). At 72 percent by far the most common use of the accusative case is as the object of a verb or participle. Combining the two most common categories, we see that eight times out of ten the accusative will be the object or subject of a verb or participle. Keep this in mind as you read.

Understanding the infinitive, optative, and subjunctive is a key to understanding the language. Again, let frequencies help you. Unmarked for case and number, the infinitive is used in the following distinct instances: (1) as a complement to verbs like βούλομαι, δοκέω, δύναμαι, ἔχω, and the like, (2) as the main verb in indirect statement, (3) as the object of verbs of commanding, advising, allowing, and so forth, (4) as an epexegete, or explanation, of a noun or adjective, (5) as a command, (6) as an articular infinitive or gerund, (7) as the main verb in natural result clauses, (8) to show purpose, and (9) after πρίν. Of these nine situations by far the most common use of the infinitive is as a complement (40 percent), followed by its use as a main verb in indirect statement (30 percent) and as an object of verbs of commanding, advising, allowing, and so forth (17.5 percent). Less common uses of the infinitive in the parsed reading selection include its use as an epexegete of a noun or adjective (8 percent), to show purpose (2 percent), as a command (1 percent), as an articular infinitive (1 percent), as the main verb in a natural result clause (0.5 percent), and finally as a verb after πρίν (0 percent in our parsed selection).

For situations (2), (7), and (9), determine who or what is doing the action of the infinitive. There are only two choices. The subject is either the subject of the main verb or the head verb that introduces the infinitive, or it is a noun or pronoun in the accusative case. For example, in the sentence "οὐκ ἐδικαίωσα φέρειν αὐτὸν ἐς ἀγορήν," the subject is either the "I" from ἐδικαίωσα or the accusative αὐτόν. You will find that often from context, the logic of the passage, intuition, or some combination of the three you will establish the answer immediately. If uncertain, pick the subject that makes the most sense from context. Also note whether the infinitive is transitive. If it is, then it typically requires a direct object. If there is only one word in the accusative case, it is most likely that the subject of the infinitive is the same as the head or main verb. In our example, "οὐκ ἐδικαίωσα φέρειν αὐτὸν ἐς ἀγορήν," the infinitive, φέρειν, is transitive, and the subject of the infinitive is the "I" from ἐδικαίωσα. Αὐτόν, then, is the object of φέρειν: "I thought it not right to carry him into the marketplace."

When the infinitive functions as a complement, which is its most common function, it completes the meaning of verbs. In such instances, English and Greek usage are similar, and thus translating the complementary infinitive will come naturally to you. Infinitives dependent on verbs, the third most common function, have nouns or pronouns in the dative or accusative case, which are to perform the action. Occasionally the person to perform the action of the infinitive is left understood: for example, Καμβύσης κελεύει αὐτὸν φέρειν ("Kambyses orders 'them' [presumably slaves] to carry him" or "Kambyses gives the order [to the slaves] to carry him"). More commonly the person to do the action of the infinitive is not left understood: thus, Καμβύσης αὐτοῖς κελεύει αὐτὸν φέρειν ("Kambyses orders them to carry him)." If an articular infinitive has a subject, it is in the accusative case. In the infinitive's next two functions—as an epexegete, or explanation, of a noun or adjective and as the infinitive of purpose—a person may perform the action. In the last function, when the infinitive is used as a command, the subject is typically an implied "you" singular or plural. The infinitive occurs regularly, and thus developing a good strategy for defining it is a big step toward gaining confidence in reading Greek.

Like the infinitive, the optative and subjunctive moods also provide keys to understanding the language. If the verb is optative and in an independent clause, it is either a potential optative (with ἄν), an optative of wish (without ἄν), or in the apodosis of a condition. The optative is in an independent clause about 21 percent of the time in the parsed reading selection, and when this is the case, the optative is always potential. In our parsed text, there are no instances of the optative in the apodosis of a condition, nor are there any instances of the optative of wish. Each of these independent uses of the optative is translated in a special way, and it is a good idea to have memorized good English equivalents for them.

You will encounter the optative in a dependent clause about 80 percent of the time, either in an indirect statement or question in secondary sequence, in the protasis of a condition, or in a purpose clause (in the pages parsed there were no instances of the optative in a fear clause). Of this 80 percent, the opta-tive stands for an original indicative in indirect statement or question 73 percent of the time. The optative will be in the protasis of a condition 13.5 percent of the time, and the optative is in a purpose clause another 13.5 percent of the time. Optatives in indirect statement and question are most often translated with the indicative in English. How you translate optatives in the protasis of conditions varies. For a theoretical understanding of the optative's meaning in conditions, review appendix C. The optative in a purpose clause may be translated with the English infinitive, or you may use the helping verb "might."

If a verb is subjunctive, the same critical process applies. Determine whether the verb is in an independent or dependent clause. If it is in an independent clause, then it is either a subjunctive of doubtful assertion (3.8 percent), a prohibitive subjunctive (3.8 percent), a deliberative subjunctive (3.8 percent), or a hortatory subjunctive (0 percent in our parsed selection). Each of these has a specific and rather formulaic translation. If the verb is in a dependent clause, it is in the protasis of a condition 61.8 percent of the time and in a purpose clause 19.2 percent of the time. In our parsed selection, the subjunctive occurs once (3.8 percent of the time) in a fear clause and once in a dependent clause expressing doubt or hesitancy. It also appears once in indirect question and stands for an original deliberative subjunctive and so is counted above. The protasis of conditions, purpose clauses, fear clauses, dependent clauses expressing doubt or hesitancy, and object clauses of effort consider events that have not occurred yet and so are hypothetical in nature. When translating them into English, take care to choose words that reflect this aspect of the subjunctive.

In considering the subjunctive and optative together, note that you may translate the optative into English as a mood expressing a fact or as a mood expressing a nonfact. The mood of the subjunctive, on the other hand, always has a nonfactual aspect to it. As you proceed though the text, create expectations for these moods and adapt them as circumstances suggest.

The Text and Dates

The origin of this text is Carolus Hude's *Herodoti Historiae*.[50] I have added additional commas and periods to encourage the reading of Greek, and

50. Carolus Hude (1927), *Herodoti Historiae*, 2 vols., 3rd ed. (New York: Oxford University Press).

I have made use of the pause to create meaning. Dates are B.C.E. unless
otherwise noted.

Herodotus and the Ionic Dialect

The text of Herodotus is a mixture of Ionic, Attic, and sometimes Doric
forms. It is uncertain whether Herodotus's text was originally purely
Ionic and later corrupted by scribes to include Attic and Doric forms,
or whether it was originally a mixture of the three. Whatever the case,
the following forms will be encountered in the text:

1. -η is found where Attic has -α, even after ε, ι, and ρ.
2. -ει, -ου for -ε, -ο before ν, ρ, λ: ξεῖνοι for ξένοι; εἵνεκα for ἕνεκα;
   κούρη for κόρη; οὔνομα for ὄνομα.
3. -ω for -αυ or -ου: θῶμα for θαῦμα; ὦν for οὖν.
4. -σσ- is found where Attic has -ττ-.
5. Consonants are often unaspirated: π, τ, κ for φ, θ, χ; ἀπῆκε instead
   of ἀφῆκε.
6. κ- is found instead of π-; for example, κοτε instead of ποτε and ὅκως
   instead of ὅπως.
7. The first declension genitive plural is -έων not -ῶν.
8. The first declension dative plural is -ῃσι not -αις.
9. The first declension genitive singular of masculine nouns is -εω not
   -ου.
10. The second declension dative plural is -οισι not -οις.
11. In the third declension, forms remain uncontracted; for example,
    γένεος not γένους.
12. In the third declension, nouns that end in -ις decline like this:

N	πόλις	πόλιες
G	πόλιος	πόλιων
D	πόλι	πόλισι (ν)
A	πόλιν	πόλιας or πόλῑς

13. Personal pronouns are not contracted; for example, σέο or σεῦ not
    σοῦ.
14. For the personal pronouns, τοι is found at times for σοι.

15. For the third person pronoun, οἱ is used for αὐτῷ and αὐτῇ.

16. For the third person regular and reflexive pronoun, μιν is found for αὐτόν, αὐτήν, αὐτό, and for ἑαυτόν and ἑαυτήν.

17. For the third person plural, σφεῖς, σφέων, σφίσι or σφι, and σφέας is found.

18. For τίς, τί and τις, τι, τέο or τεῦ for τοῦ or τίνος; τέῳ for τῷ or τίνι; τέων for τίνων; τέοισι for τίσι.

19. In cases other than the nominative, the article and the relative pronoun are identical. In specific instances Herodotus uses the customary Attic forms.

20. The past indicative augment is inconsistently used.

21. Instead of the third person plurals -νται and -ντο, Herodotus uses the third person plurals -αται and -ατο.

22. Many verb forms remain uncontracted; for example, ποιέειν not ποιεῖν.

23. For verbs ending in -οω, -οο- and -οου- contract to -ευ-.

24. For μι-verbs, ἵημι conjugates like an -εω verb; ἵστημι like an -αω verb; δίδωμι like an -οω verb.

25. Commonly occurring pronouns are the following:

	First Person	**Second Person**	**Third Person**
N	ἐγώ	σύ	—
G	ἐμέο, ἐμεῦ, μευ	σέο, σεῦ, σευ	εὑ
D	ἐμοί, μοι	σοί, τοι	οἱ (= αὐτῷ and αὐτῇ)
A	ἐμέ, με	σέ, σε	ἑ, μιν (= αὐτόν, αὐτήν, αὐτό)
N	ἡμεῖς	ὑμεῖς	σφεῖς
G	ἡμέων	ὑμέων	σφέων, σφεων
D	ἡμῖν	ὑμῖν	σφίσι (ν) σφισι (ν), σφι
A	ἡμέας	ὑμέας	σφέας, σφεας, σφεα

Transliteration of Names

Care has been taken to transliterate names by making a one-to-one correspondence with Herodotus's mixed Ionic Greek dialect and the corresponding English letters. With familiar names the Attic form or the form that results from the convention of going from Greek to Latin and then to English is added in parentheses. Note the examples below:

Ἀρισταγόρης, -ου (-εω) ὁ: Aristagores (Aristagoras), son of Herakleides and tyrant of Kyme, an Aiolian city near Lydia, c. 500 B.C.E.

Δαρεῖος, -ου ὁ: Dareios (Darius) I the Great, third king of the Akhaimenids, defeated the Magi to come to power, c. 550–486 B.C.E.

Κῦρος, -ου ὁ: Kyros (Cyrus) the Great, c. 600–530 B.C.E., Persian king who ruled for about 30 years from 559–530 B.C.E.

Μακέαι, -ων οἱ: Makeai, inhabitants of Libya

Χῖος, -α, -ον: of Khios (Chios), Khian (Chian)

Abbreviations Used in the Text

acc. = accusative	ind. = indicative
act. = active	inf. = infinitive
adj. = adjective	intrans. = intransitive
adv. = adverb	mid. = middle
app.= apposition	n. = noun
att. = attributive	n. pl. = noun, plural
c. = circa	n. s. = noun, singular
dat. = dative	nom. = nominative
dep. = deponent	obj. = object
fem. = feminine	opt. = optative
fn. = footnote	pass. = passive
fut. = future	poss. = possession
gen. = genitive	pred. = predicate
H. = Herodotus	subj. = subject
imp. = imperfect	subst. = substantive
impers. = impersonal	

Textual Marks

[ ]   indicate words believed by the editor to be spurious.

< >   indicate words, not present in the manuscript, believed by the editor to be necessary.

† †   indicate a problem with the text.

FURTHER READINGS

Herodotus has attracted many fine scholars who have devoted considerable effort to studying the *Histories*. Some of their contributions are listed below and given as entry points into the wide body of scholarship Herodotus has inspired, one reference opening the door to another.

Asheri, D., A. Lloyd, and A. Corcella. 2011. *A Commentary on Herodotus Books I–IV,* edited by O. Murray and A. Moreno. Oxford.

Bakker, E., I. J. F. de Jong, and H. van Wees. 2002. *Brill's Companion to Herodotus.* Leiden.

Bowie, A. M. 2007. *Herodotus Histories Book VIII.* Cambridge.

Dewald, C., and J. Marincola. 2006. *The Cambridge Companion to Herodotus.* Cambridge.

Fehling, D. 1989. *Herodotus and His "Sources": Citation, Invention and Narrative Art.* Leeds.

Flory, S. 1987. *The Archaic Smile of Herodotus.* Wayne State.

Flower, M. A., and J. Marincola. 2002. *Herodotus Histories Book IX.* Cambridge.

Fontenrose, J. 1978. *The Delphic Oracle: Its Responses and Operations with a Catalogue of Responses.* Berkeley.

Hornblower, S. 2013. *Herodotus Histories Book V.* Cambridge.

How, W. W., and J. Wells. 1913 [1923]. *A Commentary on Herodotus.* Reprinted with corrections. Oxford.

Jong, I. J. F. de. 2014. *Narratology and Classics.* Oxford.

Romm, J. 2003. *Herodotus on the War for Greek Freedom.* Indianapolis.

Rubincam, C. 2008. "Herodotus and His Descendants: Numbers in Ancient and Modern Narratives of Xerxes' Campaign." *Harvard Studies in Classical Philology* 104:93–138.

Scott, L. 2005. *Historical Commentary on Herodotus Book 6.* Leiden.

Smyth, H. W. 2014. *Greek Grammar.* Reprinted edition. Oxford.

Strassler, R. 2007. *The Landmark Herodotus.* New York.

Waddell, W. G. 1998 [1939]. *Herodotus Book II.* Bristol [Methuen].

West, M. L. 1993. *Greek Lyric Poetry.* Oxford.

Wilson, N. G. 2015. *Herodoti Historiae Libri V–IX.* Oxford.

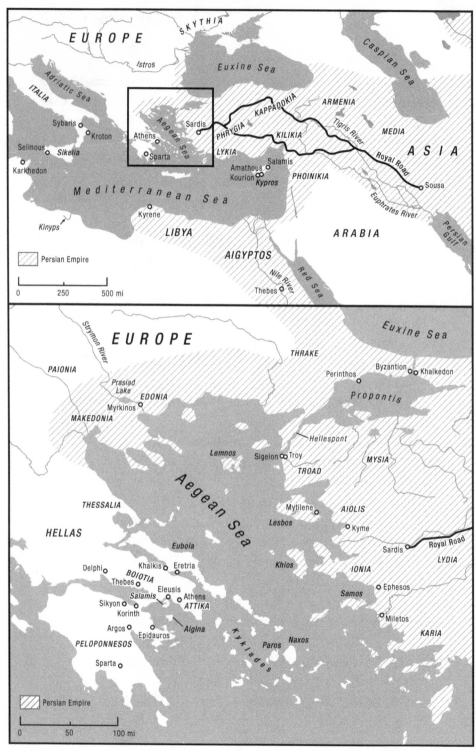

Top map labels:

EUROPE

SKYTHIA

ITALIA

Adriatic Sea

Istros

Euxine Sea

Caspian Sea

Sybaris

Kroton

Athens

Aegean Sea

Sardis

PHRYGIA

KAPPADOKIA

ARMENIA

Selinous

Sikelia

Sparta

LYKIA

KILIKIA

Tigris River

MEDIA

ASIA

Karkhedon

Mediterranean Sea

Amathous

Salamis

Kourion

Kypros

PHOINIKIA

Royal Road

Euphrates River

Sousa

Kyrene

LIBYA

ARABIA

Persian Gulf

Kinyps

Nile River

AIGYPTOS

Red Sea

Thebes

Persian Empire

0   250   500 mi

Bottom map labels:

Strymon River

EUROPE

Euxine Sea

PAIONIA

THRAKE

Prasiad Lake

Perinthos

Byzantion

Khalkedon

Myrkinos

EDONIA

Propontis

MAKEDONIA

Hellespont

Lemnos

Sigeion

Troy

MYSIA

TROAD

THESSALIA

Mytilene

AIOLIS

Lesbos

Kyme

HELLAS

Euboia

Sardis

Royal Road

LYDIA

Delphi

Khalkis

Eretria

Khios

IONIA

Thebes

BOIOTIA

Eleusis

Ephesos

Sikyon

Salamis

Athens

ATTIKA

Samos

Korinth

Aegean Sea

Argos

Aigina

Miletos

Epidauros

KARIA

PELOPONNESOS

Kyklades

Paros

Naxos

Sparta

Persian Empire

0   50   100 mi

Map by Erin Greb Cartography. Copyright © 2018 by the University of Oklahoma Press.

∿ MAP

SELECTED PLACES FROM *HISTORIES*, BOOK V

CITIES

Ἀμαθοῦς, -οῦντος ἡ: Amathous

Ἄργος, -ους (-εος) τό: Argos

Ἀθῆναι, -ῶν αἱ: Athens

Βυζαντίον, -ου τό: Byzantion (Byzantium)

Δελφαί, -ῶν αἱ: Delphi

Ἐλευσίς, -ῖνος ἡ: Eleusis

Ἐφέσος, -ου ἡ: Ephesos

Ἐπίδαυρος, -ου ἡ: Epidauros

Ἐρετρία, -ας ἡ: Eretria

Χαλκηδών, -όνος ἡ: Khalkedon (Chalcedon)

Χαλκίς, -ίδος ἡ: Khalkis (Chalcis) in Euboia

Κόρινθος, -ου ὁ and ἡ: Korinth (Corinth)

Κουρίον, -ου τό: Kourion

Κρότων, -ωνος ἡ: Kroton (Croton)

Κύμη, -ης ἡ: Kyme (Cyme)

Λακεδαίμων, -ονος ἡ: Lakedaimon (Sparta)

Μίλητος, -ου ἡ: Miletos

Μύρκινος, -ου ἡ: Myrkinos

Μυτιλήνη, -ης ἡ: Mytilene

Πέρινθος, -ου ἡ: Perinthos

Σαλαμίς, -ῖνος ἡ: Salamis

Σάρδεις, -εων (-ιων) αἱ (Σάρδις [acc.]): Sardis

Σελινοῦς, -οῦντος ἡ: Selinous

Σίγειον, -ου τό: Sigeion

Σικυών, -ῶνος ἡ: Sikyon (Sicyon)

Σοῦσα, -ων τά: Sousa

Σπάρτη, -ης ἡ: Sparta (Lakedaimon)

Σύβαρις, -εως (-ιος) ἡ: Sybaris

Θῆβαι, -ῶν αἱ: Thebes, Boiotian or Egyptian

Ἰλιάς, -άδος ἡ: Ilium, Troy

Continents

Εὐρώπη, -ης ἡ: Europe

Ἀσία, -ας ἡ: Asia

COUNTRIES AND REGIONS

Αἴγυπτος, -ου ἡ: Aigyptos (Egypt)

Αἰολίς, -ίδος ἡ: Aiolis (Aeolis)

Ἀραβία, -ας ἡ: Arabia

Ἀρμενία, -ας ἡ: Armenia

Ἀττική, -ῆς ἡ: Attika

Βοιωτία, -ας ἡ: Boiotia (Boeotia)

Ἠδωνίς, -ίδος ἡ: Edonia

Ἑλλάς, -άδος ἡ: Hellas (Greece)

Ἰωνία, -ας ἡ: Ionia

Ἰταλία, -ας ἡ: Italia (Italy)

Καππαδοκία, -ας ἡ: Kappadokia (Cappadocia)

Καρία, -ας ἡ: Karia (Caria)

Κιλικία, -ας ἡ: Kilikia (Cilicia)

Λιβύη, -ης ἡ: Libya

Λυδία, -ας ἡ: Lydia

Λυκία, -ας ἡ: Lykia (Lycia)

Μακεδονία, -ας ἡ: Makedonia (Macedon)

Μηδία, -ας ἡ: Media

Μυσία, -ας ἡ: Mysia

Παιονία, -ας ἡ: Paionia (Paeonia)

Πελοποννήσος, -ου ἡ: Peloponnesos

Περσίς γῆ: Persia

Φοινίκη, -ης ἡ: Phoinike (Phoenicia)

Φρυγία, -ας ἡ: Phrygia

Σικελία, -ας ἡ: Sikelia (Sicily)

Σκυθία, -ας ἡ: Skythia (Scythia)

Θεσσαλία, -ας ἡ: Thessalia (Thessaly)

Θράκη, -ης: Thrake (Thrace)

Τρῳάς, -άδος ἡ: Troad

ISLANDS

Αἴγινα, -ας ἡ: Aigina (Aegina)

Εὐβοία, -ας ἡ: Euboia

Χίος, -ου ἡ: Khios (Chios)

Κυκλάδες, -ων αἱ: Kyklades (Cyclades)

Κύπρος, -ου ἡ: Kypros (Cyprus)

Λῆμνος, -ου ἡ: Lemnos

Λέσβος, -ου ἡ: Lesbos

Νάξος, -ου ἡ: Naxos

Πάρος, -ου ἡ: Paros

Σαλαμίς, -ῖνος ἡ: Salamis

Σάμος, -ου ἡ: Samos

Σικελία, -ας ἡ: Sikelia (Sicily)

WATERS

Ἀδρία, -ας ἡ: Adriatic

Αἰγαῖος (πόντος), -ου ὁ: Aegean

Ἀράβιος (κόλπος), -ου ὁ: Red Sea

Ἐρυθρὴ θάλασσα: Persian Gulf

Ἐρυθρὴ θάλασσα: Red Sea (later name)

Εὐφρήτης, -ου ὁ: Euphretes

Εὔξεινος, -ου ὁ: Euxine (Black Sea)

Ἑλλήσποντος, -ου ὁ: Hellespont

Ἴστρος, -ου ὁ: Istros (Danube)

Μεσόγειος θάλασσα: Mediterranean Sea

Νεῖλος, -ου ὁ: Nile River

Πρασιάδα, -άδος ἡ: Prasiad Lake

Προποντίς, -ίδος ἡ: Propontis,

Στρυμών, -όνος ὁ: Strymon River

Τίγρης, -ου ὁ: Tigres (Tigris) River

Ὑρκανία θαλάσση: Caspian Sea

⌐ HERODOTUS, *HISTORIES*, BOOK V

V.1.1. οἱ δὲ ἐν τῇ Εὐρώπῃ τῶν Περσέων καταλειφθέντες ὑπὸ Δαρείου, τῶν ὁ Μεγάβαζος ἦρχε, πρώτους μὲν Περινθίους Ἑλλησποντίων, οὐ βουλομένους ὑπηκόους εἶναι Δαρείου, κατεστρέψαντο, περιεφθέντας πρότερον καὶ ὑπὸ Παιόνων τρηχέως. [2] οἱ γὰρ ὦν ἀπὸ Στρυμόνος Παίονες—χρήσαντος τοῦ θεοῦ στρατεύεσθαι ἐπὶ Περινθίους καὶ ἢν μὲν ἀντικατιζόμενοι ἐπικαλέσωνται σφέας οἱ Περίνθιοι ὀνομαστὶ βώσαντες, τοὺς δὲ ἐπιχειρέειν, ἢν δὲ μὴ ἐπιβώσωνται, μὴ ἐπιχειρέειν— ἐποίεον οἱ Παίονες ταῦτα. ἀντικατιζομένων δὲ τῶν Περινθίων ἐν τῷ προαστείῳ, ἐνθαῦτα μουνομαχίη τριφασίη ἐκ προκλήσιός σφι ἐγένετο. καὶ γὰρ ἄνδρα ἀνδρὶ καὶ ἵππον ἵππῳ συνέβαλον καὶ κύνα κυνί. [3] νικώντων δὲ τὰ δύο τῶν Περινθίων, ὡς ἐπαιώνιζον κεχαρηκότες, συνεβάλοντο οἱ Παίονες τὸ χρηστήριον αὐτὸ τοῦτο εἶναι. καὶ εἶπάν κου παρὰ σφίσι αὐτοῖσι· Νῦν ἂν εἴη ὁ χρησμὸς ἐπιτελεόμενος ἡμῖν· νῦν ἡμέτερον ἔργον. οὕτω τοῖσι Περινθίοισι παιωνίσασι ἐπιχειρέουσι οἱ Παίονες. καὶ πολλόν τε ἐκράτησαν καὶ ἔλιπον σφέων ὀλίγους.

V.1.1 οἱ δέ ... καταλειφθέντες: substantive, "those left behind." The article plus δέ is often used to create a substantive noun or to indicate a change of subject. Here the verb that οἱ δέ is the subject of is quite delayed.   **τῶν Περσέων:** partitive with οἱ δέ.   **τῶν = ὧν:** the relative pronoun and the article are often identical; the relative pronoun must always be translated in the order it comes in, and it always forms its

35

own clause.   **πρώτους μέν:** appears to be left unanswered.   **Ἑλλησποντίων:** partitive with Περινθίους.   **εἶναι:** complementary with βουλομένους.   **Δαρείου:** translate with ὑπηκόους.   **κατεστρέψαντο, περιεφθέντας:** the finite verb marks the end of a sense unit and the participle marks the beginning of the next.   **1.2 οἱ γάρ:** Herodotus moves back in time out of his main narrative to give a backstory. The historicity of the conflict between the Paionians and Perinthians is questioned, and it is suggested that a reason for its inclusion is the verbal similarity between "paian" and "Paionians."   **Παίονες . . . ἐποίεον οἱ Παίονες:** the subject of the finite verb is repeated; everything else in this sentence is subordinate and set up by χρήσαντος τοῦ θεοῦ.   **χρήσαντος:** has a force similar to κελεύω.   **στρατεύεσθαι . . . ἐπιχειρέειν . . . μὴ ἐπιχειρέειν:** dependent on χρήσαντος; understand an implied Paionians as the subject of στρατεύεσθαι.   **ἢν μέν:** is answered by τοὺς δέ.   **ἐπικαλέσωνται:** subjunctive, indicating a possible future occurrence.   **τοὺς δέ:** subject of ἐπιχειρέειν and of the upcoming μὴ ἐπιχειρέειν; the δέ indicates a change of subject from the Perinthians to the Paionians.   **μή:** the negative for things hypothetical.   **ἐπιβώσωνται:** see ἐπικαλέσωνται above.   **ταῦτα:** refers back to what the oracle has suggested that they do.   **σφι:** possesses μουνομαχίη.   **ἀνδρί . . . ἵππῳ . . . κυνί:** objects of the prefix συν- of συνέβαλον. Paionian dogs were famed for their fighting skills (Pollux, *Onomasticon* v. 46, 47).   **1.3 τὰ δύο:** substantive, "two of the battles."   **ὡς:** temporal.   **συνεβάλοντο:** Herodotus hands over the narrative to his subject (secondary character text). Here the Paionians figure out the oracle's meaning.   **τὸ χρηστήριον:** subject of εἶναι.   **εἶναι:** main verb in indirect statement.   **ἂν εἴη:** a potential optative, indicating some uncertainty about what is happening. For optatives decide whether εἰ ἔλθοι, for example, is best translated into English as "if he comes," "if he came," or "if he should come." As you read, use this approach to clarify why the mood is being used.   **ἔργον:** supply an implied ἐστι.   **Περινθίοισι:** object of the prefix ἐπι- of ἐπιχειρέουσι.   **πολλόν = πολύ:** substantive and accusative of respect, "completely"; adjectives in the neuter accusative are often adverbial and may be translated into English as adverbs or prepositional phrases.   **σφέων:** partitive with ὀλίγους.

⁓

V.2.1 τὰ μὲν δὴ ἀπὸ Παιόνων πρότερον γενόμενα ὧδε ἐγένετο· τότε δὲ ἀνδρῶν ἀγαθῶν περὶ τῆς ἐλευθερίης γινομένων τῶν Περινθίων οἱ Πέρσαι τε καὶ ὁ Μεγάβαζος ἐπεκράτησαν πλήθεϊ. [2] ὡς δὲ ἐχειρώθη ἡ Πέρινθος, ἤλαυνε Μεγάβαζος τὸν στρατὸν διὰ τῆς Θρηίκης, πᾶσαν πόλιν καὶ πᾶν ἔθνος τῶν ταύτῃ οἰκημένων ἡμερούμενος βασιλέϊ. ταῦτα γάρ οἱ ἐνετέταλτο ἐκ Δαρείου· Θρηίκην καταστρέφεσθαι.

V.2.1 τὰ μέν: is answered by τότε δέ.   **τά . . . πρότερον γενόμενα:** substantive, "the things which occurred previously"; πρότερον places the events at some unspecified time in the past.   **ὧδε ἐγένετο:** this marks the end of the backstory.   **τότε δέ:** marks a return back to the original story and the Persian attack on the Perinthians, which dates to approximately 512 B.C.E.   **περὶ τῆς ἐλευθερίης:** though the city-state sees a variety of different types of government, freedom is central to the Greek ethos and to Herodotus. He views ἰσηγορίη ("equality") as the best form of government in all regards (V.78).   **οἱ Πέρσαι:** founded by Kyros the Great, father of Kambyses and king of the Persians, the Akhaimenid Empire lasts some two hundred years (550–330 B.C.E.) and spans the historical time frame of Herodotus's *Histories*. By conquering Media, Lydia, and the Babylonian Empire, Kyros establishes Persian dominance in Asia Minor. At its peak the empire is believed to have ruled some 44 percent of the world's population. Throughout its territories it has a postal system, roads, and uses the language of Aramaic as a common tongue. Over this vast area the king, governors, and a professional army maintain control. In return for peace and taxes, the empire leaves local customs, religions, and businesses to perform as accustomed. The Greeks manage to keep their independence from the Persians until eventually a Greek, Alexander the Great, brings an end to their rule.   **ἐπεκράτησαν:** verbs of conquering typically take a genitive object.   **2.2 ὡς:** temporal.   **ταύτῃ:** substantive and dative of respect, "there."   **ταῦτα:** refers back to the subjugation of Thrakia.   **οἱ = αὐτῷ = Μεγαβάζῳ:** what he is commanded is expressed by the upcoming Θρηίκην καταστρέφεσθαι.   **ἐκ Δαρείου:** in addition to ὑπό, Herodotus uses a variety of prepositions to express agency; ὑπό, ἐκ, and πρός are the most common.   **Θρηίκην:** object of καταστρέφεσθαι.   **καταστρέφεσθαι:** dependent on ἐνετέταλτο.

~

V.3.1 Θρηίκων δὲ ἔθνος μέγιστον ἐστί, μετά γε Ἰνδούς, πάντων ἀνθρώπων. εἰ δὲ ὑπ' ἑνὸς ἄρχοιτο ἢ φρονέοι κατὰ τώυτό, ἄμαχόν τ' ἂν εἴη καὶ πολλῷ κράτιστον πάντων ἐθνέων κατὰ γνώμην τὴν ἐμήν. ἀλλὰ γὰρ τοῦτο ἄπορόν σφι καὶ ἀμήχανον μή κοτε ἐγγένηται. εἰσὶ δὴ κατὰ τοῦτο ἀσθενέες. [2] οὐνόματα δ' ἔχουσι πολλὰ κατὰ χώρας ἕκαστοι. νόμοισι δὲ οὗτοι παραπλησίοισι πάντες χρέωνται κατὰ πάντα, πλὴν Γετέων καὶ Τραυσῶν καὶ τῶν κατύπερθε Κρηστωναίων οἰκεόντων.

V.3.1 μετά γε Ἰνδούς: for more on the Indians, see III.98–106.   **πάντων ἀνθρώπων:** partitive with ἔθνος.   **ὑπ' ἑνός:** agency.   **ἄρχοιτο . . . φρονέοι:** hypothetical optatives, expressing a possible future outcome, no matter how unlikely; supply Θρηίκων ἔθνος as the subject.   **κατὰ τώυτό = κατὰ τὸ**

αὐτό.   **ἄμαχόν τ' ἂν εἴη:** a potential optative; supply an implied Θρηίκων ἔθνος as the subject.   **πολλῷ:** substantive and dative of degree of difference, "by far."   **ἐθνέων:** partitive with an implied Θρηίκων ἔθνος.   **μή κοτε ἐγγένηται:** a hypothetical subjunctive; μή κοτε indicates that the likelihood of the event actually occurring is nil. μή typically negates things that are hypothetical.   **κατὰ τοῦτο:** refers back to Herodotus's reason for the Thrakians' failure to dominate.   **3.2 χρέωνται = χράονται.**   **κατὰ πάντα:** substantive, "in all respects."

～

V.4.1 τούτων δὲ τὰ μὲν Γέται οἱ ἀθανατίζοντες ποιεῦσι, εἴρηταί μοι. Τραυσοὶ δὲ τὰ μὲν ἄλλα πάντα κατὰ ταὐτὰ τοῖσι ἄλλοισι Θρήιξι ἐπιτελέουσι· κατὰ δὲ τὸν γινόμενόν σφι καὶ ἀπογινόμενον, ποιεῦσι τοιάδε. [2] τὸν μὲν γενόμενον περιιζόμενοι, οἱ προσήκοντες ὀλοφύρονται ὅσα μιν δεῖ, ἐπείτε ἐγένετο, ἀναπλῆσαι κακά, ἀνηγεόμενοι τὰ ἀνθρωπήια πάντα πάθεα. τὸν δ' ἀπογενόμενον παίζοντές τε καὶ ἡδόμενοι γῇ κρύπτουσι, ἐπιλέγοντες ὅσων κακῶν ἐξαπαλλαχθεὶς ἐστὶ ἐν πάσῃ εὐδαιμονίῃ.

V.4.1 τούτων: refers back to the Getai, the Trausians, and those living above the Krestonians; partitive with Γέται.   **τὰ μέν = ταῦτα ἃ μέν:** the antecedent, ταῦτα, has dropped out; it is typical for the antecedent to drop out and for the relative pronoun to serve two functions. Here it is the object of ποιεῦσι and the subject of εἴρηται. Consider the similar use of "what" in English: "I see what is happening."   **τὰ μὲν Γέται:** is answered by Τραυσοὶ δέ.   **εἴρηται:** for what Herodotus has to say about the Getai, see IV.93.   **μοι:** the dative of agent is common with the perfect and pluperfect passive and with verbal adjectives.   **τὰ μέν:** is answered by κατὰ δέ.   **τὰ μὲν ἄλλα πάντα:** substantive, "all other things"; Herodotus tends to put the general and common first, τὰ μὲν ἄλλα, and the more specific, κατὰ δὲ τὸν γινόμενόν, second.   **κατὰ ταὐτά =** κατὰ τὰ αὐτά.   **τοῖσι ἄλλοισι Θρήιξι:** after an adjective that means "the same" or "similar," the dative case is common. Consider this example: τά σοι αὐτὰ ποιῶ ("I do the same things as you do").   **κατὰ δὲ τὸν γινόμενον:** substantive, "concerning the one born."   **ἀπογινόμενον:** substantive "concerning the one having died" and object of κατά.   **τοιάδε:** looks forward to what comes next.   **4.2 τὸν μὲν γενόμενον ... τὸν δ' ἀπογενόμενον:** substantive, "a new-born ... one having died."   **ὀλοφύρονται:** here to the end of the paragraph gives the Trausians' point of view.   **ὅσα:** modifies κακά.   **μιν = αὐτόν:** subject of ἀναπλῆσαι.   **δεῖ:** when translating δεῖ or χρή, remember to include the impersonal subject "it."   **ἐπείτε ἐγένετο:** i.e., now that he has entered the world.   **ἀναπλῆσαι:** complementary with δεῖ.   **κακά:** object of ὀλοφύρονται.   **ὅσων:** genitive of separation with ἐξαπαλλαχθείς.   **ἐπιλέγοντες ὅσων κακῶν = ἐπιλέγοντες κακά ὅσων:** κακῶν is attracted into the case of ὅσων and brought into the participial phrase. Greek literature contains at least two different strains of thought: (1) "better to never have been born at all" or "better to die as soon as possible" (the Chorus in Sophocles' *Oedipus at Colonus*, 1225) and (2) "better to be alive and a slave than dead and a king" (Akhilleus, speaking in Homer's *Odyssey*).

❧

V.5.1 οἱ δὲ κατύπερθε Κρηστωναίων ποιεῦσι τοιάδε. ἔχει γυναῖκας ἕκαστος πολλάς. ἐπεὰν ὦν τις αὐτῶν ἀποθάνῃ, κρίσις γίνεται μεγάλη τῶν γυναικῶν. καὶ φίλων σπουδαὶ ἰσχυραὶ περὶ τοῦδε· ἥτις αὐτέων ἐφιλέετο μάλιστα ὑπὸ τοῦ ἀνδρός. ἣ δ᾽ ἂν κριθῇ καὶ τιμηθῇ, ἐγκωμιασθεῖσα ὑπό τε ἀνδρῶν καὶ γυναικῶν, σφάζεται ἐς τὸν τάφον ὑπὸ τοῦ οἰκηιοτάτου ἑωυτῆς. σφαχθεῖσα δὲ συνθάπτεται τῷ ἀνδρί. αἱ δὲ ἄλλαι συμφορὴν μεγάλην ποιεῦνται· ὄνειδος γάρ σφι τοῦτο μέγιστον γίνεται.

V.5.1 οἱ δὲ κατύπερθε Κρηστωναίων: substantive, "those who live above the Krestonians."   **τοιάδε:** looks forward to what comes next.   **αὐτῶν:** partitive with τις.   **ἀποθάνῃ:** a hypothetical subjunctive, indicating an event that has occurred with frequency in the past.   **σπουδαί:** supply an implied εἰσι.   **περὶ τοῦδε:** looks forward to what comes next.   **αὐτέων:** partitive with ἥτις.   **ἣ ἂν κριθῇ . . . τιμηθῇ:** hypothetical subjunctives, indicating an event that has yet to occur.   **τοῦ οἰκηιοτάτου:** substantive, "closest relation."   **σφαχθεῖσα:** modifies an implied ἡ γυνή.   **τῷ ἀνδρί:** object of the prefix συν- of συνθάπτεται.   **ποιεῦνται = ποιοῦνται:** offers the perspective of the other wives.   **σφι:** possesses ὄνειδος.

❧

V.6.1 τῶν δὲ δὴ ἄλλων Θρηίκων ἐστὶ ὅδε νόμος· πωλεῦσι τὰ τέκνα ἐπ᾽ ἐξαγωγῇ. τὰς δὲ παρθένους οὐ φυλάσσουσι, ἀλλ᾽ ἐῶσι, τοῖσι αὐταὶ βούλονται ἀνδράσι, μίσγεσθαι. τὰς δὲ γυναῖκας ἰσχυρῶς φυλάσσουσι καὶ ὠνέονται τὰς γυναῖκας παρὰ τῶν γονέων χρημάτων μεγάλων. [2] καὶ τὸ μὲν ἐστίχθαι εὐγενὲς κέκριται· τὸ δὲ ἄστικτον ἀγεννές. ἀργὸν εἶναι κάλλιστον, γῆς δὲ ἐργάτην ἀτιμότατον. τὸ ζῆν ἀπὸ πολέμου καὶ ληιστύος κάλλιστον.

V.6.1 ὅδε: looks forward to what comes next.   **ἐπ' ἐξαγωγῇ:** "for a leading away," i.e., to non-Thrakians.   **ἐῶσι = ἐάουσι:** supply an implied παρθένους as the object; once stated, Greek tends not to restate direct and indirect objects.   **τοῖσι = οἷς:** Herodotus has placed the antecedent, ἀνδράσι, in the relative clause: e.g., εἶδεν ἐν ᾗ οἰκέω χώρᾳ ("he saw in which country I dwell") instead of εἶδεν χώραν ἐν ᾗ οἰκῶ.   **βούλονται:** supply an implied μίσγεσθαι.   **ἀνδράσι:** object of μίσγεσθαι implied with βούλονται.   **μίσγεσθαι:** dependent on ἐῶσι; supply an implied παρθένους as the subject.   **χρημάτων μεγάλων:** genitive of value, "at great cost."   **6.2 τὸ μέν:** is answered by τὸ δέ.   **τὸ μὲν ἐστίχθαι:** an articular infinitive, "being tatooed."   **κέκριται:** this judgment and what follows offer a Thrakian perspective on things.   **τὸ δὲ ἄστικτον:** supply an implied κέκριται.   **ἀργόν:** i.e., to not have to work the land to make a living; subject of εἶναι in implied indirect statement.   **ἐργάτην:** subject of εἶναι.   **τὸ ζῆν:** an articular infinitive and subject of an implied εἶναι or ἐστι.

❧

V.7.1 οὗτοι μὲν σφέων οἱ ἐπιφανέστατοι νόμοι εἰσί. θεοὺς δὲ σέβονται μούνους τούσδε, Ἄρεα καὶ Διόνυσον καὶ Ἄρτεμιν. οἱ δὲ βασιλέες αὐτῶν, πάρεξ τῶν ἄλλων πολιητέων, σέβονται Ἑρμέην μάλιστα θεῶν. καὶ ὀμνύουσι μοῦνον τοῦτον. καὶ λέγουσι γεγονέναι ἀπὸ Ἑρμέω ἑωυτούς.

V.7.1 οὗτοι μέν: is answered by θεοὺς δέ.   **οἱ ἐπιφανέστατοι νόμοι:** Herodotus selects for his narrative the information he deems most interesting to himself and his Greek audience.   **θεοὺς δὲ σέβονται:** it is customary to give a foreign deity the name of the deity from one's own culture who is judged most similar.   **τούσδε:** looks forward to what is to come.   **θεῶν:** partitive with Ἑρμέην.   **γεγονέναι:** main verb in indirect statement; the subject is the same as the subject of λέγουσι.   **ἑωυτούς:** typically when the subject of the head verb and infinitive are the same, all subject modifiers are nominative; here this is not the case.

❧

V.8.1 ταφαὶ δὲ τοῖσι εὐδαίμοσι αὐτῶν εἰσὶ αἵδε. τρεῖς μὲν ἡμέρας προτιθεῖσι τὸν νεκρόν. καὶ παντοῖα σφάξαντες ἱρήια, εὐωχέονται, προκλαύσαντες πρῶτον. ἔπειτα δὲ θάπτουσι, κατακαύσαντες ἢ ἄλλως γῇ κρύψαντες. χῶμα δὲ χέαντες, ἀγῶνα τιθεῖσι παντοῖον, ἐν τῷ τὰ μέγιστα ἄεθλα τίθεται κατὰ λόγον μουνομαχίης. ταφαὶ μὲν δὴ Θρηίκων εἰσὶ αἵδε.

V.8.1 τοῖσι εὐδαίμοσι: substantive, "those with means."   **αὐτῶν:** partitive with τοῖσι εὐδαίμοσι.   **αἵδε:** looks forward to what is to come.   **τρεῖς μέν:** is answered by ἔπειτα δέ.   **ἐν τῷ = ἐν ᾧ.**   **κατὰ λόγον μουνομαχίης:** "in the category of single combat."   **ταφαὶ μέν:** is answered by the upcoming τὸ δὲ πρὸς βορέω from 9.1.   **αἵδε:** though it typically looks ahead to what comes next, here it refers back to what has just been said.

V.9.1 τὸ δὲ πρὸς βορέω τῆς χώρης ἔτι ταύτης οὐδεὶς ἔχει φράσαι τὸ ἀτρεκὲς οἵτινες εἰσὶ ἄνθρωποι οἰκέοντες αὐτήν. ἀλλὰ τὰ πέρην ἤδη τοῦ Ἴστρου ἔρημος χώρη φαίνεται ἐοῦσα καὶ ἄπειρος. μούνους δὲ δύναμαι πυθέσθαι οἰκέοντας πέρην τοῦ Ἴστρου ἀνθρώπους, τοῖσι οὔνομα εἶναι Σιγύννας, ἐσθῆτι δὲ χρεωμένους Μηδικῇ. [2] τοὺς δὲ ἵππους αὐτῶν εἶναι λασίους ἅπαν τὸ σῶμα καὶ ἐπὶ πέντε δακτύλους τὸ βάθος τῶν τριχῶν. μικροὺς δὲ καὶ σιμοὺς καὶ ἀδυνάτους ἄνδρας φέρειν. ζευγνυμένους δὲ ὑπ᾽ ἅρματα εἶναι ὀξυτάτους. ἁρματηλατέειν δὲ πρὸς ταῦτα τοὺς ἐπιχωρίους. κατήκειν δὲ τούτων τοὺς οὔρους ἀγχοῦ Ἐνετῶν τῶν ἐν τῷ Ἀδρίῃ. [3] εἶναι δὲ Μήδων σφέας ἀποίκους λέγουσι. ὅκως δὲ οὗτοι Μήδων ἄποικοι γεγόνασι, ἐγὼ μὲν οὐκ ἔχω ἐπιφράσασθαι. γένοιτο δ᾽ ἂν πᾶν ἐν τῷ μακρῷ χρόνῳ. Σιγύννας δ᾽ ὦν καλέουσι Λίγυες, οἱ ἄνω ὑπὲρ Μασσαλίης οἰκέοντες, τοὺς καπήλους, Κύπριοι δὲ τὰ δόρατα.

V.9.1 τὸ δὲ πρὸς βορέω: substantive, "the area to the north."   **ἔχει:** the switch to the present tense indicates that this part belongs to the present day of Herodotus and his audience.   **φράσαι:** complementary with ἔχει.   **τὸ ἀτρεκές:** accusative of respect, "exactly."   **τὰ πέρην ἤδη τοῦ Ἴστρου:** substantive, "the area beyond the Istros."   **ἤδη ... φαίνεται:** indicates the current-day status of the area.   **ἐοῦσα:** supplementary with φαίνεται.   **μούνους:** substantive, "only ones" and subject of an implied εἶναι.   **πυθέσθαι:** complementary with δύναμαι.   **ἀνθρώπους:** predicate to μούνους.   **τοῖσι = οἷς:** possesses οὔνομα.   **οὔνομα:** subject of εἶναι.   **9.2 τοὺς δὲ ἵππους:** subject of εἶναι.   **εἶναι:** main verb in implied indirect statement.   **τὸ σῶμα:** accusative of respect.   **ἐπὶ πέντε δακτύλους:** predicate to τὸ βάθος.   **τὸ βάθος:** subject of an implied εἶναι.   **μικροὺς δὲ καὶ σιμοὺς καὶ ἀδυνάτους:** the three adjectives are predicate to an implied τοὺς ἵππους that is the subject of an implied εἶναι.   **φέρειν:** epexegetical with ἀδυνάτους.   **ζευγνυμένους:** modifies an implied τοὺς ἵππους.   **εἶναι:** main verb in implied indirect statement.   **ὀξυτάτους:** predicate to an implied τοὺς ἵππους that is the subject of εἶναι.   **ἁρματηλατέειν:** main verb in implied indirect statement.   **πρὸς**

ταῦτα: substantive, "consequently"; ταῦτα refers back to the swiftness of the yoked horses.   τοὺς ἐπιχωρίους: substantive, "inhabitants of the country," subject of ἁρματηλατέειν.   κατήκειν: main verb in implied indirect statement.   τοὺς οὔρους: subject of κατήκειν.   9.3 λέγουσι: Herodotus hands off narration to the Sigynnai.   εἶναι: main verb in indirect statement.   σφέας: subject of εἶναι; typically when the subject of the head verb and the infinitive are the same, all subject modifiers are nominative; here this is not the case.   λέγουσι: Herodotus typically cites his sources; he also often hands over narration to his subjects, through direct and indirect statement and other focalizing devices. He does not always make his agreement or disagreement with these other narratives explicit. Here he does.   ἐγὼ μέν: is answered by γένοιτο δ᾽ ἄν.   ἐπιφράσασθαι: complementary with ἔχω.   γένοιτο δ᾽ ἄν: potential optative.   τὰ δόρατα: supply an implied σιγύννας καλέουσι.

~

V.10.1 ὡς δὲ Θρήικες λέγουσι, μέλισσαι κατέχουσι τὰ πέρην τοῦ Ἴστρου, καὶ ὑπὸ τουτέων οὐκ εἶναι διελθεῖν τὸ προσωτέρω. ἐμοὶ μέν νυν, ταῦτα λέγοντες, δοκέουσι λέγειν οὐκ οἰκότα· τὰ γὰρ ζῷα ταῦτα φαίνεται εἶναι δύσριγα. ἀλλά μοι τὰ ὑπὸ τὴν ἄρκτον ἀοίκητα δοκέει εἶναι διὰ τὰ ψύχεα. ταῦτα μέν νυν τῆς χώρης ταύτης πέρι λέγεται. τὰ παραθαλάσσια δ᾽ ὦν αὐτῆς Μεγάβαζος Περσέων κατήκοα ἐποίεε.

V.10.1 λέγουσι: narration will be taken back by Herodotus shortly.   τὰ πέρην: substantive, "the area beyond."   τουτέων: refers back to the bees.   οὐκ εἶναι: main verb in indirect statement; impersonal, "it is not possible."   διελθεῖν: complementary with οὐκ εἶναι.   τὸ προσωτέρω: substantive, "further."   ἐμοὶ μέν νυν: is answered by ἀλλά μοι.   ταῦτα: refers back to what the Thrakians say.   λέγειν: complementary with δοκέουσι.   εἶναι: complementary with φαίνεται.   δύσριγα: inhabiting every continent but Antartica, bees live wherever there are insect-pollinated flowering plants.   τὰ ὑπὸ τὴν ἄρκτον: substantive, "the area under the Bear" or "the Big Dipper."   εἶναι: complemenatry with δοκέει.   ταῦτα μέν: refers back to what has just been said and is answered by τὰ παραθαλάσσια δέ.   τῆς χώρης ταύτης πέρι: anastrophe of the disyllabic preposition, indicated by the accent shifting to the penult.   Περσέων: translate with κατήκοα.

~

V.11.1 Δαρεῖος δέ, ὡς διαβὰς τάχιστα τὸν Ἑλλήσποντον ἀπίκετο ἐς Σάρδις, ἐμνήσθη τῆς ἐξ Ἱστιαίου τε τοῦ Μιλησίου εὐεργεσίης καὶ τῆς

παραινέσιος τοῦ Μυτιληναίου Κώεω. μεταπεμψάμενος δὲ σφέας ἐς
Σάρδις, ἐδίδου αὐτοῖσι αἵρεσιν. [2] ὁ μὲν δὴ Ἱστιαῖος, ἅτε τυραννεύων
τῆς Μιλήτου, τυραννίδος μὲν οὐδεμιῆς προσεχρήιζε. αἰτέει δὲ
Μύρκινον τὴν Ἠδωνῶν, βουλόμενος ἐν αὐτῇ πόλιν κτίσαι. οὗτος μὲν
δὴ ταύτην αἱρέεται· ὁ δὲ Κώης, οἷά τε οὐ τύραννος δημότης τε ἐών,
αἰτέει Μυτιλήνης τυραννεῦσαι.

V.11.1 ἐμνήσθη: here we see things through Dareios's eyes.   **Ἱστιαίου:** for his
good service, see IV.137–42.   **Κώεω:** for his good service, see IV.97.   **11.2 ὁ μὲν
δὴ Ἱστιαῖος:** is answered by ὁ δὲ Κώης. Herodotus offers events from both their
perspectives.   **ἅτε τυραννεύων τῆς Μιλήτου:** ἅτε (and οἷα) is typically found
with a participle in the nominative or accusative case. Use "since" or "because" to
translate it, and turn the participle into a finite verb. Thus, ἅτε αὐτὸν ὄντα καλόν
(ἅτε ὢν καλός): "since he was good."   **τυραννίδος μέν:** is answered by αἰτέει
δέ.   **κτίσαι:** complementary with βουλόμενος.   **οὗτος μέν:** repeats ὁ μὲν δὴ
Ἱστιαῖος and is answered by ὁ δὲ Κώης.   **οἷά τε οὐ τύραννος δημότης τε ἐών:**
οἷα functions just like ἅτε above, i.e., "because he was not tyrant but a private
citizen."   **τυραννεῦσαι:** complementary with αἰτέει.

◞

V.12.1 τελεωθέντων δὲ ἀμφοτέροισι, οὗτοι μέν, κατὰ τὰ εἵλοντο,
ἐτράποντο. Δαρεῖον δὲ συνήνεικε, πρῆγμα τοιόνδε ἰδόμενον,
ἐπιθυμῆσαι ἐντείλασθαι Μεγαβάζῳ, Παίονας ἑλόντα, ἀνασπάστους
ποιῆσαι ἐς τὴν Ἀσίην ἐκ τῆς Εὐρώπης. ἦν Πίγρης καὶ Μαντύης, ἄνδρες
Παίονες, οἵ, ἐπείτε Δαρεῖος διέβη ἐς τὴν Ἀσίην, αὐτοὶ ἐθέλοντες
Παιόνων τυραννεύειν, ἀπικνέονται ἐς Σάρδις, ἅμα ἀγόμενοι ἀδελφεὴν
μεγάλην τε καὶ εὐειδέα. [2] φυλάξαντες δὲ Δαρεῖον, προκατιζόμενον
ἐς τὸ προάστειον τὸ τῶν Λυδῶν, ἐποίησαν τοιόνδε. σκευάσαντες τὴν
ἀδελφεήν, ὡς εἶχον ἄριστα, ἐπ' ὕδωρ ἔπεμπον, ἄγγος ἐπὶ τῇ κεφαλῇ
ἔχουσαν καὶ ἐκ τοῦ βραχίονος ἵππον ἐπέλκουσαν καὶ κλώθουσαν λίνον.
[3] ὡς δὲ παρεξήιε ἡ γυνή, ἐπιμελὲς τῷ Δαρείῳ ἐγένετο. οὔτε γὰρ
Περσικὰ ἦν οὔτε Λύδια τὰ ποιεύμενα ἐκ τῆς γυναικός, οὔτε πρὸς τῶν ἐκ
τῆς Ἀσίης οὐδαμῶν. ἐπιμελὲς δὲ ὥς οἱ ἐγένετο, τῶν δορυφόρων τινὰς
πέμπει, κελεύων φυλάξαι ὅ τι χρήσεται τῷ ἵππῳ ἡ γυνή. [4] οἱ μὲν δὴ
ὄπισθε εἵποντο· ἡ δέ, ἐπείτε ἀπίκετο ἐπὶ τὸν ποταμόν, ἦρσε τὸν ἵππον.
ἄρσασα δὲ καὶ τὸ ἄγγος τοῦ ὕδατος ἐμπλησαμένη, τὴν αὐτὴν ὁδὸν

παρεξήιε, φέρουσα τὸ ὕδωρ ἐπὶ τῆς κεφαλῆς καὶ ἐπέλκουσα ἐκ τοῦ
βραχίονος τὸν ἵππον καὶ στρέφουσα τὸν ἄτρακτον.

V.12.1 τελεωθέντων: substantive, "these things being accomplished." **ἀμφοτέροισι:**
i.e., Histiaios and Koës.   **οὗτοι μέν:** is answered by Δαρεῖον δέ.   **κατὰ τά =
κατὰ ταῦτα, ἅ:** the antecedent ταῦτα is omitted and the relative pronoun serves as
the object of κατά and εἵλοντο.   **Δαρεῖον:** subject of ἐπιθυμῆσαι.   **συνήνεικε:**
impersonal, "it happened."   **πρῆγμα τοιόνδε ἰδόμενον:** Herodotus has us see
the upcoming events through Dareios's eyes.   **ἐντείλασθαι:** complementary
with ἐπιθυμῆσαι.   **Μεγαβάζῳ:** is to perform the action of ποιῆσαι.   **ἐλόντα:**
though the two do not agree in case, the participle modifies Μεγαβάζῳ; the lack
of agreement between the two is typical when the noun the participle modifies
is also to perform the action of an upcoming infinitive.   **ποιῆσαι:** dependent
on ἐντείλασθαι.   **ἦν Πίγρης καὶ Μαντύης:** in a declined language it is typical
for the verb to agree with the subject nearest to it, and so here the verb remains
singular.   **ἄνδρες Παίονες:** in apposition to Πίγρης καὶ Μαντύης.   **οἵ:**
subject of the upcoming ἀπικνέονται.   **τυραννεύειν:** complementary with
ἐθέλοντες.   **12.2 τοιόνδε:** looks forward to what comes next.   **ὡς . . .
ἄριστα:** "as best as."   **ἔπεμπον:** supply an implied αὐτήν as the object.   **12.3
ὡς:** temporal.   **τῷ Δαρείῳ:** translate with ἐπιμελές.   **τὰ ποιεύμενα =
τὰ ποιούμενα:** substantive, "the things being done."   **ἐκ τῆς γυναικός:**
agency.   **πρὸς τῶν . . . οὐδαμῶν:** agency.   **οἱ = αὐτῷ:** translate with
ἐπιμελές.   **τῶν δορυφόρων:** partitive with τινάς.   **κελεύων . . . φυλάξαι:**
supply an implied τῶν δορυφόρων τινὰς as the object of κελεύων and subject of
φυλάξαι.   **φυλάξαι:** dependent on κελεύων.   **ὅ τι:** accusative of respect, "in
what way."   **12.4 οἱ μέν:** is answered by ἡ δέ.   **ἄρσασα:** a bit redundant; supply
an implied τὸν ἵππον as object.

~

V.13.1 θωμάζων δὲ ὁ Δαρεῖος τά τε ἤκουσε ἐκ τῶν κατασκόπων καὶ
τὰ αὐτὸς ὥρα, ἄγειν αὐτὴν ἐκέλευε ἑωυτῷ ἐς ὄψιν. ὡς δὲ ἄχθη,
παρῆσαν καὶ οἱ ἀδελφεοὶ αὐτῆς, οὔ κῃ πρόσω σκοπιὴν ἔχοντες τούτων.
εἰρωτῶντος δὲ τοῦ Δαρείου ὁποδαπὴ εἴη, ἔφασαν οἱ νεηνίσκοι εἶναι
Παίονες καὶ ἐκείνην εἶναι σφέων ἀδελφεήν. [2] ὁ δ᾽ ἀμείβετο, τίνες δὲ
οἱ Παίονες ἄνθρωποι εἰσὶ καὶ κοῦ γῆς οἰκημένοι, καὶ τί κεῖνοι ἐθέλοντες
ἔλθοιεν ἐς Σάρδις. οἱ δέ οἱ ἔφραζον ὡς ἔλθοιεν μὲν ἐκείνῳ δώσοντες
σφέας αὐτούς· εἴη δὲ ἡ Παιονίη ἐπὶ τῷ Στρυμόνι ποταμῷ πεπολισμένη·
ὁ δὲ Στρυμὼν οὐ πρόσω τοῦ Ἑλλησπόντου· εἴησαν δὲ Τευκρῶν τῶν ἐκ
Τροίης ἄποικοι. [3] οἱ μὲν δὴ ταῦτα ἕκαστα ἔλεγον. ὁ δὲ εἰρώτα εἰ καὶ

πᾶσαι αὐτόθι αἱ γυναῖκες εἴησαν οὕτω ἐργάτιδες. οἱ δὲ καὶ τοῦτο ἔφασαν
προθύμως οὕτω ἔχειν· αὐτοῦ γὰρ ὧν τούτου εἵνεκα καὶ ἐποιέετο.

V.13.1 θωμάζων δὲ ὁ Δαρεῖος: Herodotus hands over narration to Dareios and later
to the Paionians.   **τά = ταῦτα ἅ:** the antecedent ταῦτα is omitted, and the relative
pronoun serves as the object of θωμάζων as well as the object of the upcoming
ἤκουσε.   **τε...καί:** links τά and τά.   **τά = ταῦτα ἅ:** the antecedent ταῦτα
is omitted, and the relative pronoun τά serves as the object of θωμάζων as well
as the object of ὥρα.   **ἄγειν:** dependent on ἐκέλευε; understand as subject an
implied "slaves."   **ἐκέλευε:** "he gave the order," the person being ordered is often
left implied.   **ἑωυτῷ:** possesses ὄψιν.   **τούτων:** refers back to the events just
described.   **εἴη:** optative standing for an original indicative.   **εἶναι:** main verb
in indirect statement; the subject is the same as the subject of ἔφασαν.   **ἐκείνην:**
subject of εἶναι.   **εἶναι:** main verb in indirect statement.   **13.2 εἰσί:** the
optative is typical in an indirect question in secondary sequence; here the
indicative is retained for vividness.   **ἔλθοιεν:** the optative stands for an original
indicative.   **οἱ δέ...ἔφραζον:** the Paionians take over the narration.   **οἱ
= αὐτῷ.**   **ἔλθοιεν...εἴη...εἴησαν:** the optatives stand for original
indicatives.   **ἔλθοιεν μέν:** is answered by εἴη δέ; ὁ δὲ Στρυμών; and εἴησαν
δέ.   **δώσοντες:** shows the intent of the two Paionians.   **ὁ δὲ Στρυμών:** supply
an implied εἴη.   **13.3 οἱ μέν:** is answered by ὁ δέ.   **ταῦτα:** refers back to what
they just said.   **εἴησαν:** optative standing for an original indicative.   **τοῦτο:**
subject of οὕτω ἔχειν ("this was so").   **προθύμως:** modifies ἔφασαν; adverbs
typically come right before or right after what they modify.   **ἔχειν:** main verb in
indirect statement.   **ἐποιέετο:** supply an implied ταῦτα as the subject.

⁓

V.14.1 ἐνθαῦτα Δαρεῖος γράφει γράμματα Μεγαβάζῳ, τὸν ἔλιπε ἐν
τῇ Θρηίκῃ στρατηγόν, ἐντελλόμενος ἐξαναστῆσαι ἐξ ἠθέων Παίονας
καὶ παρ' ἑωυτὸν ἀγαγεῖν καὶ αὐτοὺς καὶ τὰ τέκνα τε καὶ τὰς γυναῖκας
αὐτῶν. [2] αὐτίκα δὲ ἱππεὺς ἔθεε, φέρων τὴν ἀγγελίην ἐπὶ τὸν
Ἑλλήσποντον. περαιωθεὶς δὲ διδοῖ τὸ βυβλίον τῷ Μεγαβάζῳ. ὁ δὲ
ἐπιλεξάμενος καὶ λαβὼν ἡγεμόνας ἐκ τῆς Θρηίκης, ἐστρατεύετο ἐπὶ
τὴν Παιονίην.

V.14.1 γράφει: a historical or storytelling present.   **τόν = ὄν.**   **στρατηγόν:**
predicate to τόν.   **ἐντελλόμενος:** understand an implied Μεγαβάζῳ as the
object of the participle; an implied Μεγαβάζῳ is also to perform the action of the
upcoming infinitives.   **ἐξαναστῆσαι...ἀγαγεῖν:** dependent on ἐντελλόμενος.

～

V.15.1 πυθόμενοι δὲ οἱ Παίονες τοὺς Πέρσας ἐπὶ σφέας ἰέναι, ἁλισθέντες ἐξεστρατεύσαντο πρὸς θαλάσσης, δοκέοντες ταύτῃ ἐπιχειρήσειν τοὺς Πέρσας ἐμβάλλοντας. [2] οἱ μὲν δὴ Παίονες ἦσαν ἕτοιμοι τὸν Μεγαβάζου στρατὸν ἐπιόντα ἐρύκειν. οἱ δὲ Πέρσαι πυθόμενοι συναλίσθαι τοὺς Παίονας καὶ τὴν πρὸς θαλάσσης ἐσβολὴν φυλάσσοντας, ἔχοντες ἡγεμόνας τὴν ἄνω ὁδὸν τρέπονται. λαθόντες δὲ τοὺς Παίονας ἐσπίπτουσι ἐς τὰς πόλιας αὐτῶν, ἐούσας ἀνδρῶν ἐρήμους. οἷα δὲ κεινῇσι ἐπιπεσόντες, εὐπετέως κατέσχον. [3] οἱ δὲ Παίονες, ὡς ἐπύθοντο ἐχομένας τὰς πόλιας, αὐτίκα διασκεδασθέντες κατ᾽ ἑωυτοὺς ἕκαστοι ἐτράποντο καὶ παρεδίδοσαν σφέας αὐτοὺς τοῖσι Πέρσῃσι. οὕτω δὴ Παιόνων Σιριοπαίονές τε καὶ Παιόπλαι καὶ οἱ μέχρι τῆς Πρασιάδος λίμνης, ἐξ ἠθέων ἐξαναστάντες, ἤγοντο ἐς τὴν Ἀσίην.

V.15.1 οἱ Παίονες: are the narrators here.   **τοὺς Πέρσας:** subject of ἰέναι.   **ἰέναι:** main verb in indirect statement.   **ταύτῃ:** i.e., the area of the sea.   **ἐπιχειρήσειν:** main verb in indirect statement.   **τοὺς Πέρσας:** subject of ἐπιχειρήσειν.   **15.2 οἱ μὲν δὴ Παίονες:** is answered by οἱ δὲ Πέρσαι.   **ἐρύκειν:** epexegetical with ἕτοιμοι.   **πυθόμενοι:** the Persians take over the narration.   **συναλίσθαι:** main verb in indirect statement.   **τοὺς Παίονας:** subject of συναλίσθαι.   **τὴν ἄνω ὁδὸν:** "the upper road," which leads inland.   **λαθόντες δὲ τοὺς Παίονας:** "secretly from the Paionians"; consider the slightly different syntax that occurs when λανθάνω is the main verb, λανθάνω αὐτὸν ταῦτα ποιῶν: "I escape his notice (αὐτόν), doing these things" or "I do these things secretly from him."   **οἷα δὲ κεινῇσι ἐπιπεσόντες:** οἷα (and ἅτε) is typically found with a participle in the nominative or accusative case. Use "since" or "because" to translate it, and turn the participle into a finite verb. Thus, ἅτε αὐτὸν ὄντα καλόν (ἅτε ὢν καλός): "since he was good."   **15.3 ἐχομένας:** main verb in indirect statement.   **οὕτω:** Herodotus uses the adverb to explain to his listeners how these Thrakians were uprooted.   **Παιόνων:** partitive with Σιριοπαίονες, Παιόπλαι, and οἱ μέχρι.   **οἱ μέχρι τῆς Πρασιάδος λίμνης:** substantive, "those living as far as Prasiad Lake." Prasiad Lake has been identified with the lake of Doïran as well as with the one of Butkova.   **ἐξαναστάντες ἤγοντο:** the aorist participle emphasizes the fact of their being uprooted; the imperfect finite verb stresses the process of being led to Asia.

～

V.16.1 οἱ δὲ περί τε Πάγγαιον ὄρος [καὶ Δόβηρας καὶ Ἀγριᾶνας καὶ Ὀδομάντους] καὶ αὐτὴν τὴν λίμνην τὴν Πρασιάδα οὐκ ἐχειρώθησαν ἀρχὴν ὑπὸ Μεγαβάζου. ἐπειρήθη δὲ τοὺς ἐν τῇ λίμνῃ κατοικημένους ἐξαιρέειν ὧδε. ἴκρια, ἐπὶ σταυρῶν ὑψηλῶν ἐζευγμένα, ἐν μέσῃ ἕστηκε τῇ λίμνῃ, ἔσοδον ἐκ τῆς ἠπείρου στεινὴν ἔχοντα μιῇ γεφύρῃ. [2] τοὺς δὲ σταυροὺς τοὺς ὑπεστεῶτας τοῖσι ἰκρίοισι, τὸ μέν κου ἀρχαῖον, ἔστησαν κοινῇ πάντες οἱ πολιῆται. μετὰ δὲ νόμῳ χρεώμενοι ἱστᾶσι τοιῷδε. κομίζοντες ἐξ ὄρεος, τῷ οὔνομα ἐστὶ Ὄρβηλος, κατὰ γυναῖκα ἑκάστην ὁ γαμέων τρεῖς σταυροὺς ὑπίστησι. ἄγεται δὲ ἕκαστος συχνὰς γυναῖκας. [3] οἰκέουσι δὲ τοιοῦτον τρόπον, κρατέων ἕκαστος ἐπὶ τῶν ἰκρίων καλύβης τε ἐν τῇ διαιτᾶται καὶ θύρης καταπακτῆς διὰ τῶν ἰκρίων κάτω φερούσης ἐς τὴν λίμνην. τὰ δὲ νήπια παιδία δέουσι τοῦ ποδὸς σπάρτῳ, μὴ κατακυλισθῇ δειμαίνοντες. [4] τοῖσι δὲ ἵπποισι καὶ τοῖσι ὑποζυγίοισι παρέχουσι χόρτον ἰχθῦς. τῶν δὲ πλῆθος ἐστὶ τοσοῦτο ὥστε, ὅταν τὴν θύρην τὴν καταπακτὴν ἀνακλίνῃ, κατιεῖ σχοίνῳ σπυρίδα κεινὴν ἐς τὴν λίμνην. καὶ οὐ πολλόν τινα χρόνον ἐπισχὼν, ἀνασπᾷ πλήρεα ἰχθύων. τῶν δὲ ἰχθύων ἐστὶ γένεα δύο, τοὺς καλέουσι πάπρακάς τε καὶ τίλωνας.

V.16.1 οἱ δὲ περί τε Πάγγαιον ὄρος: substantive, "those around Mt. Pangaion." **[καὶ Δόβηρας καὶ Ἀγριᾶνας καὶ Ὀδομάντους]**: is bracketed and considered spurious by some based on geographical and ethnographical considerations, though the argument is by no means conclusive. **λίμνην**: object of περί. **ἀρχήν**: "at all." **τοὺς ἐν τῇ λίμνῃ κατοικημένους**: substantive, "those dwelling on the lake." **ἐξαιρέειν**: complementary with πειρήθη. **ὧδε**: modifies κατοικημένους and looks forward to what comes next. **ἐν μέσῃ ἕστηκε τῇ λίμνῃ**: the verb and adjective come between the preposition and its object; though we have no exact parallel in English for the delay seen here, consider this one: "in a very big and even quite deliberate hurry," where the object "hurry" is quite delayed. **ἔχοντα**: modifies ἴκρια. **16.2 τὸ μέν κου ἀρχαῖον**: "in the past," "originally." Herodotus looks back to the origin of the planks and the stakes; τὸ μέν is answered by μετὰ δέ. **κοινῇ**: "jointly," "together." Like the acc. singular and plural of neuter adjectives, the feminine dative singular adjective, when it does not modify a noun, frequently functions as a dative of respect that translates into English as an adverb. **μετὰ δέ**: adverbial, "later"; i.e., the custom for building the stakes and planks changes. **ἱστᾶσι**: supply an implied ἴκρια and σταυρούς as the object. **τοιῷδε**: looks forward to what comes next. **κομίζοντες ... ἑκάστην ὁ γαμέων**: although the numbers of the two participles are different, they each are modifying the same subject. "People come, each one bringing food" somewhat captures the idea, though in the Greek ἑκάστην modifies γυναῖκα.

Understand ἴκρια and σταυρούς as the objects of κομίζοντες.   τῷ = ᾧ: possesses οὔνομα.   **16.3 οἰκέουσι**: the narrative frame switches from the Persian conquest of c. 511 to the customs of the people of the area, which remain intact during Herodotus's own day.   **τοιοῦτον τρόπον**: accusative of respect, "in the following manner."   **τε … καί**: links καλύβης and θύρης, both objects of κρατέων.   **ἐν τῇ = ἐν ᾗ.**   **θύρης καταπακτῆς**: i.e., a trapdoor.   **μή**: the negative for hypotheticals.   **κατακυλισθῇ**: the subject is an implied νήπια παιδία; the subjunctive is hypothetical, indicating a fear for a possible future outcome.   **16.4 χόρτον**: predicate to ἰχθῦς.   **τῶν δέ**: partitive with πλῆθος.   **ἀνακλίνῃ**: a hypothetical subjunctive, referring to an event that has occurred frequently in the past.   **ἐπισχών**: a marker for a pause, indicating that everything before it up to the καὶ οὐ is to be translated together.   **πλήρεα**: modifies an implied σπυρίδα.   **ἰχθύων**: translate with πλήρεα.   **τῶν δὲ ἰχθύων**: partitive with γένεα.   **τούς = οὕς.**   **πάπρακας and τίλωνας**: predicate to τούς.

~

V.17.1 Παιόνων μὲν δὴ οἱ χειρωθέντες ἤγοντο ἐς τὴν Ἀσίην. Μεγάβαζος δέ, ὡς ἐχειρώσατο τοὺς Παίονας, πέμπει ἀγγέλους ἐς Μακεδονίην, ἄνδρας ἑπτὰ Πέρσας, οἳ μετ᾽ αὐτὸν ἐκεῖνον ἦσαν δοκιμώτατοι ἐν τῷ στρατοπέδῳ. ἐπέμποντο δὲ οὗτοι παρὰ Ἀμύντην αἰτήσοντες γῆν τε καὶ ὕδωρ Δαρείῳ βασιλέι. [2] ἔστι δὲ ἐκ τῆς Πρασιάδος λίμνης σύντομος κάρτα ἐς τὴν Μακεδονίην. πρῶτον μὲν γὰρ ἔχεται τῆς λίμνης τὸ μέταλλον, ἐξ οὗ ὕστερον τούτων τάλαντον ἀργυρίου Ἀλεξάνδρῳ ἡμέρης ἑκάστης ἐφοίτα. μετὰ δὲ τὸ μέταλλον Δύσωρον καλεόμενον ὄρος ὑπερβάντα εἶναι ἐν Μακεδονίῃ.

V.17.1 Παιόνων: partitive with οἱ χειρωθέντες.   **Παιόνων μέν**: is answered by Μεγάβαζος δέ.   **οἱ χειρωθέντες**: substantive, "those subjugated."   **ὡς**: temporal.   **πέμπει**: historical or storytelling present.   **ἄνδρας ἑπτὰ Πέρσας**: in apposition to ἀγγέλους.   **αἰτήσοντες**: the participle indicates Megabazos's reason for sending them to Amyntes.   **γῆν τε καὶ ὕδωρ Δαρείῳ βασιλέι**: the giving of land and water to the king is symbolic of surrending all rights over the land and its produce to Persian control. In modern Greek, it continues to symbolize unconditional surrender.   **17.2 πρῶτον μέν**: is answered by μετὰ δέ.   **ἔχεται**: "is near" + gen.   **ὕστερον**: the time of the story Herodotus is currently telling is about 510 B.C.E.   **τούτων**: translate with ὕστερον.   **ὄρος**: object of ὑπερβάντα.   **ὑπερβάντα**: substantive, modifying a hypothetical traveler, imagined by σύντομος; subject of the infinitive εἶναι.   **εἶναι**: main verb in implied indirect statement.

⁓

V.18.1 οἱ ὦν Πέρσαι οἱ πεμφθέντες οὗτοι παρὰ τὸν Ἀμύντην, ὡς
ἀπίκοντο, αἴτεον, ἐλθόντες ἐς ὄψιν τὴν Ἀμύντεω, Δαρείῳ βασιλέι
γῆν τε καὶ ὕδωρ. ὁ δὲ ταῦτά τε ἐδίδου καὶ σφεας ἐπὶ ξείνια καλέει.
παρασκευασάμενος δὲ δεῖπνον μεγαλοπρεπές, ἐδέκετο τοὺς Πέρσας
φιλοφρόνως. [2] ὡς δὲ ἀπὸ δείπνου ἐγένοντο, διαπίνοντες εἶπαν οἱ
Πέρσαι τάδε· Ξεῖνε Μακεδών, ἡμῖν νόμος ἐστί, τοῖσι Πέρσῃσι, ἐπεὰν
δεῖπνον προτιθώμεθα μέγα, τότε καὶ τὰς παλλακὰς καὶ τὰς κουριδίας
γυναῖκας ἐσάγεσθαι παρέδρους. σύ νυν, ἐπεί περ προθύμως μὲν
ἐδέξαο, μεγάλως δὲ ξεινίζεις, διδοῖς δὲ βασιλέι Δαρείῳ γῆν τε καὶ
ὕδωρ, ἕπεο νόμῳ τῷ ἡμετέρῳ. [3] εἶπε πρὸς ταῦτα Ἀμύντης· Ὦ Πέρσαι,
νόμος μὲν ἡμῖν γε ἐστὶ οὐκ οὗτος, ἀλλὰ κεχωρίσθαι ἄνδρας γυναικῶν.
ἐπείτε δὲ ὑμεῖς, ἐόντες δεσπόται, προσχρηίζετε τούτων, παρέσται
ὑμῖν καὶ ταῦτα. εἴπας τοσαῦτα, ὁ Ἀμύντης μετεπέμπετο τὰς γυναῖκας.
αἱ δ' ἐπείτε καλεόμεναι ἦλθον. ἐπεξῆς ἀντίαι ἵζοντο τοῖσι Πέρσῃσι.
[4] ἐνθαῦτα οἱ Πέρσαι, ἰδόμενοι γυναῖκας εὐμόρφους, ἔλεγον πρὸς
Ἀμύντην, φάμενοι τὸ ποιηθὲν τοῦτο οὐδὲν εἶναι σοφόν· κρέσσον γὰρ
εἶναι ἀρχῆθεν μὴ ἐλθεῖν τὰς γυναῖκας ἢ ἐλθούσας καὶ μὴ παριζομένας
ἀντίας ἵζεσθαι ἀλγηδόνας σφίσι ὀφθαλμῶν. [5] ἀναγκαζόμενος δὲ ὁ
Ἀμύντης ἐκέλευε παρίζειν. πειθομενέων δὲ τῶν γυναικῶν, αὐτίκα οἱ
Πέρσαι μαστῶν τε ἅπτοντο οἷα πλεόνως οἰνωμένοι, καί κού τις καὶ
φιλέειν ἐπειρᾶτο.

V.18.1 οἱ ὦν Πέρσαι: Herodotus has the Persians and Amyntes take turns narrating
much of this section.   ὡς: temporal.   ταῦτα: refers back to the earth and
water.   **18.2** ὡς: temporal.   τάδε: looks forward to what comes next.   ἡμῖν:
possesses νόμος.   τοῖσι Πέρσῃσι: in apposition to ἡμῖν.   προτιθώμεθα:
a hypothetical subjunctive, indicating an event that has occurred with some
frequency in the past.   ἐσάγεσθαι: epexegetical with νόμος.   παρέδρους: in
apposition to τὰς παλλακὰς and τὰς κουριδίας.   προθύμως μέν: is answered
by μεγάλως δέ and διδοῖς δέ.   ἐδέξαο: the form is uncontracted, and the
intervocalic sigma of the ending -ασο has dropped out. The Attic form is the
contracted –ω.   **18.3** ταῦτα: refers back to what was just said.   νόμος…
οὗτος: often two words that are to be translated together bookend or sandwich
other words that are to be translated with them, as is the case with νόμος
and οὗτος.   νόμος μέν: is answered by ἐπείτε δὲ ὑμεῖς.   ἡμῖν: possesses

νόμος.   **κεχωρίσθαι:** epexegetical with an implied νόμος ἐστι.   **γυναικῶν:**
genitive of separation.   **προσχρηίζετε:** verbs of desiring typically take a
genitive object.   **τούτων:** refers back to the request for women.   **τοῖσι**
Πέρσῃσι: translate with ἀντίαι.   **18.4 τὸ ποιηθέν:** substantive, "what was done";
subject of εἶναι.   **οὐδέν:** accusative of respect, "in no way."   **εἶναι:** main
verb in indirect statement.   **κρέσσον:** impersonal and subject of εἶναι, "it was
better."   **ἐλθεῖν … ἵζεσθαι:** epexegetical with κρέσσον; the infinitives direct
the main line of thought in this "either/or" situation.   **τὰς γυναῖκας:** subject of
ἐλθεῖν and ἵζεσθαι.   **ἀλγηδόνας:** in apposition to γυναῖκας.   **σφίσι:** possesses
ὀφθαλμῶν.   **18.5 ἐκέλευε:** understand γυναῖκας as the object.   **παρίζειν:**
dependent on ἐκέλευε; understand γυναῖκας as the subject.   **οἷα:** οἷα (and ἅτε)
is typically found with a participle in the nominative or accusative case. Use "since"
or "because" to translate it, and turn the participle into a finite verb. Thus, ἅτε
αὐτὸν ὄντα καλόν (ἅτε ὢν καλός): "since he was good."   **φιλέειν:** "to kiss,"
complementary with ἐπειρᾶτο.

&

V.19.1 Ἀμύντης μὲν δή, ταῦτα ὀρέων, ἀτρέμας εἶχε, καίπερ δυσφορέων,
οἷα ὑπερδειμαίνων τοὺς Πέρσας. Ἀλέξανδρος δὲ ὁ Ἀμύντεω, παρεών
τε καὶ ὀρέων ταῦτα, ἅτε νέος τε ἐὼν καὶ κακῶν ἀπαθής, οὐδαμῶς
ἔτι κατέχειν οἷός τε ἦν. ὥστε δὲ βαρέως φέρων εἶπε πρὸς Ἀμύντην
τάδε· Σὺ μέν, ὦ πάτερ, εἶκε τῇ ἡλικίῃ· ἀπιών τε ἀναπαύεο. μηδὲ
λιπάρεε τῇ πόσι. ἐγὼ δέ, προσμένων αὐτοῦ τῇδε, πάντα τὰ ἐπιτήδεα
παρέξω τοῖσι ξείνοισι. [2] πρὸς ταῦτα συνιεὶς Ἀμύντης ὅτι νεώτερα
πρήγματα πρήσσειν μέλλοι ὁ Ἀλέξανδρος, λέγει· Ὦ παῖ, σχεδὸν γάρ
σευ ἀνακαιομένου συνίημι τοὺς λόγους, ὅτι ἐθέλεις, ἐμὲ ἐκπέμψας,
ποιέειν τι νεώτερον. ἐγὼ ὦν σευ χρηίζω μηδὲν νεοχμῶσαι κατ' ἄνδρας
τούτους, ἵνα μὴ ἐξεργάσῃ ἡμέας. ἀλλὰ ἀνέχευ ὀρέων τὰ ποιεύμενα.
ἀμφὶ δὲ ἀπόδῳ τῇ ἐμῇ πείσομαί τοι.

V.19.1 Ἀμύντης μέν: is answered by Ἀλέξανδρος δέ; much of this section is
seen through the eyes of these two.   **ταῦτα:** refers to the Persian fondling
of the Makedonian women. This tale's historicity is questioned because of its
traditional storytelling features. Hornblower (2013) finds the crossdressing part
of the plot a fiction because, if it were true, the Makedonians would have offered
stiffer resistance when later the Persians again invade their territory (VI.44).
The crossdressing part of the tale inserts itself into the story because it lessens
for the Makedonians the shame of having to submit to the Persian regime. How
and Wells think the crossdressing an invention because it allows Alexandros to

assert himself as anti-Persian against those who would fault him for submitting
to the Persian regime and for giving his sister's hand to one of its heads.   **οἷα:**
οἷα (and ἅτε) is typically found with a participle in the nominative or accusative
case. Use "since" or "because" to translate it, and turn the participle into a finite
verb. Thus, ἅτε αὐτὸν ὄντα καλόν (ἅτε ὢν καλός): "since he was good."   **ἅτε:**
like οἷα, ἅτε is also typically found with a participle in the nominative or
accusative and may be translated in the same way. This explanation intrudes on
Alexandros's narration, indicating how Herodotus wishes his audience to view
his upcoming words.   **κατέχειν:** complementary with οἷος τε ἦν.   **αὐτοῦ
τῇδε:** adverbial, "here in this spot."   **τάδε:** looks forward to his upcoming
words.   **Σὺ μέν:** is answered by ἐγὼ δέ.   **πάντα τὰ ἐπιτήδεα:** substantive,
"all that is needed."   **19.2 πρὸς ταῦτα:** ταῦτα looks back to what has just been
said.   **πρήσσειν:** complementary with μέλλοι.   **μέλλοι:** optative standing
for an original indicative.   **λέγει:** a historical or storytelling present.   **σευ**
= σου.   **ποιέειν:** complementary with ἐθέλεις.   **σευ = σου:** object of
χρηίζω and to perform the action of νεοχμῶσαι.   **νεοχμῶσαι:** dependent on
χρηίζω.   **ἐξεργάσῃ:** a hypothetical subjunctive, indicating Amyntas's intent for
his son.   **ὁρέων = ὁράων:** supplementary with ἀνέχευ.   **τὰ ποιεύμενα = τὰ
ποιούμενα:** substantive, "what is being done."   **πείσομαί τοι = πείσομαί σοι.**

～

V.20.1 ὡς δὲ ὁ Ἀμύντης, χρήσας τούτων, οἰχώκεε, λέγει ὁ Ἀλέξανδρος
πρὸς τοὺς Πέρσας· Γυναικῶν τουτέων, ὦ ξεῖνοι, ἔστι ὑμῖν πολλὴ
εὐπετείη, καὶ εἰ πάσῃσι βούλεσθε μίσγεσθαι καὶ ὁκόσῃσι ὦν αὐτέων.
[2] τούτου μὲν πέρι αὐτοὶ ἀποσημανέετε. νῦν δέ—σχεδὸν γὰρ ἤδη τῆς
κοίτης ὥρη προσέρχεται ὑμῖν καὶ καλῶς ἔχοντας ὑμέας ὁρῶ μέθης—
γυναῖκας ταύτας, εἰ ὑμῖν φίλον ἐστί, ἄπετε λούσασθαι. λουσαμένας
δὲ ὀπίσω προσδέκεσθε. [3] εἴπας ταῦτα—συνέπαινοι γὰρ ἦσαν οἱ
Πέρσαι—γυναῖκας μὲν ἐξελθούσας ἀπέπεμπε ἐς τὴν γυναικηίην. αὐτὸς
δὲ ὁ Ἀλέξανδρος, ἴσους τῇσι γυναιξὶ ἀριθμὸν ἄνδρας λειογενείους τῇ
τῶν γυναικῶν ἐσθῆτι σκευάσας καὶ ἐγχειρίδια δούς, ἦγε ἔσω. παράγων
δὲ τούτους ἔλεγε τοῖσι Πέρσῃσι τάδε· [4] Ὦ Πέρσαι, οἴκατε πανδαισίῃ
τελέῃ ἱστιῆσθαι· τά τε γὰρ ἄλλα, ὅσα εἴχομεν, καὶ πρὸς τὰ οἷά τε ἦν
ἐξευρόντας παρέχειν, πάντα ὑμῖν πάρεστι, καὶ δὴ καὶ τόδε τὸ πάντων
μέγιστον. τάς τε ἑωυτῶν μητέρας καὶ τὰς ἀδελφεὰς ἐπιδαψιλευόμεθα
ὑμῖν, ὡς παντελέως μάθητε τιμώμενοι πρὸς ἡμέων τῶν περ ἐστὲ
ἄξιοι, πρὸς δὲ καὶ βασιλέι τῷ πέμψαντι ἀπαγγείλητε ὡς ἀνὴρ Ἕλλην,
Μακεδόνων ὕπαρχος, εὖ ὑμέας ἐδέξατο καὶ τραπέζῃ καὶ κοίτῃ. [5]

ταῦτα εἴπας, ὁ Ἀλέξανδρος παρίζει Πέρσῃ ἀνδρὶ ἄνδρα Μακεδόνα ὡς
γυναῖκα τῷ λόγῳ. οἱ δέ, ἐπείτε σφέων οἱ Πέρσαι ψαύειν ἐπειρῶντο,
διεργάζοντο αὐτούς.

V.20.1 ὡς: temporal.   **ὑμῖν:** possesses εὐπετείη.   **πάσῃσι ... ὁκόσῃσι:** modify
an implied γυναιξί.   **μίσγεσθαι:** complementary with βούλεσθε.   **αὐτέων:**
partitive with ὁκόσῃσι.   **20.2 τούτου μὲν πέρι:** anastrophe of the disyllabic
preposition. τούτου refers back to the sleeping with the women.   **μὲν πέρι:** is
answered by νῦν δέ.   **ὑμῖν:** object of the prefix προσ- of προσέρχεται.   **μέθης:**
translate with καλῶς ἔχοντας.   **γυναῖκας:** subject of λούσασθαι.   **λούσασθαι:**
purpose.   **λουσαμένας:** modifies an implied γυναῖκας.   **20.3 ταῦτα:** refers
back to what was just said.   **γυναῖκας μὲν ἐξελθούσας:** is answered by αὐτὸς
δὲ ὁ Ἀλέξανδρος.   **τῇσι γυναιξί:** translate with ἴσους.   **ἀριθμόν:** accusative
of respect, "in number."   **τάδε:** refers to what comes next.   **20.4 τά τε γὰρ
ἄλλα ... οἷά τε ... καὶ δὴ καί:** τε ... τε gives the general and καὶ δὴ καί the
specific.   **ἄλλα:** modifies πάντα of πάντα ὑμῖν πάρεστι, "for all other things are
present to you."   **πρὸς τά = πρὸς ταῦτα ἅ:** the antecedent ταῦτα has dropped
out, and the relative pronoun τά serves as the object of πρός and the subject of
οἷά τε ἦν.   **ἐξευρόντας:** modifies an implied ἡμέας and serves as the subject of
παρέχειν.   **παρέχειν:** complementary with οἷά τε ἦν.   **καὶ δὴ καί:** answers
the general τά τε γὰρ ἄλλα by providing the specific gift the Makedonians offer
the Persians.   **τόδε:** substantive, "this offering."   **τὸ πάντων μέγιστον =
ὃ πάντων μέγιστον:** supply an implied πάρεστι.   **πάντων:** partitive with
μέγιστον.   **μάθητε ... ἀπαγγείλητε:** hypothetical subjunctives, indicating the
intent behind the giving of the gifts, which is of course ironic.   **πρὸς ἡμέων:**
agency.   **τῶν περ ἐστὲ ἄξιοι = τούτοις ὧν περ ἐστὲ ἄξιοι:** the antecedent
τούτοις has dropped out, and the relative pronoun τῶν serves as a dative of means
and as an objective genitive with ἄξιοι, "with the things which you deserve." The
irony continues.   **πρὸς δέ:** adverbial, "additionally."   **βασιλέι τῷ πέμψαντι:**
understand an implied ὑμέας.   **20.5 ὡς γυναῖκα τῷ λόγῳ:** "as a woman in
word," i.e., in the guise of a woman. τῷ λόγῳ is often contrasted by τῷ ἔργῳ, "in
reality."   **ψαύειν:** complementary with ἐπειρῶντο.

❧

V.21.1 καὶ οὗτοι μὲν τούτῳ τῷ μόρῳ διεφθάρησαν, καὶ αὐτοὶ καὶ ἡ
θεραπηίη αὐτῶν. εἴπετο γὰρ δή σφι καὶ ὀχήματα καὶ θεράποντες καὶ ἡ
πᾶσα πολλὴ παρασκευή. πάντα δὴ ταῦτα ἅμα πᾶσι ἐκείνοισι ἠφάνιστο.
[2] μετὰ δὲ χρόνῳ οὐ πολλῷ ὕστερον ζήτησις τῶν ἀνδρῶν τούτων
μεγάλη ἐκ τῶν Περσέων ἐγίνετο. καί σφεας Ἀλέξανδρος κατέλαβε
σοφίῃ, χρήματά τε δοὺς πολλὰ καὶ τὴν ἑωυτοῦ ἀδελφεήν, τῇ οὔνομα

ἦν Γυγαίη. δοὺς δὲ ταῦτα κατέλαβε ὁ Ἀλέξανδρος Βουβάρῃ, ἀνδρὶ
Πέρσῃ, τῶν διζημένων τοὺς ἀπολομένους τῷ στρατηγῷ.

V.21.1 οὗτοι μέν: is answered by μετὰ δέ.   **καί . . . καί:** "both . . . and."   **εἵπετο:**
as is typical in a declined language, the verb agrees with is nearest subject, here
ὀχήματα; the neuter plural is considered a collective whole and so takes a singular
verb.   **21.2 μετὰ δέ:** adverbial, "next."   **χρόνῳ:** dative of degree of difference;
translate with ὕστερον.   **ἐκ τῶν Περσέων:** agency.   **κατέλαβε:** Herodotus's
narrative is questioned here on the grounds that it is not likely that the Persians
would be so quick to abandon retribution for such a mass killing.   **σοφίη:** a
value-laden word that may suggest approval on the part of our narrator; ethics are a
tricky business, and Herodotus may be giving an appreciative nod to Alexandros's
methods.   **τῇ = ᾗ:** possesses οὔνομα.   **ταῦτα:** refers back to the money and
sister.   **κατέλαβε:** supply as the object "the search."   **ἀνδρί:** in apposition
with Βουβάρῃ.   **τῶν διζημένων:** substantive, "those looking for."   **τοὺς**
ἀπολομένους: "the lost men."   **τῷ στρατηγῷ:** in apposition with Βουβάρῃ.

~

V.22.1 ὁ μὲν νυν τῶν Περσέων τούτων θάνατος, οὕτω καταλαμφθείς,
ἐσιγήθη. Ἕλληνας δὲ εἶναι τούτους τοὺς ἀπὸ Περδίκκεω γεγονότας,
κατά περ αὐτοὶ λέγουσι, αὐτός τε οὕτω τυγχάνω ἐπιστάμενος καὶ δὴ
καὶ ἐν τοῖσι ὄπισθε λόγοισι ἀποδέξω ὡς εἰσὶ Ἕλληνες. πρὸς δὲ καὶ
οἱ τὸν ἐν Ὀλυμπίῃ διέποντες ἀγῶνα, Ἑλληνοδίκαι, οὕτω ἔγνωσαν
εἶναι. [2] Ἀλεξάνδρου γὰρ ἀεθλεύειν ἑλομένου καὶ καταβάντος ἐπ᾽
αὐτὸ τοῦτο, οἱ ἀντιθευσόμενοι Ἑλλήνων ἐξεῖργόν μιν, φάμενοι οὐ
βαρβάρων ἀγωνιστέων εἶναι τὸν ἀγῶνα ἀλλὰ Ἑλλήνων. Ἀλέξανδρος
δέ, ἐπειδὴ ἀπέδεξε ὡς εἴη Ἀργεῖος, ἐκρίθη τε εἶναι Ἕλλην καὶ
ἀγωνιζόμενος στάδιον συνεξέπιπτε τῷ πρώτῳ.

V.22.1 ὁ μὲν νυν: is answered by Ἕλληνας δέ.   **Ἕλληνας:** subject of
εἶναι; the question of being Greek or not is of course a central one both for
Herodotus and for the Greeks of his day.   **εἶναι:** main verb in indirect
statement.   **τούτους τοὺς ἀπὸ Περδίκκεω γεγονότας:** substantive, "those
born from Perdikkes."   **Περδίκκεω:** Perdikkes, king of Makedon c. 680 B.C.E.;
for more on Perdikkes and his Argive origin, see VIII.137–39.   **ἐπιστάμενος:**
supplementary with τυγχάνω; Herodotus offers his point of view as well as that
of the Hellenodikai.   **ἐν τοῖσι ὄπισθε λόγοισι:** see VIII.137–39.   **πρὸς δέ:**
adverbial, "additionally."   **οἱ τὸν ἐν Ὀλυμπίῃ διέποντες ἀγῶνα:** substantive,
"those presiding over the games in Olympia."   **Ἑλληνοδίκαι:** a variant reading

is Ἑλλήνων. How and Wells see Herodotus's willing acceptance of Alexandros's Greek ancestry as evidence of Herodotean phil-Hellenic bias. Herodotus finds such a bias normal and argues that to be otherwise is a sign of madness (III.38). **οὕτω:** modifies εἶναι. **εἶναι:** main verb in indirect statement; supply an implied ταῦτα as the subject. **22.2 ἀεθλεύειν:** complementary with ἑλομένου. **οἱ ἀντιθευσόμενοι:** substantive, "his competitors." **Ἑλλήνων:** partitive with οἱ ἀντιθευσόμενοι. **φάμενοι:** Herodotus grants his audience still another perspective. **ἐξεῖργον:** a main aspectual meaning of the imperfect is incomplete action that remains neutral as to the success or failure of the subject. In instances like the one here, it is typically called a conative imperfect; thus, "they were trying to prevent him from competing." But as context makes clear, they were not succesful. **μιν = αὐτόν. εἶναι:** main verb in indirect statement. **τὸν ἀγῶνα:** subject of εἶναι. **εἴη:** an optative standing for an original indicative. **Ἀργεῖος:** of Argive descent, from Temenos, a son of Herakles and conqueror of Argos (VIII.137); Thoukydides' *History* accepts this genealogy (2.99). **εἶναι:** the subject is the same as the subject of ἐκρίθη. **τῷ πρώτῳ:** substantive, "first place."

〜

V.23.1 ταῦτα μέν νυν οὕτω κῃ ἐγένετο. Μεγάβαζος δέ, ἄγων τοὺς Παίονας, ἀπίκετο ἐπὶ τὸν Ἑλλήσποντον. ἐνθεῦτεν διαπεραιωθεὶς ἀπίκετο ἐς τὰς Σάρδις. ἅτε δὲ τειχέοντος ἤδη Ἱστιαίου τοῦ Μιλησίου, τὴν παρὰ Δαρείου αἰτήσας ἔτυχε μισθόν, δωρεὴν φυλακῆς τῆς σχεδίης, ἐόντος δὲ τοῦ χώρου τούτου παρὰ Στρυμόνα ποταμόν, τῷ οὔνομα ἐστὶ Μύρκινος, μαθὼν ὁ Μεγάβαζος τὸ ποιεύμενον ἐκ τοῦ Ἱστιαίου, ὡς ἦλθε τάχιστα ἐς τὰς Σάρδις ἄγων τοὺς Παίονας, ἔλεγε Δαρείῳ τάδε· [2] Ὦ βασιλεῦ, κοῖόν τι χρῆμα ἐποίησας, ἀνδρὶ Ἕλληνι, δεινῷ τε καὶ σοφῷ, δοὺς ἐγκτίσασθαι πόλιν ἐν Θρηίκῃ, ἵνα ἴδη τε ναυπηγήσιμος ἐστὶ ἄφθονος καὶ πολλοὶ κωπέες καὶ μέταλλα ἀργύρεα; ὅμιλός τε πολλὸς μὲν Ἕλλην περιοικέει, πολλὸς δὲ βάρβαρος, οἵ, προστάτεω ἐπιλαβόμενοι, ποιήσουσι τοῦτο τὸ ἂν κεῖνος ἐξηγέηται καὶ ἡμέρης καὶ νυκτός. [3] σύ νυν τοῦτον τὸν ἄνδρα παῦσον ταῦτα ποιεῦντα, ἵνα μὴ οἰκηίῳ πολέμῳ συνέχῃ. τρόπῳ δὲ ἠπίῳ μεταπεμψάμενος παῦσον. ἐπεὰν δὲ αὐτὸν περιλάβῃς, ποιέειν ὅκως μηκέτι κεῖνος ἐς Ἕλληνας ἀπίξεται.

V.23.1 ταῦτα μέν: refers back to and concludes the story of the murdered Persian envoys; is answered by Μεγάβαζος δέ. **ἅτε:** more frequently found with a nominative or accusative participle, here it is found with two genitive participles, τειχέοντος and ἐόντος. When translating the participles into English, it is helpful to turn them into finite verbs: "because he was fortifying and because the place was." Because of these two things, Megabazos comes to the conclusion that Histiaios is a threat and that he must stop him preemptively. It is his perspective that dominates this paragraph. **τήν** = ἥν. **μισθόν:** in apposition to τήν. **δωρεήν:** object of τειχέοντος. **φυλακῆς τῆς σχεδίης:** for the guarding of the bridge, see IV.136–41. **τῷ** = ᾧ: possesses οὔνομα. **τὸ ποιεύμενον** = τὸ ποιούμενον: substantive, "what was being done." **ἐκ τοῦ Ἱστιαίου:** agency. **τάδε:** looks forward to what he is about to say. **23.2 ἀνδρὶ Ἕλληνι:** is to perform the action of ἐγκτίσασθαι. **ἐγκτίσασθαι:** dependent on δούς. **ἵνα:** with the indicative ἵνα often means "where." **ἐστί:** agrees with its nearest subject. **πολλὸς μέν** = πολὺς μέν: is answered by πολλὸς δέ (πολὺς δέ). **οἵ:** plural because of the plurality implied by πολλός. **τό ἄν** = ὅ ἄν. **ἐξηγέηται:** a hypothetical subjunctive, indicating a possible future event. **23.3 συνέχῃ:** subjunctive, indicating why Megabazos thinks Histiaios must be stopped. **περιλάβῃς:** a hypothetical subjunctive, indicating a possible future event. **ποιέειν:** an infinitive standing for an original imperative.

~

V.24.1 ταῦτα λέγων ὁ Μεγάβαζος εὐπετέως ἔπειθε Δαρεῖον ὡς εὖ προορῶν τὸ μέλλον γίνεσθαι. μετὰ δὲ πέμψας ἄγγελον ἐς τὴν Μύρκινον, ὁ Δαρεῖος ἔλεγε τάδε· Ἱστιαῖε, βασιλεὺς Δαρεῖος τάδε λέγει· ἐγώ, φροντίζων, εὑρίσκω ἐμοί τε καὶ τοῖσι ἐμοῖσι πρήγμασι εἶναι οὐδένα σεῦ ἄνδρα εὐνοέστερον. τοῦτο δὲ οὐ λόγοισι ἀλλ᾽ ἔργοισι οἶδα μαθών. [2] νῦν ὦν—ἐπινοέω γὰρ πρήγματα μεγάλα κατεργάσασθαι— ἀπίκεό μοι πάντως, ἵνα τοι αὐτὰ ὑπερθέωμαι. τούτοισι τοῖσι ἔπεσι πιστεύσας, ὁ Ἱστιαῖος, καὶ ἅμα μέγα ποιεύμενος βασιλέος σύμβουλος γενέσθαι, ἀπίκετο ἐς τὰς Σάρδις. [3] ἀπικομένῳ δέ οἱ ἔλεγε Δαρεῖος τάδε· Ἱστιαῖε, ἐγώ σε μετεπεμψάμην τῶνδε εἵνεκεν. ἐπείτε τάχιστα ἐνόστησα ἀπὸ Σκυθέων καὶ σύ μοι ἐγένεο ἐξ ὀφθαλμῶν, οὐδέν κω ἄλλο χρῆμα οὕτω ἐν βραχέι ἐπεζήτησα ὡς σὲ ἰδεῖν τε καὶ ἐς λόγους μοι ἀπικέσθαι, ὅτι κτημάτων πάντων ἐστὶ τιμιώτατον ἀνὴρ φίλος συνετός τε καὶ εὔνοος· τά τοι ἐγὼ καὶ ἀμφότερα συνειδώς, ἔχω μαρτυρέειν ἐς πρήγματα τὰ ἐμά. [4] νῦν ὦν, εὖ γὰρ ἐποίησας ἀπικόμενος, τάδε τοι ἐγὼ προτείνομαι. Μίλητον μὲν ἔα καὶ τὴν νεόκτιστον ἐν Θρηίκῃ πόλιν. σὺ δέ, μοι ἑπόμενος ἐς Σοῦσα, ἔχε τά περ ἂν ἐγὼ ἔχω, ἐμός τε σύσσιτος ἐὼν καὶ σύμβουλος.

V.24.1 ταῦτα: refers back to what Megabazos has just said.   **προορῶν:** modifies Μεγάβαζος and indicates that his vision has prevailed.   **τὸ μέλλον:** substantive, "what was likely."   **γίνεσθαι:** complementary with τὸ μέλλον.   **μετὰ δέ:** adverbial, "then" or "next."   **τάδε:** looks forward to what Dareios is about to say.   **οὐδένα:** subject of εἶναι.   **σεῦ = σοῦ:** translate with εὐνοέστερον.   **τοῦτο:** refers back to being an excellent adviser.   **οὐ λόγοισι ἀλλ᾽ ἔργοισι:** the contrast is a common one in Greek, "not from reports but from your accomplishments."   **24.2 κατεργάσασθαι:** complementary with ἐπινοέω.   **τοι = σοι.**   **ὑπερθέωμαι:** a hypothetical subjunctive, indicating Dareios's stated reason for wishing Histiaios to visit him.   **μέγα ποιεύμενος = μέγα ποιούμενος:** "considering it a big deal."   **γενέσθαι:** complementary with μέγα ποιούμενος.   **24.3 οἱ = αὐτῷ.**   **τάδε:** looks forward to what comes next.   **τῶνδε εἵνεκεν:** looks forward to what comes next.   **μοι:** possesses ὀφθαλμῶν.   **οὕτω … ὡς:** "so much … as."   **ἐν βραχέι:** substantive, "quickly."   **ἰδεῖν:** complementary with ἐπεζήτησα.   **μοι:** possesses λόγους.   **ἀπικέσθαι:** complementary with ἐπεζήτησα; supply an implied σέ as subject.   **κτημάτων πάντων:** partitive with τιμιώτατον.   **τά = ἅ:** subject of an implied εἶναι.   **τοι = σοι:** possesses τά … ἀμφότερα.   **ἀμφότερα:** refers to συνετός τε καὶ εὔνοος.   **μαρτυρέειν:** complementary with ἔχω.   **24.4 τάδε:** looks forward to what comes next.   **τοι = σοι.**   **Μίλητον μέν:** is answered by σὺ δέ.   **τά = ταῦτα ἅ:** the antecedent has dropped out and τά serves as the object of ἔχε and ἔχω.

❧

V.25.1 ταῦτα Δαρεῖος εἴπας καὶ καταστήσας Ἀρταφρένεα, ἀδελφεὸν ἑωυτοῦ ὁμοπάτριον, ὕπαρχον εἶναι Σαρδίων, ἀπήλαυνε ἐς Σοῦσα ἅμα ἀγόμενος Ἱστιαῖον, Ὀτάνεα δὲ ἀποδέξας στρατηγὸν εἶναι τῶν παραθαλασσίων ἀνδρῶν, τοῦ τὸν πατέρα Σισάμνην βασιλεὺς Καμβύσης γενόμενον τῶν βασιληίων δικαστέων, ὅτι ἐπὶ χρήμασι δίκην ἄδικον ἐδίκασε, σφάξας ἀπέδειρε πᾶσαν τὴν ἀνθρωπέην. σπαδίξας δὲ αὐτοῦ τὸ δέρμα, ἱμάντας ἐξ αὐτοῦ ἔταμε καὶ ἐνέτεινε τὸν θρόνον ἐς τὸν ἵζων ἐδίκαζε. [2] ἐντανύσας δὲ ὁ Καμβύσης ἀπέδεξε δικαστὴν εἶναι ἀντὶ τοῦ Σισάμνεω, τὸν ἀποκτείνας ἀπέδειρε, τὸν παῖδα τοῦ Σισάμνεω, ἐντειλάμενός οἱ μεμνῆσθαι ἐν τῷ κατίζων θρόνῳ δικάζει.

V.25.1 ταῦτα: refers back to what Histiaios just said to Dareios.   **εἴπας:** this paragraph presents Dareios's thinking.   **Ἀρταφρένεα:** subject of εἶναι.   **ἀδελφεόν:** in apposition with Ἀρταφρένεα.   **ὕπαρχον:** predicate to Ἀρταφρένεα.   **εἶναι:** dependent on καταστήσας.   **Ὀτάνεα:** subject

of εἶναι. **στρατηγόν:** predicate to Ὀτάνεα. **εἶναι:** dependent on
ἀποδέξας. **τοῦ = οὗ.** **ἀπέδειρε:** so frequently did the Persians employ this
punishment that in late times it became known as the Persian punishment (How
and Wells 1913). **ἐς τόν = ἐς ὅν.** **25.2 δικαστήν:** subject of εἶναι. **εἶναι:**
dependent on ἀπέδεξε. **τόν = ὅν.** **τὸν παῖδα:** predicate to δικαστήν. **οἱ
= αὐτῷ:** to perform the action of μεμνῆσθαι. **μεμνῆσθαι:** dependent on
ἐντειλάμενος. **ἐν τῷ κατίζων θρόνῳ = ἐν ᾧ κατίζων θρόνῳ:** at times the
antecedent is brought into the relative clause, e.g., εἶδεν ἐν ᾗ οἰκέω χώρᾳ ("he saw
in which country I dwell") instead of εἶδεν χώραν ἐν ᾗ οἰκῶ.

~

V.26.1 οὗτος ὦν ὁ Ὀτάνης, ὁ ἐγκατιζόμενος ἐς τοῦτον τὸν θρόνον, τότε
διάδοχος γενόμενος Μεγαβάζῳ τῆς στρατηγίης, Βυζαντίους τε εἷλε
καὶ Καλχηδονίους. εἷλε δὲ Ἄντανδρον τὴν ἐν τῇ Τρῳάδι γῇ. εἷλε δὲ
Λαμπώνιον. λαβὼν δὲ παρὰ Λεσβίων νέας, εἷλε Λῆμνόν τε καὶ Ἴμβρον,
ἀμφοτέρας ἔτι τότε ὑπὸ Πελασγῶν οἰκεομένας.

V.26.1 τότε: the date is uncertain. The period of time under discussion is about
510–500 B.C.E.   **Καλχηδονίους:** that the Byzantines and Kalkhedonians are
subdued suggests that they revolted after Dareios's failed expedition to Skythia
(IV.139).   **ἀμφοτέρας:** plural because of the implied plurality of Λῆμνον τε
καὶ Ἴμβρον.   **ἔτι τότε:** another temporal marker indicating that this piece of
information is accurate within the time frame of the story. The time frame of
Herodotus and his audience is from about 450 to 425 B.C.E.   **ὑπὸ Πελασγῶν:**
there is much debate then and now as to who the Pelasgians were. For Herodotus's
conjecture on the language they spoke, see I.57.

~

V.27.1 οἱ μὲν δὴ Λήμνιοι καὶ ἐμαχέσαντο εὖ καὶ, ἀμυνόμενοι ἀνὰ χρόνον,
ἐκακώθησαν. τοῖσι δὲ περιεοῦσι αὐτῶν οἱ Πέρσαι ὕπαρχον ἐπιστᾶσι,
Λυκάρητον τὸν Μαιανδρίου τοῦ βασιλεύσαντος Σάμου ἀδελφεόν. [2]
οὗτος ὁ Λυκάρητος ἄρχων ἐν Λήμνῳ τελευτᾷ. αἰτίη δὲ τούτου ἥδε.
πάντας ἠνδραποδίζετο καὶ κατεστρέφετο, τοὺς μὲν λιποστρατίης
ἐπὶ Σκύθας αἰτιώμενος, τοὺς δὲ σίνασθαι τὸν Δαρείου στρατόν, ἀπὸ
Σκυθέων ὀπίσω ἀποκομιζόμενον.

V.27.1 οἱ μὲν δὴ Λήμνιοι: is answered by τοῖσι δὲ περιεοῦσι.   **ἐμαχέσαντο εὖ:**
whether one fights well or not matters to Herodotus and to his audience.   **τοῖσι**

δὲ περιεοῦσι: substantive, "the survivors"; object of the prefix ἐπ- of ἐπιστᾶσι. αὐτῶν: partitive with τοῖσι δὲ περιεοῦσι. ἀδελφεόν: in apposition to Λυκάρητον. 27.2 τελευτᾷ. . . . αἰτίη δὲ τούτου ἥδε: most editors see a problem with the text and print ". . ." to mark a lacuna. Faulty, inconsequential, and meaningless are three adjectives used to describe the lines. It is not clear why. It is common Herodotean practice to point out the death of a governor, especially if he dies as a result of mistreating his subjects. τούτου: refers back to the death. ἥδε: looks forward to what comes next. τοὺς μέν . . . τοὺς δέ: "some . . . others." λιποστρατίης: genitive of the charge with αἰτιώμενος. σίνασθαι: supply an implied τοῦ with σίνασθαι and translate as another genitive of the charge.

~

V.28.1 οὗτος μὲν νυν τοσαῦτα ἐξεργάσατο, στρατηγήσας. μετὰ δέ, οὐ πολλὸν χρόνον, ἄνεσις κακῶν ἦν. καὶ ἤρχετο τὸ δεύτερον ἐκ Νάξου τε καὶ Μιλήτου Ἴωσι γίνεσθαι κακά. τοῦτο μὲν γὰρ ἡ Νάξος εὐδαιμονίῃ τῶν νήσων προέφερε. τοῦτο δὲ κατὰ τὸν αὐτὸν χρόνον ἡ Μίλητος αὐτή τε ἑωυτῆς, μάλιστα δὴ τότε ἀκμάσασα, καὶ δὴ καὶ τῆς Ἰωνίης ἦν πρόσχημα, κατύπερθε δὲ τούτων ἐπὶ δύο γενεὰς ἀνδρῶν νοσήσασα ἐς τὰ μάλιστα στάσι, μέχρι οὗ μιν Πάριοι κατήρτισαν. τούτους γὰρ καταρτιστῆρας ἐκ πάντων Ἑλλήνων εἵλοντο οἱ Μιλήσιοι.

V.28.1 οὗτος μέν: is answered by μετὰ δέ; μέν concludes the narrative on Otanes, and δέ returns our attention to Ionia and its troubles. **Μιλήτου**: located at the mouth of the Meandros River and settled during the Neolithic Age, Miletos was resettled during the Dark Ages (c. 1200 B.C.E to 800 B.C.E.) by an Ionian colony from Athens, which is said to have killed the Milesian men and married their widows. In the seventh century, Miletos was a cultural hub for science and philosophy, producing three great thinkers: Thales, Anaximander, and Anaximenes. Under Akhaimenid Kyros's reign, Miletos fell to Persian rule and the Akhaimenid Empire. In this book the Ionian revolt against Persia sees its inception brought about by Aristagores in 499 B.C.E. The revolt comes to an end in Book VI, as does Miletos, whose men are killed and whose women and children are enslaved. A year later Phrynikhos, an Athenian playwright, produces his play on the capture of Miletos. He brings the Athenians to tears and they fine him 1,000 drachmas for reminding them of their sufferings (VI.19–21). **γίνεσθαι**: complementary with ἤρχετο. **τοῦτο μέν . . . τοῦτο δέ**: adverbial, "first . . . second." **τε . . . καὶ δὴ καί**: links αὐτή ἑωυτῆς and τῆς Ἰωνίης. ἑωυτῆς may be emphatic with αὐτή. Smyth (1235) has this example: αὐτοὶ ἐφ᾽ ἑαυτῶν ἐχώρουν, which is a close but not direct parallel. ἑωυτῆς may be parallel with τῆς Ἰωνίης, in which case it is to be translated with πρόσχημα. Whichever is correct, the meaning is clear and the sentence is an example of one of the few times the more specific precedes the more general.   **τούτων**: substantive, "these events." It refers back to the general prosperity; translate it with κατύπερθε.   **ἐς τὰ μάλιστα**: substantive, "most of all."   **μέχρι οὗ**: temporal, "until."   **μιν = αὐτήν.**   **ἐκ πάντων Ἑλλήνων**: partitive with τούτους.

❧

V.29.1 κατήλλαξαν δὲ σφέας ὧδε Πάριοι. ὡς ἀπίκοντο αὐτῶν ἄνδρες οἱ ἄριστοι ἐς τὴν Μίλητον—ὥρων γὰρ δή σφεας δεινῶς οἰκοφθορημένους—ἔφασαν αὐτῶν βούλεσθαι διεξελθεῖν τὴν χώρην. ποιεῦντες δὲ ταῦτα καὶ διεξιόντες πᾶσαν τὴν Μιλησίην, ὅκως τινὰ ἴδοιεν ἐν ἀνεστηκυίῃ τῇ χώρῃ ἀγρὸν εὖ ἐξεργασμένον, ἀπεγράφοντο τὸ οὔνομα τοῦ δεσπότεω τοῦ ἀγροῦ. [2] διεξελάσαντες δὲ πᾶσαν τὴν χώρην καὶ σπανίους εὑρόντες τούτους, ὡς τάχιστα κατέβησαν ἐς τὸ ἄστυ, ἁλίην ποιησάμενοι ἀπέδεξαν τούτους μὲν πόλιν νέμειν τῶν εὖρον τοὺς ἀγροὺς εὖ ἐξεργασμένους· δοκέειν γὰρ ἔφασαν καὶ τῶν δημοσίων οὕτω δή σφεας ἐπιμελήσεσθαι ὥσπερ τῶν σφετέρων· τοὺς δὲ ἄλλους Μιλησίους τοὺς πρὶν στασιάζοντας τούτων ἔταξαν πείθεσθαι.

V.29.1 ὧδε: as often looks forward to what is to come. Herodotus moves out of his main narrative frame to provide the backstory for how the Milesians recovered from civil strife, a phenomenon that plagued many Greek city-states.   **αὐτῶν**: partitive with ἄνδρες οἱ ἄριστοι.   **ἔφασαν**: Herodotus presents things from the Parian perspective.   **αὐτῶν**: translate αὐτῶν with τὴν χώρην.   **βούλεσθαι**: the subject is the same as the subject of ἔφασαν.   **διεξελθεῖν**: complementary with βούλεσθαι.   **ταῦτα**: refers back to their visiting of the land.   **ὅκως**: "whenever."   **ἴδοιεν**: an optative referring hypothetically to an event in the past that happened more than once.   **ἐξεργασμένον**: middle voice.   **29.2 τούτους**: refers back to the well-ordered farms.   **τούτους μέν**: subject of νέμειν and answered by τοὺς δὲ ἄλλους.   **νέμειν**: dependent on ἀπέδεξαν.   **τῶν = ὧν.**   **δοκέειν**: main verb in indirect statement; the subject is either impersonal or is the same as the subject of ἔφασαν.   **σφεας**: subject of ἐπιμελήσεσθαι.   **ἐπιμελήσεσθαι**: main verb in indirect statement.   **ὥσπερ**: supply an implied ἐπιμελήσεσθαι.   **Μιλησίους**: subject of πείθεσθαι.   **τούτων**: refers back to the Milesians with well-ordered farms; object of πείθεσθαι.   **πείθεσθαι**: dependent on ἔταξαν; more commonly found with the dative, the middle of this verb takes a genitive object four times in Herodotus.

⁓

V.30.1 Πάριοι μέν νυν Μιλησίους οὕτω κατήρτισαν. τότε δὲ ἐκ
τουτέων τῶν πολίων ὧδε ἤρχετο κακὰ γίνεσθαι τῇ Ἰωνίῃ. ἐκ Νάξου
ἔφυγον ἄνδρες τῶν παχέων ὑπὸ τοῦ δήμου· φυγόντες δὲ ἀπίκοντο ἐς
Μίλητον. [2] τῆς δὲ Μιλήτου ἐτύγχανε ἐπίτροπος ἐὼν Ἀρισταγόρης ὁ
Μολπαγόρεω, γαμβρός τε ἐὼν καὶ ἀνεψιὸς Ἱστιαίου τοῦ Λυσαγόρεω,
τὸν ὁ Δαρεῖος ἐν Σούσοισι κατεῖχε. ὁ γὰρ Ἱστιαῖος τύραννος ἦν
Μιλήτου καὶ ἐτύγχανε τοῦτον τὸν χρόνον ἐὼν ἐν Σούσοισι, ὅτε οἱ
Νάξιοι ἦλθον, ξεῖνοι πρὶν ἐόντες τῷ Ἱστιαίῳ. [3] ἀπικόμενοι δὲ οἱ Νάξιοι
ἐς τὴν Μίλητον ἐδέοντο τοῦ Ἀρισταγόρεω, εἴ κως αὐτοῖσι παράσχοι
δύναμίν τινα καὶ κατέλθοιεν ἐς τὴν ἑωυτῶν. ὁ δέ, ἐπιλεξάμενος ὡς,
ἢν δι᾽ αὐτοῦ κατέλθωσι ἐς τὴν πόλιν, ἄρξει τῆς Νάξου, σκῆψιν δὲ
ποιεύμενος τὴν ξεινίην τὴν Ἱστιαίου, τόνδε σφι λόγον προσέφερε· [4]
Αὐτὸς μὲν ὑμῖν οὐ φερέγγυός εἰμι δύναμιν παρασχεῖν τοσαύτην ὥστε
κατάγειν, ἀεκόντων τῶν τὴν πόλιν ἐχόντων Ναξίων· πυνθάνομαι
γὰρ ὀκτακισχιλίην ἀσπίδα Ναξίοισι εἶναι καὶ πλοῖα μακρὰ πολλά.
μηχανήσομαι δέ, πᾶσαν σπουδὴν ποιεύμενος. [5] ἐπινοέω δὲ τῇδε.
Ἀρταφρένης μοι τυγχάνει ἐὼν φίλος. ὁ δὲ Ἀρταφρένης ὑμῖν
Ὑστάσπεος μὲν ἐστὶ παῖς, Δαρείου δὲ τοῦ βασιλέος ἀδελφεός. τῶν
δ᾽ ἐπιθαλασσίων τῶν ἐν τῇ Ἀσίῃ ἄρχει πάντων, ἔχων στρατιήν τε
πολλὴν καὶ πολλὰς νέας. τοῦτον ὦν δοκέω τὸν ἄνδρα ποιήσειν τῶν ἂν
χρηίζωμεν. [6] ταῦτα ἀκούσαντες οἱ Νάξιοι προσέθεσαν τῷ Ἀρισταγόρῃ
πρήσσειν τῇ δύναιτο ἄριστα. καὶ ὑπίσχεσθαι δῶρα ἐκέλευον καὶ
δαπάνην τῇ στρατιῇ ὡς αὐτοὶ διαλύσοντες, ἐλπίδας πολλὰς ἔχοντες,
ὅταν ἐπιφανέωσι ἐς τὴν Νάξον, πάντα ποιήσειν τοὺς Ναξίους, τὰ ἂν
αὐτοὶ κελεύωσι, ὣς δὲ καὶ τοὺς ἄλλους νησιώτας. τῶν γὰρ νήσων
τουτέων τῶν Κυκλάδων οὐδεμία κω ἦν ὑπὸ Δαρείῳ.

V.30.1 Πάριοι μέν: is answered by τότε δέ. μέν ends the backstory; the temporal
marker τότε δέ resumes the current narrative thread begun in V.28.   **ἐκ τουτέων
τῶν πολίων:** refers to Naxos and Miletos and back to V.28. Having given the
backstory for troubles that had plagued the Ionians, Herodotus returns, after a brief
peaceful interlude, to the Ionians and the resumption of their troubles. In presenting
the onset of troubles, Herodotus hands over narration to the wealthy exiled Naxians
and to Aristagores, characterized as guilty of greed, self-interest, and cowardice.

Herodotus likely holds him partially responsible for the eventual slaughter of Milesian males and the enslavement of Milesian females at the hands of the Persians (VI.19–20).   ὧδε: looks forward to what comes next.   γίνεσθαι: complementary with ἤρχετο.   ἔφυγον: "they were exiled."   τῶν παχέων: substantive, "those thick with wealth"; partitive with ἄνδρες.   ὑπὸ τοῦ δήμου: agency.   30.2 ἐών: supplementary with ἐτύγχανε.   τόν = ὅν.   ἐτύγχανε … ἐών: see above note ἐών.   ὅτε οἱ Νάξιοι ἦλθον: i.e., the rich exiles.   30.3 εἴ κως … παράσχοι … κατέλθοιεν: the optatives likely stand for original subjunctives παράσχῃς ("will you provide") and κατέλθωμεν ("may we return") (Smyth 2677).   ἐς τὴν ἑωυτῶν: supply an implied χώραν.   δι' αὐτοῦ: agency.   κατέλθωσι: a hypothetical subjunctive, indicating a possible future event.   ἐπιλεξάμενος … σκῆψιν ποιεύμενος: presented from Aristagores' point of view.   τόνδε: looks forward to what comes next.   30.4 Αὐτὸς μέν: is answered by μηχανήσομαι δέ.   παρασχεῖν: epexegetical with φερέγγυος.   κατάγειν: main verb in a result clause; the subject is the same as the subject of εἰμί. Supply an implied ὑμέας as the object.   ἀσπίδα: subject of εἶναι.   Ναξίοισι: possesses ἀσπίδα and πλοῖα.   εἶναι: main verb in indirect statement.   πλοῖα: subject of an implied εἶναι.   30.5 τῇδε: substantive, "the following"; looks forward to what comes next.   ἐών: supplementary with τυγχάνει.   ὑμῖν: seems parallel to μοι, i.e., Artaphrenes to me is a friend; Artaphrenes to you has connections to the Persian court.   Ὑστάσπεος μέν: is answered by Δαρείου δέ.   ἀδελφεός: in apposition with Ἀρταφρένης.   τὸν ἄνδρα: subject of ποιήσειν.   τῶν = ταῦτα ὧν: the antecedent ταῦτα has dropped out and the relative τῶν serves as the object of ποιήσειν and χρηίζωμεν.   ἂν χρηίζωμεν: a hypothetical subjunctive indicating whatever possible desires they may have.   30.6 ταῦτα: refers back to what Artaphrenes has just said.   οἱ Νάξιοι: their perspective colors this section.   τῷ Ἀρισταγόρῃ: subject of πρήσσειν.   τῇ = ᾗ: "in whatever way."   δύναιτο: a hypothetical optative looking forward to a future action.   ἄριστα: adverbial, "best"; translate with an implied πρήσσειν that is complementary with δύναιτο.   ὑπίσχεσθαι: dependent on ἐκέλευον; understand τῷ Ἀρισταγόρῃ or τὸν Ἀρισταγόρην as the implied subject.   διαλύσοντες: the participle looks to the future and expresses the reason why the Naxians encourage Aristogoras to promise these things.   ἐπιφανέωσι: a hypothetical subjunctive that looks forward to an upcoming event.   ποιήσειν: main verb in indirect statement.   τοὺς Ναξίους: the subject of ποιήσειν.   τὰ ἂν αὐτοὶ κελεύωσι = ταῦτα ἃ ἂν αὐτοὶ κελεύωσι: the antecedent ταῦτα has dropped out, and τά serves as the object of ποιήσειν and the ποιήσειν that is to be understood with κελεύωσι.   νησιώτας: subject of an implied ποιήσειν.   τῶν γὰρ νήσων: partitive with οὐδεμία.   ὑπὸ Δαρείῳ: "subject to Dareios." The backstory of the Naxians sets the stage for their successful defense in 502 against Aristagores and the Persians. The largest of the Kykladic islands, Naxos gained its wealth through trade.   τῶν γὰρ νήσων: Herodotus intrudes on the Naxian narration so as to explain things for his audience.

~

V.31.1 ἀπικόμενος δὲ ὁ Ἀρισταγόρης ἐς τὰς Σάρδις λέγει πρὸς τὸν Ἀρταφρένεα ὡς Νάξος εἴη νῆσος μεγάθεϊ μὲν οὐ μεγάλη. ἄλλως δὲ καλή τε καὶ ἀγαθὴ καὶ ἀγχοῦ Ἰωνίης. χρήματα δὲ ἔνι πολλὰ καὶ ἀνδράποδα. Σὺ ὦν ἐπὶ ταύτην τὴν χώρην στρατηλάτεε, κατάγων ἐς αὐτὴν τοὺς φυγάδας ἐξ αὐτῆς. [2] καί τοι ταῦτα ποιήσαντι, τοῦτο μέν, ἐστὶ ἕτοιμα παρ᾽ ἐμοὶ χρήματα μεγάλα πάρεξ τῶν ἀναισιμωμάτων τῇ στρατιῇ. ταῦτα μὲν γὰρ δίκαιον ἡμέας, τοὺς ἄγοντας, παρέχειν. τοῦτο δέ νήσους βασιλέι προσκτήσεαι, αὐτήν τε Νάξον καὶ τὰς ἐκ ταύτης ἠρτημένας, Πάρον καὶ Ἄνδρον καὶ ἄλλας τὰς Κυκλάδας καλευμένας. [3] ἐνθεῦτεν δὲ ὁρμώμενος εὐπετέως ἐπιθήσεαι Εὐβοίῃ, νήσῳ μεγάλῃ τε καὶ εὐδαίμονι, οὐκ ἐλάσσονι Κύπρου καὶ κάρτα εὐπετέϊ αἱρεθῆναι. ἀποχρῶσι δὲ ἑκατὸν νέες ταύτας πάσας χειρώσασθαι. ὁ δὲ ἀμείβετο αὐτὸν τοῖσιδε· [4] Σὺ ἐς οἶκον τὸν βασιλέος ἐξηγητὴς γίνεαι πρηγμάτων ἀγαθῶν. καὶ ταῦτα εὖ παραινέεις πάντα, πλὴν τῶν νεῶν τοῦ ἀριθμοῦ. ἀντὶ δὲ ἑκατὸν νεῶν διηκόσιαί τοι ἕτοιμοι ἔσονται ἅμα τῷ ἔαρι. δεῖ δὲ τούτοισι καὶ αὐτὸν βασιλέα συνέπαινον γίνεσθαι.

V.31.1 ὁ Ἀρισταγόρης: in this section Herodotus presents us with Aristagores' attempt to gain political power for himself. The events of Naxos lead directly to Aristagores' fomenting the Ionian revolt (499–493 B.C.E.). As such, much of the information in this section forms part of Aristagores' narrative—a narrative designed to persuade Artaphrenes to agree to go to war. Presented as οὐ μεγάλη and ἀγχοῦ Ἰωνίης, Naxos is the largest of the Kykladic isles and is located some 100 miles from Miletos. Euboia, introduced as οὐκ ἐλάσσονι Κύπρου, is about a third the size of Kypros. Herodotus's Aristagores crafts his tale to make it as persuasive as possible.   **λέγει:** a historic or storytelling present.   **εἴη:** optative standing for an original indicative.   **μεγάθεϊ:** dative of respect, "in size."   **καλή:** supply an implied Νάξος εἴη.   **31.2 τοι = σοι.**   **ταῦτα:** refers back to the campaign and return of the exiles.   **τοῦτο μέν ... τοῦτο δέ:** adverbial, "first of all" ... "second of all."   **ταῦτα μέν:** refers back to the expenses and is left unanswered.   **δίκαιον:** supply an implied ἐστιν.   **ἡμέας:** subject of παρέχειν.   **τοὺς ἄγοντας:** substantive, "the ones leading"; in apposition to ἡμέας; supply an implied "expedition."   **παρέχειν:** epexegetical with δίκαιον.   **προσκτήσεαι:** intervocalic sigma (-εσαι) has dropped out, but the contraction to -ει or -ῃ has not occurred.   **τὰς ἐκ ταύτης ἠρτημένας:** modifies an implied νήσους.   **Πάρον καὶ Ἄνδρον καὶ ἄλλας:** in apposition to νήσους.   **31.3 ἐπιθήσεαι:** intervocalic sigma (-εσαι) has dropped out, and the contraction to -ει or -ῃ has not occurred.   **νήσῳ:** in apposition with Εὐβοίη.   **αἱρεθῆναι:** epexegetical with εὐπετέϊ.   **χειρώσασθαι:** complementary with ἀποχρῶσι; as object supply an implied νήσους.   **τοῖσιδε:** looks forward to what comes next.   **31.4** **γίνεαι = γίγνεαι:** note the loss of the intervocalic sigma, γίνεσαι.   **ταῦτα:** refers back to what Aristagores has just said.   **τοι = σοι.**   **τούτοισι:** refers back to the agreed-on plans; translate with συνέπαινον.   **βασιλέα:** subject of γίνεσθαι.   **γίνεσθαι:** complementary with δεῖ.

❧

V.32.1 ὁ μὲν δὴ Ἀρισταγόρης, ὡς ταῦτα ἤκουσε, περιχαρὴς ἐὼν ἀπήιε ἐς Μίλητον. ὁ δὲ Ἀρταφρένης—ὡς οἱ πέμψαντι ἐς Σοῦσα καὶ ὑπερθέντι τὰ ἐκ τοῦ Ἀρισταγόρεω λεγόμενα συνέπαινος καὶ αὐτὸς Δαρεῖος ἐγένετο—παρεσκευάσατο μὲν διηκοσίας τριήρεας, πολλὸν δὲ κάρτα ὅμιλον Περσέων τε καὶ τῶν ἄλλων συμμάχων. στρατηγὸν δὲ τούτων ἀπέδεξε Μεγαβάτην, ἄνδρα Πέρσην τῶν Ἀχαιμενιδέων, ἑωυτοῦ τε καὶ Δαρείου ἀνεψιόν, τοῦ Παυσανίης ὁ Κλεομβρότου Λακεδαιμόνιος—εἰ δὴ ἀληθής γε ἐστὶ ὁ λόγος—ὑστέρῳ χρόνῳ τούτων ἡρμόσατο θυγατέρα, ἔρωτα σχὼν τῆς Ἑλλάδος τύραννος γενέσθαι. ἀποδέξας δὲ Μεγαβάτην στρατηγόν, Ἀρταφρένης ἀπέστειλε τὸν στρατὸν παρὰ τὸν Ἀρισταγόρεα.

V.32.1 ὁ μὲν δὴ Ἀρισταγόρης: is answered by ὁ δὲ Ἀρταφρένης.   **ὡς:** temporal, "when."   **ταῦτα:** refers back to Artaphrenes' response.   **οἱ =** **αὐτῷ:** i.e., Artaphrenes.   **τὰ ... λεγόμενα:** substantive, "what was said."   **ἐκ** **τοῦ Ἀρισταγόρεω:** agency.   **παρεσκευάσατο μέν:** answered by πολλὸν δὲ κάρτα ὅμιλον.   **πολλόν = πολύν.**   **ἄνδρα ... ἀνεψιόν:** in apposition to Μεγαβάτην.   **τοῦ = οὗ:** translate with θυγατέρα. The separation of the relative pronoun from the noun it possesses is roughly equivalent to the following English sentence: "see that man, the one whose—if the story be true and not a malicious lie intended to defame him and her—daughter sits over there?" Thoukydides (1.128) writes that Pausanias wished to marry the daughter of Xerxes, not of Megabates, and he cites as proof a letter written by Pausanias. An oral culture may look askance at written documentation, coming from a new and suspicious technology. It is uncertain how fifth-century Greek intellectuals would weigh good written accounts against good oral ones. Herodotus and Thoukydides used both.   **τούτων:** translate with ὑστέρῳ.   **γενέσθαι:** epexegetical with ἔρωτα.

～

V.33.1 παραλαβὼν δὲ ὁ Μεγαβάτης τόν τε Ἀρισταγόρεα ἐκ τῆς
Μιλήτου καὶ τὴν Ἰάδα στρατιὴν καὶ τοὺς Ναξίους ἔπλεε πρόφασιν ἐπ᾽
Ἑλλησπόντου. ἐπείτε δὲ ἐγένετο ἐν Χίῳ, ἔσχε τὰς νέας ἐς Καύκασα,
ὡς ἐνθεῦτεν βορέῃ ἀνέμῳ ἐς τὴν Νάξον διαβάλοι. [2] καὶ οὐ γὰρ ἔδεε
τούτῳ τῷ στόλῳ Ναξίους ἀπολέσθαι, πρῆγμα τοιόνδε συνηνείχθη
γενέσθαι. περιιόντος Μεγαβάτεω τὰς ἐπὶ τῶν νεῶν φυλακάς, ἐπὶ
νεὸς Μυνδίης ἔτυχε οὐδεὶς φυλάσσων. ὁ δέ, δεινόν τι ποιησάμενος,
ἐκέλευσε τοὺς δορυφόρους, ἐξευρόντας τὸν ἄρχοντα ταύτης τῆς νεός,
τῷ οὔνομα ἦν Σκύλαξ, τοῦτον δῆσαι, διὰ θαλαμίης διελόντας τῆς νεὸς
κατὰ τοῦτο· ἔξω μὲν κεφαλὴν ποιεῦντας ἔσω δὲ τὸ σῶμα. [3] δεθέντος
δὲ τοῦ Σκύλακος, ἐξαγγέλλει τις τῷ Ἀρισταγόρῃ ὅτι τὸν ξεῖνόν οἱ
τὸν Μύνδιον Μεγαβάτης δήσας λυμαίνοιτο. ὁ δ᾽ ἐλθὼν παραιτέετο
τὸν Πέρσην. τυγχάνων δὲ οὐδενὸς τῶν ἐδέετο, αὐτὸς ἐλθὼν ἔλυσε.
πυθόμενος δέ, κάρτα δεινὸν ἐποιήσατο ὁ Μεγαβάτης καὶ ἐσπέρχετο τῷ
Ἀρισταγόρῃ. [4] ὁ δὲ εἶπε· Σοὶ δὲ καὶ τούτοισι τοῖσι πρήγμασι τί ἐστι;
οὐ σὲ ἀπέστειλε Ἀρταφρένης ἐμέο πείθεσθαι καὶ πλέειν τῇ ἂν ἐγὼ
κελεύω; τί πολλὰ πρήσσεις; ταῦτα εἶπε ὁ Ἀρισταγόρης. ὁ δὲ θυμωθεὶς
τούτοισι, ὡς νὺξ ἐγένετο, ἔπεμπε ἐς Νάξον πλοίῳ ἄνδρας φράσοντας
τοῖσι Ναξίοισι πάντα τὰ παρεόντα σφι πρήγματα.

V.33.1 πρόφασιν: accusative of respect, "ostensibly." The events in chapter
33 begin with the failure of the Naxian invasion (499 B.C.E.) and serve as the
rationale for what Megabates does next. However well justified from a personal
standpoint, Megabates' subsequent actions are treasonous, and thus historians
question Herodotus's account, wondering whether it be reasonable to think
that a Persian of royal blood would act as Megabates is about to because of his
treatment at the hands of Aristagores. Also at issue is whether he could act in
this way and keep his favor at court. Finally, it is suggested that given the fate of
Samos, Khios, Lesbos, and Lemnos, the antennae of the Naxians would have
been on high alert.   **τε … καί … καί:** links τὸν Ἀρισταγόρεα, τὴν Ἰάδα, and
τοὺς Ναξίους.   **διαβάλοι:** a hypothetical optative giving Megabates' reason
for halting the ships at Kaukasa.   **33.2 ἔδεε … συνηνείχθη:** impersonals; it
is unclear whether Herodotus sees fate, chance, or both at work.   **Ναξίους:**
subject of ἀπολέσθαι.   **πρῆγμα τοιόνδε:** τοιόνδε looks forward to what is
about to come.   **γενέσθαι:** complementary with συνηνείχθη.   **φυλάσσων:**
supplementary with ἔτυχε.   **δεινόν τι ποιησάμενος:** supply an implied

εἶναι, which δεινόν is the subject of. Megabates' perspective is given.   τοὺς
δορυφόρους: subject of δῆσαι.   τῷ = ᾧ: possesses οὔνομα.   τοῦτον:
refers back to Skylax.   διελόντας: modifies τοὺς δορυφόρους; supply an
implied αὐτόν, i.e., Skylax.   κατὰ τοῦτο: looks forward to what comes
next.   ποιεῦντας = ποιοῦντας: modifies τοὺς δορυφόρους.   ἔξω μέν: is
answered by ἔσω δέ.   33.3 οἱ = αὐτῷ = Ἀρισταγόρῃ: possesses ξεῖνον. Herodotus
switches between Aristagores' point of view and Megabates.   λυμαίνοιτο: an
optative standing for an original indicative.   τῶν ἐδέετο = τούτων ὧν ἐδέετο:
the antecedent τούτων has dropped out, and τῶν serves as a partitive genitive
with οὐδενός and the object of ἐδέετο.   ἔλυσε: the object, Skylax, must be
supplied from context.   δεινόν: subject of an implied εἶναι.   33.4 σέ: subject
of πείθεσθαι and πλέειν.   ἐμέο = ἐμοῦ: more commonly found with the dative,
the middle of πείθω takes a genitive object four times in Herodotus.   πείθεσθαι
...πλέειν: infinitives of purpose.   τῇ: "whereever."   ἂν ... κελεύω: a
hypothetical subjunctive, looking forward to whatever orders may be given.   τί:
accusative of respect, "why."   τί πολλὰ πρήσσεις: "why are you doing many
things," i.e., why are you being a troublemaker.   ταῦτα: refers back to what
Aristagoras has just said.   φράσοντας: the participle indicates Megabates' reason
for sending the men.

❧

V.34.1 οἱ γὰρ ὧν Νάξιοι οὐδὲν πάντως προσεδέκοντο ἐπὶ σφέας
τὸν στόλον τοῦτον ὁρμήσεσθαι. ἐπεὶ μέντοι ἐπύθοντο, αὐτίκα μὲν
ἐσηνείκαντο τὰ ἐκ τῶν ἀγρῶν ἐς τὸ τεῖχος. παρεσκευάσαντο δέ, ὡς
πολιορκησόμενοι, καὶ σῖτα καὶ ποτά· καὶ τὸ τεῖχος ἐσάξαντο. [2] καὶ
οὗτοι μὲν παρεσκευάζοντο ὡς παρεσομένου σφι πολέμου. οἱ δ᾽ ἐπείτε
διέβαλον ἐκ τῆς Χίου τὰς νέας ἐς τὴν Νάξον, πρὸς πεφραγμένους
προσεφέροντο καὶ ἐπολιόρκεον μῆνας τέσσερας. [3] ὡς δέ, τά τε
ἔχοντες ἦλθον χρήματα οἱ Πέρσαι, ταῦτα κατεδεδαπάνητό σφι καὶ
αὐτῷ τῷ Ἀρισταγόρῃ προσαναισίμωτο πολλά τοῦ πλεῦνός τε ἐδέετο ἡ
πολιορκίη, ἐνθαῦτα τείχεα τοῖσι φυγάσι τῶν Ναξίων οἰκοδομήσαντες
ἀπαλλάσσοντο ἐς τὴν ἤπειρον, κακῶς πρήσσοντες.

V.34.1 Νάξιοι οὐδὲν πάντως προσεδέκοντο: historians question Herodotus's
account, thinking it not reasonable that the Naxians should not have some
expectation that the armada could be sailing against them. From a narratological
standpoint, the passage serves as a typical Herodotean correction to the mistaken
narratives of Aristagores and Artaphrenes in 31.   **τὸν στόλον**: subject of
ὁρμήσεσθαι.   **αὐτίκα μέν**: is answered by παρεσκευάσαντο δέ.   **τὰ ἐκ τῶν**

ἀγρῶν: substantive, "the things from the fields." πολιορκησόμενοι: the tense of the participle looks toward the upcoming siege; the middle has a passive sense.   34.2 καὶ οὗτοι μέν: is answered by οἱ δ᾽ ἐπείτε; μέν concludes the narration on the actions of the Naxians, and δέ begins telling of the armada sailing against them.   παρεσομένου: looks forward to the upcoming war and indicates that the Naxians were acting on certain foreknowledge.   πεφραγμένους: substantive, "men well-fortified."   34.3 ὡς δέ: introduces three subordinate clauses, the verbs of which are κατεδεδαπάνητο, προσαναισίμωτο, and ἐδέετο.   τά ... χρήματα = ἅ ... χρήματα: Herodotus has placed the antecedent in the relative clause, "what money," as in, for example, εἶδεν ἐν ᾗ οἰκέω χώρᾳ ("he saw in which country I dwell") instead of εἶδεν χώραν ἐν ᾗ οἰκῶ.   ταῦτα: refers back to the money.   σφι ... Ἀρισταγόρῃ: agency, as is typical with the perfect and pluperfect passive.   ἐνθαῦτα: marks the start of the independent clause.   τῶν Ναξίων: partitive with τοῖσι φυγάσι.

❧

V.35.1 Ἀρισταγόρης δὲ οὐκ εἶχε τὴν ὑπόσχεσιν τῷ Ἀρταφρένεϊ ἐκτελέσαι. ἅμα δὲ ἐπίεζέ μιν ἡ δαπάνη τῆς στρατιῆς, ἀπαιτεομένη. ἀρρώδεέ τε τοῦ στρατοῦ πρήξαντος κακῶς καὶ Μεγαβάτῃ διαβεβλημένος. ἐδόκεέ τε τὴν βασιληίην τῆς Μιλήτου ἀπαιρεθήσεσθαι. [2] ἀρρωδέων δὲ τούτων ἕκαστα, ἐβουλεύετο ἀπόστασιν· συνέπιπτε γὰρ καὶ τὸν ἐστιγμένον τὴν κεφαλὴν ἀπῖχθαι ἐκ Σούσων παρὰ Ἱστιαίου, σημαίνοντα ἀπίστασθαι Ἀρισταγόρην ἀπὸ βασιλέος. [3] ὁ γὰρ Ἱστιαῖος, βουλόμενος τῷ Ἀρισταγόρῃ σημῆναι ἀποστῆναι, ἄλλως μὲν οὐδαμῶς εἶχε ἀσφαλέως σημῆναι ὥστε φυλασσομενέων τῶν ὁδῶν. ὁ δέ, τῶν δούλων τὸν πιστότατον ἀποξυρήσας, τὴν κεφαλὴν ἔστιξε καὶ ἀνέμεινε ἀναφῦναι τὰς τρίχας. ὡς δὲ ἀνέφυσαν τάχιστα, ἀπέπεμπε ἐς Μίλητον, ἐντειλάμενος αὐτῷ ἄλλο μὲν οὐδέν, ἐπεὰν δὲ ἀπίκηται ἐς Μίλητον, κελεύειν Ἀρισταγόρην, ξυρήσαντά μιν τὰς τρίχας, κατιδέσθαι ἐς τὴν κεφαλήν. τὰ δὲ στίγματα ἐσήμαινε, ὡς καὶ πρότερόν μοι εἴρηται, ἀπόστασιν. [4] ταῦτα δὲ ὁ Ἱστιαῖος ἐποίεε, συμφορὴν ποιεύμενος μεγάλην τὴν ἑωυτοῦ κατοχὴν τὴν ἐν Σούσοισι. ἀποστάσιος ὦν γινομένης, πολλὰς εἶχε ἐλπίδας μετήσεσθαι ἐπὶ θάλασσαν. μὴ δὲ νεώτερόν τι ποιεύσης τῆς Μιλήτου, οὐδαμὰ ἐς αὐτὴν ἥξειν ἔτι ἐλογίζετο.

V.35.1 Ἀρισταγόρης: this paragraph offers an explanation of events mainly from the perspectives of Aristagores and Histiaios.   ἐκτελέσαι:

complementary with εἶχε. **μιν = αὐτόν.** **τε … καί:** give the two reasons behind his being afraid. **Μεγαβάτῃ:** agency. **τὴν βασιληίην:** subject of ἀπαιρεθήσεσθαι. **35.2 τούτων:** partitive with ἕκαστα. **ἀρρωδέων:** Herodotus sees a variety of things causing events to play out as they do. The divine has its role. Other times he sees the particular at work: revenge, greed, and desire. Here we see fear at work. **συνέπιπτε:** chance also has a role to play. **τὸν ἐστιγμένον:** substantive, "the man with the tattoo" and subject of ἀπῖχθαι; the backstory comes next. **τὴν κεφαλήν:** accusative of respect. **ἀπῖχθαι:** complementary with συνέπιπτε. **σημαίνοντα:** modifies τὸν ἐστιγμένον ("the man with the tattoo"). **ἀπίστασθαι:** dependent on σημαίνοντα. **Ἀρισταγόρην:** subject of ἀπίστασθαι. **35.3 τῷ Ἀρισταγόρῃ:** to perform the action of ἀποστῆναι. **σημῆναι:** complementary with βουλόμενος. **ἀποστῆναι:** dependent on σημῆναι. **ἄλλως μὲν οὐδαμῶς:** is answered by ὁ δέ. **σημῆναι:** complementary with εἶχε. **τῶν δούλων:** partitive with τὸν πιστότατον. **τὸν πιστότατον:** substantive, "the most trusted." **ἀναφῦναι:** dependent on ἀνέμεινε. **τὰς τρίχας:** subject of ἀναφῦναι. **αὐτῷ:** to perform the action of κελεύειν. **ἄλλο μὲν οὐδέν:** is answered by ἐπεὰν δὲ ἀπίκηται. **ἀπίκηται:** a hypothetical subjunctive, looking forward to an event that is yet to occur. **κελεύειν:** dependent on ἐντειλάμενος; supply an implied ἤ before κελεύειν. **Ἀρισταγόρην:** object of κελεύειν and subject of κατιδέσθαι. **μιν = αὐτόν = δούλων τὸν πιστότατον.** **κατιδέσθαι:** dependent on κελεύειν. **πρότερον:** an internal temporal reference, referring to 35.2. **μοι:** agency. **35.4 ταῦτα:** refers back to the shaving and tattooing of the head. **συμφορὴν ποιεύμενος μεγάλην:** represents Histiaios's point of view. **συμφορήν … μεγάλην:** predicate to τὴν ἑωυτοῦ κατοχὴν τὴν ἐν Σούσοισι; understand an implied εἶναι. **μετήσεσθαι:** epexegetical with ἐλπίδας. **μή:** the negative for hypotheticals. **ἥξειν:** main verb in indirect statement; the subject is the same as the subject of ἐλογίζετο. Unlike Aristagores, Histiaios is prompted to revolt by a yearning for his metropolis.

~

V.36.1 Ἱστιαῖος μέν νυν, ταῦτα διανοεύμενος, ἀπέπεμπε τὸν ἄγγελον. Ἀρισταγόρῃ δὲ συνέπιπτε τοῦ αὐτοῦ χρόνου πάντα ταῦτα συνελθόντα. ἐβουλεύετο ὦν μετὰ τῶν στασιωτέων, ἐκφήνας τήν τε ἑωυτοῦ γνώμην καὶ τὰ παρὰ τοῦ Ἱστιαίου ἀπιγμένα. [2] οἱ μὲν δὴ ἄλλοι πάντες γνώμην κατὰ τὠυτὸ ἐξεφέροντο, κελεύοντες ἀπίστασθαι. Ἑκαταῖος δ᾿ ὁ λογοποιὸς πρῶτα μὲν οὐκ ἔα πόλεμον βασιλέι τῶν Περσέων ἀναιρέεσθαι, καταλέγων τά τε ἔθνεα πάντα, τῶν ἦρχε Δαρεῖος, καὶ τὴν δύναμιν αὐτοῦ. ἐπείτε δὲ οὐκ ἔπειθε, δεύτερα συνεβούλευε ποιέειν ὅκως ναυκρατέες τῆς θαλάσσης ἔσονται. [3] ἄλλως μέν νυν οὐδαμῶς

ἔφη λέγων ἐνορᾶν ἐσόμενον τοῦτο· ἐπίστασθαι γὰρ τὴν δύναμιν
τῶν Μιλησίων ἐοῦσαν ἀσθενέα. εἰ δὲ τὰ χρήματα καταιρεθείη τὰ ἐκ
τοῦ ἱροῦ τοῦ ἐν Βραγχίδῃσι, τὰ Κροῖσος ὁ Λυδὸς ἀνέθηκε, πολλὰς
εἶχε ἐλπίδας ἐπικρατήσειν τῆς θαλάσσης. καὶ οὕτω αὐτούς τε ἕξειν
τοῖσι χρήμασι χρᾶσθαι καὶ τοὺς πολεμίους οὐ συλήσειν αὐτά. [4] τὰ δὲ
χρήματα ἦν ταῦτα μεγάλα, ὡς δεδήλωταί μοι ἐν τῷ πρώτῳ τῶν λόγων.
αὕτη μὲν δὴ οὐκ ἐνίκα ἡ γνώμη. ἐδόκεε δὲ ὅμως ἀπίστασθαι, ἕνα τε
αὐτῶν πλώσαντα ἐς Μυοῦντα ἐς τὸ στρατόπεδον, τὸ ἀπὸ τῆς Νάξου
ἀπελθόν, ἐὸν ἐνθαῦτα, συλλαμβάνειν πειρᾶσθαι τοὺς ἐπὶ τῶν νεῶν
ἐπιπλέοντας στρατηγούς.

V.36.1 Ἱστιαῖος μέν: is answered by Ἀρισταγόρῃ δέ; μέν ends Histiaios's
narrative, and δέ takes us back to Aristagores and his tale.   **ταῦτα:** refers
back to the reasons behind Histiaios's actions in 35.   **Ἀρισταγόρῃ:** object of
the prefix συν- of συνέπιπτε.   **συνέπιπτε:** by chance all factors converge;
refers back to the συνέπιπτε of 35.2 above.   **τὰ παρὰ τοῦ Ἱστιαίου ἀπιγμένα:**
substantive, "the information that came from Histiaios."   **36.2 οἱ μὲν δὴ ἄλλοι:**
is answered by Ἑκαταῖος δ᾽.   **κατὰ τὠυτό = κατὰ τὸ αὐτό:** substantive,
"to the same conclusion."   **κελεύοντες:** supply an implied Ἀρισταγόρην as
object.   **ἀπίστασθαι:** dependent on κελεύοντες; supply an implied Ἀρισταγόρην
as subject.   **Ἑκαταῖος δ᾽ ὁ λογοποιός:** author of geographical and historical
accounts of Asia Minor and the East. Hekataios is cited by Herodotus in a few
passages (II.143; V.36; V.125–26; VI.137). Herodotus offers Hekataios's counsel on
the best course of action.   **πρῶτα μέν... ἐπείτε δέ... δεύτερα:** "at first... but
when... then."   **οὐκ ἔα:** "he disagrees with."   **ἀναιρέεσθαι:** complementary
with οὐκ ἔα.   **τῶν = ὧν.**   **συνεβούλευε:** supply an implied αὐτοῖς.   **ποιέειν:**
"to make sure," dependent on συνεβούλευε; an implied αὐτοῖς is to perform the
action.   **36.3 ἄλλως μέν:** is answered by εἰ δέ.   **ἄλλως μέν νυν οὐδαμῶς:**
translate with ἐσόμενον τοῦτο.   **ἔφη λέγων:** though redundant, this finite
verb and participle combination is common.   **ἐνορᾶν:** main verb in indirect
statement; the subject is the same as the subject of ἔφη.   **τοῦτο:** refers back to
their taking control of the sea.   **ἐπίστασθαι:** main verb in indirect statement; the
subject is the same as the subject of ἔφη.   **καταιρεθείη:** a hypothetical optative
indicating a possible future event.   **τά = ἅ.**   **Κροῖσος ὁ Λυδὸς ἀνέθηκε:** for the
dedication see I.92.2.   **ἐπικρατήσειν:** epexegetical with ἐλπίδας.   **οὕτω:** refers
back to their taking the funds.   **αὐτούς:** subject of ἕξειν.   **ἕξειν:** main verb in
indirect statement.   **χρᾶσθαι:** complementary with ἕξειν.   **τοὺς πολεμίους:**
subject of συλήσειν.   **συλήσειν:** main verb in indirect statement.   **αὐτά =
τὰ χρήματα.**   **36.4 μοι:** agency with the perfect passive.   **ἐν τῷ πρώτῳ:**
substantive, "in the first part"; see I.92.2.   **τῶν λόγων:** partitive with τῷ

πρώτῳ. **αὕτη μέν:** is answered by ἐδόκεε δέ. **οὐκ ἐνίκα ἡ γνώμη:** though what Herodotus thinks about the failure to follow either of the two things Hekataios advises is not certain, his *Histories* do show the advantage superior forces and funds have, and his portrayal of Aristagores, who presents the Persians as easy to defeat, is not very flattering. Both suggest that he would prefer Hekataios's advice. Contrary to Herodotus's depiction, an attempt has been made in modern scholarship to portray Aristagores as a freedom fighter and hero of the cause of liberty. See George Cawkwell (2005), *The Greek Wars: The Failure of Persia* (Oxford: Oxford University Press), 61–86. **ἐδόκεε:** impersonal; supply an implied αὐτοῖς. **ἀπίστασθαι... πειρᾶσθαι:** complementary with ἐδόκεε. **ἕνα:** subject of πειρᾶσθαι. **αὐτῶν:** partitive with ἕνα. **ἐὸν ἐνθαῦτα:** i.e., at Myous. **συλλαμβάνειν:** complementary with πειρᾶσθαι.

~

V.37.1 ἀποπεμφθέντος δὲ ᾽Ιητραγόρεω κατ᾽ αὐτὸ τοῦτο καὶ συλλαβόντος δόλῳ ᾽Ολίατον ᾽Ιβανώλλιος Μυλασσέα καὶ Ἱστιαῖον Τύμνεω Τερμερέα καὶ Κώην Ἐρξάνδρου, τῷ Δαρεῖος Μυτιλήνην ἐδωρήσατο, καὶ Ἀρισταγόρην Ἡρακλείδεω Κυμαῖον καὶ ἄλλους συχνούς, οὕτω δὴ ἐκ τοῦ ἐμφανέος ὁ Ἀρισταγόρης ἀπεστήκεε, πᾶν ἐπὶ Δαρείῳ μηχανώμενος. [2] καὶ πρῶτα μέν, λόγῳ μετεὶς τὴν τυραννίδα, ἰσονομίην ἐποίεε τῇ Μιλήτῳ, ὡς ἂν ἑκόντες αὐτῷ οἱ Μιλήσιοι συναπισταίατο. μετὰ δὲ καὶ ἐν τῇ ἄλλῃ ᾽Ιωνίῃ τὠυτὸ τοῦτο ἐποίεε, τοὺς μὲν ἐξελαύνων τῶν τυράννων. τοὺς δ᾽ ἔλαβε τυράννους ἀπὸ τῶν νεῶν τῶν συμπλευσασέων ἐπὶ Νάξον, τούτους δέ, φίλα βουλόμενος ποιέεσθαι τῇσι πόλισι, ἐξεδίδου, ἄλλον ἐς ἄλλην πόλιν παραδιδούς, ὅθεν εἴη ἕκαστος.

V.37.1 κατ᾽ αὐτὸ τοῦτο: refers back to the decision to arrest the generals. **τῷ = ᾧ.** **πᾶν ἐπὶ Δαρείῳ μηχανώμενος:** Aristagores' perspective colors much of this section. **37.2 πρῶτα μέν... μετὰ δέ:** "first of all ... second." **λόγῳ:** dative of respect, "in word." At 49.1 Herodotus calls Aristagores "the tyrant of Miletos." For this reason the exact meaning of λόγῳ μετεὶς τὴν τυραννίδα is debated. Various solutions are offered, including emendation. Rather than suggest that Herodotus has forgotten what he wrote in 37, as Hornblower (2013) does, it is perhaps best to understand λόγῳ as part of Herodotus's narrative. Thus, though he renounces the office in word, in deed Aristagores continues to act as tyrant and Herodotus continues to call him one. **αὐτῷ:** object of the prefix συν- of συναπισταίατο. **συναπισταίατο:** optative giving the reason why he establishes ἰσονομία ("equality" or "equality of rights"); the optative with ἄν occurs in purpose clauses in Homer and Herodotus (Smyth 2201).   **τοῦτο:** refers back to establishing ἰσονομία.   **τοὺς μέν:** is answered by τοὺς δ'.   **τυράννων:** partitive with τοὺς μέν.   **τοὺς δ' ἔλαβε τυράννους = οὓς δ' ἔλαβε τυράννους:** at times the antecedent is brought into the relative clause, e.g., εἶδεν ἐν ᾗ οἰκέω χώρᾳ ("he saw in which country I dwell") instead of εἶδεν χώραν ἐν ᾗ οἰκῶ.   **τούτους δέ:** refers back to τοὺς δ' ἔλαβε τυράννους.   **φίλα:** substantive, "kindness."   **ποιέεσθαι:** complementary with βουλόμενος.   **ἄλλον ἐς ἄλλην πόλιν:** the repetition of ἄλλος indicates, idiomatically, that he handed over each of the tyrants to their respective cities.   **εἴη:** optative standing for an original indicative.

V.38.1 Κώην μέν νυν Μυτιληναῖοι ἐπείτε τάχιστα παρέλαβον, ἐξαγαγόντες κατέλευσαν. Κυμαῖοι δὲ τὸν σφέτερον αὐτῶν ἀπῆκαν. ὡς δὲ καὶ ἄλλοι οἱ πλεῦνες ἀπίεσαν. [2] τυράννων μέν νυν κατάπαυσις ἐγίνετο ἀνὰ τὰς πόλιας. Ἀρισταγόρης δὲ ὁ Μιλήσιος ὡς τοὺς τυράννους κατέπαυσε, στρατηγοὺς ἐν ἑκάστῃ τῶν πολίων κελεύσας ἑκάστους καταστῆσαι, δεύτερα αὐτὸς ἐς Λακεδαίμονα τριήρεϊ ἀπόστολος ἐγίνετο. ἔδεε γὰρ δὴ συμμαχίης τινός οἱ μεγάλης ἐξευρεθῆναι.

V.38.1 Κώην μέν: is answered by Κυμαῖοι δέ.   **τὸν σφέτερον:** modifies an understood τύραννον.   **ὥς:** refers back to the letting go of their tyrant.   **ἀπίεσαν:** supply an implied τὸν σφέτερον τύραννον αὐτῶν.   **38.2 τυράννων μέν:** is answered by Ἀρισταγόρης δέ.   **στρατηγούς:** object of καταστῆσαι.   **ἑκάστους:** subject of καταστῆσαι.   **καταστῆσαι:** dependent on κελεύσας.   **οἱ = αὐτῷ.**   **συμμαχίης:** is to perform the action of ἐξευρεθῆναι.   **ἐξευρεθῆναι:** complementary with ἔδεε.

V.39.1 τῆς δὲ Σπάρτης Ἀναξανδρίδης μὲν ὁ Λέοντος, οὐκέτι περιεών, ἐβασίλευε ἀλλὰ ἐτετελευτήκεε. Κλεομένης δὲ ὁ Ἀναξανδρίδεω εἶχε τὴν βασιληίην, οὐ κατ' ἀνδραγαθίην σχὼν ἀλλὰ κατὰ γένος. Ἀναξανδρίδῃ γὰρ ἔχοντι γυναῖκα, ἀδελφεῆς ἑωυτοῦ θυγατέρα, καὶ ἐούσης ταύτης οἱ καταθυμίης, παῖδες οὐκ ἐγίνοντο. [2] τούτου δὲ τοιούτου ἐόντος, οἱ ἔφοροι εἶπαν, ἐπικαλεσάμενοι αὐτόν· Εἴ τοι σὺ σεωυτοῦ μὴ προορᾷς, ἀλλ' ἡμῖν τοῦτ' ἐστὶ οὐ περιοπτέον γένος τὸ Εὐρυσθένεος γενέσθαι ἐξίτηλον. σύ νυν, τὴν μὲν ἔχεις γυναῖκα, ἐπείτε τοι οὐ τίκτει, ἔξεο, ἄλλην δὲ γῆμον. καὶ ποιέων ταῦτα Σπαρτιήτῃσι ἀδήσεις. ὁ δ᾽ ἀμείβετο, φὰς τούτων οὐδέτερα ποιήσειν· ἐκείνους τε οὐ καλῶς συμβουλεύειν παραινέοντας, τὴν ἔχει γυναῖκα, ἐοῦσαν ἀναμάρτητον ἑωυτῷ, ταύτην ἀπέντα, ἄλλην ἐσαγαγέσθαι· οὐδέ σφι πείσεσθαι.

V.39.1 Ἀναξανδρίδης μέν: is answered by Κλεομένης δέ. **ἐβασίλευε...**
ἐτετελευτήκεε: the aspect of the first verb stresses continuous action in the past, "he used to be king"; the aspect of the second stresses a completed action of the past. **Κλεομένης:** comes to the Spartan throne in about 520 B.C.E. In Book VI he will be imprisoned by his countrymen. While in prison he obtains a knife and slashes himself to death. Herodotus gives the various possible reasons for his madness as the following: his bribery of the Pythia to drive his colleague Demaratos from the throne (VI.66); his destruction of the precinct of the goddesses during his invasion of Eleusis (V.74–77); his killing of the suppliants he drove from Argos (VI.76–84); or his drinking of wine neat, which he learned from the Skythians (VI.84). All but the last see the divine at work. Herodotus thinks his treatment of Demaratos the most likely reason (VI.84). **οὐ κατ᾽ ἀνδραγαθίην:** Hornblower (2013) notes that ἀνδραγαθία had no influence in Sparta on kingship. If true, then why mention it? Later at 42.1 the same phrase is used in indirect statement of Dorieus's expectations. It could be that here, like in 42.1, the phrase is part of Dorieus's narrative and that Herodotus is highlighting his delusion. It could also be that we are mistaken in the possibilities concerning royal succession at Sparta. In this reading the phrase belongs to Herodotus's narrative, one that is open to the possibility of Spartan norms being broken, as they are in the case of Anaxandrides and his two wives. **σχών:** supply an implied τὴν βασιληίην as object. **Ἀναξανδρίδῃ:** possesses παῖδες. **θυγατέρα:** in apposition to γυναῖκα. **ταύτης:** refers back to his wife/niece. **οἱ = αὐτῷ:** translate with καταθυμίης. **39.2 τούτου:** refers back to his having no children. **οἱ ἔφοροι εἶπαν:** the narration switches between them and Anaxandrides. **σεωυτοῦ = σεαυτοῦ:** object of the prefix προ- of προορᾷς. **μή:** the negative for hypotheticals. **προορᾷς:** subjunctive referring to an event that may or may not happen. **ἡμῖν:** agency with a verbal adjective. **τοῦτ᾽:** refers back to Kleomenes' looking out for his future by having children. **ἐστὶ οὐ περιοπτέον:** impersonal and having obligation, "it must not be ignored." **γένος:** subject of γενέσθαι. **γενέσθαι:** main verb in indirect statement. **τὴν μέν = ἣν μέν:** is answered by ἄλλην δὲ γῆμον. **γυναῖκα:** at times the antecedent is brought into the relative clause, e.g., εἶδεν ἐν ᾗ οἰκέω χώρᾳ ("he saw in which country I dwell") instead of εἶδεν χώραν ἐν ᾗ οἰκῶ. **τοι = σοι. ταῦτα:** refers back to doing what the Spartans ask. **φάς:** he makes three points, each one an infinitive: (1) ποιήσειν; (2) συμβουλεύειν; and (3) πείσεσθαι. **οὐδέτερα:** partitive with

τούτων.   ποιήσειν: main verb in indirect statement; the subject is the same as
the subject of ἀμείβετο.   ἐκείνους: subject of συμβουλεύειν.   συμβουλεύειν:
main verb in indirect statement.   ταύτην: refers back to γυναῖκα.   ἀπέντα
= ἀφέντα: substantive, modifying an understood αὐτόν = Ἀναξανδρίδην,
which is the subject of ἐσαγαγέσθαι.   ἐσαγαγέσθαι: dependent on
παραινέοντας.   πείσεσθαι: the subject is the same as the subject of ἀμείβετο.

～

V.40.1 πρὸς ταῦτα οἱ ἔφοροι καὶ οἱ γέροντες, βουλευσάμενοι,
προσέφερον Ἀναξανδρίδῃ τάδε· Ἐπεὶ τοίνυν τοι περιεχόμενόν σε
ὁρῶμεν τῆς ἔχεις γυναικός, σὺ δὲ ταῦτα ποίεε καὶ μὴ ἀντίβαινε
τούτοισι, ἵνα μή τι ἀλλοῖον περὶ σεῦ Σπαρτιῆται βουλεύσωνται. [2]
γυναικὸς μὲν τῆς ἔχεις οὐ προσδεόμεθά σευ τῆς ἐξέσιος. σὺ δὲ ταύτῃ
τε πάντα, ὅσα νῦν παρέχεις, πάρεχε. καὶ ἄλλην πρὸς ταύτῃ ἐσάγαγε
γυναῖκα τεκνοποιόν. ταῦτά κη λεγόντων, συνεχώρησε ὁ Ἀναξανδρίδης.
μετὰ δὲ γυναῖκας ἔχων δύο, διξὰς ἱστίας οἴκεε, ποιέων οὐδαμῶς
Σπαρτιητικά.

V.40.1 πρὸς ταῦτα: refers back to what has just been said in 39.   οἱ ἔφοροι
καὶ οἱ γέροντες: they narrate much of this section.   τάδε: looks forward to
what comes next.   τῆς = ἧς = ἥν: the relative pronoun is attracted into the
case of its antecedent, γυναικός, which Herodotus has placed in the relative
clause.   γυναικός: object of the prefix περι- of περιεχόμενον.   ταῦτα: refers to
what comes next.   τούτοισι: object of the prefix ἀντί- of ἀντίβαινε; looks forward
to what comes next.   περὶ σεῦ = περὶ σοῦ.   βουλεύσωνται: a hypothetical
subjunctive, indicating the reason why they think Anaxandrides should follow their
advice.   40.2 γυναικός: translate with ἐξέσιος.   γυναικὸς μέν: is answered
by σὺ δέ.   τῆς = ἧς = ἥν: the relative pronoun is attracted into the case of its
antecedent, γυναικός, which Herodotus has placed in the relative clause.   σευ =
σου.   ταύτῃ = γυναικί.   ταῦτα: refers back to his taking another wife.   μετὰ
δέ: adverbial, "next."   Σπαρτιητικά: substantive, "Spartan customs"; aware of
the dangers of cultural relativism, Herodotus insists that not to think one's own
customs best is the sign of a madman (III.38). Bigamy was generally not permissible
throughout Greece, and this incidence of two wives at Sparta is exceptional.

～

V.41.1 χρόνου δὲ οὐ πολλοῦ διελθόντος, ἡ ἐσύστερον ἐπελθοῦσα
γυνὴ τίκτει τὸν δὴ Κλεομένεα τοῦτον. καὶ αὕτη τε ἔφεδρον βασιλέα

Σπαρτιήτησι ἀπέφαινε. καὶ ἡ προτέρη γυνή, τὸν πρότερον χρόνον
ἄτοκος ἐοῦσα, τότε κως ἐκύησε, συντυχίῃ ταύτῃ χρησαμένη. [2]
ἔχουσαν δὲ αὐτὴν ἀληθεῖ λόγῳ οἱ τῆς ἐπελθούσης γυναικὸς οἰκήιοι
πυθόμενοι ὤχλεον, φάμενοι αὐτὴν κομπέειν, ἄλλως βουλομένην
ὑποβαλέσθαι. δεινὰ δὲ ποιεύντων αὐτῶν, τοῦ χρόνου συντάμνοντος,
ὑπ᾽ ἀπιστίης οἱ ἔφοροι τίκτουσαν τὴν γυναῖκα περιιζόμενοι ἐφύλαξαν.
[3] ἡ δὲ ὡς ἔτεκε Δωριέα, ἰθέως ἴσχει Λεωνίδην· καὶ μετὰ τοῦτον
ἰθέως ἴσχει Κλεόμβροτον. οἱ δὲ καὶ διδύμους λέγουσι Κλεόμβροτον
καὶ Λεωνίδην γενέσθαι. ἡ δὲ Κλεομένεα τεκοῦσα καὶ τὸ δεύτερον
ἐπελθοῦσα γυνή, ἐοῦσα θυγάτηρ Πρινητάδεω τοῦ Δημαρμένου, οὐκέτι
ἔτικτε τὸ δεύτερον.

V.41.1 Κλεομένεα τοῦτον: τοῦτον refers back to the Kleomenes mentioned in
39.1.   **συντυχίῃ ταύτῃ χρησαμένη:** Herodotus narrates this as another chance
event.   **41.2 ἔχουσαν δὲ αὐτήν:** supply an implied ἐν γαστρί.   **ἀληθεῖ λόγῳ:**
i.e., she really is pregnant. Herodotus intrudes his commentary into the narrative of
the relatives claiming that she is lying.   **αὐτήν:** subject of κομπέειν.   **κομπέειν:**
main verb in indirect statement.   **ὑποβαλέσθαι:** complementary with
βουλομένην; supply an implied παιδίον as the object.   **δεινά:** substantive,
"trouble"; their actions are δεινά both from the perspectives of the first wife and
Herodotus.   **41.3 ὡς:** temporal.   **οἱ δέ ... λέγουσι:** Herodotus offers another
version.   **διδύμους:** predicate to Κλεόμβροτον and Λεωνίδην and plural
because of the implied plurality.   **Κλεόμβροτον ... Λεωνίδην:** subjects of
γενέσθαι.   **γενέσθαι:** main verb in indirect statement.

~

V.42.1 ὁ μὲν δὴ Κλεομένης, ὡς λέγεται, ἦν τε οὐ φρενήρης ἀκρομανής
τε. ὁ δὲ Δωριεὺς ἦν τῶν ἡλίκων πάντων πρῶτος, εὖ τε ἐπίστατο
κατ᾽ ἀνδραγαθίην αὐτὸς σχήσων τὴν βασιληίην. [2] ὥστε ὦν οὕτω
φρονέων, ἐπειδὴ ὅ τε Ἀναξανδρίδης ἀπέθανε καὶ οἱ Λακεδαιμόνιοι,
χρεώμενοι τῷ νόμῳ, ἐστήσαντο βασιλέα τὸν πρεσβύτατον Κλεομένεα,
ὁ Δωριεύς, δεινόν τε ποιεύμενος καὶ οὐκ ἀξιῶν ὑπὸ Κλεομένεος
βασιλεύεσθαι, αἰτήσας λεὼν Σπαρτιήτας ἦγε ἐς ἀποικίην, οὔτε τῷ
ἐν Δελφοῖσι χρηστηρίῳ χρησάμενος ἐς ἥντινα γῆν κτίσων ἴῃ, οὔτε
ποιήσας οὐδὲν τῶν νομιζομένων. οἷα δὲ βαρέως φέρων, ἀπίει ἐς τὴν
Λιβύην τὰ πλοῖα· κατηγέοντο δέ οἱ ἄνδρες Θηραῖοι. [3] ἀπικόμενος

δὲ ἐς Λιβύην, οἴκισε χῶρον κάλλιστον τῶν Λιβύων παρὰ Κίνυπα
ποταμόν. ἐξελασθεὶς δὲ ἐνθεῦτεν τρίτῳ ἔτεϊ ὑπὸ Μακέων τε Λιβύων
καὶ Καρχηδονίων, ἀπίκετο ἐς Πελοπόννησον.

V.42.1 ὁ μὲν δὴ Κλεομένης: is answered by ὁ δὲ Δωριεύς.   **ὡς λέγεται:** indicates
an unknown source for this part of the narrative.   **τῶν ἡλίκων:** partitive with
πρῶτος; Dorieus is a natural leader.   **εὖ τε ἐπίστατο:** in Dorieus's ideal narrative,
he becomes king.   **σχήσων:** future because it indicates time subsequent to
ἐπίστατο.   **42.2 οὕτω:** refers back to his expectation of becoming king; much
of this paragraph represents Dorieus's view of things.   **δεινόν:** subject of an
implied εἶναι.   **βασιλεύεσθαι:** complementary with ἀξιῶν.   **χρησάμενος:**
it was Greek custom to obtain the sanction of an oracle before establishing a
colony or undertaking a war.   **κτίσων:** future showing Dorieus's intent.   **ἴῃ:** a
hypothetical subjunctive, standing for an original deliberative subjunctive.   **τῶν
νομιζομένων:** substantive, "what was customary"; it is partitive with οὐδέν. By
stating what Dorieus did not do, Herodotus offers a corrective that suggests what
a better course of action could have been.   **οἷα:** οἷα (and ἅτε) is typically found
with a participle in the nominative or accusative case. Use "since" or "because" to
translate it, and turn the participle into a finite verb. Thus, ἅτε αὐτὸν ὄντα καλόν
(ἅτε ὢν καλός): "since he was good."   **κατηγέοντο δέ οἱ ἄνδρες Θηραῖοι:**
colonists from Sparta (IV.147) and founders of Kyrene (IV.150); they serve as
guides.   **42.3 Λιβύων:** the Greeks colonized eastern Libya and founded Kyrene c.
630 B.C.E.

❧

V.43.1 ἐνθαῦτα δέ οἱ Ἀντιχάρης, ἀνὴρ Ἐλεώνιος, συνεβούλευσε ἐκ τῶν
Λαΐου χρησμῶν Ἡρακλείην τὴν ἐν Σικελίῃ κτίζειν, φὰς τὴν Ἔρυκος
χώρην πᾶσαν εἶναι Ἡρακλειδέων, αὐτοῦ Ἡρακλέος κτησαμένου. ὁ
δέ, ἀκούσας ταῦτα, ἐς Δελφοὺς οἴχετο χρησόμενος τῷ χρηστηρίῳ,
εἰ αἱρέει, ἐπ' ἣν στέλλεται χώρην. ἡ δὲ Πυθίη οἱ χρᾷ, αἱρήσειν.
παραλαβὼν δὲ Δωριεὺς τὸν στόλον, τὸν καὶ ἐς Λιβύην ἦγε, ἐκομίζετο
παρὰ τὴν Ἰταλίην.

V.43.1 οἱ = αὐτῷ: object of the prefix συν- of συνεβούλευσε; the pronoun is to
perform the action of κτίζειν.   **Ἐλεώνιος:** the legendary seer Bakis is said to
have come from Eleon.   **ἐκ τῶν Λαΐου χρησμῶν:** because they are not otherwise
attested, their historicity is challenged by scholars.   **Ἔρυκος:** founded by the
indigineous hero Eryx, who hosted Herakles when he traveled to Sikelia and
lost to him in a wrestling match. Greece and Phoinikia both claimed rights over

western Sikelia. The story of Herakles' defeat of Eryx was used by the Greeks to claim ascendancy in the area. Poets and their stories are legitimate historical sources. This may seem strange, but for the Greeks of this time it was not at all. Before writing, history is preserved by the poets in their stories and passed down from one generation to the next. These stories preserve culture and history, and foundation stories tell how and who founded what city. These foundation accounts could be used as evidence for a city-state's claim to a particular land or for a person's claim to a particular lineage. **χώρην:** subject of εἶναι. **εἶναι:** main verb in indirect statement. **Ἡρακλειδέων:** the sons of Herakles conquered several areas in Greece. **κτησαμένου:** supply an implied αὐτήν. **ταῦτα:** refers back to what Antikhares says. **χρησόμενος:** indicates Dorieus's reason for going to Delphi. **χώρην:** at times the antecedent is brought into the relative clause, e.g., εἶδεν ἐν ᾗ οἰκέω χώρᾳ ("he saw in which country I dwell") instead of εἶδεν χώραν ἐν ᾗ οἰκῶ. **οἱ = αὐτῷ:** is to perform the action of αἱρήσειν. **τόν = ὅν.**

❧

V.44.1 τὸν χρόνον δὲ τοῦτον, ὡς λέγουσι Συβαρῖται, σφέας τε αὐτοὺς καὶ Τῆλυν τὸν ἑωυτῶν βασιλέα ἐπὶ Κρότωνα μέλλειν στρατεύεσθαι. τοὺς δὲ Κροτωνιήτας, περιδεέας γενομένους, δεηθῆναι Δωριέος σφίσι τιμωρῆσαι καὶ τυχεῖν, δεηθέντας. συστρατεύεσθαί τε δὴ ἐπὶ Σύβαριν Δωριέα καὶ συνελεῖν τὴν Σύβαριν. [2] ταῦτα μέν νυν Συβαρῖται λέγουσι ποιῆσαι Δωριέα τε καὶ τοὺς μετ' αὐτοῦ. Κροτωνιῆται δὲ οὐδένα σφίσι φασὶ ξεῖνον προσεπιλαβέσθαι τοῦ πρὸς Συβαρίτας πολέμου εἰ μὴ Καλλίην, τῶν Ἰαμιδέων μάντιν Ἠλεῖον μοῦνον, καὶ τοῦτον τρόπῳ τοιῷδε. παρὰ Τήλυος τοῦ Συβαριτέων τυράννου ἀποδράντα ἀπικέσθαι παρὰ σφέας, ἐπείτε οἱ τὰ ἱρὰ οὐ προεχώρεε χρηστά, θυομένῳ ἐπὶ Κρότωνα.

V.44.1 τὸν χρόνον δὲ τοῦτον: about 510 B.C.E. **ὡς λέγουσι Συβαρῖται:** the narrative focus starts with the Sybarites, then goes to the Krotoniates, and then to the seer Kallies. **σφέας:** subject of μέλλειν. **Τῆλυν:** subject of μέλλειν. **βασιλέα:** in apposition to Τῆλυν; Hornblower (2013) mistakenly defines this secondary character text (indirect statement) as authorial. Reference to Telys as king belongs to the narrative of the Sybarites. **μέλλειν:** main verb in indirect statement. **στρατεύεσθαι:** complementary with μέλλειν. **τοὺς δὲ Κροτωνιήτας:** subject of δεηθῆναι and τυχεῖν. **δεηθῆναι ... τυχεῖν:** main verbs in indirect statement. **Δωριέος:** is to perform the action of τιμωρῆσαι. **τιμωρῆσαι:** dependent on δεηθῆναι. **τυχεῖν:** supply the object, τούτου, from context. **συστρατεύεσθαι ... συνελεῖν:**

main verbs in indirect statement.   ἐπὶ Σύβαριν: a Greek town in Lukania, Italia, Sybaris was founded in 720 B.C.E. and destroyed, as we see here, in 510 B.C.E.   Δωριέα: subject of συστρατεύεσθαι and συνελεῖν along with an implied Κροτωνιήτας.   44.2 ταῦτα: refers back to the conquering of Sybaris.   ταῦτα μέν νυν: is answered by Κροτωνιῆται δέ.   τοὺς μετ᾽ αὐτοῦ: substantive, "those with him"; subject of ποιῆσαι.   σφίσι: translate with ξεῖνον.   ξεῖνον: subject of προσεπιλαβέσθαι.   προσεπιλαβέσθαι: main verb in indirect statement.   Καλλίην: subject of an implied προσεπιλαβέσθαι.   μάντιν: in apposition to Καλλίην.   τοῦτον: refers back to Kallies.   τρόπῳ τοιῷδε: looks forward to what comes next.   τυράννου: in the Sybarite narrative he is called βασιλεύς, but in the Krotoniate one τύραννος.   ἀποδράντα: substantive modifying an implied Καλλίην and subject of ἀπικέσθαι.   ἀπικέσθαι: main verb in indirect statement.   οἱ = αὐτῷ: modified by θυομένῳ.   προεχώρεε: the aspect stresses the repetition of the sacrificing.

~

V.45.1 ταῦτα δὲ οὗτοι λέγουσι. μαρτύρια δὲ τούτων ἑκάτεροι ἀποδεικνύουσι τάδε. Συβαρῖται μὲν τέμενός τε καὶ νηὸν ἐόντα παρὰ τὸν ξηρὸν Κρᾶθιν, τὸν ἱδρύσασθαι, συνελόντα τὴν πόλιν, Δωριέα λέγουσι Ἀθηναίῃ ἐπωνύμῳ Κραθίῃ. τοῦτο δὲ αὐτοῦ Δωριέος τὸν θάνατον μαρτύριον μέγιστον ποιεῦνται, ὅτι παρὰ τὰ μεμαντευμένα ποιέων διεφθάρη. εἰ γὰρ δὴ μὴ παρέπρηξε μηδέν, ἐπ᾽ ὃ δὲ ἐστάλη ἐποίεε, εἷλε ἂν τὴν Ἐρυκίνην χώρην καὶ ἑλὼν κατέσχε, οὐδ᾽ ἂν αὐτός τε καὶ ἡ στρατιὴ διεφθάρη. [2] οἱ δ᾽ αὖ Κροτωνιῆται ἀποδεικνῦσι Καλλίῃ μὲν τῷ Ἠλείῳ ἐξαίρετα ἐν γῇ τῇ Κροτωνιήτιδι πολλὰ δοθέντα—τὰ καὶ ἐς ἐμὲ ἔτι ἐνέμοντο οἱ Καλλίεω ἀπόγονοι—Δωριέι δὲ καὶ τοῖσι Δωριέος ἀπογόνοισι οὐδέν. καίτοι εἰ συνεπελάβετό γε τοῦ Συβαριτικοῦ πολέμου Δωριεύς, δοθῆναι ἄν οἱ πολλαπλήσια ἢ Καλλίῃ. ταῦτα μέν νυν ἑκάτεροι αὐτῶν μαρτύρια ἀποφαίνονται. καὶ πάρεστι, ὁκοτέροισί τις πείθεται αὐτῶν, τούτοισι προσχωρέειν.

V.45.1 ταῦτα: refers back to what both sides claim.   **τούτων:** refers back to what both sides claim.   **ἑκάτεροι ἀποδεικνύουσι:** Herodotus presents without stating a preference the evidence the Sybarites and the Krotoniates offer.   **τάδε:** looks forward to what comes next.   **Συβαρῖται μέν:** is answered by οἱ δ᾽ αὖ Κροτωνιῆται from 45.2 and subject of the delayed λέγουσι. The whole of 45.1 offers the Sybarites' point of view.   **τέμενός τε καὶ νηόν:** subjects of an implied εἶναι; the grove and temple are the μαρτύρια.   **τόν = ὅν:** the relative pronoun is singular because it agrees with its nearest antecedent. **ἱδρύσασθαι:** main verb in the relative clause in indirect statement. **συνελόντα:** shows time prior to ἱδρύσασθαι and serves as evidence for their version of events. **Δωριέα:** subject of ἱδρύσασθαι. **Ἀθηναίῃ ἐπωνύμῳ Κραθίῃ:** translate with ἱδρύσασθαι. **τοῦτο δέ:** gives the second piece of evidence. **τὸν θάνατον:** subject of an implied εἶναι. **τὰ μεμαντευμένα:** substantive, "the advice of the oracle." **ἐπ' ὅ δὲ ἐστάλη ἐποίεε = τοῦτο δέ, ἐπ' ὅ ἐστάλη, ἐποίεε:** the antecedent τοῦτο has dropped out, and the relative pronoun ὅ serves as the object of the preposition ἐπί and as the object of ἐποίεε. **εἷλε ἄν ... κατέσχε ... ἄν διεφθάρη:** ἄν renders the indicatives counterfactual; the condition is part of the narrative of the Sybarites. **διεφθάρη:** the verb agrees with its nearest subject. **45.2 Κροτωνιῆται:** Herodotus now offers the other side's perspective. **Καλλίῃ μέν:** is answered by Δωριέι δέ. **ἐξαίρετα ἐν γῇ τῇ Κροτωνιήτιδι:** substantive, "choice estates on Krotonian land." **τά = ἅ.** **ἐς ἐμέ:** a temporal marker that Herodotus inserts into the Krotonian narrative. **οὐδέν:** supply an implied δοθέν. **δοθῆναι:** main verb in indirect statement, standing for an original aorist indicative. **ἄν:** renders δοθῆναι counterfactual; the condition forms part of the narrative of the Krotoniates. **οἱ = αὐτῷ.** **πολλαπλήσια:** substantive, "much more land"; it is the subject of δοθῆναι. **ταῦτα μέν:** sums up the arguments on both sides and is answered by συνέπλεον δέ of the next paragraph. **αὐτῶν:** partitive with ἑκάτεροι. **ἀποφαίνονται:** Herodotus resumes narration. **πάρεστι:** impersonal. **αὐτῶν:** partitive with ὁκοτέροισι. **τούτοισι:** refers back to ὁκοτέροισι αὐτῶν. **προσχωρέειν:** complementary with πάρεστι.

❧

V.46.1 συνέπλεον δὲ Δωριέϊ καὶ ἄλλοι συγκτίσται Σπαρτιητέων, Θεσσαλὸς καὶ Παραιβάτης καὶ Κελέης καὶ Εὐρυλέων, οἵ, ἐπείτε ἀπίκοντο παντὶ στόλῳ ἐς τὴν Σικελίην, ἀπέθανον, μάχῃ ἐσσωθέντες ὑπό τε Φοινίκων καὶ Ἐγεσταίων. μοῦνος δὲ Εὐρυλέων τῶν συγκτιστέων περιεγένετο τούτου τοῦ πάθεος. [2] συλλαβὼν δὲ οὗτος τῆς στρατιῆς τοὺς περιγενομένους ἔσχε Μινώην, τὴν Σελινουσίων ἀποικίην. καὶ συνελευθέρου Σελινουσίους τοῦ μουνάρχου Πειθαγόρεω. μετὰ δέ, ὡς τοῦτον κατεῖλε, αὐτὸς τυραννίδι ἐπεχείρησε Σελινοῦντος. καὶ ἐμουνάρχησε χρόνον ἐπ' ὀλίγον. οἱ γάρ μιν Σελινούσιοι ἐπαναστάντες ἀπέκτειναν, καταφυγόντα ἐπὶ Διὸς ἀγοραίου βωμόν.

V.46.1 Δωριέϊ: object of the prefix συν- of συνέπλεον. **Σπαρτιητέων:** partitive with ἄλλοι. **Φοινίκων:** the Phoinikians colonized Karthage and parts of

Sikelia. When the Greeks sent colonies to Sikelia, the Phoinikians concentrated themselves in the west and made an alliance with the indigenous Elymian people, whose three major cities were Egesta, Eryx, and Entella. Ἐγεσταίων: indigenous Elymians. τῶν συγκτιστέων: partitive with μοῦνος δὲ Εὐρυλέων. τοῦ πάθεος: object of the prefix περι- of περιεγένετο. 46.2 τοὺς περιγενομένους: substantive, "the survivors." ἀποικίην: in apposition with Μινώην. μετὰ δέ: adverbial, "next." ὡς: temporal. τοῦτον: refers back to Peithagoras. τυραννίδι: object of the prefix ἐπι- of ἐπεχείρησε. The majority of Greeks of Herodotus's day had enough experience with tyrants to conclude that tyranny was to be avoided. That the Spartan Euryleon is quick to grasp at tyranny uncovers that segment of Greek society that considered tyranny an acceptable form of government. For the general Greek disapproval of the Spartans' proposal to establish tyranny at Athens, see V.92–93. μιν = αὐτόν. καταφυγόντα: modifies μιν, i.e., Euryleon.

❧

V.47.1 συνέσπετο δὲ Δωριέϊ καὶ συναπέθανε Φίλιππος ὁ Βουτακίδεω, Κροτωνιήτης ἀνήρ, ὅς, ἁρμοσάμενος Τήλυος τοῦ Συβαρίτεω θυγατέρα, ἔφυγε ἐκ Κρότωνος. ψευσθεὶς δὲ τοῦ γάμου, οἴχετο πλέων ἐς Κυρήνην. ἐκ ταύτης δὲ ὁρμώμενος συνέσπετο οἰκηίῃ τε τριήρεϊ καὶ οἰκηίῃ ἀνδρῶν δαπάνῃ, ἐών τε Ὀλυμπιονίκης καὶ κάλλιστος Ἑλλήνων τῶν κατ' ἑωυτόν. [2] διὰ δὲ τὸ ἑωυτοῦ κάλλος ἠνείκατο παρὰ Ἐγεσταίων τὰ οὐδεὶς ἄλλος· ἐπὶ γὰρ τοῦ τάφου αὐτοῦ ἡρώιον ἱδρυσάμενοι, θυσίῃσι αὐτὸν ἱλάσκονται.

V.47.1 Ἑλλήνων: partitive with κάλλιστος. κατ' ἑωυτόν = κατὰ ἑωυτοῦ χρόνον. 47.2 τά = ταῦτα ἅ: the antecedent ταῦτα has dropped out, and τά serves as the object of ἠνείκατο and of an ἠνείκατο implied with οὐδεὶς ἄλλος. ἡρώιον ἱδρυσάμενοι: as well as patron deities, Greeks worshipped heroes, more than human but less than divine, whose good will could keep them safe. Built from stone and smaller than a temple, the hero cult was an impressive grave marker. Since the Egestaians were not Greek, scholars wonder why they built a Greek monument.

❧

V.48.1 Δωριεὺς μέν νυν τρόπῳ τοιούτῳ ἐτελεύτησε. εἰ δὲ ἠνέσχετο βασιλευόμενος ὑπὸ Κλεομένεος καὶ κατέμενε ἐν Σπάρτῃ, ἐβασίλευσε ἂν Λακεδαίμονος· οὐ γάρ τινα πολλὸν χρόνον ἦρξε ὁ Κλεομένης, ἀλλ' ἀπέθανε ἄπαις, θυγατέρα μούνην λιπών, τῇ οὔνομα ἦν Γοργώ.

V.48.1 Δωριεὺς μέν: sums up Dorieus's backstory and is answered by εἰ δὲ ἠνέσχετο. **τρόπῳ τοιούτῳ:** refers back to 46.1. **εἰ δέ:** Herodotus uses this counterfactual to state an alternate arc for Dorieus's narrative. By stating what could have been, Herodotus colors the choices that Dorieus made with a critical brush. **ἠνέσχετο < ἀνέχω:** note the double augment. **βασιλευόμενος:** supplementary with ἠνέσχετο. **ἄν:** renders the indicative ἐβασίλευσε counterfactual. **ἦρξε ὁ Κλεομένης:** there are problems of chronology. It may be that Kleomenes ruled for some thirty years. If this duration of his reign is true, then its length is at odds with what Herodotus says. **τῇ = ᾗ:** possesses οὔνομα.

∿

V.49.1 ἀπικνέεται δὲ ὦν ὁ Ἀρισταγόρης, ὁ Μιλήτου τύραννος, ἐς τὴν Σπάρτην, Κλεομένεος ἔχοντος τὴν ἀρχήν, τῷ δὴ ἐς λόγους ἤιε, ὡς Λακεδαιμόνιοι λέγουσι, ἔχων χάλκεον πίνακα, ἐν τῷ γῆς ἁπάσης περίοδος ἐνετέτμητο καὶ θάλασσά τε πᾶσα καὶ ποταμοὶ πάντες. [2] ἀπικνεόμενος δὲ ἐς λόγους, ὁ Ἀρισταγόρης ἔλεγε πρὸς αὐτὸν τάδε· Κλεόμενες, σπουδὴν μὲν τὴν ἐμὴν μὴ θωμάσῃς τῆς ἐνθαῦτα ἀπίξιος· τὰ γὰρ κατήκοντα ἐστὶ τοιαῦτα. Ἰώνων παῖδας δούλους εἶναι ἀντ' ἐλευθέρων ὄνειδος καὶ ἄλγος μέγιστον μὲν αὐτοῖσι ἡμῖν, ἔτι δὲ τῶν λοιπῶν ὑμῖν, ὅσῳ προέστατε τῆς Ἑλλάδος. [3] νῦν ὦν, πρὸς θεῶν τῶν Ἑλληνίων, ῥύσασθε Ἴωνας ἐκ δουλοσύνης, ἄνδρας ὁμαίμονας. εὐπετέως δὲ ὑμῖν ταῦτα οἷά τε χωρέειν ἐστί. οὔτε γὰρ οἱ βάρβαροι ἄλκιμοι εἰσί. ὑμεῖς τε, τὰ ἐς τὸν πόλεμον, ἐς τὰ μέγιστα ἀνήκετε ἀρετῆς πέρι. ἥ τε μάχη αὐτῶν ἐστὶ τοιήδε· τόξα καὶ αἰχμὴ βραχέα. ἀναξυρίδας δὲ ἔχοντες ἔρχονται ἐς τὰς μάχας καὶ κυρβασίας ἐπὶ τῇσι κεφαλῇσι. [4] οὕτω εὐπετέες χειρωθῆναι εἰσί. ἔστι δὲ καὶ ἀγαθὰ τοῖσι τὴν ἤπειρον ἐκείνην νεμομένοισι, ὅσα οὐδὲ τοῖσι συνάπασι ἄλλοισι. ἀπὸ χρυσοῦ ἀρξαμένοισι ἄργυρος καὶ χαλκὸς καὶ ἐσθὴς ποικίλη καὶ ὑποζύγιά τε καὶ ἀνδράποδα, τά, θυμῷ βουλόμενοι, αὐτοὶ ἂν ἔχοιτε. [5] κατοίκηνται δέ, ἀλλήλων ἐχόμενοι, ὡς ἐγὼ φράσω. Ἰώνων μὲν τῶνδε οἵδε Λυδοί, οἰκέοντές τε χώρην ἀγαθὴν καὶ πολυαργυρώτατοι ἐόντες—δεικνὺς δέ, ἔλεγε ταῦτα, ἐς τῆς γῆς τὴν περίοδον, τὴν ἐφέρετο ἐν τῷ πίνακι ἐντετμημένην—Λυδῶν δέ, ἔφη λέγων ὁ Ἀρισταγόρης, οἵδε ἔχονται Φρύγες οἱ πρὸς τὴν ἠῶ, πολυπροβατώτατοί τε ἐόντες πάντων, τῶν ἐγὼ οἶδα, καὶ πολυκαρπότατοι. [6] Φρυγῶν δὲ ἔχονται Καππαδόκαι, τοὺς ἡμεῖς Συρίους καλέομεν. τούτοισι δὲ πρόσουροι Κίλικες, κατήκοντες

ἐπὶ θάλασσαν τήνδε, ἐν τῇ ἥδε Κύπρος νῆσος κέεται, οἳ πεντακόσια
τάλαντα βασιλέι τὸν ἐπέτειον φόρον ἐπιτελεῦσι. Κιλίκων δὲ τῶνδε
ἔχονται Ἀρμένιοι οἵδε, καὶ οὗτοι ἐόντες πολυπρόβατοι. Ἀρμενίων δὲ
Ματιηνοὶ χώρην τήνδε ἔχοντες. [7] ἔχεται δὲ τούτων γῆ ἥδε Κισσίη,
ἐν τῇ δὴ παρὰ ποταμὸν τόνδε Χοάσπην κείμενα ἐστὶ τὰ Σοῦσα ταῦτα,
ἔνθα βασιλεύς τε μέγας δίαιταν ποιέεται, καὶ τῶν χρημάτων οἱ
θησαυροὶ ἐνθαῦτα εἰσί. ἑλόντες δὲ ταύτην τὴν πόλιν, θαρσέοντες ἤδη
τῷ Διὶ πλούτου πέρι ἐρίζετε. [8] ἀλλὰ περὶ μὲν χώρης ἄρα οὐ πολλῆς
οὐδὲ οὕτω χρηστῆς καὶ οὔρων σμικρῶν χρεόν ἐστι ὑμέας μάχας
ἀναβάλλεσθαι πρός τε Μεσσηνίους ἐόντας ἰσοπαλέας καὶ Ἀρκάδας τε
καὶ Ἀργείους, τοῖσι οὔτε χρυσοῦ ἐχόμενον ἐστι οὐδὲν οὔτε ἀργύρου,
τῶν πέρι καί τινα ἐνάγει προθυμίη μαχόμενον ἀποθνήσκειν. παρέχον δὲ
τῆς Ἀσίης πάσης ἄρχειν εὐπετέως, ἄλλο τι αἱρήσεσθε; [9] Ἀρισταγόρης
μὲν ταῦτα ἔλεξε· Κλεομένης δὲ ἀμείβετο τοῖσιδε· Ὦ ξεῖνε Μιλήσιε,
ἀναβάλλομαί τοι ἐς τρίτην ἡμέρην ὑποκρινέεσθαι.

V.49.1 ὁ Ἀρισταγόρης: Herodotus now returns to Aristagores and his quest to
obtain assistance from the Spartans, as he seeks an ally in Sparta for the Ionian
revolt.   **τύραννος:** in apposition to Ἀρισταγόρης; for Aristagores' resigning
his rule in name, see 37.2.   **τῷ = ᾧ.   Λακεδαιμόνιοι λέγουσι:** the Spartans
are the source for this part of the narrative.   **ἐν τῷ = ἐν ᾧ.   ἐνετέτμητο:** the
verb agrees with its nearest subject.   **49.2 τάδε:** looks forward to what comes
next.   **σπουδὴν μέν:** appears to be answered by τὰ γὰρ κατήκοντα.   **μὴ
θωμάσῃς:** a prohibitive subjunctive, requesting Kleomenes' understanding.   **τὰ
... κατήκοντα:** substantive, "the situation."   **παῖδας:** subject of εἶναι.   **εἶναι:**
understand as an articular infinitive and subject of an implied εἶναι.   **ὄνειδος
καὶ ἄλγος:** predicate to an implied εἶναι.   **μέγιστον μέν:** is answered by ἔτι
δέ.   **τῶν λοιπῶν:** partitive with ὑμῖν.   **ὅσῳ:** substantive, "in so far as."   **49.3
ἐκ δουλοσύνης:** an oft-used rally cry. In Thoukydides, Greeks will ask the Spartans
to save them from enslavement at the hands of the Athenians. It is worth noting
that in a bit, Herodotus will recount the Spartan desire to reinstall tyranny at
Athens and the Greek reaction against it.   **ἄνδρας ὁμαίμονας:** in apposition
to Ἴωνας.   **χωρέειν:** complementary with οἷά τε ἐστί.   **τὰ ἐς τὸν πόλεμον:**
substantive and accusative of respect, "as regards the things of war."   **ἐς τὰ
μέγιστα ἀνήκετε:** "you have reached the zenith."   **πέρι:** anastrophe.   **τοιήδε:**
looks forward to what comes next.   **κυρβασίας:** supply an implied
ἔχοντες.   **49.4 οὕτω:** refers back to their dress and weapons.   **χειρωθῆναι:**
epexegetical with εὐπετέες.   **ἀγαθά:** substantive, "goods."   **τοῖσι τὴν ἤπειρον
ἐκείνην νεμομένοισι:** substantive, "to those inhabiting that land"; possesses

ἀγαθά. ὅσα: supply an implied ἐστι. ἄλλοισι: possesses ὅσα. ἀπὸ χρυσοῦ
ἀρξαμένοισι: the participle modifies the same people as τοῖσι τὴν ἤπειρον ἐκείνην
νεμομένοισι and possesses ἄργυρος, χαλκός, ἐσθής, ὑποζύγια, and ἀνδράποδα, "to
them having begun with gold." τά = ταῦτα ἅ: the antecedent ταῦτα has dropped
out, and the pronoun τά serves as the object of βουλόμενοι and ἔχοιτε. ἂν
ἔχοιτε: potential optative. 49.5 ἀλλήλων ἐχόμενοι: "being right next to one
another." Ἰώνων μέν: is answered by Λυδῶν δέ. οἵδε: in this paragraph,
ὅδε, ἥδε, τόδε indicates a pointing at the map. Λυδοί: supply an implied
ἔχονται. δεικνὺς δέ: Herodotus intrudes on Aristagores' narration. τήν
= ἥν. πάντων: partitive with πολυπροβατώτατοι. τῶν = ὧν = οὕς: the
relative pronoun has been attracted into the case of its antecedent. 49.6
τούς = οὕς. τούτοισι: refers back to the Syrians. τήνδε: indicates that
Aristagores is pointing at the map. ἐν τῇ = ἐν ᾗ. φόρον: in apposition to
τάλαντα. Ματιηνοί: subject of an implied ἔχονται. 49.7 τούτων: refers back
to the Matienoi. ἐν τῇ = ἐν ᾗ. πέρι: anastrophe. 49.8 περὶ μὲν χώρης: is
answered by παρέχον δέ. οὔρων σμικρῶν: translate with χώρης. ὑμέας:
subject of ἀναβάλλεσθαι. ἀναβάλλεσθαι: epexegetical with χρεόν. τοῖσι
= οἷς: possesses οὐδέν. τῶν πέρι = ὧν πέρι: anastrophe of the disyllabic
preposition. τινα: subject of ἀποθνήσκειν. ἀποθνήσκειν: dependent
on ἐνάγει. παρέχον: accusative absolute, "it being possible." ἄρχειν:
complementary with παρέχον. 49.9 Ἀρισταγόρης μέν: is answered by
Κλεομένης δέ. τοῖσιδε: looks forward to what comes next. ξεῖνε Μιλήσιε:
citing Dickey, Hornblower (2013) suggests that the tone is severe, though
Dickey suggests that addresses using ξένε tend to be neutral (Eleanor Dickey
[1996], *Greek Forms of Address* [Oxford: Clarendon Press], 145–49). τοι =
σοι. ὑποκρινέεσθαι: complementary with ἀναβάλλομαι.

~

V.50.1 τότε μὲν ἐς τοσοῦτον ἤλασαν. ἐπείτε δὲ ἡ κυρίη ἡμέρη ἐγένετο
τῆς ὑποκρίσιος καὶ ἦλθον ἐς τὸ συγκείμενον, εἴρετο ὁ Κλεομένης τὸν
Ἀρισταγόρην ὁκοσέων ἡμερέων ἀπὸ θαλάσσης τῆς Ἰώνων ὁδὸς εἴη
παρὰ βασιλέα. [2] ὁ δὲ Ἀρισταγόρης, τἆλλα ἐὼν σοφὸς καὶ διαβάλλων
ἐκεῖνον εὖ, ἐν τούτῳ ἐσφάλη. χρεὸν γάρ μιν μὴ λέγειν τὸ ἐόν,
βουλόμενόν γε Σπαρτιήτας ἐξαγαγεῖν ἐς τὴν Ἀσίην. λέγει δ' ὢν τριῶν
μηνῶν φὰς εἶναι τὴν ἄνοδον. ὁ δὲ ὑπαρπάσας τὸν ἐπίλοιπον λόγον, τὸν
ὁ Ἀρισταγόρης ὥρμητο λέγειν περὶ τῆς ὁδοῦ, εἶπε· [3] Ὦ ξεῖνε Μιλήσιε,
ἀπαλλάσσεο ἐκ Σπάρτης πρὸ δύντος ἡλίου. οὐδένα γὰρ λόγον εὐεπέα
λέγεις Λακεδαιμονίοισι, ἐθέλων σφέας ἀπὸ θαλάσσης τριῶν μηνῶν
ὁδὸν ἀγαγεῖν.

V.50.1 τότε μέν: is answered by ἐπείτε δέ.   **ἐς τοσοῦτον ἤλασαν:** a metaphor, i.e., they marched thus far in their talks.   **ἐς τὸ συγκείμενον:** substantive, "to the appointed spot."   **ὁκοσέων ἡμερέων:** translate with ὁδός.   **εἴη:** optative standing for an original indicative.   **50.2 τἄλλα = τὰ ἄλλα:** accusative of respect; the general is given first and is followed by Aristagores' specific mistake.   **ἐν τούτῳ:** substantive, "on this detail."   **ἐσφάλη:** Herodotus intrudes his own commentary into the narratives of Aristagores and Kleomenes. Thus far Aristagores has painted a completely unrealistic picture of what is involved in defeating the Persians. Upon telling the truth, he errs and loses his audience.   **χρεόν:** supply an implied ἐστι.   **μιν = αὐτόν.**   **μή:** the negative for hypotheticals.   **λέγειν:** epexegetical with χρεόν.   **τὸ ἐόν:** substantive, "the truth."   **ἐξαγαγεῖν:** complementary with βουλόμενον.   **εἶναι:** main verb in indirect statement.   **τὴν ἄνοδον:** subject of εἶναι.   **τόν = ὅν.**   **λέγειν:** complementary with ὥρμητο.   **50.3 λόγον:** subject of an implied εἶναι.   **Λακεδαιμονίοισι:** translate with εὐπέα.   **ὁδόν:** translate with ἀγαγεῖν, "to lead on a journey."   **ἀγαγεῖν:** complementary with ἐθέλων.

～

V.51.1 ὁ μὲν Κλεομένης, ταῦτα εἴπας, ἤιε ἐς τὰ οἰκία. ὁ δὲ Ἀρισταγόρης, λαβὼν ἱκετηρίην, ἤιε ἐς τοῦ Κλεομένεος. ἐσελθὼν δὲ ἔσω, ἅτε ἱκετεύων, ἐπακοῦσαι ἐκέλευε τὸν Κλεομένεα, ἀποπέμψαντα τὸ παιδίον. προσεστήκεε γὰρ δὴ τῷ Κλεομένεϊ ἡ θυγάτηρ, τῇ οὔνομα ἦν Γοργώ. τοῦτο δέ οἱ καὶ μοῦνον τέκνον ἐτύγχανε ἐὸν ἐτέων ὀκτὼ ἢ ἐννέα ἡλικίην. Κλεομένης δὲ λέγειν μιν ἐκέλευε τὰ βούλεται μηδὲ ἐπισχεῖν τοῦ παιδίου εἵνεκα. [2] ἐνθαῦτα δὴ ὁ Ἀρισταγόρης ἄρχετο ἐκ δέκα ταλάντων ὑπισχνεόμενος, ἤν οἱ ἐπιτελέσῃ τῶν ἐδέετο. ἀνανεύοντος δὲ τοῦ Κλεομένεος, προέβαινε τοῖσι χρήμασι ὑπερβάλλων ὁ Ἀρισταγόρης, ἐς οὗ πεντήκοντά τε τάλαντα ὑπεδέδεκτο καὶ τὸ παιδίον ηὐδάξατο· Πάτερ, διαφθερέει σε ὁ ξεῖνος, ἢν μὴ ἀποστὰς ἴῃς. [3] ὅ τε δὴ Κλεομένης, ἡσθεὶς τοῦ παιδίου τῇ παραινέσι, ἤιε ἐς ἕτερον οἴκημα. καὶ ὁ Ἀρισταγόρης ἀπαλλάσσετο τὸ παράπαν ἐκ τῆς Σπάρτης. οὐδέ οἱ ἐξεγένετο ἐπὶ πλέον ἔτι σημῆναι περὶ τῆς ἀνόδου τῆς παρὰ βασιλέα.

V.51.1 ὁ μὲν Κλεομένης: is answered by ὁ δὲ Ἀρισταγόρης.   **ταῦτα:** refers back to what Kleomenes says at the end of chapter 50.   **λαβὼν ἱκετηρίην:** the olive branch marks him as a suppliant and thereby places him under divine protection. For Christians, the cross or bible could function similarly.   **ἐς τοῦ**

Κλεομένεος: "to Kleomenes"; supply an implied δόμους. ἅτε ἱκετεύων: ἅτε (and οἷα) is typically found with a participle in the nominative or accusative case. Use "since" or "because" to translate it, and turn the participle into a finite verb. Thus, ἅτε αὐτὸν ὄντα καλόν (ἅτε ὢν καλός): "since he was good." ἐπακοῦσαι: dependent on ἐκέλευε. Κλεομένεα: subject of ἐπακοῦσαι. τῷ Κλεομένεϊ: object of the prefix προσ- of προσεστήκεε. τῇ = ᾗ: possesses οὔνομα. τοῦτο δέ: modifies τέκνον. οἱ = αὐτῷ: possesses τέκνον. ἐόν: supplementary with ἐτύγχανε. ἡλικίην: accusative of respect. λέγειν ... ἐπισχεῖν: dependent on ἐκέλευε. μιν = αὐτόν: subject of λέγειν and the upcoming ἐπισχεῖν. τά = ταῦτα ἅ: the antecedent ταῦτα has dropped out, and τά serves as the object of λέγειν, which is understood with βούλεται. ἐπισχεῖν: supply an implied τὰ βούλεται. 51.2 ὑπισχνεόμενος: supplementary with ἄρχετο. ἀνανεύοντος: in modern Greece, a tilting back of the head continues to be a gesture of refusal or disagreement. οἱ = αὐτῷ. ἐπιτελέσῃ: a hypothetical subjunctive, indicating a possible future event. τῶν = ταῦτα ὧν: the antecedent ταῦτα has dropped out; though serving as the object of both ἐπιτελέσῃ and ἐδέετο, τῶν is in the genitive case because of ἐδέετο. ἐς οὗ: temporal, "until." ἵῃς: a hypothetical subjunctive, indicating a possible future event. 51.3 τὸ παράπαν: adverbial, "completely," "absolutely." οἱ = αὐτῷ. ἐξεγένετο: impersonal. σημῆναι: complementary with ἐξεγένετο.

〜

V.52.1 Ἔχει γὰρ ἀμφὶ τῇ ὁδῷ ταύτῃ ὧδε. σταθμοί τε πανταχῇ εἰσι βασιλήιοι καὶ καταλύσιες κάλλισται, διὰ οἰκεομένης τε ἡ ὁδὸς ἅπασα καὶ ἀσφαλέος. διὰ μέν γε Λυδίης καὶ Φρυγίης σταθμοὶ τείνοντες εἴκοσι εἰσί, παρασάγγαι δὲ τέσσερες καὶ ἐνενήκοντα καὶ ἥμισυ. [2] ἐκδέκεται δὲ ἐκ τῆς Φρυγίης ὁ Ἅλυς ποταμός, ἐπ᾽ ᾧ πύλαι τε ἔπεισι, τὰς διεξελάσαι πᾶσα ἀνάγκη καὶ οὕτω διεκπερᾶν τὸν ποταμόν. καὶ φυλακτήριον μέγα ἐπ᾽ αὐτῷ. διαβάντι δὲ ἐς τὴν Καππαδοκίην καὶ ταύτῃ πορευομένῳ μέχρι οὔρων τῶν Κιλικίων σταθμοὶ δυῶν δέοντες εἰσὶ τριήκοντα, παρασάγγαι δὲ τέσσερες καὶ ἑκατόν. ἐπὶ δὲ τοῖσι τούτων οὔροισι διξάς τε πύλας διεξελᾷς καὶ διξὰ φυλακτήρια παραμείψεαι. [3] ταῦτα δὲ διεξελάσαντι καὶ διὰ τῆς Κιλικίης ὁδὸν ποιευμένῳ τρεῖς εἰσι σταθμοί, παρασάγγαι δὲ πεντεκαίδεκα καὶ ἥμισυ. οὖρος δὲ Κιλικίης καὶ τῆς Ἀρμενίης ἐστὶ ποταμὸς νηυσιπέρητος, τῷ οὔνομα Εὐφρήτης. ἐν δὲ τῇ Ἀρμενίῃ σταθμοὶ μὲν εἰσὶ καταγωγέων πεντεκαίδεκα, παρασάγγαι δὲ ἓξ καὶ πεντήκοντα καὶ ἥμισυ. καὶ φυλακτήριον ἐν αὐτοῖσι. [4] ποταμοὶ δὲ νηυσιπέρητοι τέσσερες διὰ ταύτης ῥέουσι, τοὺς πᾶσα ἀνάγκη διαπορθμεῦσαι ἐστί. πρῶτος μὲν Τίγρης· μετὰ δὲ δεύτερός τε καὶ τρίτος, ὡυτὸς ὀνομαζόμενος, οὐκ ὡυτὸς ἐὼν ποταμὸς οὐδὲ ἐκ τοῦ αὐτοῦ ῥέων. ὁ μὲν γὰρ πρότερον αὐτῶν καταλεχθεὶς ἐξ Ἀρμενίων ῥέει, ὁ δ᾽ ὕστερον ἐκ Ματιηνῶν. [5] ὁ δὲ τέταρτος τῶν ποταμῶν οὔνομα ἔχει Γύνδης, τὸν Κῦρος διέλαβε κοτὲ ἐς διώρυχας ἑξήκοντα καὶ τριηκοσίας. ἐκ δὲ ταύτης τῆς Ἀρμενίης ἐσβάλλοντι ἐς τὴν Ματιηνὴν γῆν σταθμοί εἰσι τέσσερες καὶ τριήκοντα, παρασάγγαι δὲ ἑπτὰ καὶ τριήκοντα καὶ ἑκατόν. [6] ἐκ δὲ ταύτης ἐς τὴν Κισσίην χώρην μεταβαίνοντι ἕνδεκα σταθμοί, παρασάγγαι δὲ δύο καὶ τεσσεράκοντα καὶ ἥμισυ ἐστὶ ἐπὶ ποταμὸν Χοάσπην, ἐόντα καὶ τοῦτον νηυσιπέρητον· ἐπ᾽ ᾧ Σοῦσα πόλις πεπόλισται.

V.52.1 Ἔχει ... ὧδε: impersonal, "it is like this." Facilitating communication for the Akhaimenid Empire, the Royal Road stretched about two thousand miles, with stations located about one day's journey from each other. Built in stages over time and connecting smaller roads into a larger one, it has been identified along two major routes. Herodotus's account does not resolve the ambiguity because the geography and his description are at times at odds and because his distances are at times off. Dareios is credited with establishing the road as it is recognized today. It lasted into Roman times, and from these times a bridge at Diyarbakır in Turkey still stands. **διὰ οἰκεομένης**: supply an implied γῆς. **τε ... καί**: links οἰκεομένης and ἀσφαλέος. **ἀσφαλέος**: supply an implied γῆς. **διὰ μέν γε Λυδίης**: is answered by ἐκδέκεται δέ. **παρασάγγαι δὲ τέσσερες καὶ ἐνενήκοντα καὶ ἥμισυ**: about 330 miles. The equivalents assume that Herodotus uses the Attic standard, where 1 stade = 583 feet, 30 stades = 1 parasang = 5,830 yards or about 3 1/3 miles. **52.2 τάς = ἅς**. **διεξελάσαι ... διεκπερᾶν**: epexegetical with ἀνάγκη. **φυλακτήριον**: supply an implied ἐστι. **διαβάντι ... πορευομένῳ**: supply a σοι or a hypothetical traveler as the noun the participle modifies. **ταύτῃ**: dative of respect, "there." **παρασάγγαι δὲ τέσσερες καὶ ἑκατόν**: about 490 miles. **διεξελᾷς**: Herodotus addresses his audience directly. **παραμείψεαι**: intervocalic sigma has dropped out and the form remains uncontracted. **52.3 διεξελάσαντι ... ποιευμένῳ**: supply a σοι or a hypothetical traveler as the noun the participle modifies. **παρασάγγαι δὲ πεντεκαίδεκα καὶ ἥμισυ**: about 50 miles. **τῷ = ᾧ**: possesses οὔνομα. **ἐν δὲ τῇ Ἀρμενίῃ**: is answered by ἐκ δὲ ταύτης τῆς Ἀρμενίης. **παρασάγγαι δὲ ἓξ καὶ πεντήκοντα καὶ ἥμισυ**: about 200 miles long. **φυλακτήριον**: supply an implied ἐστι. **52.4 τούς = οὕς**. **διαπορθμεῦσαι**: epexegetical with ἀνάγκη. **πρῶτος μέν**: is answered by μετὰ δέ. **μετὰ δέ**: adverbial, "next." **ὡυτός = ὁ αὐτός**. **ἐκ τοῦ αὐτοῦ**: substantive, "from the same source." **ὁ μὲν γάρ**: is answered by ὁ δ᾽ ὕστερον. **ὁ μὲν γὰρ πρότερον ... καταλεχθείς**: substantive, "the one

---

mentioned first." **αὐτῶν:** partitive with ὁ μέν. **ὁ δ' ὕστερον:** supply an implied αὐτῶν καταλεχθείς; substantive, "the one mentioned second." **52.5 τόν** = ὅν. **ἐσβάλλοντι:** supply a σοι or a hypothetical traveler as the noun the participle modifies. **παρασάγγαι δὲ ἑπτὰ καὶ τριήκοντα καὶ ἑκατόν:** about 480 miles. **52.6 μεταβαίνοντι:** supply a σοι or a hypothetical traveler as the noun the participle modifies. **παρασάγγαι δὲ δύο καὶ τεσσεράκοντα καὶ ἥμισυ:** about 150 miles.

V.53.1 οὗτοι οἱ πάντες σταθμοί εἰσι ἕνδεκα καὶ ἑκατόν. καταγωγαὶ μέν νυν σταθμῶν τοσαῦται εἰσὶ ἐκ Σαρδίων ἐς Σοῦσα ἀναβαίνοντι. εἰ δὲ ὀρθῶς μεμέτρηται ἡ ὁδὸς ἡ βασιληίη τοῖσι παρασάγγῃσι καὶ ὁ παρασάγγης δύναται τριήκοντα στάδια, ὥσπερ οὗτός γε δύναται ταῦτα, ἐκ Σαρδίων στάδια ἐστὶ ἐς τὰ βασιλήια τὰ Μεμνόνια καλεόμενα πεντακόσια καὶ τρισχίλια καὶ μύρια, παρασαγγέων ἐόντων πεντήκοντα καὶ τετρακοσίων. πεντήκοντα δὲ καὶ ἑκατὸν στάδια ἐπ' ἡμέρῃ ἑκάστῃ διεξιοῦσι ἀναισιμοῦνται ἡμέραι ἀπαρτὶ ἐνενήκοντα.

V.53.1 ἀναβαίνοντι: supply a σοι or a hypothetical traveler as the noun the participle modifies. **οὗτος** = ὁ παρασάγγης. **ταῦτα:** ταῦτα refers back to τριήκοντα στάδια. **πεντήκοντα δὲ καὶ ἑκατὸν στάδια:** about 17 miles. **διεξιοῦσι:** though plural, the construction is similar to διαβάντι and ἀναβαίνοντι from above.

V.54.1 οὕτω τῷ Μιλησίῳ Ἀρισταγόρῃ εἴπαντι πρὸς Κλεομένεα τὸν Λακεδαιμόνιον εἶναι τριῶν μηνῶν τὴν ἄνοδον τὴν παρὰ βασιλέα, ὀρθῶς εἴρητο. εἰ δέ τις τὸ ἀτρεκέστερον τούτων ἔτι δίζηται, ἐγὼ καὶ τοῦτο σημανέω· τὴν γὰρ ἐξ Ἐφέσου ἐς Σάρδις ὁδὸν δεῖ προσλογίσασθαι ταύτῃ. [2] καὶ δὴ λέγω σταδίους εἶναι τοὺς πάντας ἀπὸ θαλάσσης τῆς Ἑλληνικῆς μέχρι Σούσων—τοῦτο γὰρ Μεμνόνειον ἄστυ καλέεται—τεσσεράκοντα καὶ τετρακισχιλίους καὶ μυρίους· οἱ γὰρ ἐξ Ἐφέσου ἐς Σάρδις εἰσὶ τεσσεράκοντα καὶ πεντακόσιοι στάδιοι, καὶ οὕτω τρισὶ ἡμέρῃσι μηκύνεται ἡ τρίμηνος ὁδός.

V.54.1 οὕτω: refers back to the calculated distance of the royal road. **Ἀρισταγόρῃ:** agency. **εἶναι:** main verb in indirect statement. **τριῶν μηνῶν:** predicate to τὴν ἄνοδον.   **τὴν ἄνοδον:** subject of εἶναι.   **ὀρθῶς εἴρητο:** impersonal, "it was correctly stated."   **τούτων:** refers back to the distances just calculated; translate with τὸ ἀτρεκέστερον.   **ταύτῃ:** object of the prefix προς- of προσλογίσασθαι and substantive, "this distance."   **προσλογίσασθαι:** complementary with δεῖ.   **54.2 σταδίους:** subject of εἶναι.   **εἶναι:** main verb in indirect statement.   **ἀπὸ θαλάσσης τῆς Ἑλληνικῆς:** the Aegean.   **ἐξ Ἐφέσου ἐς Σάρδις:** soon the Greeks will march from Ephesos to Sardis and capture much of the city (V.99–100).   **μηκύνεται ἡ τρίμηνος ὁδός:** the total number of miles is 1,615; the distance from Ephesos to Sardis is 60 miles. The distances over, Herodotus returns us to Aristagores and to how the Athenians became freed from tyranny.

❧

V.55.1 ἀπελαυνόμενος δὲ ὁ Ἀρισταγόρης ἐκ τῆς Σπάρτης ἤιε ἐς τὰς Ἀθήνας, γενομένας τυράννων ὧδε ἐλευθέρας. ἐπεὶ Ἵππαρχον τὸν Πεισιστράτου, Ἱππίεω δὲ τοῦ τυράννου ἀδελφεόν, ἰδόντα ὄψιν ἐνυπνίου τῷ ἑωυτοῦ πάθεϊ ἐναργεστάτην κτείνουσι Ἀριστογείτων καὶ Ἁρμόδιος, γένος ἐόντες τὰ ἀνέκαθεν Γεφυραῖοι, μετὰ ταῦτα ἐτυραννεύοντο Ἀθηναῖοι ἐπ᾽ ἔτεα τέσσερα οὐδὲν ἧσσον ἀλλὰ καὶ μᾶλλον ἢ πρὸ τοῦ.

V.55.1 ὧδε: as often, it looks forward to what comes next, which, in this case, is an explanation of how Athens became free of tyranny. Note that Herodotus continues to characterize Aristagores as a tyrant, as in 49.1.   **ἐπεί:** is answered by μετὰ ταῦτα.   **Ἵππαρχον ... κτείνουσι Ἀριστογείτων καὶ Ἁρμόδιος:** complicated by modifiers, this subordinate clause contains a subject, verb, and direct object.   **ἀδελφεόν:** in apposition to Ἵππαρχον.   **ἰδόντα:** the tense shows time prior to κτείνουσι.   **τῷ ἑωυτοῦ πάθεϊ:** translate with ἐναργεστάτην; he catches a glimpse of the future and his own death.   **γένος:** accusative of respect, "in origin."   **τὰ ἀνέκαθεν:** accusative of respect and substantive, "from the first."   **μετὰ ταῦτα:** refers back to the murder of Hipparkhos.   **πρὸ τοῦ:** temporal, "before this time."

❧

V.56.1 ἡ μέν νυν ὄψις τοῦ Ἱππάρχου ἐνυπνίου ἦν ἥδε· ἐν τῇ προτέρῃ νυκτὶ τῶν Παναθηναίων ἐδόκεε ὁ Ἵππαρχος ἄνδρα, οἱ ἐπιστάντα μέγαν καὶ εὐειδέα, αἰνίσσεσθαι τάδε τὰ ἔπεα·

> τλῆθι λέων ἄτλητα παθὼν τετληότι θυμῷ·
> οὐδεὶς ἀνθρώπων ἀδικῶν τίσιν οὐκ ἀποτίσει.

[2] ταῦτα δέ, ὡς ἡμέρη ἐγένετο τάχιστα, φανερὸς ἦν ὑπερτιθέμενος ὀνειροπόλοισι. μετὰ δέ, ἀπειπάμενος τὴν ὄψιν, ἔπεμπε τὴν πομπήν, ἐν τῇ δὴ τελευτᾷ.

V.56.1 ἡ μέν: is answered by οἱ δὲ Γεφυραῖοι of chapter 57.   **ἥδε:** looks forward to what comes next.   **Παναθηναίων:** the Panathenaia, festivals in honor of Athene. Since 566 B.C.E. in Athens, the greater Panathenaia festival was held every four years, and the lesser Panathenaia, shorter by a few days, every year. Honoring Athene and the other gods, the religious festival celebrated them through sacrifices and through athletic, music, and poetry competitions. The athletic events were boxing, wrestling, the pankration, the pentathlon, and chariot racing. Of these events the chariot race was the most prestigious.   **ἄνδρα:** subject of αἰνίσσεσθαι.   **οἱ =** **αὐτῷ:** object of the prefix ἐπι- of ἐπιστάντα.   **αἰνίσσεσθαι:** main verb in indirect statement.   **ἀνθρώπων:** partitive with οὐδείς.   **οὐκ:** the negative applies.   **56.2** **ταῦτα:** refers back to the dream.   **μετὰ δέ:** adverbial, "but then."   **ἐν τῇ = ἐν ᾗ.**

~

V.57.1 οἱ δὲ Γεφυραῖοι, τῶν ἦσαν οἱ φονέες οἱ Ἱππάρχου, ὡς μὲν αὐτοὶ λέγουσι, ἐγεγόνεσαν ἐξ Ἐρετρίης τὴν ἀρχήν. ὡς δὲ ἐγὼ ἀναπυνθανόμενος εὑρίσκω, ἦσαν Φοίνικες τῶν σὺν Κάδμῳ ἀπικομένων Φοινίκων ἐς γῆν τὴν νῦν Βοιωτίην καλεομένην. οἴκεον δὲ τῆς χώρης ταύτης ἀπολαχόντες τὴν Ταναγρικὴν μοῖραν. [2] ἐνθεῦτεν δὲ Καδμείων πρότερον ἐξαναστάντων ὑπ᾽ Ἀργείων, οἱ Γεφυραῖοι οὗτοι, δεύτερα ὑπὸ Βοιωτῶν ἐξαναστάντες, ἐτράποντο ἐπ᾽ Ἀθηνέων. Ἀθηναῖοι δὲ σφέας ἐπὶ ῥητοῖσι ἐδέξαντο σφέων αὐτῶν εἶναι πολιήτας, πολλῶν τεῶν καὶ οὐκ ἀξιαπηγήτων ἐπιτάξαντες ἔργεσθαι.

V.57.1 τῶν = ὧν: partitive with φονέες.   **οἱ φονέες οἱ Ἱππάρχου:** Hipparkhos is killed in 514/13 B.C.E.   **ὡς μέν ... ὡς δέ:** contrast the two claims.   **τὴν ἀρχήν:** accusative of respect, "originally."   **Φοινίκων:** partitive with Φοίνικες. A Semitic peoples, the Phoinikians spread throughout the Mediterranean from 1500 to 300 B.C.E. Said to possess the first world economy, the Phoinikians had their heyday from 1200 to 800 B.C.E. In 539 B.C.E., the Phoinikians are conquered by the Persians under Kyros the Great.   **τῆς χώρης ταύτης:** chorographic genitive (Smyth 1311).   **57.2 πρότερον:** is answered by δεύτερα.   **ὑπ᾽ Ἀργείων ... ὑπὸ Βοιωτῶν:** agency.   **σφέας:** subject of εἶναι.   **ἐπὶ ῥητοῖσι:** substantive, "upon set terms."   **εἶναι:** dependent on ἐδέξαντο.   **ἐπιτάξαντες:** supply an implied τούτους as object of ἐπιτάξαντες and subject of ἔργεσθαι.   **ἔργεσθαι:** dependent on ἐπιτάξαντες.

◞

V.58.1 οἱ δὲ Φοίνικες οὗτοι οἱ σὺν Κάδμῳ ἀπικόμενοι, τῶν ἦσαν οἱ
Γεφυραῖοι, ἄλλα τε πολλά, οἰκήσαντες ταύτην τὴν χώρην, ἐσήγαγον
διδασκάλια ἐς τοὺς Ἕλληνας καὶ δὴ καὶ γράμματα, οὐκ ἐόντα πρὶν
Ἕλλησι, ὡς ἐμοὶ δοκέειν. πρῶτα μὲν τοῖσι καὶ ἅπαντες χρέωνται
Φοίνικες. μετὰ δὲ χρόνου προβαίνοντος ἅμα τῇ φωνῇ μετέβαλλον
καὶ τὸν ῥυθμὸν τῶν γραμμάτων. [2] περιοίκεον δὲ σφέας τὰ πολλὰ
τῶν χώρων τοῦτον τὸν χρόνον Ἑλλήνων Ἴωνες, οἵ, παραλαβόντες
διδαχῇ παρὰ τῶν Φοινίκων τὰ γράμματα, μεταρρυθμίσαντες σφέων
ὀλίγα, ἐχρέωντο. χρεώμενοι δὲ ἐφάτισαν, ὥσπερ καὶ τὸ δίκαιον ἔφερε,
ἐσαγαγόντων Φοινίκων ἐς τὴν Ἑλλάδα, Φοινικήια κεκλῆσθαι. [3] καὶ
τὰς βύβλους "διφθέρας" καλέουσι ἀπὸ τοῦ παλαιοῦ οἱ Ἴωνες, ὅτι κοτὲ
ἐν σπάνι βύβλων ἐχρέωντο διφθέρῃσι αἰγέῃσί τε καὶ οἰέῃσι. ἔτι δὲ καὶ
τὸ κατ᾽ ἐμὲ πολλοὶ τῶν βαρβάρων ἐς τοιαύτας διφθέρας γράφουσι.

V.58.1 τῶν = ὧν: partitive with Γεφυραῖοι.   **ἄλλα τε πολλά ... καὶ δὴ καὶ
γράμματα:** ἄλλα τε πολλά modifies διδασκάλια; τε introduces the general and καὶ
δὴ καί the specific. Based on the Phoinikian script, which had twenty-two letters
for consonants only, the Greek alphabet is the first to have letters corresponding
to the sounds of consonants and vowels. Most specialists today date the birth of
the Greek alphabet to 750 B.C.E. The earliest known Greek inscriptions date to this
time. A few specialists date the alphabet earlier. Their guesses range in time from
the eighteenth to the ninth centuries B.C.E. Herodotus dates Kadmos to about
2,000 B.C.E. and cites inscriptional evidence from this time.   **ὡς ἐμοὶ δοκέειν:**
impersonal, "as it seems to me."   **πρῶτα μέν ... μετὰ δὲ χρόνου προβαίνοντος:**
"initially ... then after some time."   **τοῖσι = οἷς:** the antecedent τούτοις has
dropped out, and the relative pronoun τοῖσι serves as the object of χρέωνται and an
understood χρέωνται. The full expression is this: οἱ Ἕλληνες πρῶτα μέν, τοῖσι καὶ
ἅπαντες χρέωνται Φοίνικες, χρέωνται.   **58.2 σφέας = Φοίνικας.   τὰ πολλὰ
τῶν χώρων:** substantive, "in the majority of the places."   **Ἑλλήνων:** partitive
with Ἴωνες.   **σφέων:** partitive with ὀλίγα.   **ὀλίγα:** modifies an implied
γράμματα.   **ἐχρέωντο:** supply the implied object from context.   **τὸ δίκαιον
ἔφερε:** "as justice brought about" or "as was just"; the statement forms a part of
Herodotus's narrative.   **Φοινικήια:** subject of κεκλῆσθαι.   **58.3 τὸ κατ᾽ ἐμέ:**
substantive, "even in my day."   **τῶν βαρβάρων:** partitive with πολλοί.

∾

V.59.1 εἶδον δὲ καὶ αὐτὸς Καδμήια γράμματα ἐν τῷ ἱρῷ τοῦ
Ἀπόλλωνος τοῦ Ἰσμηνίου ἐν Θήβῃσι τῇσι Βοιωτῶν, ἐπὶ τρίποσι τισὶ
ἐγκεκολαμμένα, τὰ πολλὰ ὅμοια ἐόντα τοῖσι Ἰωνικοῖσι. ὁ μὲν δὴ εἷς τῶν
τριπόδων ἐπίγραμμα ἔχει·

> Ἀμφιτρύων μ᾽ ἀνέθηκ᾽ ἐὼν ἀπὸ Τηλεβοάων.

ταῦτα ἡλικίην εἴη ἂν κατὰ Λάιον τὸν Λαβδάκου τοῦ Πολυδώρου τοῦ
Κάδμου.

V.59.1 εἶδον δὲ καὶ αὐτός: his claim to autopsy is questioned. It is argued
that Herodotus's claims for autopsy tend to coincide with matters known
to be controversial.   **τὰ πολλά:** substantive and accusative of respect,
"for the most part."   **τοῖσι Ἰωνικοῖσι:** translate with ὅμοια and supply
an implied γράμμασι.   **ὁ μὲν δὴ εἷς:** is answered by ἕτερος δὲ τρίπους of
chapter 60 and by τρίτος δὲ τρίπους of chapter 61.   **τριπόδων:** partitive
with εἷς.   **ταῦτα = γράμματα.**   **ἐών:** most scholars are unhappy with the
meaning; various emendations are suggested, including ἀνέθηκε νέων and
ἀνέθηκε νεῶν.   **ἡλικίην:** accusative of respect, "in age."   **εἴη ἄν:** potential
optative.   **κατά:** translate with ἡλικίην.

∾

V.60.1 ἕτερος δὲ τρίπους ἐν ἐξαμέτρῳ τόνῳ λέγει·

> Σκαῖος πυγμαχέων με ἑκηβόλῳ Ἀπόλλωνι
> νικήσας ἀνέθηκε τεῒν περικαλλὲς ἄγαλμα.

Σκαῖος δ᾽ ἂν εἴη ὁ Ἱπποκόωντος, εἰ δὴ οὗτός γε ἐστὶ ὁ ἀναθεὶς καὶ μὴ
ἄλλος τώυτὸ οὔνομα ἔχων τῷ Ἱπποκόωντος, ἡλικίην κατὰ Οἰδίπουν
τὸν Λαΐου.

V.60.1 τεῒν = σοι.   **ἄγαλμα:** in apposition to με.   **Σκαῖος:** the name means
"Southpaw," and his lineage, as Herodotus suggests, is uncertain.   **ἂν εἴη:** a
potential optative.   **ὁ ἀναθείς:** substantive, "the one having dedicated."   **τώυτό
= τὸ αὐτό.**   **τῷ Ἱπποκόωντος = τῷ υἱῷ Ἱπποκόωντος:** note this similar
construction, ταὐτά σοι ποιῶ: "I do the same things as you."   **ἡλικίην:** accusative
of respect, "in age."   **κατά:** translate with ἡλικίην.

❧

V.61.1 τρίτος δὲ τρίπους λέγει καὶ οὗτος ἐν ἑξαμέτρῳ·

Λαοδάμας τρίποδ᾽ αὐτὸς ἐυσκόπῳ Ἀπόλλωνι
μουναρχέων ἀνέθηκε τεΐν περικαλλὲς ἄγαλμα.

[2] ἐπὶ τούτου δὴ τοῦ Λαοδάμαντος τοῦ Ἐτεοκλέος μουναρχέοντος
ἐξανιστέαται Καδμεῖοι ὑπ᾽ Ἀργείων καὶ τρέπονται ἐς τοὺς Ἐγχελέας.
οἱ δὲ Γεφυραῖοι, ὑπολειφθέντες, ὕστερον ὑπὸ Βοιωτῶν ἀναχωρέουσι
ἐς Ἀθήνας. καί σφι ἱρά ἐστι ἐν Ἀθήνῃσι ἱδρυμένα, τῶν οὐδὲν μέτα τοῖσι
λοιποῖσι Ἀθηναίοισι. ἄλλα τε κεχωρισμένα τῶν ἄλλων ἱρῶν καὶ δὴ καὶ
Ἀχαιίης Δήμητρος ἱρόν τε καὶ ὄργια.

V.61.1 τεΐν = σοι.   **61.2** ὕστερον: translate with ἀναχωρέουσι.   ὑπὸ Βοιωτῶν:
agency, "because of the Boiotians."   σφι: agency.   τῶν = ὧν: partitive with
οὐδέν.   ἄλλα τε … καὶ δὴ καὶ Ἀχαιίης Δήμητρος ἱρόν: ἄλλα τε refers generally
to the other temples; καὶ δὴ καὶ … ἱρόν refers specifically to the temple of Demeter.

❧

V.62.1 ἡ μὲν δὴ ὄψις τοῦ Ἱππάρχου ἐνυπνίου καὶ οἱ Γεφυραῖοι ὅθεν
ἐγεγόνεσαν, τῶν ἦσαν οἱ Ἱππάρχου φονέες, ἀπήγηταί μοι. δεῖ δὲ
πρὸς τούτοισι ἔτι ἀναλαβεῖν, τὸν κατ᾽ ἀρχὰς ἦια λέξων λόγον, ὡς
τυράννων ἐλευθερώθησαν Ἀθηναῖοι. [2] Ἱππίεω τυραννεύοντος καὶ
ἐμπικραινομένου Ἀθηναίοισι διὰ τὸν Ἱππάρχου θάνατον, Ἀλκμεωνίδαι,
γένος ἐόντες Ἀθηναῖοι καὶ φεύγοντες Πεισιστρατίδας—ἐπείτε σφι
ἅμα τοῖσι ἄλλοισι Ἀθηναίων φυγάσι πειρωμένοισι κατὰ τὸ ἰσχυρὸν οὐ
προεχώρεε κάτοδος ἀλλὰ προσέπταιον μεγάλως πειρώμενοι κατιέναι τε
καὶ ἐλευθεροῦν τὰς Ἀθήνας, Λειψύδριον τὸ ὑπὲρ Παιονίης τειχίσαντες—
ἐνθαῦτα οἱ Ἀλκμεωνίδαι, πᾶν ἐπὶ τοῖσι Πεισιστρατίδῃσι μηχανώμενοι,
παρ᾽ Ἀμφικτυόνων τὸν νηὸν μισθοῦνται, τὸν ἐν Δελφοῖσι τὸν νῦν ἐόντα
τότε δὲ οὔκω, τοῦτον ἐξοικοδομῆσαι. [3] οἷα δὲ χρημάτων εὖ ἥκοντες
καὶ ἐόντες ἄνδρες δόκιμοι ἀνέκαθεν ἔτι, τόν τε νηὸν ἐξεργάσαντο τοῦ
παραδείγματος κάλλιον· τά τε ἄλλα καί—συγκειμένου σφι πωρίνου
λίθου ποιέειν τὸν νηόν—Παρίου τὰ ἔμπροσθε αὐτοῦ ἐξεποίησαν.

V.62.1 ἡ μὲν δὴ ὄψις: is answered by δεῖ δέ; μέν marks the end of the narrative on Hipparkhos, his dream, and his murderers the Gephyraians.   **οἱ Γεφυραῖοι ὅθεν:** English typically flips the order, ὅθεν οἱ Γεφυραῖοι.   **τῶν = ὧν:** partitive with οἱ φονέες.   **μοι:** agency.   **πρὸς τούτοισι:** refers back to the accounts just given.   **τόν = ὅν:** at times the antecedent, here λόγον, is brought into the relative clause, e.g., εἶδεν ἐν ᾗ οἰκέω χώρᾳ ("he saw in which country I dwell") instead of εἶδεν χώραν ἐν ᾗ οἰκῶ.   **ἀναλαβεῖν:** complementary with δεῖ.   **κατ' ἀρχάς:** see V.55.   **λέξων:** supplementary with ἤια; the participle translates nicely into English as an infinitive.   **62.2 Ἱππίεω τυραννεύοντος:** so begins a lengthy and complicated sentence, whose subject, direct object, verb, and complementary infinitive are the following: οἱ Ἀλκμεωνίδαι, τὸν νηὸν, μισθοῦνται, ἐξοικοδομῆσαι.   **Ἀλκμεωνίδαι:** the Alkmeonids claimed descent from Alkmaion, the great-grandson of Nestor. In 632 B.C.E., Kylon attempted to become tyrant of Athens. The Alkmeonid Megakles killed his followers, even though they had taken refuge at the temple of Athene. The murder of these suppliants taints the Alkmeonids with a curse. Curses bring bad luck and destruction. To protect itself against the curse, the city of Athens exiles the Alkmeonids and has the bones of long-deceased members of the family dug up and removed from the city limits.   **γένος:** accusative of respect, "by birth."   **Πεισιστρατίδας:** Peisistratos rules Athens as tyrant from 561 to 527 B.C.E. His sons, the Peisistratids, are Hippias and Hipparkhos. Peisistratos comes to power by currying favor with the poor, the most numerous of the Athenian populace. After Peisistratos's death, Hippias takes over until he is ousted from the city in 508 B.C.E. by the Alkmeonids and Sparta. In exile and hoping to be restored to power, Hippias aids the Persians in their attack against the Greeks (VI.102–109). For Thoukydides' narrative on the ousting of the Peisistratids, see 1.20.   **σφι...πειρωμένοισι:** supply an implied κατιέναι.   **κατὰ τὸ ἰσχυρόν:** "by force."   **κατιέναι... ἐλευθεροῦν:** complementary with πειρώμενοι.   **οἱ Ἀλκμεωνίδαι:** the subject is repeated.   **παρ' Ἀμφικτυόνων:** agency.   **τόν = ὅν.   τὸν νῦν ἐόντα:** substantive, "the one there now."   **ἐξοικοδομῆσαι:** complementary with μισθοῦνται.   **62.3 οἷα...ἥκοντες καὶ ἐόντες:** οἷα (and ἅτε) is typically found with a participle in the nominative or accusative case. Use "since" or "because" to translate it, and turn the participle into a finite verb. Thus, ἅτε αὐτὸν ὄντα καλόν (ἅτε ὢν καλός): "since he was good."   **χρημάτων:** translate with εὖ ἥκοντες.   **τά τε ἄλλα...Παρίου τὰ ἔμπροσθε αὐτοῦ ἐξεποίησαν:** τε introduces the generic and καί the specific, "they did other things ... and they made the front of it of Parian marble."   **συγκειμένου:** impersonal.   **σφι:** to perform the action of ποιέειν.   **ποιέειν:** complementary with συγκειμένου.

~

V.63.1 ὡς ὦν δὴ οἱ Ἀθηναῖοι λέγουσι, οὗτοι οἱ ἄνδρες ἐν Δελφοῖσι κατήμενοι ἀνέπειθον τὴν Πυθίην χρήμασι, ὅκως ἔλθοιεν Σπαρτιητέων

ἄνδρες εἴτε ἰδίῳ στόλῳ εἴτε δημοσίῳ χρησόμενοι, προφέρειν σφι
τὰς Ἀθήνας ἐλευθεροῦν. [2] Λακεδαιμόνιοι δέ, ὥς σφι αἰεὶ τὠυτὸ
πρόφαντον ἐγίνετο, πέμπουσι Ἀγχιμόλιον τὸν Ἀστέρος, ἐόντα τῶν
ἀστῶν ἄνδρα δόκιμον, σὺν στρατῷ ἐξελῶντα Πεισιστρατίδας ἐξ
Ἀθηνέων, ὅμως καὶ ξεινίους σφι ἐόντας τὰ μάλιστα· τὰ γὰρ τοῦ θεοῦ
πρεσβύτερα ἐποιεῦντο ἢ τὰ τῶν ἀνδρῶν. πέμπουσι δὲ τούτους κατὰ
θάλασσαν πλοίοισι. [3] ὁ μὲν δὴ προσσχὼν ἐς Φάληρον τὴν στρατιὴν
ἀπέβησε. οἱ δὲ Πεισιστρατίδαι, προπυνθανόμενοι ταῦτα, ἐπεκαλέοντο
ἐκ Θεσσαλίης ἐπικουρίην· ἐπεποίητο γάρ σφι συμμαχίη πρὸς αὐτούς.
Θεσσαλοὶ δέ σφι δεομένοισι ἀπέπεμψαν, κοινῇ γνώμῃ χρεώμενοι,
χιλίην τε ἵππον καὶ τὸν βασιλέα τὸν σφέτερον, Κινέην, ἄνδρα Κονδαῖον.
τοὺς ἐπείτε ἔσχον συμμάχους, οἱ Πεισιστρατίδαι ἐμηχανῶντο τοιάδε·
[4] κείραντες τῶν Φαληρέων τὸ πεδίον καὶ ἱππάσιμον ποιήσαντες τοῦτον
τὸν χῶρον, ἐπῆκαν τῷ στρατοπέδῳ τὴν ἵππον. ἐμπεσοῦσα δὲ διέφθειρε
ἄλλους τε πολλοὺς τῶν Λακεδαιμονίων καὶ δὴ καὶ τὸν Ἀγχιμόλιον.
τοὺς δὲ περιγενομένους αὐτῶν ἐς τὰς νέας κατεῖρξαν. ὁ μὲν δὴ πρῶτος
στόλος ἐκ Λακεδαίμονος οὕτω ἀπήλλαξε. καὶ Ἀγχιμολίου εἰσὶ ταφαὶ τῆς
Ἀττικῆς Ἀλωπεκῆσι, ἀγχοῦ τοῦ Ἡρακλείου τοῦ ἐν Κυνοσάργεϊ.

V.63.1 ὡς ὦν δὴ οἱ Ἀθηναῖοι λέγουσι: the Athenian narrative begins.   **οὗτοι
οἱ ἄνδρες:** οὗτοι refers back to the previously mentioned Ἀλκμεωνίδαι.   **τὴν
Πυθίην:** subject of προφέρειν.   **ὅκως:** "whenever."   **ἔλθοιεν:** an optative
hypothetically referring to an event in the past that happened with some
regularity.   **Σπαρτιητέων:** partitive with ἄνδρες.   **σφι = Σπαρτιητέων
ἀνδράσι:** to perform the action of ἐλευθεροῦν.   **ἐλευθεροῦν:** complementary
with προφέρειν.   **63.2 τὠυτό = τὸ αὐτό.   τῶν ἀστῶν:** partitive with
ἄνδρα.   **ἐξελῶντα:** the tense indicates the reason why the Spartans send
him.   **τὰ μάλιστα:** substantive and accusative of respect, "very much."   **τὰ γὰρ
τοῦ θεοῦ ... τὰ τῶν ἀνδρῶν:** substantive, "the things of the gods ... the things
of men," subjects of an implied εἶναι.   **τούτους:** refers back to the army.   **63.3
ὁ μὲν δὴ προσσχών:** modifies an implied Ankhimolios and is answered οἱ
δὲ Πεισιστρατίδαι.   **ταῦτα:** refers back to the landing of the army.   **σφι:**
agency.   **Κινέην:** in apposition to βασιλέα.   **ἄνδρα:** in apposition to
Κινέην.   **τοὺς ἐπείτε = τούτους ἐπείτε:** English word order would be ἐπείτε
τούτους.   **τοιάδε:** looks forward to what comes next.   **63.4 τῷ στρατοπέδῳ:**
object of the prefix ἐπι- of ἐπῆκαν.   **ἐμπεσοῦσα:** modifies an implied ἡ
ἵππος.   **διέφθειρε ἄλλους τε πολλούς ... καὶ δὴ καί:** τε introduces the general
and καὶ δὴ καί the specific.   **τῶν Λακεδαιμονίων:** partitive with ἄλλους τε

πολλούς.   **αὐτῶν:** partitive with τοὺς δὲ περιγενομένους.   **ὁ μὲν δὴ πρῶτος**
στόλος: is answered by μετὰ δὲ Λακεδαιμόνιοι.   **οὕτω:** refers back to the death
of the Spartans and their being driven onto their ships.

V.64.1 μετὰ δὲ Λακεδαιμόνιοι, μέζω στόλον στείλαντες, ἀπέπεμψαν
ἐπὶ τὰς Ἀθήνας, στρατηγὸν τῆς στρατιῆς ἀποδέξαντες βασιλέα
Κλεομένεα τὸν Ἀναξανδρίδεω, οὐκέτι κατὰ θάλασσαν στείλαντες
ἀλλὰ κατ᾽ ἤπειρον. [2] τοῖσι ἐσβαλοῦσι ἐς τὴν Ἀττικὴν χώρην ἡ τῶν
Θεσσαλῶν ἵππος πρώτη προσέμιξε καὶ οὐ μετὰ πολλὸν ἐτράπετο.
καὶ σφεων ἔπεσον ὑπὲρ τεσσεράκοντα ἄνδρας. οἱ δὲ περιγενόμενοι
ἀπαλλάσσοντο, ὡς εἶχον, εὐθὺς ἐπὶ Θεσσαλίης. Κλεομένης δέ,
ἀπικόμενος ἐς τὸ ἄστυ ἅμα Ἀθηναίων τοῖσι βουλομένοισι εἶναι
ἐλευθέροισι, ἐπολιόρκεε τοὺς τυράννους ἀπεργμένους ἐν τῷ
Πελασγικῷ τείχεϊ.

V.64.1 μετὰ δέ: adverbial, "next."   **στρατηγόν:** predicate to βασιλέα.   **64.2**
τοῖσι ἐσβαλοῦσι: substantive, "those invading," object of the prefix προσ- of
προσέμιξε.   **οὐ μετὰ πολλόν:** temporal, "after a short time."   **σφεων:**
partitive with ὑπὲρ τεσσεράκοντα ἄνδρας.   **οἱ δὲ περιγενόμενοι:** substantive,
"the survivors."   **Ἀθηναίων:** partitive with τοῖσι βουλομένοισι.   **τοῖσι**
βουλομένοισι: substantive, "those wishing."   **εἶναι:** complementary with τοῖσι
βουλομένοισι.

V.65.1 καὶ οὐδέν τι πάντως ἂν ἐξεῖλον Πεισιστρατίδας οἱ
Λακεδαιμόνιοι. οὔ τε γὰρ ἐπέδρην ἐπενόεον ποιήσασθαι. οἵ τε
Πεισιστρατίδαι σίτοισι καὶ ποτοῖσι εὖ παρεσκευάδατο. πολιορκήσαντές
τε ἂν ἡμέρας ὀλίγας ἀπαλλάσσοντο ἐς τὴν Σπάρτην. νῦν δὲ
συντυχίη τοῖσι μὲν κακὴ ἐπεγένετο, τοῖσι δὲ ἡ αὐτὴ αὕτη σύμμαχος.
ὑπεκτιθέμενοι γὰρ ἔξω τῆς χώρης, οἱ παῖδες τῶν Πεισιστρατιδέων
ἥλωσαν. [2] τοῦτο δὲ ὡς ἐγένετο, πάντα αὐτῶν τὰ πρήγματα
συνετετάρακτο. παρέστησαν δὲ ἐπὶ μισθῷ τοῖσι τέκνοισι, ἐπ᾽ οἷσι
ἐβούλοντο οἱ Ἀθηναῖοι, ὥστε ἐν πέντε ἡμέρῃσι ἐκχωρῆσαι ἐκ τῆς
Ἀττικῆς. [3] μετὰ δὲ ἐξεχώρησαν ἐς Σίγειον τὸ ἐπὶ τῷ Σκαμάνδρῳ,
ἄρξαντες μὲν Ἀθηναίων ἐπ᾽ ἔτεα ἕξ τε καὶ τριήκοντα, ἐόντες δὲ καὶ

οὗτοι ἀνέκαθεν Πύλιοί τε καὶ Νηλεῖδαι, ἐκ τῶν αὐτῶν γεγονότες καὶ
οἱ ἀμφὶ Κόδρον τε καὶ Μέλανθον, οἵ, πρότερον ἐπήλυδες ἐόντες,
ἐγένοντο Ἀθηναίων βασιλέες. [4] ἐπὶ τούτου δὲ καὶ τὠυτὸ οὔνομα
ἀπεμνημόνευσε Ἱπποκράτης, τῷ παιδὶ θέσθαι "τὸν Πεισίστρατον," ἐπὶ
τοῦ Νέστορος Πεισιστράτου ποιεύμενος τὴν ἐπωνυμίην. [5] οὕτω μὲν
Ἀθηναῖοι τυράννων ἀπαλλάχθησαν. ὅσα δὲ ἐλευθερωθέντες ἔρξαν ἢ
ἔπαθον ἀξιόχρεα ἀπηγήσιος, πρὶν ἢ Ἰωνίην τε ἀποστῆναι ἀπὸ Δαρείου
καὶ Ἀρισταγόρεα τὸν Μιλήσιον, ἀπικόμενον ἐς Ἀθήνας, χρηίσαι σφέων
βοηθέειν, ταῦτα πρῶτα φράσω.

V.65.1 οὐδέν: accusative of respect, "in no way."   **ἂν ἐξεῖλον ... ἀπαλλάσσοντο**:
ἄν renders the indicatives counterfactual; the negation offers a reality that
would have occurred had chance not intervened. Statements like these are
part of Herodotus's narrative and are clear indications of the way he views
history.   **παρεσκευάδατο = παρεσκευάδαντο**: pluperfect.   **συντυχίη ...
κακή**: the adjective indicates how events were viewed by the Peisistratids, as does
σύμμαχος for their opponents.   **τοῖσι μέν ... τοῖσι δέ**: substantive, "to the one
side ... to the other side."   **65.2 ὡς**: temporal.   **ἐπ' οἷσι**: a noun like "terms"
can be supplied from context, "on whichever terms."   **ἐκχωρῆσαι**: main verb in
the dependent clause; the subject is the same as the subject of παρέστησαν.   **65.3
μετὰ δέ**: adverbial, "next."   **ἄρξαντες μέν**: is answered by ἐόντες δέ.   **ἐκ
τῶν αὐτῶν**: substantive, "from the same ancestors as."   **οἱ ἀμφὶ Κόδρον τε καὶ
Μέλανθον**: substantive, "the families around Kodros and Melanthos."   **65.4 ἐπὶ
τούτου δὲ καὶ τὠυτὸ οὔνομα ἀπεμνημόνευσε Ἱπποκράτης τῷ παιδὶ θέσθαι
τὸν Πεισίστρατον**: the syntax is difficult; perhaps the infinitive is articular:
"for this reason Hippokrates called to mind the same name by giving (the name)
'Peisistratos' to his son."   **65.5 οὕτω μέν**: sums up the discussion on the end
of tyranny at Athens and is answered by ὅσα δέ.   **ὅσα**: the antecedent ταῦτα
is delayed.   **Ἰωνίην**: subject of ἀποστῆναι.   **ἀποστῆναι ... χρηίσαι**: main
verbs in the dependent clause.   **Ἀρισταγόρεα**: subject of χρηίσαι.   **σφέων**: to
perform the action of βοηθέειν.   **βοηθέειν**: dependent on χρηίσαι.   **πρῶτα**:
adverbial, "first."

V.66.1 Ἀθῆναι, ἐοῦσαι καὶ πρὶν μεγάλαι, τότε, ἀπαλλαχθεῖσαι
τυράννων, ἐγίνοντο μέζονες. ἐν δὲ αὐτῇσι δύο ἄνδρες ἐδυνάστευον,

Κλεισθένης τε ἀνὴρ Ἀλκμεωνίδης, ὅς περ δὴ λόγον ἔχει τὴν Πυθίην ἀναπεῖσαι, καὶ Ἰσαγόρης Τεισάνδρου οἰκίης μὲν ἐὼν δοκίμου. ἀτὰρ τὰ ἀνέκαθεν οὐκ ἔχω φράσαι· θύουσι δὲ οἱ συγγενέες αὐτοῦ Διὶ Καρίῳ. [2] οὗτοι οἱ ἄνδρες ἐστασίασαν περὶ δυνάμιος, ἑσσούμενος δὲ ὁ Κλεισθένης τὸν δῆμον προσεταιρίζεται. μετὰ δὲ τετραφύλους ἐόντας Ἀθηναίους δεκαφύλους ἐποίησε, τῶν Ἴωνος παίδων, Γελέοντος καὶ Αἰγικόρεος καὶ Ἀργάδεω καὶ Ὅπλητος, ἀπαλλάξας τὰς ἐπωνυμίας, ἐξευρὼν δὲ ἑτέρων ἡρώων ἐπωνυμίας ἐπιχωρίων, πάρεξ Αἴαντος. τοῦτον δέ, ἅτε ἀστυγείτονα καὶ σύμμαχον ξεῖνον ἐόντα, προσέθετο.

V.66.1 τότε ἀπαλλαχθεῖσαι τυράννων: the date is approximately 508 B.C.E. **ἐν δὲ αὐτῇσι:** names of cities are often feminine plural. **ἀνήρ:** in apposition with Κλεισθένης. **ὅς περ δὴ λόγον ἔχει τὴν Πυθίην ἀναπεῖσαι** = ὅς περ δὴ λέγεται τὴν Πυθίην ἀναπεῖσαι: λόγον ἔχει sets up ἀναπεῖσαι. **οἰκίης μὲν ἐὼν δοκίμου:** is answered by θύουσι δὲ οἱ συγγενέες. **τὰ ἀνέκαθεν:** substantive, "his origins." **φράσαι:** complementary with ἔχω. **Διὶ Καρίῳ:** Plutarch argues that Herodotus is making a racial gibe at Isagoras by suggesting he may have a Karian origin. Karians and Phoinikians, it seems, are two ethnicities that a Greek would not want an association with (Plutarch, *On the Malice of Herodotus* 23). **66.2 μετὰ δέ:** adverbial, "next." **δεκαφύλους:** predicate to Ἀθηναίους; supply an implied εἶναι. Kleisthenes' genius in reorganizing Athens in accordance with geography rather than with lineage does not quite come across in Herodotus's narrative. **τῶν Ἴωνος παίδων:** translate with τὰς ἐπωνυμίας. **Γελέοντος, Αἰγικόρεος, Ἀργάδεω, Ὅπλητος:** in apposition with παίδων. **τοῦτον:** refers back to Aias. **ἅτε ἀστυγείτονα καὶ σύμμαχον ξεῖνον ἐόντα:** ἅτε (and οἷα) is typically found with a participle in the nominative or accusative case. Use "since" or "because" to translate it, and turn the participle into a finite verb. Thus, ἅτε αὐτὸν ὄντα καλόν (ἅτε ὢν καλός): "since he was good."

V.67.1 ταῦτα δέ, δοκέειν ἐμοί, ἐμιμέετο ὁ Κλεισθένης οὗτος τὸν ἑωυτοῦ μητροπάτορα, Κλεισθένεα, τὸν Σικυῶνος τύραννον. Κλεισθένης γάρ, Ἀργείοισι πολεμήσας, τοῦτο μὲν ῥαψῳδοὺς ἔπαυσε ἐν Σικυῶνι ἀγωνίζεσθαι τῶν Ὁμηρείων ἐπέων εἵνεκα, ὅτι Ἀργεῖοί τε καὶ Ἄργος τὰ πολλὰ πάντα ὑμνέαται. τοῦτο δέ—ἡρώιον γὰρ ἦν καὶ ἔστι ἐν αὐτῇ τῇ ἀγορῇ τῶν Σικυωνίων Ἀδρήστου τοῦ Ταλαοῦ—τοῦτον ἐπεθύμησε ὁ Κλεισθένης, ἐόντα Ἀργεῖον, ἐκβαλεῖν ἐκ τῆς χώρης. [2] ἐλθὼν δὲ ἐς Δελφοὺς ἐχρηστηριάζετο εἰ ἐκβάλοι τὸν Ἄδρηστον. ἡ δὲ Πυθίη οἱ χρᾷ, φᾶσα Ἄδρηστον μὲν εἶναι Σικυωνίων βασιλέα, κεῖνον δὲ λευστῆρα. ἐπεὶ δὲ ὁ θεὸς τοῦτό γε οὐ παρεδίδου, ἀπελθὼν ὀπίσω ἐφρόντιζε μηχανὴν τῇ αὐτὸς ὁ Ἄδρηστος ἀπαλλάξεται. ὡς δέ οἱ ἐξευρῆσθαι ἐδόκεε, πέμψας ἐς Θήβας τὰς Βοιωτίας ἔφη θέλειν ἐπαγαγέσθαι Μελάνιππον τὸν Ἀστακοῦ· οἱ δὲ Θηβαῖοι ἔδοσαν. [3] ἐπαγαγόμενος δὲ ὁ Κλεισθένης τὸν Μελάνιππον τέμενός οἱ ἀπέδεξε ἐν αὐτῷ τῷ πρυτανηίῳ καί μιν ἵδρυσε ἐνθαῦτα ἐν τῷ ἰσχυροτάτῳ. ἐπηγάγετο δὲ τὸν Μελάνιππον ὁ Κλεισθένης—καὶ γὰρ τοῦτο δεῖ ἀπηγήσασθαι—ὡς ἔχθιστον ἐόντα Ἀδρήστῳ, ὃς τόν τε ἀδελφεόν οἱ Μηκιστέα ἀπεκτόνεε καὶ τὸν γαμβρὸν Τυδέα. [4] ἐπείτε δέ οἱ τὸ τέμενος ἀπέδεξε, θυσίας τε καὶ ὁρτὰς Ἀδρήστου ἀπελόμενος ἔδωκε τῷ Μελανίππῳ. οἱ δὲ Σικυώνιοι ἐώθεσαν μεγαλωστὶ κάρτα τιμᾶν τὸν Ἄδρηστον. ἡ γὰρ χώρη ἦν αὕτη Πολύβου· ὁ δὲ Ἄδρηστος ἦν Πολύβου θυγατριδέος. ἄπαις δὲ Πόλυβος τελευτῶν διδοῖ Ἀδρήστῳ τὴν ἀρχήν. [5] τά τε δὴ ἄλλα οἱ Σικυώνιοι ἐτίμων τὸν Ἄδρηστον καὶ δὴ πρὸς τὰ πάθεα αὐτοῦ τραγικοῖσι χοροῖσι ἐγέραιρον, τὸν μὲν Διόνυσον οὐ τιμῶντες, τὸν δὲ Ἄδρηστον. Κλεισθένης δὲ χοροὺς μὲν τῷ Διονύσῳ ἀπέδωκε, τὴν δὲ ἄλλην θυσίην Μελανίππῳ.

V.67.1 ταῦτα δέ: refers back to the reforms of Kleisthenes; accusative of respect, "in regard to these things."   **δοκέειν**: impersonal, "it seems."   **Κλεισθένεα ... τύραννον**: in apposition to μητροπάτορα; the marriage that connects the two is narrated at VI.126–31.   **Σικυῶνος**: a settlement from the time preceding the Trojan War; it was originally independent and comprised of Dorians and Ionians. Around the time of Agamemnon, Sikyon became subject to Dorian Argos. In 676 B.C.E., Orthagoras freed Sikyon of Dorian Argive rule and established himelf as tyrant. His grandson Kleisthenes, uncle of the Kleisthenes of Athens, succeeded as tyrant and ruled from 600 to 560 B.C.E. He revised the city's constitution to favor the Ionian population. He also replaced Dorian cults with the worship of Dionysos. The Orthagorids continued as tyrants until 556 B.C.E., when the Dorian Spartans exiled them and established an alliance with the city. Sikyon became known for its arts: sculpting, wood carving, bronze work, pottery, and painting, which it is said to have invented.   **τοῦτο μέν ... τοῦτο δέ**: "first ... second."   **ῥαψῳδούς**: subject of ἀγωνίζεσθαι.   **ἀγωνίζεσθαι**: dependent on ἔπαυσε.   **τὰ πολλὰ πάντα**: accusative of respect, "in almost all cases."   **τοῦτον**: refers back to Adrastos.   **ἐκβαλεῖν**: complementary with ἐπεθύμησε.   **67.2 ἐκβάλοι**: a hypothetical optative, standing for a deliberative subjunctive (Smyth 2599).   **οἱ = αὐτῷ**.   **Ἄδρηστον**: subject of εἶναι.   **Ἄδρηστον μέν**: is answered by κεῖνον δέ.   εἶναι: main verb in indirect statement.   κεῖνον δέ: i.e., Κλεισθένεα; supply an implied εἶναι.   τοῦτο: refers back to Kleisthenes' desire to expel Adrastos.   ἐφρόντιζε: as context makes clear, Kleisthenes is in a state of devising a plan. This section and the next offer his story.   τῇ = ᾗ.   ὡς: temporal.   οἱ = αὐτῷ.   ἐξευρῆσθαι: complementary with ἐδόκεε.   θέλειν: main verb in indirect statement; the subject is the same as the subject of ἔφη.   ἐπαγαγέσθαι: complementary with θέλειν.   ἔδοσαν: supply an implied Μελάνιππον.   67.3 οἱ = αὐτῷ.   μιν = αὐτόν.   ἐν τῷ ἰσχυροτάτῳ: substantive, "in the strongest spot."   ἀπηγήσασθαι: complementary with δεῖ.   Ἀδρήστῳ: translate with ἔχθιστον.   οἱ = αὐτῷ: possesses ἀδελφεόν.   Μηκιστέα: in apposition to ἀδελφεόν.   Τυδέα: in apposition to γαμβρόν.   67.4 οἱ = αὐτῷ.   τιμᾶν: complementary with ἐώθεσαν.   67.5 τά τε δὴ ἄλλα … καὶ δὴ πρὸς τὰ πάθεα αὐτοῦ: τε introduces the general ("both in other ways") and καί the specific ("and on account of his sufferings").   τὸν μὲν Διόνυσον: is answered by τὸν δὲ Ἄδρηστον.   χοροὺς μέν: is answered by τὴν δὲ ἄλλην θυσίην; at Athens these choruses developed into the tragedies we enjoy today.

~

V.68.1 ταῦτα μὲν ἐς Ἄδρηστόν οἱ ἐπεποίητο. φυλὰς δὲ τὰς Δωριέων, ἵνα δὴ μὴ αἱ αὐταὶ ἔωσι τοῖσι Σικυωνίοισι καὶ τοῖσι Ἀργείοισι, μετέβαλε ἐς ἄλλα οὐνόματα. ἔνθα καὶ πλεῖστον κατεγέλασε τῶν Σικυωνίων· ἐπὶ γὰρ ὑός τε καὶ ὄνου τὰς ἐπωνυμίας, μετατιθείς, αὐτὰ τὰ τελευταῖα ἐπέθηκε, πλὴν τῆς ἑωυτοῦ φυλῆς. ταύτῃ δὲ τὸ οὔνομα ἀπὸ τῆς ἑωυτοῦ ἀρχῆς ἔθετο. οὗτοι μὲν δὴ Ἀρχέλαοι ἐκαλέοντο, ἕτεροι δὲ Ὑᾶται, ἄλλοι δὲ Ὀνεᾶται, ἕτεροι δὲ Χοιρεᾶται. [2] τούτοισι τοῖσι οὐνόμασι τῶν φυλέων ἐχρέωντο οἱ Σικυώνιοι καὶ ἐπὶ Κλεισθένεος ἄρχοντος καὶ ἐκείνου τεθνεῶτος ἔτι ἐπ' ἔτεα ἑξήκοντα. μετέπειτα μέντοι, λόγον σφίσι δόντες, μετέβαλον ἐς τοὺς Ὑλλέας καὶ Παμφύλους καὶ Δυμανάτας. τετάρτους δὲ αὐτοῖσι προσέθεντο, ἐπὶ τοῦ Ἀδρήστου παιδός, Αἰγιαλέος, τὴν ἐπωνυμίην ποιεύμενοι κεκλῆσθαι Αἰγιαλέας.

V.68.1 ταῦτα: refers back to the changes that Kleisthenes enacted.   **ταῦτα μέν**: is answered by φυλὰς δέ.   **οἱ = αὐτῷ**: agency.   **ἔωσι = ὦσι**: subjunctive, indicating Kleisthenes' reason for changing the names of the Dorian tribes.   **Σικυωνίοισι … Ἀργείοισι**: translate with αὐταί; the expression is similar to τὰ αὐτά σοι ποιῶ ("I do the same things as you").   **πλεῖστον**: adverbial, "vehemently."   **τελευταῖα**: Ὑᾶται comes from ὗς, ὑός ἡ: sow, pig; Ὀνεᾶται, from ὄνος, -ου ὁ or ἡ: ass; and Χοιρεᾶται from χοῖρος, -ου ὁ: young pig, porker. Because the names are so offensive, the credibility of this story is questioned.   **ταύτῃ**:

refers back to φυλῆς.   **οὗτοι μέν:** is answered by ἕτεροι δέ, ἄλλοι δέ, and ἕτεροι δέ.   **ἕτεροι δέ ... ἄλλοι δέ ... ἕτεροι δέ:** supply an implied ἐκαλέοντο.   **68.2 μετέπειτα μέντοι:** is answered by τετάρτους δέ.   **κεκλῆσθαι:** dependent on ποιεύμενοι; supply an implied αὐτούς as subject.   **Αἰγιαλέας:** predicate to an implied αὐτούς.

~

V.69.1 ταῦτα μέν νυν ὁ Σικυώνιος Κλεισθένης ἐπεποιήκεε. ὁ δὲ δὴ Ἀθηναῖος Κλεισθένης, ἐὼν τοῦ Σικυωνίου τούτου θυγατριδέος καὶ τὸ οὔνομα ἐπὶ τούτου ἔχων, δοκέειν ἐμοί, καὶ οὗτος ὑπεριδὼν Ἴωνας, ἵνα μὴ σφίσι αἱ αὐταὶ ἔωσι φυλαὶ καὶ Ἴωσι, τὸν ὁμώνυμον Κλεισθένεα ἐμιμήσατο. [2] ὡς γὰρ δὴ τὸν Ἀθηναίων δῆμον, πρότερον ἀπωσμένον τότε πάντων, πρὸς τὴν ἑωυτοῦ μοῖραν προσεθήκατο, τὰς φυλὰς μετωνόμασε καὶ ἐποίησε πλεῦνας ἐξ ἐλασσόνων. δέκα τε δὴ φυλάρχους ἀντὶ τεσσέρων ἐποίησε. δέκαχα δὲ καὶ τοὺς δήμους κατένειμε ἐς τὰς φυλάς. ἤν τε, τὸν δῆμον προσθέμενος, πολλῷ κατύπερθε τῶν ἀντιστασιωτέων.

V.69.1 ταῦτα μέν νυν ὁ Σικυώνιος: concludes the narrative on Kleisthenes of Sikyon and is answered by ὁ δὲ δὴ Ἀθηναῖος.   **ἐπὶ τούτου:** refers back to Kleisthenes of Sikyon.   **δοκέειν:** impersonal, "it seems."   **καὶ οὗτος:** refers back to and repeats the subject, Ἀθηναῖος Κλεισθένης. Hornblower (2013) translates the καί as "also," which creates a discrepancy in the narrative since Sikyonian Kleisthenes did not disdain the Ionians. See note on 67.1. A simple solution is to translate the καί as intensive.   **ὑπεριδὼν Ἴωνας:** just as his namesake favored his own tribe over the three other nastily named ones, so does Kleisthenes favor his own faction over the rest of the Ionian Athenians. That said, Kleisthenes' reforms, both to the increase in the number of tribes and to their basis in geography, broke the cultural and traditional stranglehold noble lineage held on the masses.   **σφίσι ... Ἴωσι:** translate with αἱ αὐταί; σφίσι refers to Kleisthenes and his newly formed political faction.   **ἔωσι = ὦσι:** a subjunctive, indicating Kleisthenes' reason for changing the names of the Dorian tribes.   **69.2 ὡς:** temporal.   **τὸν Ἀθηναίων δῆμον:** the populace at large.   **πάντων:** object of the prefix ἀπο- of ἀπωσμένον.   **τοὺς δήμους κατένειμε ἐς τὰς φυλάς:** previously townships, the demes now became official political units, and each citizen identified himself by his name and deme. For hundreds of years the dominant paradigm in Greece had been that lineage was one of the determinants of a person's prestige and influence. By making this change, Kleisthenes took power and influence away from established families and clans. He also enfranchised many who previously were without citizenship: (cf. Aristotle, *Athenian Constitution* 20: "ἀποδιδοὺς τῷ πλήθει τὴν πολιτείαν"; and Aristotle, *Politics* book 3, chapter 2, 1275b37: "πολλοὺς γὰρ ἐφυλέτευσε ξένους καὶ δούλους μετοίκους"). **πολλῷ**: adverbial, "by far."

~

V.70.1 ἐν τῷ μέρεϊ δὲ ἑσσούμενος, ὁ Ἰσαγόρης ἀντιτεχνᾶται τάδε· ἐπικαλέεται Κλεομένεα τὸν Λακεδαιμόνιον, γενόμενον ἑωυτῷ ξεῖνον ἀπὸ τῆς Πεισιστρατιδέων πολιορκίης. τὸν δὲ Κλεομένεα εἶχε αἰτίη φοιτᾶν παρὰ τοῦ Ἰσαγόρεω τὴν γυναῖκα. [2] τὰ μὲν δὴ πρῶτα πέμπων ὁ Κλεομένης ἐς τὰς Ἀθήνας κήρυκα ἐξέβαλλε Κλεισθένεα καὶ μετ᾽ αὐτοῦ ἄλλους πολλοὺς Ἀθηναίων, τοὺς ἐναγέας ἐπιλέγων. ταῦτα δέ, πέμπων, ἔλεγε ἐκ διδαχῆς τοῦ Ἰσαγόρεω. οἱ μὲν γὰρ Ἀλκμεωνίδαι καὶ οἱ συστασιῶται αὐτῶν εἶχον αἰτίην τοῦ φόνου τούτου· αὐτὸς δὲ οὐ μετεῖχε οὐδ᾽ οἱ φίλοι αὐτοῦ.

V.70.1 τάδε: looks forward to what comes next.   **ἑωυτῷ**: possesses ξεῖνον.   **ἀπό**: temporal, "ever since."   **Κλεομένεα**: subject of φοιτᾶν.   **εἶχε αἰτίη**: "there was an accusation that."   **φοιτᾶν**: main verb in indirect statement; whatever the truth of the relations among Kleomenes, Isagores, and Isagores' wife, Spartan men were accustomed to share their wives.   **70.2 τὰ μὲν δὴ πρῶτα**: substantive, "first"; it is not answered until ταῦτα δὲ ποιήσας of chapter 72.1.   **ἐξέβαλλε**: the aspect of the imperfect indicates that the action is incomplete; this use of the imperfect is commonly called "conative."   **τοὺς ἐναγέας ἐπιλέγων**: supply an implied τούτους: "calling them the accursed." Murder caused a pollution that, like a disease, was catching; banishment was one way to cleanse the stain.   **ταῦτα**: refers back to his calling them accursed.   **πέμπων**: supply an implied κήρυκα.   **οἱ μὲν γὰρ Ἀλκμεωνίδαι**: is answered by αὐτὸς δέ.   **αὐτός** = Ἰσαγόρης.

~

V.71.1 οἱ δ᾽ ἐναγέες Ἀθηναίων ὧδε ὠνομάσθησαν. ἦν Κύλων τῶν Ἀθηναίων ἀνὴρ Ὀλυμπιονίκης. οὗτος ἐπὶ τυραννίδι ἐκόμησε. προσποιησάμενος δὲ ἑταιρηίην τῶν ἡλικιωτέων, καταλαβεῖν τὴν ἀκρόπολιν ἐπειρήθη. οὐ δυνάμενος δὲ ἐπικρατῆσαι, ἱκέτης ἵζετο πρὸς τὸ ἄγαλμα. [2] τούτους ἀνιστᾶσι μὲν οἱ πρυτάνιες τῶν ναυκράρων, οἵπερ ἔνεμον τότε τὰς Ἀθήνας, ὑπεγγύους πλὴν θανάτου. φονεῦσαι δὲ αὐτοὺς αἰτίη ἔχει Ἀλκμεωνίδας. ταῦτα πρὸ τῆς Πεισιστράτου ἡλικίης ἐγένετο.

V.71.1 ὧδε: looks forward to what comes next.   **Κύλων:** Kylon's attempted coup is dated to 632 B.C.E. For two additional versions of this tale, see Thoukydides 1.126 and Plutarch's *Solon* 12. In both, the Alkmeonids kill Kylon's followers, who depart the temple thinking that they will not be killed. That Herodotus says only that the Alkmeonids "were accused" of murder is often taken as evidence of Herodotus's or his sources' pro-Alkmeonid bias.   **Ὀλυμπιονίκης:** Kylon's name is in the Olympic victors list of the year 640 B.C.E. Begun in 776 B.C.E., the Olympic games were held in Olympia in honor of Zeus and Pelops. The events were boxing, discus and javelin throwing, equestrian races, foot races, jumping, the pankration (somewhat similar to the MMA bouts of today), and wrestling. Winners were admired and immortalized in poems and statues.   **οὗτος:** refers back to Kylon.   **καταλαβεῖν:** complementary with ἐπειρήθη.   **ἐπικρατῆσαι:** complementary with δυνάμενος.   **ἱκέτης ἵζετο:** suppliants are inviolable and under divine protection.   **71.2 τούτους:** refers back to Kylon and his supporters.   **ἀνιστᾶσι μέν:** is answered by φονεῦσαι δέ.   **οἵ περ ἔνεμον τότε τὰς Ἀθήνας:** Thoukydides writes that the archons, not the prytanies, were in charge (1.126.8). The question as to who was in charge remains unanswered.   **Ἀλκμεωνίδας:** subject of φονεῦσαι.   **ταῦτα:** refers back to the events just described.   **πρὸ τῆς Πεισιστράτου ἡλικίης:** the date is somewhere around 640–632 B.C.E.

~

V.72.1 Κλεομένης δέ, ὡς πέμπων, ἐξέβαλλε Κλεισθένεα καὶ τοὺς ἐναγέας. Κλεισθένης μὲν αὐτὸς ὑπεξέσχε· μετὰ δὲ οὐδὲν ἧσσον παρῆν ἐς τὰς Ἀθήνας ὁ Κλεομένης οὐ σὺν μεγάλῃ χειρί. ἀπικόμενος δὲ ἀγηλατέει ἑπτακόσια ἐπίστια Ἀθηναίων, τά οἱ ὑπέθετο ὁ Ἰσαγόρης. ταῦτα δὲ ποιήσας, δεύτερα τὴν βουλὴν καταλύειν ἐπειρᾶτο. τριηκοσίοισι δὲ τοῖσι Ἰσαγόρεω στασιώτῃσι τὰς ἀρχὰς ἐνεχείριζε. [2] ἀντισταθείσης δὲ τῆς βουλῆς καὶ οὐ βουλομένης πείθεσθαι, ὅ τε Κλεομένης καὶ ὁ Ἰσαγόρης καὶ οἱ στασιῶται αὐτοῦ καταλαμβάνουσι τὴν ἀκρόπολιν. Ἀθηναίων δὲ οἱ λοιποί, τὰ αὐτὰ φρονήσαντες, ἐπολιόρκεον αὐτοὺς ἡμέρας δύο. τῇ δὲ τρίτῃ ὑπόσπονδοι ἐξέρχονται ἐκ τῆς χώρης, ὅσοι ἦσαν αὐτῶν Λακεδαιμόνιοι. ἐπετελέετο δὲ τῷ Κλεομένεϊ ἡ φήμη. [3] ὡς γὰρ ἀνέβη ἐς τὴν ἀκρόπολιν, μέλλων δὴ αὐτὴν κατασχήσειν, ἤιε ἐς τὸ ἄδυτον τῆς θεοῦ ὡς προσερέων. ἡ δὲ ἱρείη ἐξαναστᾶσα ἐκ τοῦ θρόνου, πρὶν ἢ τὰς θύρας αὐτὸν ἀμεῖψαι, εἶπε· Ὦ ξεῖνε Λακεδαιμόνιε, πάλιν χώρεε μηδὲ ἔσιθι ἐς τὸ ἱρόν· οὐ γὰρ θεμιτὸν Δωριεῦσι παριέναι ἐνθαῦτα. ὁ δὲ εἶπε· Ὦ γύναι, ἀλλ᾽ οὐ Δωριεύς εἰμι

ἀλλ' Ἀχαιός. [4] ὁ μὲν δή, τῇ κλεηδόνι οὐδὲν χρεώμενος, ἐπεχείρησέ
τε καὶ τότε πάλιν ἐξέπιπτε μετὰ τῶν Λακεδαιμονίων. τοὺς δὲ ἄλλους
Ἀθηναῖοι κατέδησαν τὴν ἐπὶ θανάτῳ, ἐν δὲ αὐτοῖσι καὶ Τιμησίθεον τὸν
Δελφόν, τοῦ ἔργα χειρῶν τε καὶ λήματος ἔχοιμ' ἂν μέγιστα καταλέξαι.

V.72.1 Κλεομένης δὲ ὡς πέμπων: after explaining why the Alkmeonids have
blood on their hands, Herodotus returns us to Kleomenes and his sending of the
herald in chapter 70.2.   **ἐξέβαλλε . . . ἀγηλατέει . . . ἐπειρᾶτο . . . ἐνεχείριζε**: the
aspect of these imperfects indicates that the action is incomplete.   **Κλεισθένης
μέν**: is answered by μετὰ δέ.   **μετὰ δέ**: adverbial, "next."   **οὐδὲν ἧσσον**:
accusative of respect, "nonetheless."   **ἑπτακόσια ἐπίστια**: substantive,
"seven hundred families"; the large number is widely disbelieved.   **τά
οἱ ὑπέθετο = ἃ αὐτῷ ὑπέθετο**.   **ταῦτα δὲ ποιήσας**: ταῦτα refers back
to driving out the families, and ποιήσας indicates Kleomenes' success in
doing so.   **καταλύειν**: complementary with ἐπειρᾶτο.   **72.2 πείθεσθαι**:
complementary with βουλομένης.   **Ἀθηναίων**: partitive with οἱ λοιποί.   **τὰ
αὐτά**: substantive, "the same things."   **αὐτῶν**: partitive with ὅσοι.   **72.3 ὡς**:
temporal.   **κατασχήσειν**: complementary with μέλλων.   **προσερέων**: the
tense indicates his reason for entering the inner chamber.   **αὐτόν**: subject of
ἀμεῖψαι.   **ἀμεῖψαι**: main verb in the dependent clause.   **Δωριεῦσι**: to perform
the action of παριέναι.   **παριέναι**: epexegetical with θεμιτόν.   **οὐ Δωριεύς
εἰμι ἀλλ' Ἀχαιός**: Akhaian is a generic term for a Greek and is one of the four main
Greek tribes. The other three are Aiolian, Dorian, and Ionian. Greek tribes tended
to side with each other in disputes with other Greeks.   **72.4 ὁ μέν**: is answered
by τοὺς δὲ ἄλλους.   **οὐδέν**: accusative of respect, "in no way."   **χρεώμενος**:
"heeding."   **τοὺς δὲ ἄλλους . . . Τιμησίθεον τὸν Δελφόν**: the general is noted
first and then followed by the specific.   **τὴν ἐπὶ θανάτῳ**: in certain instances
nouns commonly understood by native speakers in specific contexts are elipsed.
In this case, the Liddell, Scott, Jones lexicon suggests δέσιν, a "binding." And
so the accusative is either an accusative of respect, or the verb takes a double
accusative like ποιεῖ αὐτοὺς κακά: "he does bad things to them."   **τοῦ ἔργα = οὗ
ἔργα**.   **ἔχοιμ' ἄν**: potential optative, indicating Herodotus's capability in listing
Timesitheos's achievements. From Pausanias we learn that Timesitheos won the
pankration twice at Olympia and three times at Delphi and that he was a formidable
warrior (*Korinthiaka* 6.8.6).   **καταλέξαι**: complementary with ἔχοιμ'.

**V.73.1 οὗτοι μέν νυν δεδεμένοι ἐτελεύτησαν. Ἀθηναῖοι δὲ μετὰ
ταῦτα, Κλεισθένεα καὶ τὰ ἑπτακόσια ἐπίστια, τὰ διωχθέντα ὑπὸ
Κλεομένεος, μεταπεμψάμενοι, πέμπουσι ἀγγέλους ἐς Σάρδις,**

συμμαχίην βουλόμενοι ποιήσασθαι πρὸς Πέρσας· ἠπιστέατο γὰρ σφίσι
Λακεδαιμονίους τε καὶ Κλεομένεα ἐκπεπολεμῶσθαι. [2] ἀπικομένων
δὲ τῶν ἀγγέλων ἐς τὰς Σάρδις καὶ λεγόντων τὰ ἐντεταλμένα,
Ἀρταφρένης ὁ Ὑστάσπεος, Σαρδίων ὕπαρχος, ἐπειρώτα τίνες ἐόντες
ἄνθρωποι καὶ κοῦ γῆς οἰκημένοι δεοίατο Περσέων σύμμαχοι γενέσθαι.
πυθόμενος δὲ πρὸς τῶν ἀγγέλων, ἀπεκορύφου σφι τάδε· εἰ μὲν
διδοῦσι βασιλέι Δαρείῳ Ἀθηναῖοι γῆν τε καὶ ὕδωρ, ὁ δὲ συμμαχίην σφι
συνετίθετο. εἰ δὲ μὴ διδοῦσι, ἀπαλλάσσεσθαι αὐτοὺς ἐκέλευε. [3] οἱ δὲ
ἄγγελοι, ἐπὶ σφέων αὐτῶν βαλόμενοι, διδόναι ἔφασαν, βουλόμενοι
τὴν συμμαχίην ποιήσασθαι. οὗτοι μὲν δή, ἀπελθόντες ἐς τὴν ἑωυτῶν,
αἰτίας μεγάλας εἶχον.

V.73.1 οὗτοι μέν: is answered by Ἀθηναῖοι δέ; μέν ends the narrative on
the attack of Kleomenes, and δέ returns us to Kleisthenes.   **μετὰ ταῦτα:**
refers back to the events of Isagores and his partisans.   **ποιήσασθαι:**
complementary with βουλόμενοι.   **ἠπιστέατο:** they are correct in their
assessment. See chapter 74.   **Λακεδαιμονίους . . . Κλεομένεα:** subjects of
ἐκπεπολεμῶσθαι.   **ἐκπεπολεμῶσθαι:** main verb in indirect statement.   73.2
τὰ ἐντεταλμένα: substantive, "what was ordered."   **ὕπαρχος:** in apposition
with Ἀρταφρένης.   **δεοίατο = δέοιντο:** optative standing for an original
indicative.   **γενέσθαι:** complementary with δεοίατο.   **τάδε:** looks forward
to what comes next. The ensuing dialogue, presented indirectly, offers the
perspectives of the Persians and the Athenians.   **εἰ μὲν διδοῦσι:** is answered
by εἰ δὲ μὴ διδοῦσι.   **εἰ δὲ μὴ διδοῦσι:** εἰ and μή work together to render the
indicative hypothetical.   **ἀπαλλάσσεσθαι:** dependent on ἐκέλευε.   **αὐτούς:**
subject of ἀπαλλάσσεσθαι.   73.3 **διδόναι:** main verb in indirect statement. The
subject is the same as the subject of ἔφασαν; as object supply an implied γῆν τε καὶ
ὕδωρ.   **ποιήσασθαι:** complementary with βουλόμενοι.   **ἐς τὴν ἑωυτῶν = ἐς**
τὴν ἑωυτῶν γῆν.   **οὗτοι μὲν δή:** refers back to the envoys and is answered by
Κλεομένης δέ.   **αἰτίας μεγάλας εἶχον:** commentators think that Herodotus is
politely concealing the fact that the Athenians medized, that is, they sided with the
Persians.

⌒

V.74.1 Κλεομένης δέ, ἐπιστάμενος περιυβρίσθαι ἔπεσι καὶ ἔργοισι ὑπ᾽
Ἀθηναίων, συνέλεγε ἐκ πάσης Πελοποννήσου στρατόν, οὐ φράζων
ἐς τὸ συλλέγει· τίσασθαι τε ἐθέλων τὸν δῆμον τὸν Ἀθηναίων καὶ
Ἰσαγόρην βουλόμενος τύραννον καταστῆσαι. συνεξῆλθε γάρ οἱ οὗτος

ἐκ τῆς ἀκροπόλιος. [2] Κλεομένης τε δὴ στόλῳ μεγάλῳ ἐσέβαλε ἐς
Ἐλευσῖνα. καὶ οἱ Βοιωτοί, ἀπὸ συνθήματος, Οἰνόην αἱρέουσι καὶ Ὑσιὰς
δήμους τοὺς ἐσχάτους τῆς Ἀττικῆς. Χαλκιδέες τε ἐπὶ τὰ ἕτερα ἐσίνοντο
ἐπιόντες χώρους τῆς Ἀττικῆς. Ἀθηναῖοι δέ, καίπερ ἀμφιβολίῃ ἐχόμενοι,
Βοιωτῶν μὲν καὶ Χαλκιδέων ἐς ὕστερον ἔμελλον μνήμην ποιήσεσθαι.
Πελοποννησίοισι δὲ ἐοῦσι ἐν Ἐλευσῖνι ἀντία ἔθεντο τὰ ὅπλα.

V.74.1 ἐπιστάμενος περιυβρίσθαι: forms part of Kleomenes' narrative. Causation
in Herodotus often involves retribution for harms done or assistance for services
rendered.   **περιυβρίσθαι:** main verb in indirect statement; the subject is the
same as the subject of συνέλεγε.   **οὐ φράζων ἐς τὸ = οὐ φράζων τοῦτο ἐς ὅ:**
the antecedent τοῦτο has dropped out, and ἐς τό serves as the object of φράζων
and ἐς.   **συλλέγει:** supply an implied στρατόν from context.   **τίσασθαι:**
complementary with ἐθέλων; Herodotus tells what Kleomenes does
not.   **τύραννον:** predicate to Ἰσαγόρην.   **καταστῆσαι:** complementary with
βουλόμενος; the Athenians destroyed the homes, distributed the property, and
condemned to death Isagores and his faction (Scholiast to Aristophanes, *Lysistrata*
273).   **οἱ = αὐτῷ:** object of the prefix συν- of συνεξῆλθε.   **74.2 ἐς Ἐλευσῖνα:**
fortified, Eleusis is a strategic town to capture for an army invading from the
Peloponnesos.   **ἀπὸ συνθήματος:** the allies were bound by agreement to provide
military assistance.   **αἱρέουσι:** a historic or storytelling present.   **δήμους:**
in apposition with Οἰνόην and Ὑσιάς.   **τὰ ἕτερα:** substantive, "the other side,
opposite."   **Βοιωτῶν μὲν καὶ Χαλκιδέων:** is answered by Πελοποννησίοισι δὲ
ἐοῦσι.   **ἐς ὕστερον:** substantive, "until later."   **ποιήσεσθαι:** complementary
with ἔμελλον.   **Πελοποννησίοισι:** translate with ἀντία.

❧

V.75.1 μελλόντων δὲ συνάψειν τὰ στρατόπεδα ἐς μάχην, Κορίνθιοι
μέν πρῶτοι, σφίσι αὐτοῖσι δόντες λόγον ὡς οὐ ποιέοιεν δίκαια,
μετεβάλλοντό τε καὶ ἀπαλλάσσοντο. μετὰ δὲ Δημάρητος ὁ Ἀρίστωνος,
ἐὼν καὶ οὗτος βασιλεὺς Σπαρτιητέων καὶ συνεξαγαγών τε τὴν
στρατιὴν ἐκ Λακεδαίμονος καὶ οὐκ ἐὼν διάφορος ἐν τῷ πρόσθε
χρόνῳ Κλεομένεϊ. [2] ἀπὸ δὲ ταύτης τῆς διχοστασίης ἐτέθη νόμος
ἐν Σπάρτῃ μὴ ἐξεῖναι ἕπεσθαι ἀμφοτέρους τοὺς βασιλέας ἐξιούσης
στρατιῆς—τέως γὰρ ἀμφότεροι εἵποντο. παραλυομένου δὲ τούτων τοῦ
ἑτέρου, καταλείπεσθαι καὶ τῶν Τυνδαριδέων τὸν ἕτερον. πρὸ τοῦ γὰρ
δὴ καὶ οὗτοι ἀμφότεροι ἐπίκλητοί σφι ἐόντες εἵποντο. [3] τότε δὴ ἐν
τῇ Ἐλευσῖνι ὁρῶντες οἱ λοιποὶ τῶν συμμάχων τούς τε βασιλέας τῶν

Λακεδαιμονίων οὐκ ὁμολογέοντας καὶ Κορινθίους ἐκλιπόντας τὴν
τάξιν, οἴχοντο καὶ αὐτοὶ ἀπαλλασσόμενοι.

V.75.1 μελλόντων: modifies an implied Peloponnesians.   **συνάψειν:**
complementary with μελλόντων.   **Κορίνθιοι:** part of the allied forces gathered
by Kleomenes: συνέλεγε ἐκ πάσης Πελοποννήσου στρατόν.   **Κορίνθιοι**
μέν πρῶτοι: is answered by μετὰ δὲ Δημάρητος.   **αὐτοῖσι δόντες λόγον:**
part of the Korinthian narrative.   **ποιέοιεν:** optative standing for an original
indicative.   **δίκαια:** though obligated to help, they were not required to with no
exception; their reason for leaving displays a strong current in Greek culture: to
act unjustly is to incur the anger of the gods. Others suggest that the given reason
is unconvincing and think that the invasion was called off because it became
known that the Athenians had medized: the allies did not wish to invite Persian
hostilities.   **μετὰ δέ:** adverbial, "next."   **Δημάρητος:** supply an implied
μεταβάλλεταί τε καὶ ἀπαλλάσσεται.   **75.2 ἐξεῖναι:** impersonal and introduced by
ἐτέθη νόμος.   **ἔπεσθαι:** complementary with ἐξεῖναι.   **τοὺς βασιλέας:** subject
of ἔπεσθαι.   **τέως:** a temporal marker for Herodotus's audience.   **τούτων:**
refers back to the two kings and is partitive with τοῦ ἑτέρου.   **Τυνδαριδέων:**
partitive with τὸν ἕτερον. The Spartan kings are referred to as the sons of Tyndareos
because Kastor and Polydeukes, raised in Sparta and to immortality, represent
for the Spartans the tradition of dual kingship. Their images would be taken on
campaign as talismans.   **καταλείπεσθαι:** main verb in indirect statement.   **τὸν**
ἕτερον: subject of καταλείπεσθαι.   **πρὸ τοῦ:** substantive, "previously."   **75.3**
τότε δή: indicates a return to Herodotus's main narrative.   **οἱ λοιποί:**
substantive, "the rest."   **τῶν συμμάχων:** partitive with οἱ λοιποί.   **τε ... καί:**
links βασιλέας and Κορινθίους.

～

V.76.1 τέταρτον δὴ τοῦτο ἐπὶ τὴν Ἀττικὴν ἀπικόμενοι Δωριέες, δίς τε
ἐπὶ πολέμῳ ἐσβαλόντες καὶ δὶς ἐπ᾽ ἀγαθῷ τοῦ πλήθεος τοῦ Ἀθηναίων.
πρῶτον μὲν ὅτε καὶ Μέγαρα κατοίκισαν. οὗτος ὁ στόλος ἐπὶ Κόδρου
βασιλεύοντος Ἀθηναίων ὀρθῶς ἂν καλέοιτο. δεύτερον δὲ καὶ τρίτον
ὅτε ἐπὶ Πεισιστρατιδέων ἐξέλασιν ὁρμηθέντες ἐκ Σπάρτης ἀπίκοντο.
τέταρτον δὲ τότε ὅτε ἐς Ἐλευσῖνα Κλεομένης ἄγων Πελοποννησίους
ἐσέβαλε. οὕτω τέταρτον τότε Δωριέες ἐσέβαλον ἐς Ἀθήνας.

V.76.1 τέταρτον δὴ τοῦτο: substantive, "for the fourth time." In chapter 19 of
Book IX, the Spartans arrive at Eleusis on their way to fight the Persians at Plataia.
Herodotus's contemporary audience is well aware of continued Dorian aggression
against the Ionians. In 446 and 431 B.C.E., the Spartans invade Athens. In later

years the attacks continue. **Δωριέες:** there are four main tribes of Hellas: Dorian, Aiolian, Akhaian, and Ionian. Herodotus notes that the Ionians are the weakest and of least repute of the Hellenes, with Athens being the only Ionian city of significance (I.143). The Skythians view the Ionians as cowards (IV.142). **ἐπ' ἀγαθῷ:** substantive, "for the welfare." **πρῶτον μέν:** is answered by δεύτερον δὲ καὶ τρίτον and τέταρτον δέ; supply an implied ἦν. **οὗτος ὁ στόλος:** refers back to the founding of Megara. **ἐπί:** temporal. **ἂν καλέοιτο:** a potential optative, indicating Herodotus's assertion that this is the correct temporal designation. **δεύτερον δὲ καὶ τρίτον:** substantive, "the second and third times"; supply an implied ἦν. These are the two that are ἐπ' ἀγαθῷ τοῦ πλήθεος τοῦ Ἀθηναίων. **τέταρτον δέ:** substantive, "the fourth"; supply an implied ἦν.

V.77.1 διαλυθέντος ὦν τοῦ στόλου τούτου ἀκλεῶς, ἐνθαῦτα Ἀθηναῖοι, τίνυσθαι βουλόμενοι, πρῶτα στρατηίην ποιεῦνται ἐπὶ Χαλκιδέας. Βοιωτοὶ δὲ τοῖσι Χαλκιδεῦσι βοηθέουσι ἐπὶ τὸν Εὔριπον. Ἀθηναίοισι δὲ ἰδοῦσι τοὺς Βοιωτοὺς ἔδοξε πρότερον τοῖσι Βοιωτοῖσι ἢ τοῖσι Χαλκιδεῦσι ἐπιχειρέειν. [2] συμβάλλουσί τε δὴ τοῖσι Βοιωτοῖσι οἱ Ἀθηναῖοι καὶ πολλῷ ἐκράτησαν, κάρτα δὲ πολλοὺς φονεύσαντες, ἑπτακοσίους αὐτῶν ἐζώγρησαν. τῆς δὲ αὐτῆς ταύτης ἡμέρης οἱ Ἀθηναῖοι, διαβάντες ἐς τὴν Εὔβοιαν, συμβάλλουσι καὶ τοῖσι Χαλκιδεῦσι. νικήσαντες δὲ καὶ τούτους, τετρακισχιλίους κληρούχους ἐπὶ τῶν ἱπποβοτέων τῇ χώρῃ λείπουσι. οἱ δὲ ἱπποβόται ἐκαλέοντο οἱ παχέες τῶν Χαλκιδέων. [3] ὅσους δὲ καὶ τούτων ἐζώγρησαν, ἅμα τοῖσι Βοιωτῶν ἐζωγρημένοισι, εἶχον ἐν φυλακῇ, ἐς πέδας δήσαντες. χρόνῳ δὲ ἔλυσαν σφέας, δίμνεως ἀποτιμησάμενοι. τὰς δὲ πέδας αὐτῶν, ἐν τῇσι ἐδεδέατο, ἀνεκρέμασαν ἐς τὴν ἀκρόπολιν, αἵ περ ἔτι καὶ ἐς ἐμὲ ἦσαν περιεοῦσαι, κρεμάμεναι ἐκ τειχέων περιπεφλευσμένων πυρὶ ὑπὸ τοῦ Μήδου, ἀντίον δὲ τοῦ μεγάρου τοῦ πρὸς ἑσπέρην τετραμμένου. [4] καὶ τῶν λύτρων τὴν δεκάτην ἀνέθηκαν, ποιησάμενοι τέθριππον χάλκεον, τὸ δὲ ἀριστερῆς χειρὸς ἕστηκε πρῶτον ἐσιόντι ἐς τὰ προπύλαια τὰ ἐν τῇ ἀκροπόλι. ἐπιγέγραπται δέ οἱ τάδε·

> ἔθνεα Βοιωτῶν καὶ Χαλκιδέων δαμάσαντες
>   παῖδες Ἀθηναίων ἔργμασιν ἐν πολέμου,
> δεσμῷ ἐν ἀχλυόεντι σιδηρέῳ ἔσβεσαν ὕβριν·
>   τῶν ἵππους δεκάτην Παλλάδι τάσδ' ἔθεσαν.

V.77.1 τίνυσθαι: complementary with βουλόμενοι.　Ἀθηναίοισι: to perform the action of ἐπιχειρέειν.　ἥ: translate with πρότερον.　ἐπιχειρέειν: complementary with ἔδοξε.　**77.2 τε ... καί:** connects συμβάλλουσι and ἐκράτησαν.　αὐτῶν: partitive with ἑπτακοσίους.　τετρακισχιλίους κληρούχους: this was a way to enfranchise Athens' poor, who retained Athenian citizenship and were still subject to military and naval service.　ἐπὶ τῶν ἱπποβοτέων: the Athenians take from the wealthy of the Khalkideans.　τῶν Χαλκιδέων: partitive with οἱ παχέες.　**77.3 τούτων:** partitive with ὅσους.　τοῖσι ... ἐζωγρημένοισι: substantive, "those captured."　Βοιωτῶν: partitive with ἐζωγρημένοισι.　δίμνεως ἀποτιμησάμενοι: toward the end of the fifth century B.C.E., a rower on an Athenian warship earned a drachma a day. There are 100 drachmas in a mina.　ἐν τῆσι = ἐν αἷς.　ἐς ἐμέ: temporal.　ὑπὸ τοῦ Μήδου: see VIII.51–55.　**77.4 τῶν λύτρων:** partitive with τὴν δεκάτην.　τὸ δέ = ὃ δέ.　ἀριστερῆς χειρός: "on the left," a genitive denoting place.　ἐσιόντι: the participle modifies a hypothetical visitor and possesses χειρός, "of one entering."　οἱ = αὐτῷ: object of the prefix ἐπι- of ἐπιγέγραπται.　ἔργμασιν ἐν: the object precedes its preposition.　τῶν = ὧν: translate with δεκάτην as "a tenth of which things."　δεκάτην: in apposition with ἵππους. The dedication is made in about 505 B.C.E.; the Persians attack and burn Athens in 480 B.C.E.

～

V.78.1 Ἀθηναῖοι μέν νυν ηὔξηντο. δηλοῖ δὲ οὐ κατ' ἓν μοῦνον ἀλλὰ πανταχῇ ἡ ἰσηγορίη ὡς ἔστι χρῆμα σπουδαῖον, εἰ καὶ Ἀθηναῖοι, τυραννευόμενοι μέν, οὐδαμῶν τῶν σφέας περιοικεόντων ἦσαν τὰ πολέμια ἀμείνους, ἀπαλλαχθέντες δὲ τυράννων, μακρῷ πρῶτοι ἐγένοντο. δηλοῖ ὧν ταῦτα ὅτι, κατεχόμενοι μέν, ἐθελοκάκεον ὡς δεσπότῃ ἐργαζόμενοι, ἐλευθερωθέντων δέ, αὐτὸς ἕκαστος ἑωυτῷ προεθυμέετο κατεργάζεσθαι.

V.78.1 Ἀθηναῖοι μέν νυν: is answered, it seems, by Θηβαῖοι δὲ μετὰ ταῦτα from chapter 79.1.　δηλοῖ δέ: Herodotus offers his analysis of what makes human beings excel.　κατ' ἓν μοῦνον: substantive, "in one way."　ἡ ἰσηγορίη ὡς ἔστι: in English the word order would be ὡς ἡ ἰσηγορίη ἔστι. In the *Iliad*, status is established by fighting prowess, by intellect, and by lineage. Of the three, we read in Greek lyric poetry of the eighth century B.C.E. poems attacking lineage's privilege. In Athens, once the Peisistratids are expelled, though wealth and nobility remain influential, Kleisthenes extends the reach of ἰσηγορίη beyond the barriers of birthright. As a result, Herodotus sees Athens become stronger than it ever was. Note that the standard by which Herodotus judges excellence is martial excellence.　χρῆμα σπουδαῖον: in Herodotus's day, the best form of government was a hot topic. Here Herodotus makes clear that freedom from tyranny is desirable but does not state a preference beyond this. Thoukydides writes that during the rule of the five thousand, Athens is governed best (8.97). In the *Republic* Plato prefers an aristocracy, ruled by philosopher-kings. Aristotle argues for a mixed constitution and a strong middle class, noting that polarization of wealth leads to civic unrest (*Politics*).   **τυραννευόμενοι μέν**: is answered by ἀπαλλαχθέντες δέ.   **τῶν σφέας περιοικεόντων**: substantive, "those dwelling around them"; translate with ἀμείνους.   **τὰ πολέμια**: accusative of respect, "in things of war."   **κατεχόμενοι μέν**: is answered by ἐλευθερωθέντων δέ.   **ἐλευθερωθέντων**: substantive, modifying an implied Ἀθηναίων, "once freed."   **κατεργάζεσθαι**: complementary with προεθυμέετο.

~

V.79.1 οὗτοι μέν νυν ταῦτα ἔπρησσον. Θηβαῖοι δὲ μετὰ ταῦτα ἐς θεὸν ἔπεμπον, βουλόμενοι τίσασθαι Ἀθηναίους. ἡ δὲ Πυθίη ἀπὸ σφέων μὲν αὐτῶν οὐκ ἔφη αὐτοῖσι εἶναι τίσιν. ἐς πολύφημον δὲ ἐξενείκαντας ἐκέλευε τῶν ἄγχιστα δέεσθαι. [2] ἀπελθόντων ὦν τῶν θεοπρόπων, ἐξέφερον τὸ χρηστήριον, ἁλίην ποιησάμενοι. ὡς ἐπυνθάνοντο δὲ λεγόντων αὐτῶν τῶν ἄγχιστα δέεσθαι, εἶπαν οἱ Θηβαῖοι ἀκούσαντες τούτων· Οὐκ ὦν ἄγχιστα ἡμέων οἰκέουσι Ταναγραῖοί τε καὶ Κορωναῖοι καὶ Θεσπιέες; καὶ οὗτοί γε, ἅμα ἡμῖν αἰεὶ μαχόμενοι, προθύμως συνδιαφέρουσι τὸν πόλεμον. τί δεῖ τούτων γε δέεσθαι; ἀλλὰ μᾶλλον μὴ οὐ τοῦτο ᾖ τὸ χρηστήριον.

V.79.1 **οὗτοι μέν νυν**: refers back to Ἀθηναῖοι μέν νυν from chapter 78.1 and is answered by Θηβαῖοι δέ.   **μετὰ ταῦτα**: refers back to their defeat by the Athenians (77).   **τίσασθαι**: complementary with βουλόμενοι; Thebes is the leading city among the just-defeated Boiotians. Much of this section is presented from the Thebans' perspective.   **ἀπὸ σφέων μέν**: is answered by ἐς πολύφημον δὲ ἐξενείκαντας.   **εἶναι**: main verb in indirect statement.   **τίσιν**: subject of εἶναι.   **ἐξενείκαντας**: modifies an implied Θηβαίους and subject of δέεσθαι.   **τῶν ἄγχιστα**: substantive, "those closest."   **79.2 τῶν ἄγχιστα**: substantive; see previous.   **δέεσθαι**: the subject is the same as the subject of ἐπυνθάνοντο.   **οὗτοι**: refers back to the three peoples just mentioned.   **δέεσθαι**: complementary with δεῖ.   **μὴ οὐ ... ᾖ**: a hypothetical subjunctive expressing doubt.

~

V.80.1 τοιαῦτα ἐπιλεγομένων, εἶπε δή κοτε μαθών τις· Ἐγώ μοι δοκέω συνιέναι τὸ θέλει λέγειν ἡμῖν τὸ μαντήιον. Ἀσωποῦ λέγονται γενέσθαι

θυγατέρες Θήβη τε καὶ Αἴγινα· τουτέων ἀδελφεῶν ἐουσέων, δοκέω
ἡμῖν Αἰγινητέων δέεσθαι τὸν θεὸν χρῆσαι τιμωρητήρων γενέσθαι.
[2] καὶ οὐ γάρ τις ταύτης ἀμείνων γνώμη ἐδόκεε φαίνεσθαι. αὐτίκα
πέμψαντες ἐδέοντο Αἰγινητέων, ἐπικαλεόμενοι κατὰ τὸ χρηστήριόν,
σφι βοηθέειν, ὡς ἐόντων ἀγχίστων. οἱ δέ σφι αἰτέουσι ἐπικουρίην τοὺς
Αἰακίδας συμπέμπειν ἔφασαν.

V.80.1 Ἐγώ μοι δοκέω: English prefers the impersonal: "it seems to me."　**μαθών
τις:** cataloguing examples of the one mind who solves the riddle, Hornblower
(2013) views this as not history but clever Herodotean storytelling. Hornblower
notwithstanding, history is replete with the perspicuity of clever souls who see what
others do not.　**συνιέναι:** complementary with δοκέω.　**τὸ θέλει = τοῦτο ὃ
θέλει:** the antecedent τοῦτο has dropped out, and τό serves as the object of συνιέναι
and of λέγειν.　**λέγειν:** complementary with θέλει.　**Ἀσωποῦ:** a river god and
father of Aigina and Thebe.　**γενέσθαι:** complementary with λέγονται.　**ἡμῖν:**
to perform the action of δέεσθαι.　**Αἰγινητέων:** subject of γενέσθαι; so
begins the backstory of fighting between the Athenians and the Aiginetans. As
Herodotus's *Histories* unfold, the Athenians and Aiginetans will play crucial
roles in defeating the Persians. The Boiotians medize.　**δέεσθαι:** dependent
on χρῆσαι.　**τὸν θεόν:** subject of χρῆσαι.　**χρῆσαι:** main verb in indirect
statement.　**τιμωρητήρων:** predicate to Αἰγινητέων.　**γενέσθαι:** dependent on
δέεσθαι.　**80.2 ταύτης:** translate with ἀμείνων.　**φαίνεσθαι:** complementary
with ἐδόκεε.　**Αἰγινητέων:** to perform the action of βοηθέειν.　**βοηθέειν:**
dependent on ἐδέοντο.　**αἰτέουσι:** the forms of the finite verb and participle are
look-alikes.　**ἐπικουρίην:** predicate to τοὺς Αἰακίδας.　**τοὺς Αἰακίδας:** the
images of Aiakos's sons, probably Telamon and Peleus.　**συμπέμπειν:** main verb
in indirect statement; the subject is the same as the subject of ἔφασαν.

V.81.1 πειρησαμένων δὲ τῶν Θηβαίων κατὰ τὴν συμμαχίην τῶν
Αἰακιδέων καὶ τρηχέως περιεφθέντων ὑπὸ τῶν Ἀθηναίων, αὖτις οἱ
Θηβαῖοι πέμψαντες τοὺς μὲν Αἰακίδας σφι ἀπεδίδοσαν, τῶν δὲ ἀνδρῶν
ἐδέοντο. [2] Αἰγινῆται δέ, εὐδαιμονίῃ τε μεγάλῃ ἐπαερθέντες καὶ
ἔχθρης παλαιῆς ἀναμνησθέντες ἐχούσης ἐς Ἀθηναίους, τότε, Θηβαίων
δεηθέντων, πόλεμον ἀκήρυκτον Ἀθηναίοισι ἐπέφερον. [3] ἐπικειμένων
γὰρ αὐτῶν Βοιωτοῖσι, ἐπιπλώσαντες μακρῇσι νηυσὶ ἐς τὴν Ἀττικήν,
κατὰ μέν, ἔσυραν Φάληρον, κατὰ δέ, τῆς ἄλλης παραλίης πολλοὺς
δήμους. ποιεῦντες δὲ ταῦτα μεγάλως Ἀθηναίους ἐσίνοντο.

V.81.1 πειρησαμένων δὲ τῶν Θηβαίων: often in conjunction with a complementary infinitive, here the participle means that the Thebans gave it a go and attacked the Athenians.   **οἱ Θηβαῖοι:** Greek syntax allows for the subject of the genitive absolute also to be the subject of the main verb.   **τοὺς μὲν Αἰακίδας:** is answered by τῶν δὲ ἀνδρῶν.   **τῶν δὲ ἀνδρῶν ἐδέοντο:** i.e., not the statues (80.2).   **81.2 εὐδαιμονίη τε μεγάλῃ:** the wealth of Aigina rested in its trade; for the theme of great fortune in Herodotus, see the stories of Kyros (I.210) and Polykrates (III.125).   **ἔχθρης παλαιῆς:** the reason is explained in chapter 82 below.   **πόλεμον ἀκήρυκτον:** war was customarily announced by heralds. Not bothering to do so could bring down the wrath of the gods. See also Thoukydides 1.146 and 2.1.   **Ἀθηναίοισι:** object of the prefix ἐπι- of ἐπέφερον.   **81.3 ἐπικειμένων:** modifies an implied Ἀθηναίων.   **κατὰ μέν ... κατὰ δέ:** "first ... second."   **ἔσυραν Φάληρον:** the date is about 504 B.C.E.

~

V.82.1 ἡ δὲ ἔχθρη ἡ προοφειλομένη ἐς Ἀθηναίους ἐκ τῶν Αἰγινητέων ἐγένετο ἐξ ἀρχῆς τοιῆσδε. Ἐπιδαυρίοισι ἡ γῆ καρπὸν οὐδένα ἀνεδίδου. περὶ ταύτης ὦν τῆς συμφορῆς οἱ Ἐπιδαύριοι ἐχρέωντο ἐν Δελφοῖσι. ἡ δὲ Πυθίη σφέας ἐκέλευε Δαμίης τε καὶ Αὐξησίης ἀγάλματα ἱδρύσασθαι καί σφι ἱδρυσαμένοισι ἄμεινον συνοίσεσθαι. [2] ἐπειρώτεον ὦν οἱ Ἐπιδαύριοι κότερα χαλκοῦ ποιέωνται τὰ ἀγάλματα ἢ λίθου. ἡ δὲ Πυθίη οὐδέτερα τούτων ἔα, ἀλλὰ ξύλου ἡμέρης ἐλαίης. ἐδέοντο ὦν οἱ Ἐπιδαύριοι Ἀθηναίων ἐλαίην σφι δοῦναι ταμέσθαι, ἱρωτάτας δὴ κείνας νομίζοντες εἶναι. λέγεται δὲ καὶ ὡς ἐλαῖαι ἦσαν ἄλλοθι γῆς οὐδαμοῦ κατὰ χρόνον ἐκεῖνον ἢ ἐν Ἀθήνῃσι. [3] οἱ δὲ ἐπὶ τοῖσιδε δώσειν ἔφασαν, ἐπ᾽ ᾧ ἀπάξουσι ἔτεος ἑκάστου τῇ Ἀθηναίῃ τε τῇ Πολιάδι ἱρὰ καὶ τῷ Ἐρεχθέι. καταινέσαντες δὲ ἐπὶ τούτοισι, οἱ Ἐπιδαύριοι τῶν τε ἐδέοντο ἔτυχον καὶ ἀγάλματα ἐκ τῶν ἐλαιέων τουτέων ποιησάμενοι ἱδρύσαντο. καὶ ἥ τε γῆ σφι ἔφερε καρπὸν καὶ Ἀθηναίοισι ἐπετέλεον τὰ συνέθεντο.

V.82.1 ἐξ ἀρχῆς τοιῆσδε: refers back to the previous explanation.   **σφέας:** subject of ἱδρύσασθαι.   **Δαμίης τε καὶ Αὐξησίης:** both deities are concerned with the bounty of the earth.   **ἱδρύσασθαι:** dependent on ἐκέλευε.   **ἄμεινον:** translate with συνοίσεσθαι.   **συνοίσεσθαι:** main verb in indirect statement; impersonal, "it would go."   **82.2 ποιέωνται:** a deliberative subjunctive.   **τούτων:** partitive with οὐδέτερα.   **Ἀθηναίων:** to perform the action of δοῦναι.   **σφι:** to perform the action of ταμέσθαι.   **δοῦναι:** dependent on ἐδέοντο.   **ταμέσθαι:** purpose.   **κείνας:** subject of εἶναι.   **εἶναι:** main verb in indirect statement. **λέγεται:** impersonal. **82.3 ἐπὶ τοῖσιδε:** substantive, "on the following terms." **δώσειν:** main verb in indirect statement; the subject is the same as the subject of ἔφασαν. **ἐπ' ᾧ:** "on condition that." **τε … καί:** links τῇ Ἀθηναίῃ and τῷ Ἐρεχθέι. **τῇ Πολιάδι:** Athene Polias is the protectress of Athens. **ἐπὶ τούτοισι:** refers back to the conditions. **τῶν τε ἐδέοντο ἔτυχον = τούτων, ὧν τε ἐδέοντο, ἔτυχον:** the antecedent τούτων has dropped out, and τῶν serves as the object of ἐδέοντο and ἔτυχον. **τὰ συνέθεντο = ταῦτα ἃ συνέθεντο:** the antecedent ταῦτα has dropped out, and τά serves as the object of ἐπετέλεον and συνέθεντο.

~

V.83.1 τοῦτον δ' ἔτι τὸν χρόνον καὶ πρὸ τοῦ Αἰγινῆται Ἐπιδαυρίων ἤκουον τά τε ἄλλα καὶ δίκας· διαβαίνοντες ἐς Ἐπίδαυρον ἐδίδοσάν τε καὶ ἐλάμβανον παρ' ἀλλήλων οἱ Αἰγινῆται. τὸ δὲ ἀπὸ τοῦδε νέας τε πηξάμενοι καὶ ἀγνωμοσύνῃ χρησάμενοι ἀπέστησαν ἀπὸ τῶν Ἐπιδαυρίων. [2] ἅτε δὲ ἐόντες διάφοροι, ἐδηλέοντο αὐτούς, ὥστε θαλασσοκράτορες ἐόντες, καὶ δὴ καὶ τὰ ἀγάλματα ταῦτα τῆς τε Δαμίης καὶ τῆς Αὐξησίης ὑπαιρέονται αὐτῶν. καί σφεα ἐκόμισάν τε καὶ ἱδρύσαντο τῆς σφετέρης χώρης ἐς τὴν μεσόγαιαν, τῇ Οἴῃ μὲν ἐστὶ οὔνομα. στάδια δὲ μάλιστά κῃ ἀπὸ τῆς πόλιος ὡς εἴκοσι ἀπέχει. [3] ἱδρυσάμενοι δὲ ἐν τούτῳ τῷ χώρῳ θυσίῃσί τε σφέα καὶ χοροῖσι γυναικηίοισι κερτομίοισι ἱλάσκοντο, χορηγῶν ἀποδεικνυμένων ἑκατέρῃ τῶν δαιμόνων δέκα ἀνδρῶν. κακῶς δὲ ἠγόρευον οἱ χοροὶ ἄνδρα μὲν οὐδένα, τὰς δὲ ἐπιχωρίας γυναῖκας. ἦσαν δὲ καὶ τοῖσι Ἐπιδαυρίοισι αἱ αὐταὶ ἱροεργίαι· εἰσὶ δέ σφι καὶ ἄρρητοι ἱρουργίαι.

V.83.1 καὶ πρὸ τοῦ: temporal, "and before"; the time period under discussion is probably about 650 B.C.E. **Αἰγινῆται Ἐπιδαυρίων ἤκουον:** Dorians from Epidauros colonized Aigina (Pausanias, *Korinthiaka* 29.5). **τά τε ἄλλα καὶ δίκας:** accusatives of respect; τε introduces the general and καί the specific. **ἐδίδοσάν τε καὶ ἐλάμβανον:** supply an implied δίκας. **τὸ δὲ ἀπὸ τοῦδε:** substantive, "during the time after this." **83.2 ἅτε δὲ ἐόντες διάφοροι:** ἅτε (and οἷα) is typically found with a participle in the nominative or accusative case. Use "since" or "because" to translate it, and turn the participle into a finite verb. Thus, ἅτε αὐτὸν ὄντα καλόν (ἅτε ὢν καλός): "since he was good." **ἐδηλέοντο αὐτούς:** the imperfect stresses the repetitive aspect of their plundering. **θαλασσοκράτορες ἐόντες:** from which comes their wealth; in the ancient thalassocracy lists, the Aiginetans are the seventeenth and last one, reigning from 490 to 480 B.C.E.

(Diodorus, from Eusebius, 7 fr. 11). **καὶ δὴ καὶ … ὑπαιρέονται:** gives a specific example of their plundering. **τῇ = ᾗ:** possesses οὔνομα. **Οἵη μέν:** is answered by στάδια δέ. **στάδια δὲ μάλιστα … ὡς εἴκοσι:** about two miles. **ἀπέχει:** as subject supply an implied Οἵη. **83.3 χοροῖσι γυναικηίοισι κερτομίοισι:** propitiary rites of abuse are apotropaic and designed to maintain the prosperity these fertility and earth goddesses promise. **τῶν δαιμόνων:** partitive with ἑκατέρῃ. **ἄνδρα μέν:** is answered by τὰς δέ. **γυναῖκας:** supply an implied κακῶς δὲ ἠγόρευον.

~

V.84.1 κλεφθέντων δὲ τῶνδε τῶν ἀγαλμάτων, οἱ Ἐπιδαύριοι τοῖσι Ἀθηναίοισι τὰ συνέθεντο οὐκ ἐπετέλεον. πέμψαντες δέ, οἱ Ἀθηναῖοι ἐμήνιον τοῖσι Ἐπιδαυρίοισι. οἱ δὲ ἀπέφαινον λόγῳ ὡς οὐκ ἀδικέοιεν· ὅσον μὲν γὰρ χρόνον εἶχον τὰ ἀγάλματα ἐν τῇ χώρῃ, ἐπιτελέειν τὰ συνέθεντο. ἐπεὶ δὲ ἐστερῆσθαι αὐτῶν, οὐ δίκαιον εἶναι ἀποφέρειν ἔτι. ἀλλὰ τοὺς ἔχοντας αὐτά, Αἰγινήτας, πρήσσεσθαι ἐκέλευον. [2] πρὸς ταῦτα οἱ Ἀθηναῖοι, ἐς Αἴγιναν πέμψαντες, ἀπαίτεον τὰ ἀγάλματα. οἱ δὲ Αἰγινῆται ἔφασαν σφίσι τε καὶ Ἀθηναίοισι εἶναι οὐδὲν πρῆγμα.

V.84.1 τὰ συνέθεντο οὐκ ἐπετέλεον = ταῦτα ἃ συνέθεντο οὐκ ἐπετέλεον: the antecedent ταῦτα has dropped out, and τά serves as the object of συνέθεντο and ἐπετέλεον. **πέμψαντες:** supply an implied ἄγγελον. **οἱ δὲ ἀπέφαινον:** as the story unfolds, three different perspectives are offered: the Athenians', the Epidaurians', and the Aiginetans'. **ἀδικέοιεν:** the optative stands for an original indicative; note the presence of οὐ, the negative for statements of fact. **ἐπιτελέειν … ἐστερῆσθαι:** main verbs in indirect statement; the subject is the same as the subject of ἀπέφαινον. **ἐπιτελέειν τὰ συνέθεντο = ἐπιτελέειν ταῦτα ἃ συνέθεντο:** the antecedent ταῦτα has dropped out, and τά serves as the object of ἐπιτελέειν and συνέθεντο. **δίκαιον:** impersonal and subject of εἶναι. **εἶναι:** main verb in indirect statement. **ἀποφέρειν:** epexegetical with δίκαιον; as subject supply an implied αὐτούς. **τοὺς ἔχοντας αὐτά:** substantive, "those in possession of them"; subject of πρήσσεσθαι. **Αἰγινήτας:** in apposition with τοὺς ἔχοντας αὐτά. **πρήσσεσθαι:** dependent on ἐκέλευον; supply an implied τὰ συνέθεντο. **84.2 πρὸς ταῦτα:** refers back to what the Epidaurians just said. **εἶναι:** main verb in indirect statement. **πρῆγμα:** subject of εἶναι.

~

V.85.1 Ἀθηναῖοι μέν νυν λέγουσι μετὰ τὴν ἀπαίτησιν ἀποσταλῆναι τριήρεϊ μιῇ τῶν ἀστῶν τούτους οἵ, ἀποπεμφθέντες ἀπὸ τοῦ κοινοῦ καὶ

ἀπικόμενοι ἐς Αἴγιναν, τὰ ἀγάλματα ταῦτα, ὡς σφετέρων ξύλων ἐόντα,
ἐπειρῶντο ἐκ τῶν βάθρων ἐξανασπᾶν, ἵνα σφέα ἀνακομίσωνται. [2]
οὐ δυναμένους δὲ τούτῳ τῷ τρόπῳ αὐτῶν κρατῆσαι, περιβαλόντας
σχοινία ἕλκειν τὰ ἀγάλματα. καί σφι ἕλκουσι βροντήν τε καὶ ἅμα τῇ
βροντῇ σεισμὸν ἐπιγενέσθαι. τοὺς δὲ τριηρίτας τοὺς ἕλκοντας ὑπὸ
τούτων ἀλλοφρονῆσαι. παθόντας δὲ τοῦτο κτείνειν ἀλλήλους ἅτε
πολεμίους, ἐς ὃ ἐκ πάντων ἕνα λειφθέντα ἀνακομισθῆναι αὐτὸν ἐς
Φάληρον.

V.85.1 Ἀθηναῖοι μέν νυν: is answered by Αἰγινῆται δέ from chapter 86.1.
This paragraph offers the Athenian version; the next offers the Aiginetan
version.   **τῶν ἀστῶν:** partitive with τούτους.   **ἀποσταλῆναι:** main verb in
indirect statement.   **τούτους:** subject of ἀποσταλῆναι.   **ἀπὸ τοῦ κοινοῦ:**
agency.   **ἐξανασπᾶν:** complementary with ἐπειρῶντο.   **ἀνακομίσωνται:**
a hypothetical subjunctive indicating the Athenians' reason for sending the
trireme.   **85.2 οὐ δυναμένους ... περιβαλόντας:** substantive modifying
an implied ἄνδρας and subject of ἕλκειν.   **κρατῆσαι:** complementary with
δυναμένους.   **ἕλκειν:** main verb in indirect statement.   **σφι:** object of
the prefix ἐπι- of ἐπιγενέσθαι.   **ἕλκουσι:** the dative plural masculine and
neuter participle is identical to the third-person plural present indicative
active.   **βροντήν ... σεισμόν:** subjects of ἐπιγενέσθαι.   **ἐπιγενέσθαι:** main
verb in indirect statement.   **τοὺς δὲ τριηρίτας:** subject of ἀλλοφρονῆσαι and
κτείνειν.   **ὑπὸ τούτων:** refers back to βροντή and σεισμός.   **τοῦτο:** refers
back to the loss of sanity.   **ἐς ὃ:** temporal, "until."   **ἐκ πάντων:** translate with
ἕνα.   **ἕνα:** subject of ἀνακομισθῆναι.

V.86.1 Ἀθηναῖοι μὲν οὕτω γενέσθαι λέγουσι. Αἰγινῆται δὲ οὐ μιῇ νηὶ
ἀπικέσθαι Ἀθηναίους—μίαν μὲν γὰρ καὶ ὀλίγῳ πλεῦνας μιῆς, καὶ
εἰ σφίσι μὴ ἔτυχον ἐοῦσαι νέες, ἀπαμύνεσθαι ἂν εὐπετέως—ἀλλὰ
πολλῇσι νηυσὶ ἐπιπλέειν σφίσι ἐπὶ τὴν χώρην. αὐτοὶ δέ σφι εἶξαι καὶ
οὐ ναυμαχῆσαι. [2] οὐκ ἔχουσι δὲ τοῦτο διασημῆναι ἀτρεκέως, οὔτε εἰ
ἥσσονες συγγινωσκόμενοι εἶναι τῇ ναυμαχίῃ κατὰ τοῦτο εἶξαν, οὔτε εἰ
βουλόμενοι ποιῆσαι οἷόν τι καὶ ἐποίησαν. [3] Ἀθηναίους μέν νυν, ἐπείτε
σφι οὐδεὶς ἐς μάχην κατίστατο, ἀποβάντας ἀπὸ τῶν νεῶν τραπέσθαι
πρὸς τὰ ἀγάλματα. οὐ δυναμένους δὲ ἀνασπάσαι ἐκ τῶν βάθρων
αὐτὰ οὕτω δὴ περιβαλομένους σχοινία ἕλκειν, ἐς οὗ ἑλκόμενα τὰ

ἀγάλματα ἀμφότερα τὠυτὸ ποιῆσαι. ἐμοὶ μὲν οὐ πιστὰ λέγοντες, ἄλλῳ
δὲ τεῷ, ἐς γούνατα γάρ σφι αὐτὰ πεσεῖν, καὶ τὸν ἀπὸ τούτου χρόνον
διατελέειν οὕτω ἔχοντα. [4] Ἀθηναίους μὲν δὴ ταῦτα ποιέειν· σφέας δὲ
Αἰγινῆται λέγουσι πυθομένους τοὺς Ἀθηναίους ὡς μέλλοιεν ἐπὶ σφέας
στρατεύεσθαι, ἑτοίμους Ἀργείους ποιέεσθαι. τούς τε δὴ Ἀθηναίους
ἀποβεβάναι ἐς τὴν Αἰγιναίην. καὶ παρεῖναι βοηθέοντας σφίσι τοὺς
Ἀργείους καὶ λαθεῖν τε ἐξ Ἐπιδαύρου διαβάντας ἐς τὴν νῆσον. καὶ
οὐ προακηκόόσι τοῖσι Ἀθηναίοισι ἐπιπεσεῖν ὑποταμομένους τὸ ἀπὸ
τῶν νεῶν. ἅμα τε ἐν τούτῳ τὴν βροντήν τε γενέσθαι καὶ τὸν σεισμὸν
αὐτοῖσι.

V.86.1 Ἀθηναῖοι μὲν οὕτω: repeats Ἀθηναῖοι μέν νυν from chapter 85.1 and
is answered by Αἰγινῆται δέ.   **γενέσθαι:** main verb in indirect statement;
as subject supply an implied ταῦτα.   **Αἰγινῆται δέ:** supply an implied
λέγουσι.   **ἀπικέσθαι:** main verb in indirect statement.   **Ἀθηναίους:** subject
of ἀπικέσθαι.   **μίαν μέν:** is answered by ἀλλὰ πολλῇσι νηυσί.   **ὀλίγῳ:** dative
of degree of difference.   **ἐοῦσαι:** supplementary with ἔτυχον.   **ἀπαμύνεσθαι:**
main verb in indirect statement; the subject is the same as the subject of the
implied λέγουσι.   **ἄν:** indicates that the infinitive, ἀπαμύνεσθαι, stands for an
original optative, not an original indicative.   **ἐπιπλέειν:** main verb in indirect
statement; supply an implied Ἀθηναίους as subject.   **αὐτοὶ δέ:** δέ notes a
change in subject; supply an implied λέγουσι.   **εἶξαι ... οὐ ναυμαχῆσαι:**
main verbs in indirect statement; the subject is the same as the subject of the
implied λέγουσι; οὐ is the negative for statements of fact.   **86.2 διασημῆναι:**
complementary with ἔχουσι.   **οὔτε εἰ ... οὔτε εἰ:** the main verb in each is
εἶξαν.   **εἶναι:** main verb in indirect statement; the subject is the same as the
subject of ἔχουσι.   **ποιῆσαι:** complementary with βουλόμενοι.   **οἷόν τι:**
object of ποιῆσαι and ἐποίησαν.   **86.3 Ἀθηναίους:** subject of τραπέσθαι and
the upcoming ἕλκειν.   **Ἀθηναίους μέν νυν:** is answered by οὐ δυναμένους
δέ.   **τραπέσθαι:** main verb in indirect statement.   **ἀνασπάσαι:** complementary
with δυναμένους.   **ἕλκειν:** main verb in indirect statement.   **ἐς οὗ:**
temporal, "until."   **ἀγάλματα:** subject of ποιῆσαι.   **ποιῆσαι:** main verb in
indirect statement.   **ἐμοὶ μέν:** is answered by ἄλλῳ δέ.   **οὐ πιστὰ λέγοντες:**
part of Herodotus's narrative.   **ἄλλῳ δὲ τεῷ:** supply an implied πιστὰ
λέγοντες.   **σφι:** possesses γούνατα.   **αὐτά:** subject of πεσεῖν and the upcoming
διατελέειν.   **πεσεῖν ... διατελέειν:** main verbs in indirect statement.   **ἔχοντα:**
supplementary with διατελέειν. The kneeling statue of Auge fell to her knees before
giving birth (Pausanias, *Korinthiaka* 8.48.7). If the kneeling does not indicate
childbirth, it is suggested that Damie and Auxie are kneeling as suppliants.   **86.4**
Ἀθηναίους: subject of ποιέειν.   **Ἀθηναίους μέν:** is answered by σφέας δὲ

Αἰγινῆται.   **ποιέειν:** main verb in indirect statement.   **σφέας δὲ Αἰγινῆται
λέγουσι:** σφέας is the subject of the upcomping ποιέεσθαι; typically when the
subjects of the head verb and infinitive are the same, there is not a separate subject
accusative, and all subject modifiers remain nominative. Here the two subjects are
the same, but there is still a separate subject accusative, σφέας.   **πυθομένους
τοὺς Ἀθηναίους ὡς μέλλοιεν** = πυθομένους ὡς οἱ Ἀθηναῖοι μέλλοιεν:
compare the colloquial English expression, "I asked about the game, how it
went."   **μέλλοιεν:** optative standing for an original indicative.   **στρατεύεσθαι:**
complementary with μέλλοιεν.   **ἑτοίμους:** predicate to Ἀργείους.   **ποιέεσθαι:**
main verb in indirect statement.   **τούς τε δὴ Ἀθηναίους:** subject of
ἀποβεβάναι.   **ἀποβεβάναι:** main verb in indirect statement.   **παρεῖναι...
λαθεῖν:** main verbs in indirect statement.   **τοὺς Ἀργείους:** subject of παρεῖναι,
λαθεῖν, and ἐπιπεσεῖν.   **διαβάντας:** supplementary with λαθεῖν.   **τοῖσι
Ἀθηναίοισι:** object of the prefix ἐπι- of ἐπιπεσεῖν.   **ἐπιπεσεῖν:** main verb in
indirect statement.   **ὑποταμομένους:** modifies an implied Ἀργείους.   **τὸ
ἀπὸ τῶν νεῶν:** substantive, "the area around the ships."   **τὴν βροντήν... τὸν
σεισμόν:** subjects of γενέσθαι.   **γενέσθαι:** main verb in indirect statement.

～

V.87.1 λέγεται μέν νυν ὑπ᾽ Ἀργείων τε καὶ Αἰγινητέων τάδε.
ὁμολογέεται δὲ καὶ ὑπ᾽ Ἀθηναίων ἕνα μοῦνον τὸν ἀποσωθέντα αὐτῶν
ἐς τὴν Ἀττικὴν γενέσθαι. [2] πλὴν Ἀργεῖοι μὲν λέγουσι, αὐτῶν τὸ
Ἀττικὸν στρατόπεδον διαφθειράντων, τὸν ἕνα τοῦτον περιγενέσθαι·
Ἀθηναῖοι δὲ τοῦ δαιμονίου. περιγενέσθαι μέντοι οὐδὲ τοῦτον τὸν
ἕνα, ἀλλ᾽ ἀπολέσθαι τρόπῳ τοιῷδε. κομισθεὶς ἄρα ἐς τὰς Ἀθήνας,
ἀπήγγελλε τὸ πάθος. πυθομένας δὲ τὰς γυναῖκας τῶν ἐπ᾽ Αἴγιναν
στρατευσαμένων ἀνδρῶν, δεινόν τι ποιησαμένας κεῖνον μοῦνον
ἐξ ἁπάντων σωθῆναι, πέριξ τὸν ἄνθρωπον τοῦτον λαβούσας καὶ
κεντεύσας τῇσι περόνῃσι τῶν ἱματίων εἰρωτᾶν, ἑκάστην αὐτέων, ὅκου
εἴη ὁ ἑωυτῆς ἀνήρ. [3] καὶ τοῦτον μὲν οὕτω διαφθαρῆναι. Ἀθηναίοισι
δὲ ἔτι τοῦ πάθεος δεινότερόν τι δόξαι εἶναι τὸ τῶν γυναικῶν ἔργον.
ἄλλῳ μὲν δὴ οὐκ ἔχειν ὅτεῳ ζημιώσωσι τὰς γυναῖκας. τὴν δὲ ἐσθῆτα
μετέβαλον αὐτέων ἐς τὴν Ἰάδα. ἐφόρεον γὰρ δὴ πρὸ τοῦ αἱ τῶν
Ἀθηναίων γυναῖκες ἐσθῆτα Δωρίδα, τῇ Κορινθίῃ παραπλησιωτάτην.
μετέβαλον ὦν ἐς τὸν λίνεον κιθῶνα, ἵνα δὴ περόνῃσι μὴ χρέωνται.

V.87.1 **λέγεται μέν νυν:** is answered by ὁμολογέεται δέ.   **τάδε:** often translated
in this instance as looking back to the events of the previous paragraph, τάδε

again looks forward to what comes next, specifically to the general agreement about the sole survivor. **ἕνα μοῦνον**: subject of γενέσθαι. **αὐτῶν**: partitive with ἕνα. **γενέσθαι**: main verb in indirect statement. **87.2 πλήν**: adverb, "conversely." **Ἀργεῖοι μέν**: is answered by Ἀθηναῖοι δέ. **τὸν ἕνα**: subject of περιγενέσθαι. **περιγενέσθαι**: main verb in indirect statement. **Ἀθηναῖοι δὲ τοῦ δαιμονίου** = Ἀθηναῖοι δὲ λέγουσι τὸν ἕνα τοῦτον ὑπὸ τοῦ δαιμονίου περιγενέσθαι. **περιγενέσθαι... ἀπολέσθαι**: main verbs in indirect statement. **τοῦτον τὸν ἕνα**: subject of περιγενέσθαι and ἀπολέσθαι. **τρόπῳ τοιῷδε**: looks forward to what comes next. **τὰς γυναῖκας**: the expectation is that this noun will be the subject of an upcoming infinitive; this expectation is fulfilled but is done by restating the subject of the infinitive as ἑκάστην αὐτέων, which is the subject of εἰρωτᾶν, "the women ... each one of them asked." **δεινόν**: impersonal and subject of an implied εἶναι. **κεῖνον μοῦνον**: subject of σωθῆναι. **σωθῆναι**: epexegetical with δεινόν. **εἰρωτᾶν**: main verb in indirect statement. **αὐτέων**: partitive with ἑκάστην. **εἴη**: the optative stands for an original indicative. **87.3 τοῦτον**: refers back to the sole survivor and subject of διαφθαρῆναι. **καὶ τοῦτον μέν**: is answered by Ἀθηναίοισι δέ. **οὕτω**: looks back to the description of his death. **διαφθαρῆναι**: main verb in implied indirect statement. **τοῦ πάθεος**: translate with δεινότερον. **δόξαι**: main verb in implied indirect statement. **εἶναι**: complementary with δόξαι. **τὸ τῶν γυναικῶν ἔργον**: subject of δόξαι. **ἄλλῳ μέν**: is answered by τὴν δὲ ἐσθῆτα. **ἄλλῳ μέν ... ὅτεῳ**: substantive, "in another way." **ἔχειν**: impersonal. **ζημιώσωσι**: a hypothetical subjunctive indicating their desire to punish the women. **πρὸ τοῦ**: temporal, "previously." **χρέωνται**: a hypothetical subjunctive indicating their reason for changing the dress.

~

V.88.1 ἔστι δέ, ἀληθέι λόγῳ χρεωμένοισι, οὐκ Ἰὰς αὕτη ἡ ἐσθὴς τὸ παλαιὸν ἀλλὰ Κάειρα, ἐπεὶ ἥ γε Ἑλληνικὴ ἐσθὴς πᾶσα ἡ ἀρχαίη τῶν γυναικῶν ἡ αὐτὴ ἦν τὴν νῦν Δωρίδα καλέομεν. [2] τοῖσι δὲ Ἀργείοισι καὶ τοῖσι Αἰγινήτῃσι καὶ πρὸς ταῦτα ἔτι τόδε ποιῆσαι νόμον εἶναι· παρὰ σφίσι ἑκατέροισι τὰς περόνας ἡμιολίας ποιέεσθαι τοῦ τότε κατεστεῶτος μέτρου, καὶ ἐς τὸ ἱρὸν τῶν θεῶν τουτέων περόνας μάλιστα ἀνατιθέναι τὰς γυναῖκας, Ἀττικὸν δὲ μήτε τι ἄλλο προσφέρειν πρὸς τὸ ἱρὸν μήτε κέραμον. ἀλλ᾽ ἐκ χυτρίδων ἐπιχωριέων νόμον τὸ λοιπὸν αὐτόθι εἶναι πίνειν. [3] Ἀργείων μέν νυν καὶ Αἰγινητέων αἱ γυναῖκες ἐκ τόσου κατ᾽ ἔριν τὴν Ἀθηναίων περόνας ἔτι καὶ ἐς ἐμὲ ἐφόρεον μέζονας ἢ πρὸ τοῦ.

V.88.1 χρεωμένοισι: substantive, modifying hypothetical truth-seekers, "those employing a true account."   **τὸ παλαιόν:** accusative of respect, "originally."   **ἡ αὐτὴ ἦν τὴν νῦν Δωρίδα καλέομεν = ἡ αὐτὴ ἦν ταύτῃ ἦν νῦν Δωρίδα καλέομεν:** the antecedent ταύτῃ has dropped out, and τήν functions as the word to be translated with ἡ αὐτή and the object of καλέομεν. Fabrics in general were costly and made of silk, linen, and most often wool.   **88.2 Ἀργείοισι καὶ τοῖσι Αἰγινήτῃσι:** possess νόμον.   **πρὸς ταῦτα:** refers back to the events behind the reasons for the change in dress.   **ἔτι τόδε:** looks forward to what comes next and is the object of ποιῆσαι.   **ποιῆσαι:** epexegetical with νόμον.   **νόμον:** subject of εἶναι.   **εἶναι:** infinitive in implied indirect statement.   **ποιέεσθαι … ἀνατιθέναι … προσφέρειν:** epexegetical with τόδε.   **τὰς γυναῖκας:** subject of ἀνατιθέναι.   **κέραμον:** excavations corroborate that the embargo on Athenian pottery was successful.   **νόμον:** subject of εἶναι.   **τὸ λοιπόν:** temporal, "from then on."   **πίνειν:** epexegetical with νόμον.   **Ἀργείων μέν νυν:** is answered by τῆς δὲ ἔχθρης.   **88.3 ἐκ τόσου … ἔτι καὶ ἐς ἐμέ:** ἐκ τόσου and ἐς ἐμέ establish the time frame.   **πρὸ τοῦ:** temporal, "before."

~

V.89.1 Τῆς δὲ ἔχθρης τῆς πρὸς Αἰγινήτας ἐξ Ἀθηναίων γενομένης ἀρχή, κατὰ τὰ εἴρηται, ἐγένετο. τότε δὲ Θηβαίων ἐπικαλεομένων, προθύμως τῶν περὶ τὰ ἀγάλματα γενομένων ἀναμιμνησκόμενοι, οἱ Αἰγινῆται ἐβοήθεον τοῖσι Βοιωτοῖσι. [2] Αἰγινῆταί τε δὴ ἐδηίουν τῆς Ἀττικῆς τὰ παραθαλάσσια. καὶ Ἀθηναίοισι ὁρμημένοισι ἐπ᾽ Αἰγινήτας στρατεύεσθαι ἦλθε μαντήιον ἐκ Δελφῶν· ἐπισχόντας ἀπὸ τοῦ Αἰγινητέων ἀδικίου τριήκοντα ἔτεα, τῷ ἑνὶ καὶ τριηκοστῷ, Αἰακῷ τέμενος ἀποδέξαντας, ἄρχεσθαι τοῦ πρὸς Αἰγινήτας πολέμου. καί σφι χωρήσειν τὰ βούλονται. ἢν δὲ αὐτίκα ἐπιστρατεύωνται, πολλὰ μὲν σφέας ἐν τῷ μεταξὺ τοῦ χρόνου πείσεσθαι, πολλὰ δὲ καὶ ποιήσειν, τέλος μέντοι καταστρέψεσθαι. [3] ταῦτα ὡς ἀπενειχθέντα ἤκουσαν οἱ Ἀθηναῖοι, τῷ μὲν Αἰακῷ τέμενος ἀπέδεξαν τοῦτο τὸ νῦν ἐπὶ τῆς ἀγορῆς ἵδρυται. τριήκοντα δὲ ἔτεα οὐκ ἀνέσχοντο, ἀκούσαντες ὅκως χρεὸν εἴη ἐπισχεῖν, πεπονθότας ὑπ᾽ Αἰγινητέων ἀνάρσια.

V.89.1 κατὰ τὰ εἴρηται = κατὰ ταῦτα ἃ εἴρηται: the antecedent ταῦτα has dropped out, and τά serves as the object of κατά and the subject of εἴρηται.   **τότε δέ:** marks a return back to the main narrative started in chapter 80. The time is about 498 B.C.E.   **τῶν περὶ τὰ ἀγάλματα γενομένων:** substantive, "the events concerning the statues."   **89.2 στρατεύεσθαι:** complementary with ὁρμημένοισι.   **ἐπισχόντας . . . ἀποδέξαντας:** modify an implied Ἀθηναίους, which is the subject of ἄρχεσθαι.   **ἄρχεσθαι:** dependent on ἦλθε μαντήιον ἐκ Δελφῶν, the infinitive probably stands for an original imperative.   **χωρήσειν:** dependent on ἦλθε μαντήιον ἐκ Δελφῶν.   **τὰ βούλονται = ταῦτα, ἃ βούλονται:** the antecedent ταῦτα has dropped out, and τά serves as the subject of χωρήσειν and the subject of χωρήσειν understood with βούλονται.   **ἐπιστρατεύωνται:** a hypothetical subjunctive, indicating a possible future outcome.   **πολλὰ μέν:** is answered by πολλὰ δέ.   **σφέας:** subject of πείσεσθαι, ποιήσειν, and καταστρέψεσθαι.   **ἐν τῷ μεταξὺ τοῦ χρόνου:** substantive, "in the intervening time."   **πείσεσθαι . . . ποιήσειν . . . καταστρέψεσθαι:** main verbs in indirect statement.   **89.3 ταῦτα . . . ἀπενειχθέντα:** substantive, "what was said."   **ὡς:** temporal.   **τῷ μὲν Αἰακῷ τέμενος:** recently fixed on the south side of the agora. Its location can be viewed on the Athenian agora website of the American School.   **τὸ νῦν = ὃ νῦν.**   **χρεὸν εἴη:** optative standing for an original indicative.   **ἐπισχεῖν:** complementary with χρεὸν εἴη.   **πεπονθότας:** modifies an implied Ἀθηναίους.   **ὑπ᾽ Αἰγινητέων ἀνάρσια:** forms part of the Athenian narrative.

❧

V.90.1 ἐς τιμωρίην δὲ παρασκευαζομένοισι αὐτοῖσι, ἐκ Λακεδαιμονίων πρῆγμα ἐγειρόμενον ἐμπόδιον ἐγένετο. πυθόμενοι γὰρ Λακεδαιμόνιοι τὰ ἐκ τῶν Ἀλκμεωνιδέων ἐς τὴν Πυθίην μεμηχανημένα καὶ τὰ ἐκ τῆς Πυθίης ἐπὶ σφέας τε καὶ τοὺς Πεισιστρατίδας, συμφορὴν ἐποιεῦντο διπλῆν, ὅτι τε ἄνδρας ξείνους σφίσι ἐόντας ἐξεληλάκεσαν ἐκ τῆς ἐκείνων, καὶ ὅτι, ταῦτα ποιήσασι, χάρις οὐδεμία ἐφαίνετο πρὸς Ἀθηναίων. [2] ἔτι τε πρὸς τούτοισι ἐνῆγον σφέας οἱ χρησμοί, λέγοντες πολλά τε καὶ ἀνάρσια ἔσεσθαι αὐτοῖσι ἐξ Ἀθηναίων, τῶν πρότερον μὲν ἦσαν ἀδαέες. τότε δὲ Κλεομένεος κομίσαντος ἐς Σπάρτην ἐξέμαθον. ἐκτήσατο δὲ ὁ Κλεομένης ἐκ τῆς Ἀθηναίων ἀκροπόλιος τοὺς χρησμούς, τοὺς ἔκτηντο μὲν πρότερον οἱ Πεισιστρατίδαι.

ἐξελαυνόμενοι δέ, ἔλιπον ἐν τῷ ἱρῷ. καταλειφθέντας δὲ ὁ Κλεομένης
ἀνέλαβε.

V.90.1 παρασκευαζομένοισι αὐτοῖσι: modifies an implied Ἀθηναίοις;
translate with ἐμπόδιον.   **πυθόμενοι γὰρ Λακεδαιμόνιοι:** much of this
section offers events from the Spartan perspective.   **ἐκ Λακεδαιμονίων ...
ἐκ τῶν Ἀλκμεωνιδέων ... ἐκ τῆς Πυθίης:** agency.   **τὰ ... μεμηχανημένα:**
substantive, "the things contrived."   **τὰ ἐκ τῆς Πυθίης:** supply an implied
μεμηχανημένα.   **ἐπί:** governs both σφέας and τοὺς Πεισιστρατίδας.   **τε ...
καί:** joins ὅτι and ὅτι.   **ἐκ τῆς ἐκείνων = ἐκ τῆς ἐκείνων γῆς.**   **ταῦτα:** refers
back to the Spartans' helping to rid Athens of the Peisistratids.   **ποιήσασι:**
modifies an implied Λακεδαιμονίοις.   **90.2 πρὸς τούτοισι:** refers back to
the two points just made.   **πολλά ... ἀνάρσια:** subject of ἔσεσθαι.   **τῶν
πρότερον = ὧν πρότερον:** i.e., οἱ χρησμοί.   **πρότερον μέν:** is answered by
τότε δέ.   **κομίσαντος:** supply an implied τοὺς χρησμούς.   **τοὺς ἔκτηντο
= οὓς ἔκτηντο.**   **ἔκτηντο μὲν πρότερον:** is answered by ἐξελαυνόμενοι δὲ
ἔλιπον.   **ἔλιπον:** supply an implied τοὺς χρησμούς.   **καταλειφθέντας:**
substantive, modifying an implied τοὺς χρησμούς.

～

V.91.1 τότε δὲ ὡς ἀνέλαβον οἱ Λακεδαιμόνιοι τοὺς χρησμοὺς καὶ
τοὺς Ἀθηναίους ὥρων αὐξομένους καὶ οὐδαμῶς ἑτοίμους ἐόντας
πείθεσθαι σφίσι, νόῳ λαβόντες ὡς ἐλεύθερον μὲν ἐὸν τὸ γένος
τὸ Ἀττικὸν ἰσόρροπον ἂν τῷ ἑωυτῶν γίνοιτο, κατεχόμενον δὲ ὑπὸ
τυραννίδος ἀσθενὲς καὶ πειθαρχέεσθαι ἕτοιμον—μαθόντες δὲ τούτων
ἕκαστα, μετεπέμποντο Ἱππίην τὸν Πεισιστράτου ἀπὸ Σιγείου τοῦ
ἐν Ἑλλησπόντῳ, ἐς ὃ καταφεύγουσι οἱ Πεισιστρατίδαι. [2] ἐπείτε
δέ σφι Ἱππίης καλεόμενος ἧκε, μεταπεμψάμενοι καὶ τῶν ἄλλων
συμμάχων ἀγγέλους, ἔλεγόν σφι Σπαρτιῆται τάδε· Ἄνδρες σύμμαχοι,
συγγινώσκομεν αὐτοῖσι ἡμῖν, οὐ ποιήσασι ὀρθῶς· ἐπαερθέντες γὰρ
κιβδήλοισι μαντηίοισι ἄνδρας, ξείνους ἐόντας ἡμῖν τὰ μάλιστα καὶ
ἀναδεκομένους ὑποχειρίας παρέξειν τὰς Ἀθήνας, τούτους ἐκ τῆς
πατρίδος ἐξηλάσαμεν. καὶ ἔπειτα, ποιήσαντες ταῦτα, δήμῳ ἀχαρίστῳ
παρεδώκαμεν τὴν πόλιν, ὅς, ἐπείτε δι' ἡμέας ἐλευθερωθείς, ἀνέκυψε.
ἡμέας μὲν καὶ τὸν βασιλέα ἡμέων περιυβρίσας ἐξέβαλε. δόξαν δὲ
φύσας αὐξάνεται, ὥστε ἐκμεμαθήκασι μάλιστα μὲν οἱ περίοικοι αὐτῶν,
Βοιωτοὶ καὶ Χαλκιδέες, τάχα δέ τις καὶ ἄλλος ἐκμαθήσεται ἁμαρτών.

[3] ἐπείτε δὲ ἐκεῖνα ποιήσαντες ἡμάρτομεν, νῦν πειρησόμεθα σφέας, ἅμα ὑμῖν ἀκεόμενοι, τίσασθαι· αὐτοῦ γὰρ τούτου εἵνεκεν τόνδε τε Ἱππίην μετεπεμψάμεθα καὶ ὑμέας ἀπὸ τῶν πολίων, ἵνα κοινῷ τε λόγῳ καὶ κοινῷ στόλῳ ἐσαγαγόντες αὐτὸν ἐς τὰς Ἀθήνας, ἀποδῶμεν τὰ καὶ ἀπειλόμεθα.

V.91.1 τότε δέ: about 504 B.C.E.   ὡς: temporal, governs ἀνέλαβον and ὥρων.   πείθεσθαι: epexegetical with ἑτοίμους.   νόῳ λαβόντες ὡς: governs γίνοιτο and a γίνοιτο implied with ἀσθενές . . . ἕτοιμον. The main verb in this rather long sentence is μετεπέμποντο.   ἐλεύθερον μέν: is answered by κατεχόμενον δέ.   ἰσόρροπον ἂν τῷ ἑωυτῶν: focalization often presents a nuanced view of events. For example, as we saw earlier Aristagores thinks that it will be fairly easy to restore the Naxian exiles, but the narrative does not play out the way that he predicts (30–31). That the Spartan viewpoint here (91.1), impossible for us to verify, so closely aligns with Herodotus's view that a free Athens is a very powerful Athens may be an example of the two sharing the same point of view, or it may be that Herodotus has placed these words into their speech. Even if Herodotus has embedded his own analysis into their speech, in his Pentekontaetia, the fifty year period preceding the Peloponnesian War, Thoukydides argues that Athens' rise to an imperial power leads directly to that conflict (1.23.6). And so it is true that the analysis Herodotus presents here was a typical way of analyzing the power politics of the time.   ἄν . . . γίνοιτο: a hypothetical optative, indicating a conclusion the Spartans have drawn regarding a future event.   τῷ ἑωυτῶν = τῷ ἑωυτῶν γένει.   κατεχόμενον: modifies an implied γένος.   ἀσθενές . . . ἕτοιμον: predicate to an implied ἄν . . . γίνοιτο.   πειθαρχέεσθαι: epexegetical with ἕτοιμον.   μαθόντες δέ: repeats the information from the previous dependent clauses and prepares for the long-awaited main verb μετεπέμποντο.   τούτων: partitive with ἕκαστα.   91.2 τάδε: looks forward to what comes next.   ποιήσασι: modifies αὐτοῖσι ἡμῖν.   κιβδήλοισι μαντηίοισι: the Spartans' assertion that the oracle was deceptive serves as a reminder of how politicized Delphi could be.   ἡμῖν: translate with ξείνους.   παρέξειν: complementary with ἀναδεκομένους.   τὰ μάλιστα: accusative of respect, "exceptionally."   τούτους: the direct object, ἄνδρας, is repeated by τούτους.   ταῦτα: refers back to the kicking out of their guest-friends.   δι' ἡμέας: agency.   ἡμέας μέν: is answered by δόξαν δέ.   δόξαν: accusative of respect.   φύσας: modifies δῆμος, the subject of αὐξάνεται.   ὥστε ἐκμεμαθήκασι: supply an implied ἁμαρτόντες, obtained from the upcoming ἐκμαθήσεται ἁμαρτῶν; the mistake, in each instance, consists of not realizing Athens' growing power.   οἱ περίοικοι αὐτῶν: substantive, "their neighbors."   Βοιωτοὶ καὶ Χαλκιδέες: in apposition with οἱ περίοικοι αὐτῶν.   91.3 τίσασθαι: complementary with πειρησόμεθα.   τε . . . καί: links τόνδε Ἱππίην and ὑμέας.   ἀποδῶμεν: a hypothetical subjunctive indicating the Spartans' reason for sending for Hippias and the others; supply an implied τούτῳ.   **τὰ καὶ ἀπειλόμεθα = ταῦτα ἃ καὶ ἀπειλόμεθα:** the antecedent ταῦτα has dropped out, and τά serves as the object of ἀποδῶμεν and ἀπειλόμεθα.

~

V.92.1 οἱ μὲν ταῦτα ἔλεγον· τῶν δὲ συμμάχων τὸ πλῆθος οὐκ ἐνεδέκετο τοὺς λόγους. οἱ μέν νυν ἄλλοι ἡσυχίην ἦγον· Κορίνθιος δὲ Σωσικλέης ἔλεξε τάδε·

V.92.1 οἱ μέν: is answered by τῶν δὲ συμμάχων.   **ταῦτα:** looks back to what was just said.   **τῶν δὲ συμμάχων:** partitive with τὸ πλῆθος.   **οἱ μέν νυν:** is answered by Κορίνθιος δὲ Σωσικλέης.   **τάδε:** looks forward to what comes next.

~

V.92α.1 Ἦ δὴ ὅ τε οὐρανὸς ἔνερθε ἔσται τῆς γῆς καὶ ἡ γῆ μετέωρος ὑπὲρ τοῦ οὐρανοῦ, καὶ ἄνθρωποι νομὸν ἐν θαλάσσῃ ἕξουσι καὶ ἰχθύες, τὸν πρότερον ἄνθρωποι, ὅτε γε ὑμεῖς, ὦ Λακεδαιμόνιοι, ἰσοκρατίας καταλύοντες, τυραννίδας ἐς τὰς πόλις κατάγειν παρασκευάζεσθε, τοῦ οὔτε ἀδικώτερον ἐστὶ οὐδὲν κατ᾽ ἀνθρώπους οὔτε μιαιφονώτερον. [2] εἰ γὰρ δὴ τοῦτό γε δοκέει ὑμῖν εἶναι χρηστὸν ὥστε τυραννεύεσθαι τὰς πόλις, αὐτοὶ πρῶτοι, τύραννον καταστησάμενοι παρὰ σφίσι αὐτοῖσι, οὕτω καὶ τοῖσι ἄλλοισι δίζησθε κατιστάναι. νῦν δὲ αὐτοί, τυράννων ἄπειροι ἐόντες καὶ φυλάσσοντες τοῦτο δεινότατα ἐν τῇ Σπάρτῃ μὴ γενέσθαι, παραχρᾶσθε ἐς τοὺς συμμάχους. εἰ δὲ αὐτοῦ ἔμπειροι ἔατε κατά περ ἡμεῖς, εἴχετε ἂν περὶ αὐτοῦ γνώμας ἀμείνονας συμβαλέσθαι ἤ περ νῦν.

V.92α.1 τῆς γῆς: translate with ἔνερθε.   **ἡ γῆ:** supply an implied ἔσται.   **ἰχθύες τὸν πρότερον ἄνθρωποι:** the full expression is ἰχθύες ἕξουσι ὃν πρότερον νομὸν ἄνθρωποι.   **κατάγειν:** complementary with παρασκευάζεσθε.   **τοῦ = οὗ:** translate with ἀδικώτερον and μιαιφονώτερον; the antecedent is the general act of establishing tyrannies.   **92α.2 εἶναι:** complementary with δοκέει.   **τυραννεύεσθαι:** main verb after ὥστε.   **τὰς πόλις:** subject of τυραννεύεσθαι.   **οὕτω καί:** "and then."   **δίζησθε:** imperative.   **κατιστάναι:** complementary with δίζησθε; supply an implied τύραννον.   **καταστησάμενοι:** the time is prior to πρῶτοι... δίζησθε.   **τοῦτο:** refers back to the idea of establishing tyranny; subject of γενέσθαι.   **δεινότατα:** adverbial, "most fearsomely"; translate with φυλάσσοντες.   **αὐτοῦ:** i.e., tyranny.   **κατά περ**

ἡμεῖς: the full expression is καθ᾽ ἅ περ τούτου ἡμεῖς ἔμπειροι ἐσμέν.   εἴχετε ἄν:
ἄν renders the indicative counterfactual.   συμβαλέσθαι: complementary with
εἴχετε.   ἤ περ νῦν: supply an implied συμβαλέσθαι ἔχετε.

～

V.92β.1 Κορινθίοισι γὰρ ἦν πόλιος κατάστασις τοιήδε. ἦν ὀλιγαρχίη καὶ
οὗτοι Βακχιάδαι καλεόμενοι ἔνεμον τὴν πόλιν. ἐδίδοσαν δὲ καὶ ἤγοντο
ἐξ ἀλλήλων. Ἀμφίονι δὲ ἐόντι τούτων τῶν ἀνδρῶν γίνεται θυγάτηρ
χωλή· οὔνομα δέ οἱ ἦν Λάβδα. ταύτην Βακχιαδέων γὰρ οὐδεὶς ἤθελε
γῆμαι. ἴσχει Ἠετίων ὁ Ἐχεκράτεος, δήμου μὲν ἐὼν ἐκ Πέτρης, ἀτὰρ τὰ
ἀνέκαθεν Λαπίθης τε καὶ Καινείδης. [2] ἐκ δέ οἱ ταύτης τῆς γυναικὸς
οὐδ᾽ ἐξ ἄλλης παῖδες ἐγίνοντο. ἐστάλη ὦν ἐς Δελφοὺς περὶ γόνου.
ἐσιόντα δὲ αὐτὸν ἰθέως ἡ Πυθίη προσαγορεύει τοῖσιδε τοῖσι ἔπεσι·

> Ἠετίων, οὔτις σε τίει πολύτιτον ἐόντα.
> Λάβδα κύει, τέξει δ᾽ ὀλοοίτροχον· ἐν δὲ πεσεῖται
> ἀνδράσι μουνάρχοισι, δικαιώσει δὲ Κόρινθον.

[3] ταῦτα, χρησθέντα τῷ Ἠετίωνι, ἐξαγγέλλεταί κως τοῖσι Βακχιάδησι,
τοῖσι τὸ μὲν πρότερον γενόμενον χρηστήριον ἐς Κόρινθον ἦν ἄσημον,
φέρον τε ἐς τὠυτὸ καὶ τὸ τοῦ Ἠετίωνος καὶ λέγον ὧδε·

> αἰετὸς ἐν πέτρῃσι κύει, τέξει δὲ λέοντα
> καρτερὸν ὠμηστήν· πολλῶν δ᾽ ὑπὸ γούνατα λύσει.
> ταῦτά νυν εὖ φράζεσθε, Κορίνθιοι, οἳ περὶ καλὴν
> Πειρήνην οἰκεῖτε καὶ ὀφρυόεντα Κόρινθον.

V.92β.1 τοιήδε: looks forward to what comes next.   **ἐδίδοσαν δὲ καὶ
ἤγοντο:** supply an implied ἐπιγαμίαν ("marriage").   **Ἀμφίονι:** possesses
θυγάτηρ.   **ἀνδρῶν:** partitive with Ἀμφίονι.   **οἱ = αὐτῇ:** possesses
οὔνομα.   **Βακχιαδέων:** partitive with οὐδείς.   **γῆμαι:** complementary with
ἤθελε.   **ἴσχει:** supply an implied ταύτην.   **δήμου μέν:** is answered by ἀτὰρ
τὰ ἀνέκαθεν.   **τὰ ἀνέκαθεν:** substantive, "in origin."   **92β.2 ἐκ δέ οἱ = ἐκ δὲ
αὐτῷ:** οἱ possesses γυναικός.   **ἐν δὲ πεσεῖται:** as subject supply an implied τὸ
παιδίον.   **ἀνδράσι μουνάρχοισι:** object of ἐν δέ.   **92β.3 ταῦτα:** looks back to
the oracle just stated.   **τοῖσι = οἷς.**   **τὸ μὲν πρότερον:** is answered by τότε δὲ
τὸ Ἠετίωνι from 92γ.1.   **ἐς τὠυτὸ καί = ἐς τὸ αὐτὸ καί:** "into the same place
as."   **τὸ τοῦ Ἠετίωνος:** substantive, "the prophecy of Eetion"; supply an implied
φέρει.   **πολλῶν δ᾽ ὑπὸ γούνατα λύσει = πολλῶν δ᾽ γούνατα ὑπολύσει:** the

separation of the prefix, ὑπο-, from its verb is commonly called tmesis.   ταῦτα:
refers back to the previous two lines.

~

V.92γ.1 τοῦτο μὲν δή, τοῖσι Βακχιάδῃσι πρότερον γενόμενον, ἦν
ἀτέκμαρτον· τότε δέ, τὸ Ἠετίωνι γενόμενον ὡς ἐπύθοντο, αὐτίκα
καὶ τὸ πρότερον συνῆκαν ἐὸν συνῳδὸν τῷ Ἠετίωνος. συνέντες δὲ
καὶ τοῦτο εἶχον ἐν ἡσυχίῃ, ἐθέλοντες τὸν μέλλοντα Ἠετίωνι γίνεσθαι
γόνον διαφθεῖραι. ὡς δ᾽ ἔτεκε ἡ γυνὴ τάχιστα, πέμπουσι σφέων αὐτῶν
δέκα ἐς τὸν δῆμον, ἐν τῷ κατοίκητο ὁ Ἠετίων, ἀποκτενέοντας τὸ
παιδίον. [2] ἀπικόμενοι δὲ οὗτοι ἐς τὴν Πέτρην καὶ παρελθόντες ἐς τὴν
αὐλὴν τὴν Ἠετίωνος, αἴτεον τὸ παιδίον. ἡ δὲ Λάβδα, εἰδυῖά τε οὐδὲν
τῶν εἵνεκα ἐκεῖνοι ἀπικοίατο καὶ δοκέουσα σφέας φιλοφροσύνης
τοῦ πατρὸς εἵνεκα αἰτέειν, φέρουσα ἐνεχείρισε αὐτῶν ἑνί. τοῖσι δὲ
ἄρα ἐβεβούλευτο κατ᾽ ὁδὸν τὸν πρῶτον αὐτῶν λαβόντα τὸ παιδίον
προσουδίσαι. [3] ἐπεὶ ὦν ἔδωκε φέρουσα ἡ Λάβδα, τὸν λαβόντα τῶν
ἀνδρῶν θείῃ τύχῃ προσεγέλασε τὸ παιδίον. καὶ τὸν φρασθέντα τοῦτο
οἶκτός τις ἴσχει ἀποκτεῖναι. κατοικτείρας δὲ παραδιδοῖ τῷ δευτέρῳ, ὁ
δὲ τῷ τρίτῳ. οὕτω δὴ διεξῆλθε διὰ πάντων τῶν δέκα παραδιδόμενον,
οὐδενὸς βουλομένου διεργάσασθαι. [4] ἀποδόντες ὦν ὀπίσω τῇ
τεκούσῃ τὸ παιδίον καὶ ἐξελθόντες ἔξω, ἑστεῶτες ἐπὶ τῶν θυρέων,
ἀλλήλων ἅπτοντο καταιτιώμενοι, καὶ μάλιστα τοῦ πρώτου λαβόντος
ὅτι οὐκ ἐποίησε κατὰ τὰ δεδογμένα, ἐς ὃ δή σφι, χρόνου ἐγγινομένου,
ἔδοξε αὖτις παρελθόντας πάντας τοῦ φόνου μετίσχειν.

V.92γ.1 τοῦτο μὲν δή: refers back to τὸ μὲν πρότερον χρηστήριον from 92β.3 above
and is answered by τότε δὲ τὸ Ἠετίωνι.   **τότε δὲ τὸ Ἠετίωνι γενόμενον ὡς
ἐπύθοντο** = τότε δὲ ὡς τὸ Ἠετίωνι γενόμενον ἐπύθοντο.   **τῷ Ἠετίωνος**
= τῷ Ἠετίωνος χρηστηρίῳ: translate with συνῳδόν.   **τοῦτο**: refers back
to χρηστήριον.   **γίνεσθαι**: complementary with μέλλοντα.   **διαφθεῖραι**:
complementary with ἐθέλοντες.   **σφέων αὐτῶν**: partitive with δέκα.   **δέκα**:
modifies an implied ἀνδρᾶς.   **ἐν τῷ** = ἐν ᾧ.   **ἀποκτενέοντας**: the tense shows
the reason for sending the ten men.   **92γ.2 ἀπικόμενοι δὲ οὗτοι**: the narrative
switches between the murderers and Labda. Keep in mind that Herodotus is
reporting a direct speech given by Soklees, who tells a tale secondarily narrated
by its characters.   **τε … καί**: links εἰδυῖα and δοκέουσα.   **οὐδὲν τῶν
εἵνεκα** = οὐδὲν τούτων ὧν εἵνεκα: the antecedent τούτων has dropped out,

and the relative pronoun τῶν serves as a partitive genitive with οὐδέν and is the object of εἵνεκα.   ἀπικοίατο = ἀφίκοιντο: the optative stands for an original indicative.   σφέας: subject of αἰτέειν.   αὐτῶν: partitive with ἑνί.   τοῖσι δέ: agency; as often at the start of a sentence, the article with δέ indicates a subject change. Here, because the verb is impersonal, the change in subject is conveyed via agency.   ἐβεβούλευτο: impersonal.   τὸν πρῶτον: substantive, "the first one"; it is the subject of προσουδίσαι.   αὐτῶν: partitive with τὸν πρῶτον.   προσουδίσαι: complementary with ἐβεβούλευτο.   92γ.3 ἔδωκε: supply an implied παιδίον.   τὸν λαβόντα: substantive, "the one taking."   τῶν ἀνδρῶν: partitive with τὸν λαβόντα.   θείη τύχῃ: it is unclear whether Soklees sees the divine, chance, or both at work.   τὸν φρασθέντα: substantive, "the one appointed."   τοῦτο = τὸ παιδίον.   ἀποκτεῖναι: complementary with τὸν φρασθέντα.   παραδιδοῖ = παραδίδωσι: supply an implied παιδίον.   διεξῆλθε: the subject is τὸ παιδίον.   διεργάσασθαι: complementary with βουλομένου.   92γ.4 τοῦ πρώτου λαβόντος: substantive, "the first to take hold of"; understand an implied ἅπτοντο καταιτιώμενοι.   τὰ δεδογμένα: substantive, "what had been decided."   ἐς ὅ: temporal, "until"; it marks an end to ἅπτοντο καταιτιώμενοι.   σφι: translate with ἔδοξε.   παρελθόντας: though the two do not agree in case, the participle modifies σφι; the lack of agreement between the two is typical when the noun the participle modifies is also to perform the action of an upcoming infinitive.   μετίσχειν: complementary with ἔδοξε.

⁓

V.92δ.1 ἔδει δὲ ἐκ τοῦ Ἠετίωνος γόνου Κορίνθῳ κακὰ ἀναβλαστεῖν. ἡ Λάβδα γὰρ πάντα ἤκουε, ἑστεῶσα πρὸς αὐτῇσι τῇσι θύρῃσι. δείσασα δὲ μή σφι μεταδόξῃ καὶ τὸ δεύτερον λαβόντες τὸ παιδίον ἀποκτείνωσι, φέρουσα κατακρύπτει ἐς τὸ ἀφραστότατόν οἱ ἐφαίνετο εἶναι, ἐς κυψέλην, ἐπισταμένη ὡς εἰ ὑποστρέψαντες ἐς ζήτησιν ἀπικνεοίατο, πάντα ἐρευνήσειν μέλλοιεν, τὰ δὴ καὶ ἐγίνετο. [2] ἐλθοῦσι δὲ καὶ διζημένοισι αὐτοῖσι ὡς οὐκ ἐφαίνετο, ἐδόκεε ἀπαλλάσσεσθαι καὶ λέγειν πρὸς τοὺς ἀποπέμψαντας ὡς πάντα ποιήσειαν τὰ ἐκεῖνοι ἐνετείλαντο. οἱ μὲν δὴ ἀπελθόντες ἔλεγον ταῦτα.

V.92δ.1 ἔδει: Soklees' assertion that fate was at work.   **κακά:** subject of ἀναβλαστεῖν.   **ἀναβλαστεῖν:** complementary with ἔδει.   **μεταδόξῃ:** a hypothetical subjunctive that is impersonal and expresses a possible future outcome.   **ἀποκτείνωσι:** a hypothetical subjunctive expressing a possible future outcome.   **ἐς τὸ ἀφραστότατόν οἱ ἐφαίνετο = ἐς τοῦτο ὃ ἀφραστότατόν αὐτῇ ἐφαίνετο:** the antecedent τοῦτο has dropped out, and τό serves as the object of ἐς and the subject of ἐφαίνετο.   **εἶναι:** complementary with ἐφαίνετο.   ἀπικνεοίατο = ἀφικνέοιντο: a hypothetical optative indicating a possible future outcome.   ἐρευνήσειν: complementary with μέλλοιεν.   μέλλοιεν: an optative standing for an original indicative.   τὰ δὴ καὶ ἐγίνετο = ἃ δὴ καὶ ἐγίνετο: Soklees inserts his narrative into Labda's.   92δ.2 ἀπαλλάσσεσθαι . . . λέγειν: complementary with ἐδόκεε.   τοὺς ἀποπέμψαντας: substantive, "those sending them out."   ποιήσειαν: optative standing for an original indicative.   τὰ ἐκεῖνοι ἐνετείλαντο = ἃ ἐκεῖνοι ἐνετείλαντο.   οἱ μὲν δὴ ἀπελθόντες: is answered by Ἠετίωνι δέ of chapter 92ε.   ἔλεγον ταῦτα: since the previous sentence is focalized by the ten Bakkhiadai, Soklees asserts that they actually did say what they intended to.

~

V.92ε.1 Ἠετίωνι δὲ μετὰ ταῦτα ὁ παῖς ηὐξάνετο. καί οἱ διαφυγόντι τοῦτον τὸν κίνδυνον ἀπὸ τῆς κυψέλης ἐπωνυμίην Κύψελος οὔνομα ἐτέθη. ἀνδρωθέντι δὲ καὶ μαντευομένῳ Κυψέλῳ ἐγένετο ἀμφιδέξιον χρηστήριον ἐν Δελφοῖσι, τῷ πίσυνος γενόμενος ἐπεχείρησέ τε καὶ ἔσχε Κόρινθον. ὁ δὲ χρησμὸς ὅδε ἦν· [2]

> ὄλβιος οὗτος ἀνὴρ ὃς ἐμὸν δόμον ἐσκαταβαίνει,
> Κύψελος Ἠετίδης, βασιλεὺς κλειτοῖο Κορίνθου
> αὐτὸς καὶ παῖδες, παίδων γε μὲν οὐκέτι παῖδες.

τὸ μὲν δὴ χρηστήριον τοῦτο ἦν. τυραννεύσας δὲ ὁ Κύψελος τοιοῦτος δή τις ἀνὴρ ἐγένετο· πολλοὺς μὲν Κορινθίων ἐδίωξε, πολλοὺς δὲ χρημάτων ἀπεστέρησε, πολλῷ δέ τι πλείστους τῆς ψυχῆς.

V.92ε.1 μετὰ ταῦτα: temporal, refers back to the attempted murder.   **οἱ διαφυγόντι = αὐτῷ διαφυγόντι**.   **ἐπωνυμίην**: accusative of respect, "named after, called after."   **οὔνομα**: in apposition to Κύψελος.   **τῷ = ᾧ**: translate with πίσυνος.   **ὅδε**: looks forward to what comes next.   **92ε.2 κλειτοῖο =κλειτοῦ**.   **μέν = μήν**.   **οὐκέτι παῖδες**: supply an implied βασιλεῖς.   **τὸ μὲν δὴ χρηστήριον**: is answered by τυραννεύσας δέ.   **τοιοῦτος**: looks forward to what comes next; Soklees' story stresses the inhumanity of tyranny.   **πολλοὺς μέν . . . δέ . . . δέ**: organize the three things that Kypselos does.   **Κορινθίων**: partitive with πολλούς.   **πολλῷ**: dative of degree of difference.   **πλείστους τῆς ψυχῆς**: supply an implied ἀπεστέρησε.

~

V.92ζ.1 ἄρξαντος δὲ τούτου ἐπὶ τριήκοντα ἔτεα καὶ διαπλέξαντος

τὸν βίον εὖ, διάδοχός οἱ τῆς τυραννίδος ὁ παῖς Περίανδρος γίνεται.
ὁ τοίνυν Περίανδρος κατ᾽ ἀρχὰς μὲν ἦν ἠπιώτερος τοῦ πατρός.
ἐπείτε δὲ ὡμίλησε δι᾽ ἀγγέλων Θρασυβούλῳ, τῷ Μιλήτου τυράννῳ,
πολλῷ ἔτι ἐγένετο Κυψέλου μιαιφονώτερος. [2] πέμψας γὰρ παρὰ
Θρασύβουλον κήρυκα, ἐπυνθάνετο ὅντινα ἂν τρόπον, ἀσφαλέστατον
καταστησάμενος τῶν πρηγμάτων, κάλλιστα τὴν πόλιν ἐπιτροπεύοι.
Θρασύβουλος δὲ τὸν ἐλθόντα παρὰ τοῦ Περιάνδρου ἐξῆγαγε ἔξω τοῦ
ἄστεος. ἐσβὰς δὲ ἐς ἄρουραν ἐσπαρμένην ἅμα τε διεξήιε τὸ λήιον,
ἐπειρωτῶν τε καὶ ἀναποδίζων τὸν κήρυκα κατὰ τὴν ἀπὸ Κορίνθου
ἄπιξιν, καὶ ἐκόλουε αἰεὶ ὅκως τινὰ ἴδοι τῶν ἀσταχύων ὑπερέχοντα.
κολούων δὲ ἔρριπτε, ἐς ὃ τοῦ ληίου τὸ κάλλιστόν τε καὶ βαθύτατον
διέφθειρε τρόπῳ τοιούτῳ. [3] διεξελθὼν δὲ τὸ χωρίον καὶ ὑποθέμενος
ἔπος οὐδέν, ἀποπέμπει τὸν κήρυκα. νοστήσαντος δὲ τοῦ κήρυκος ἐς
τὴν Κόρινθον, ἦν πρόθυμος πυνθάνεσθαι τὴν ὑποθήκην ὁ Περίανδρος.
ὁ δὲ οὐδέν οἱ ἔφη Θρασύβουλον ὑποθέσθαι. θωμάζειν τε αὐτοῦ
παρ᾽ οἷόν μιν ἄνδρα ἀποπέμψειε, ὡς παραπλῆγά τε καὶ τῶν ἑωυτοῦ
σινάμωρον, ἀπηγεόμενος τά περ πρὸς Θρασυβούλου ὀπώπεε.

V.92ζ.1 τούτου: refers back to Kypselos.   **διαπλέξαντος τὸν βίον εὖ:** a neutral
observation given that Soklees is speaking against tyranny.   **οἱ = αὐτῷ:**
possesses διάδοχος.   **κατ᾽ ἀρχὰς μέν:** temporal and is answered by ἐπείτε
δέ.   **τοῦ πατρός:** translate with ἠπιώτερος.   **πολλῷ:** dative of degree of
difference.   **Κυψέλου:** translate with μιαιφονώτερος.   **92ζ.2 ὅντινα ...**
τρόπον: accusative of respect.   **ἄν ... ἐπιτροπεύοι:** potential optative.   **τῶν**
πρηγμάτων: partitive with ἀσφαλέστατον.   **τὸν ἐλθόντα:** substantive, "the
one coming," i.e., the ἄγγελος.   **τε ... καί:** links διεξήιε and ἐκόλουε.   **ὅκως:**
"whenever."   **ἴδοι:** an optative hypothetically referring to an event in the past
that happened with some frequency.   **τῶν ἀσταχύων:** partitive with τινά; the
first syllable is possibly a pun on ἀστός.   **ἐς ὅ:** until.   **92ζ.3 πυνθάνεσθαι:**
epexegetical with πρόθυμος.   **ὁ δέ = ὁ ἄγγελος.**   **οἱ = αὐτῷ.**   **Θρασύβουλον:**
subject of ὑποθέσθαι.   **ὑποθέσθαι:** main verb in indirect statement.   **θωμάζειν:**
main verb in indirect statement; the subject is the same as the subject of
ἔφη.   **αὐτοῦ = Περιάνδρου:** object of θωμάζειν.   **παρ᾽ οἷον:** modifies
ἄνδρα.   **μιν = αὐτόν:** i.e., ἄγγελον.   **ἀποπέμψειε:** the optative stands for
an original indicative.   **ὡς παραπλῆγά ... σινάμωρον:** predicate to οἷον
ἄνδρα.   **τῶν ἑωυτοῦ:** substantive, "of his own possessions."   **ἀπηγεόμενος τά**
περ = ἀφηγεόμενος ταῦτα ἅ περ: the antecedent ταῦτα has dropped out, and τά
serves as the object of ἀπηγεόμενος and ὀπώπεε.

❧

V.92η.1 Περίανδρος δέ, συνιεὶς τὸ ποιηθὲν καὶ νόῳ ἴσχων ὥς οἱ
ὑπετίθετο Θρασύβουλος τοὺς ὑπειρόχους τῶν ἀστῶν φονεύειν,
ἐνθαῦτα δὴ πᾶσαν κακότητα ἐξέφαινε ἐς τοὺς πολιήτας. ὅσα
γὰρ Κύψελος ἀπέλιπε κτείνων τε καὶ διώκων, Περίανδρος σφέα
ἀπετέλεσε. μιῇ δὲ ἡμέρῃ ἀπέδυσε πάσας τὰς Κορινθίων γυναῖκας διὰ
τὴν ἑωυτοῦ γυναῖκα, Μέλισσαν. [2] πέμψαντι γάρ οἱ ἐς Θεσπρωτοὺς
ἐπ' Ἀχέροντα ποταμὸν ἀγγέλους ἐπὶ τὸ νεκυομαντήιον παρακαταθήκης
πέρι ξεινικῆς οὔτε σημανέειν ἔφη ἡ Μέλισσα ἐπιφανεῖσα οὔτε
κατερέειν ἐν τῷ κέεται χώρῳ ἡ παρακαταθήκη· ῥιγοῦν τε γὰρ καὶ
εἶναι γυμνή. τῶν γάρ οἱ συγκατέθαψε ἱματίων ὄφελος εἶναι οὐδὲν οὐ
κατακαυθέντων. μαρτύριον δέ οἱ εἶναι ὡς ἀληθέα ταῦτα λέγει, ὅτι ἐπὶ
ψυχρὸν τὸν ἰπνὸν Περίανδρος τοὺς ἄρτους ἐπέβαλε. [3] ταῦτα δὲ ὡς
ὀπίσω ἀπηγγέλθη τῷ Περιάνδρῳ—πιστὸν γάρ οἱ ἦν τὸ συμβόλαιον ὃς
νεκρῷ ἐούσῃ Μελίσσῃ ἐμίγη—ἰθέως δὴ μετὰ τὴν ἀγγελίην κήρυγμα
ἐποιήσατο ἐς τὸ Ἥραιον ἐξιέναι πάσας τὰς Κορινθίων γυναῖκας. αἱ μὲν
δή, ὡς ἐς ὁρτήν, ἤισαν κόσμῳ τῷ καλλίστῳ χρεώμεναι. ὁ δ' ὑποστήσας
τοὺς δορυφόρους ἀπέδυσε σφέας πάσας ὁμοίως, τάς τε ἐλευθέρας καὶ
τὰς ἀμφιπόλους. συμφορήσας δὲ ἐς ὄρυγμα Μελίσσῃ ἐπευχόμενος
κατέκαιε. [4] ταῦτα δέ οἱ ποιήσαντι καὶ τὸ δεύτερον πέμψαντι ἔφρασε
τὸ εἴδωλον τὸ Μελίσσης, ἐς τὸν κατέθηκε χῶρον τοῦ ξείνου τὴν
παρακαταθήκην. τοιοῦτο μὲν ὑμῖν ἐστὶ ἡ τυραννίς, ὦ Λακεδαιμόνιοι,
καὶ τοιούτων ἔργων. [5] ἡμέας δέ, τοὺς Κορινθίους, τότε αὐτίκα
θῶμα μέγα εἶχε ὅτε ὑμέας εἴδομεν μεταπεμπομένους Ἱππίην. νῦν
τε δὴ καὶ μεζόνως θωμάζομεν λέγοντας ταῦτα. ἐπιμαρτυρόμεθά τε,
ἐπικαλεόμενοι ὑμῖν θεοὺς τοὺς Ἑλληνίους, μὴ κατιστάναι τυραννίδας
ἐς τὰς πόλις. οὔκ ὧν παύσεσθε ἀλλὰ πειρήσεσθε παρὰ τὸ δίκαιον
κατάγοντες Ἱππίην; ἴστε ὑμῖν Κορινθίους γε οὐ συναινέοντας.

V.92η.1 τὸ ποιηθέν: substantive, "what happened."   **οἱ = αὐτῷ**: to perform the
action of φονεύειν.   **τοὺς ὑπειρόχους**: substantive, "the high-ranking."   **τῶν
ἀστῶν**: partitive with τοὺς ὑπειρόχους.   **ὅσα ... σφέα**: "as many things as ...
these things."   **κτείνων ... διώκων**: supplementary with ἀπέλιπε.   **92η.2**
πέμψαντι γάρ οἱ = πέμψαντι γάρ αὐτῷ.   **παρακαταθήκης πέρι**:
anastrophe of the disyllabic preposition.   **οὔτε ... οὔτε**: links σημανέειν and

κατερέειν.   σημανέειν … κατερέειν: the subect is the same as the subject of ἔφη.   ἐν τῷ κέεται χώρῳ = ἐν ᾧ κέεται χώρῳ: at times the antecedent is brought into the relative clause, e.g., εἶδεν ἐν ᾗ οἰκέω χώρᾳ ("he saw in which country I dwell") instead of εἶδεν χώραν ἐν ᾗ οἰκῶ.   ῥιγοῦν … εἶναι: main verbs in indirect statement; the subject is the same as the subject of an implied ἔφη.   τῶν = ὧν: the relative pronoun τῶν has been attracted into the case of its antecedent and serves as the object of συγκατέθαψε and as a modifier of ἱματίων.   οἱ = αὐτῇ = Μελίσσῃ: the object of the prefix συν- of συγκατέθαψε.   ἱματίων: translate with ὄφελος.   ὄφελος: subject of εἶναι; supply an implied ἔφη.   εἶναι: main verb in indirect statement.   οὐδέν: accusative of respect.   οὐ κατακαυθέντων: provides the reason why she cannot use the clothes.   μαρτύριον: subject of εἶναι.   οἱ = αὐτῇ: possesses μαρτύριον.   εἶναι: main verb in indirect statement; supply an implied ἔφη.   92η.3 ταῦτα: refers back to what was just said.   οἱ = αὐτῷ: translate with πιστόν.   ὅς: the antecedent is οἱ.   ἐξιέναι: main verb in indirect statement.   γυναῖκας: subject of ἐξιέναι.   αἱ μὲν δή: is answered by ὁ δ᾽ ὑποστήσας.   συμφορήσας … κατέκαιε: supply an implied τὰ ἱμάτια.   92η.4 ταῦτα: refers back to what was just said.   οἱ ποιήσαντι = αὐτῷ ποιήσαντι.   ἔφρασε: the object is τὴν παρακαταθήκην.   ἐς τὸν κατέθηκε χῶρον = ἐς ὃν κατέθηκε χῶρον: at times the antecedent is brought into the relative clause, e.g., εἶδεν ἐν ᾗ οἰκέω χώρᾳ ("he saw in which country I dwell") instead of εἶδεν χώραν ἐν ᾗ οἰκῶ.   τοιοῦτο μέν: is answered by ἡμέας δέ.   τοιούτων ἔργων: supply an implied ἐστὶ ἡ τυραννίς.   92η.5 τοὺς Κορινθίους: in apposition to ἡμέας.   τότε: is answered by ὅτε.   λέγοντας: modifies an implied ὑμέας.   ὑμῖν: object of the prefix ἐπι- of ἐπικαλεόμενοι.   κατιστάναι: complementary with ἐπιμαρτυρόμεθα.   κατάγοντες: supplementary with πειρήσεσθε.   ὑμῖν: object of the prefix συν- of συναινέοντας.

⤚

V.93.1 Σωκλέης μέν, ἀπὸ Κορίνθου πρεσβεύων, ἔλεξε τάδε. Ἱππίης δὲ αὐτὸν ἀμείβετο, τοὺς αὐτοὺς ἐπικαλέσας θεοὺς ἐκείνῳ· ἦ μὲν Κορινθίους μάλιστα πάντων ἐπιποθήσειν Πεισιστρατίδας, ὅταν σφι ἥκωσι ἡμέραι αἱ κύριαι ἀνιᾶσθαι ὑπ᾽ Ἀθηναίων. [2] Ἱππίης μὲν τούτοισι ἀμείψατο οἷα τοὺς χρησμοὺς ἀτρεκέστατα ἀνδρῶν ἐξεπιστάμενος. οἱ δὲ λοιποὶ τῶν συμμάχων τέως μὲν εἶχον ἐν ἡσυχίῃ σφέας αὐτούς. ἐπείτε δὲ Σωκλέος ἤκουσαν ἐλευθέρως, ἅπας τις αὐτῶν, φωνὴν ῥήξας, αἱρέετο τοῦ Κορινθίου τὴν γνώμην. Λακεδαιμονίοισί τε ἐπεμαρτυρέοντο μὴ ποιέειν μηδὲν νεώτερον περὶ πόλιν Ἑλλάδα.

128   HERODOTUS, *HISTORIES*, BOOK V

V.93.1 Σωκλέης μέν: is answered by Ἱππίης δέ.   **τάδε:** one of the few times in Herodotus that τάδε refers back to what has just been said.   **ἐκείνῳ:** object of the prefix ἐπι- of ἐπικαλέσας.   **ἦ μέν = ἦ μήν:** Hippias offers an assessment from his perspective and attempts to persuade by an appeal to divine knowledge.   **Κορινθίους:** subject of ἐπιποθήσειν.   **μάλιστα πάντων:** partitive with Κορινθίους.   **σφι:** to perform the action of ἀνιᾶσθαι.   **ἥκωσι:** a hypothetical subjunctive, indicating an event that may happen at some future time.   **ἀνιᾶσθαι:** complementary with ἥκωσι.   **93.2 Ἱππίης μέν:** is answered by οἱ δὲ λοιποί.   **τούτοισι:** refers back to the Korinthians.   **οἷα:** οἷα (and ἅτε) is typically found with a participle in the nominative or accusative case. Use "since" or "because" to translate it, and turn the participle into a finite verb. Thus, ἅτε αὐτὸν ὄντα καλόν (ἅτε ὢν καλός): "since he was good."   **ἀτρεκέστατα ἀνδρῶν:** partitive with ἐξεπιστάμενος.   **τῶν συμμάχων:** partitive with οἱ δὲ λοιποί.   **τέως μὲν εἶχον:** is answered by ἐπείτε δέ.   **αὐτῶν:** partitive with ἅπας τις.   **αἱρέετο = ᾑρέετο.**   **Λακεδαιμονίοισι:** to perform the action of ποιέειν.   **ποιέειν:** dependent on ἐπεμαρτυρέοντο.

⁓

V.94.1 οὕτω μὲν τοῦτο ἐπαύσθη. Ἱππίη δὲ ἐνθεῦτεν ἀπελαυνομένῳ ἐδίδου μὲν Ἀμύντης, ὁ Μακεδόνων βασιλεύς, Ἀνθεμοῦντα· ἐδίδοσαν δὲ Θεσσαλοὶ Ἰωλκόν. ὁ δὲ τούτων μὲν οὐδέτερα αἱρέετο. ἀνεχώρεε δὲ ὀπίσω ἐς Σίγειον, τὸ εἷλε Πεισίστρατος αἰχμῇ παρὰ Μυτιληναίων. κρατήσας δὲ αὐτοῦ, κατέστησε τύραννον εἶναι παῖδα τὸν ἑωυτοῦ νόθον, Ἡγησίστρατον, γεγονότα ἐξ Ἀργείης γυναικός, ὃς οὐκ ἀμαχητὶ εἶχε τὰ παρέλαβε παρὰ Πεισιστράτου. [2] ἐπολέμεον γὰρ ἔκ τε Ἀχιληίου πόλιος ὁρμώμενοι καὶ Σιγείου ἐπὶ χρόνον συχνὸν Μυτιληναῖοί τε καὶ Ἀθηναῖοι, οἱ μὲν ἀπαιτέοντες τὴν χώρην, Ἀθηναῖοι δὲ οὔτε συγγινωσκόμενοι ἀποδεικνύντες τε λόγῳ οὐδὲν μᾶλλον Αἰολεῦσι μετεὸν τῆς Ἰλιάδος χώρης ἢ οὐ καὶ σφίσι καὶ τοῖσι ἄλλοισι, ὅσοι Ἑλλήνων συνεπρήξαντο Μενέλεῳ τὰς Ἑλένης ἁρπαγάς.

V.94.1 οὕτω μέν: is answered by Ἱππίη δέ; μέν concludes the narrative on the Spartans' attempt to restore Hippias to Athens; δέ introduces his next move. Hippias's flight to Asia and his subsequent slander of the Athenians mark the start of public antagonism between the Athenians and the Persians.   **τοῦτο:** i.e., establishing Hippias as tyrant.   **ἐδίδου μὲν Ἀμύντης:** is answered by ἐδίδοσαν δὲ Θεσσαλοί.   **βασιλεύς:** in apposition with Ἀμύντης.   **τούτων:** partitive with οὐδέτερα.   **τούτων μὲν οὐδέτερα:** is answered by ἀνεχώρεε δὲ ὀπίσω.   **τὸ εἷλε = ὃ εἷλε.**   **τύραννον:** subject of εἶναι.   **εἶναι:** dependent on

κατέστησε.   Ἡγησίστρατον: in apposition to παῖδα.   εἶχε τὰ παρέλαβε =
εἶχε ταῦτα ἃ παρέλαβε: the antecedent ταῦτα has dropped out, and τά serves as
the object of εἶχε and παρέλαβε.   94.2 ἔκ τε Ἀχιλληίου πόλιος ... καὶ Σιγείου:
τε and καί link the two objects.   οἱ μὲν ἀπαιτέοντες: is answered by Ἀθηναῖοι
δέ.   οὔτε ... τε: links the two participles, συγγινωσκόμενοι and ἀποδεικνύντες,
the first negative and the second affirmative.   ἀποδεικνύντες τε λόγῳ:
epigraphic evidence concerning Hellenistic territorial disputes suggests officials
carrying texts, especially Homer, so as to settle the disagreement.   οὐδέν:
accusative of respect, "in no way."   μετεόν: impersonal.   Ἑλλήνων: partitive
with ὅσοι.   Μενέλεῳ: object of the prefix συν- of συνεπρήξαντο.

～

V.95.1 πολεμεόντων δὲ σφέων, παντοῖα καὶ ἄλλα ἐγένετο ἐν τῇσι
μάχῃσι. ἐν δὲ δὴ καὶ Ἀλκαῖος ὁ ποιητής, συμβολῆς γενομένης καὶ
νικώντων Ἀθηναίων, αὐτὸς μὲν φεύγων ἐκφεύγει· τὰ δέ οἱ ὅπλα
ἴσχουσι Ἀθηναῖοι. καί σφεα ἀνεκρέμασαν πρὸς τὸ Ἀθήναιον τὸ ἐν
Σιγείῳ. [2] ταῦτα δὲ Ἀλκαῖος ἐν μέλεϊ ποιήσας ἐπιτιθεῖ ἐς Μυτιλήνην,
ἐξαγγελλόμενος τὸ ἑωυτοῦ πάθος Μελανίππῳ, ἀνδρὶ ἑταίρῳ.
Μυτιληναίους δὲ καὶ Ἀθηναίους κατήλλαξε Περίανδρος ὁ Κυψέλου·
τούτῳ γὰρ διαιτητῇ ἐπετράποντο. κατήλλαξε δὲ ὧδε, νέμεσθαι
ἑκατέρους τὴν ἔχουσι.

V.95.1 ἐν δὲ δὴ καί: "including also."   αὐτὸς μὲν φεύγων: is answered by τὰ δέ
οἱ ὅπλα.   οἱ = αὐτῷ: possesses ὅπλα.   95.2 ταῦτα: refers back to his fleeing and
losing his weapons.   ἀνδρὶ ἑταίρῳ: in apposition to Μελανίππῳ.   διαιτητῇ:
predicate to τούτῳ.   νέμεσθαι ἑκατέρους τὴν ἔχουσι = νέμεσθαι χώρην
ἑκατέρους ἣν ἔχουσι: the antecedent χώρην has dropped out, and τήν serves as
the object of νέμεσθαι and ἔχουσι.   νέμεσθαι: dependent on an implied verb of
advising or commanding.   ἑκατέρους: subject of νέμεσθαι.

～

V.96.1 Σίγειον μέν νυν οὕτω ἐγένετο ὑπ' Ἀθηναίοισι. Ἱππίης δὲ
ἐπείτε ἀπίκετο ἐκ τῆς Λακεδαίμονος ἐς τὴν Ἀσίην, πᾶν χρῆμα ἐκίνεε,
διαβάλλων τε τοὺς Ἀθηναίους πρὸς τὸν Ἀρταφρένεα καὶ ποιέων
ἅπαντα ὅκως αἱ Ἀθῆναι γενοίατο ὑπ' ἑωυτῷ τε καὶ Δαρείῳ. [2] Ἱππίης
τε δὴ ταῦτα ἔπρησσε καὶ οἱ Ἀθηναῖοι, πυθόμενοι ταῦτα, πέμπουσι
ἐς Σάρδις ἀγγέλους, οὐκ ἐῶντες τοὺς Πέρσας πείθεσθαι Ἀθηναίων

130   HERODOTUS, *HISTORIES*, BOOK V

τοῖσι φυγάσι. ὁ δὲ Ἀρταφρένης ἐκέλευε σφέας, εἰ βουλοίατο σόοι
εἶναι, καταδέκεσθαι ὀπίσω Ἱππίην. οὔκων δὴ ἐνεδέκοντο τοὺς λόγους
ἀποφερομένους οἱ Ἀθηναῖοι. οὐκ ἐνδεκομένοισι δέ σφι ἐδέδοκτο ἐκ
τοῦ φανεροῦ τοῖσι Πέρσῃσι πολεμίους εἶναι.

V.96.1 Σίγειον μέν νυν: is answered by Ἱππίης δὲ ἐπείτε; μέν concludes the
backstory on Sigeion, and δέ returns us again to Hippias.   **τε . . . καί**: links
διαβάλλων and ποιέων.   **γενοίατο = γένοιντο**: a hypothetical optative,
indicating why Hippias acts as he does.   **96.2 τε . . . καί**: links Ἱππίης and οἱ
Ἀθηναῖοι.   **πυθόμενοι ταῦτα**: ταῦτα refers back to Hippias's actions.   **τοὺς**
Πέρσας: subject of πείθεσθαι.   **πείθεσθαι**: dependent on ἐῶντες.   **σφέας**:
subject of καταδέκεσθαι.   **καταδέκεσθαι**: dependent on ἐκέλευε.   **βουλοίατο**
= βούλοιντο.   **εἶναι**: complementary with βουλοίατο.   **σφι**:
agency.   **ἐδέδοκτο**: impersonal; the Athenian current state of mind is integral to
what happens in the next section.   **πολεμίους**: the expectation is for πολεμίους to
agree with σφι in gender, case, and number, but it does not. The lack of agreement
between the two is typical when the noun the participle modifies is also to
perform the action of an upcoming infinitive.   **τοῖσι Πέρσῃσι**: translate with
πολεμίους.   **εἶναι**: complementary with ἐδέδοκτο.

❧

V.97.1 νομίζουσι δὲ ταῦτα καὶ διαβεβλημένοισι ἐς τοὺς Πέρσας, ἐν
τούτῳ δὴ τῷ καιρῷ ὁ Μιλήσιος Ἀρισταγόρης, ὑπὸ Κλεομένεος τοῦ
Λακεδαιμονίου ἐξελασθεὶς ἐκ τῆς Σπάρτης, ἀπίκετο ἐς τὰς Ἀθήνας·
αὕτη γὰρ ἡ πόλις τῶν λοιπέων ἐδυνάστευε μέγιστον. ἐπελθὼν δὲ ἐπὶ
τὸν δῆμον, ὁ Ἀρισταγόρης ταὐτὰ ἔλεγε τὰ καὶ ἐν τῇ Σπάρτῃ περὶ τῶν
ἀγαθῶν τῶν ἐν τῇ Ἀσίῃ καὶ τοῦ πολέμου τοῦ Περσικοῦ, ὡς οὔτε ἀσπίδα
οὔτε δόρυ νομίζουσι εὐπετέες τε χειρωθῆναι εἴησαν. [2] ταῦτά τε δὴ
ἔλεγε καὶ πρὸς τοῖσι τάδε, ὡς οἱ Μιλήσιοι τῶν Ἀθηναίων εἰσὶ ἄποικοι, καὶ
οἰκός σφεας εἴη ῥύεσθαι δυναμένους μέγα. καὶ οὐδὲν ὅ τι οὐκ ὑπίσχετο,
οἷα κάρτα δεόμενος, ἐς ὃ ἀνέπεισε σφέας. πολλοὺς γὰρ οἶκε εἶναι
εὐπετέστερον διαβάλλειν ἢ ἕνα, εἰ Κλεομένεα μὲν τὸν Λακεδαιμόνιον
μοῦνον οὐκ οἷός τε ἐγένετο διαβάλλειν, τρεῖς δὲ μυριάδας Ἀθηναίων
ἐποίησε τοῦτο. [3] Ἀθηναῖοι μὲν δὴ ἀναπεισθέντες ἐψηφίσαντο εἴκοσι
νέας ἀποστεῖλαι βοηθοὺς Ἴωσι, στρατηγὸν ἀποδέξαντες αὐτῶν εἶναι
Μελάνθιον, ἄνδρα τῶν ἀστῶν ἐόντα τὰ πάντα δόκιμον. αὗται δὲ αἱ νέες
ἀρχὴ κακῶν ἐγένοντο Ἕλλησί τε καὶ βαρβάροισι.

V.97.1 νομίζουσι ... διαβεβλημένοισι: translate with ἀπίκετο.   **ταῦτα:** refers
back to the Athenians' refusal to take Hippias back.   **τῶν λοιπέων:** partitive
with ἡ πόλις.   **ταῦτα = τὰ αὐτά.**   **τὰ καὶ ἐν τῇ Σπάρτῃ = ἃ καὶ ἐν τῇ Σπάρτῃ:**
supply an implied ἔλεγε.   **τῶν ἀγαθῶν:** substantive, "the wealth."   **νομίζουσι:**
indicative stating what the Persian custom is.   **χειρωθῆναι:** epexegetical with
εὐπετέες.   **εἴησαν:** probably a potential optative without ἄν (Smyth 1821);
Herodotus's later narrative corrects Aristagores' hyperbole.   **97.2 ταῦτα:** looks
back to what was just said.   **καὶ πρὸς τοῖσι:** "and in addition to them."   **τάδε:**
looks forward to what comes next; supply an implied ἔλεγε.   **σφεας =**
Μιλησίους: object of ῥύεσθαι.   **εἴη:** an optative standing for an original
indicative.   **ῥύεσθαι:** epexegetical with οἰκός.   **δυναμένους:** modifies an
implied Ἀθηναίους.   **μέγα:** accusative of respect, "very."   **οὐδέν:** supply
an implied ἦν.   **οἷα κάρτα:** οἷα (and ἅτε) is typically found with a participle
in the nominative or accusative case. Use "since" or "because" to translate it,
and turn the participle into a finite verb. Thus, ἅτε αὐτὸν ὄντα καλόν (ἅτε
ὢν καλός): "since he was good."   **ἐς ὅ:** temporal, "until."   **οἶκε = ἔοικε:**
impersonal.   **εἶναι:** complementary with οἶκε.   **διαβάλλειν:** complementary
with εὐπετέστερον.   **ἢ ἕνα:** supply an implied διαβάλλειν.   **διαβάλλειν:**
complementary with οἷός τε ἐγένετο.   **εἰ Κλεομένεα μέν:** is answered by
τρεῖς δὲ μυριάδας.   **Ἀθηναίων:** partitive with τρεῖς δὲ μυριάδας.   **τρεῖς**
δὲ μυριάδας: it is possible that this number represents the actual number of
Athenian adult males enrolled on the deme registers. Though the statement may
be a joking observation, crowd behavior intrigues Herodotus.   **ἐποίησε:** often
takes a double accusative.   **τοῦτο:** i.e., διαβάλλειν.   **97.3 Ἀθηναῖοι μέν:** is
answered by Ἀρισταγόρης δέ of chapter 98.1.   **ἀποστεῖλαι:** complementary
with ἐψηφίσαντο.   **βοηθούς:** predicate to νέας.   **Ἴωσι:** translate with
βοηθούς.   **στρατηγόν:** subject of εἶναι.   **ἄνδρα:** in apposition with
Μελάνθιον.   **τὰ πάντα:** accusative of respect, "in all ways."

~

V.98.1 Ἀρισταγόρης δέ, προπλώσας καὶ ἀπικόμενος ἐς τὴν Μίλητον,
ἐξευρὼν βούλευμα ἀπ' οὗ Ἴωσι μὲν οὐδεμία ἔμελλε ὠφελίη ἔσεσθαι—
οὐδ' ὦν οὐδὲ τούτου εἵνεκα ἐποίεε ἀλλ' ὅκως βασιλέα Δαρεῖον
λυπήσειε—ἔπεμψε ἐς τὴν Φρυγίην ἄνδρα ἐπὶ τοὺς Παίονας τοὺς
ἀπὸ Στρυμόνος ποταμοῦ αἰχμαλώτους γενομένους ὑπὸ Μεγαβάζου,
οἰκέοντας δὲ τῆς Φρυγίης χῶρόν τε καὶ κώμην ἐπ' ἑωυτῶν, ὅς, ἐπειδὴ
ἀπίκετο ἐς τοὺς Παίονας, ἔλεγε τάδε· [2] Ἄνδρες Παίονες, ἔπεμψέ
με Ἀρισταγόρης, ὁ Μιλήτου τύραννος, σωτηρίην ὑποθησόμενον
ὑμῖν, ἤν περ βούλησθε πείθεσθαι. νῦν γὰρ Ἰωνίη πᾶσα ἀπέστηκε ἀπὸ
βασιλέος. καὶ ὑμῖν παρέχει σώζεσθαι ἐπὶ τὴν ὑμετέρην αὐτῶν. μέχρι

μὲν θαλάσσης αὐτοῖσι ὑμῖν, τὸ δὲ ἀπὸ τούτου ἡμῖν ἤδη μελήσει. [3]
ταῦτα δὲ ἀκούσαντες, οἱ Παίονες κάρτα τε ἀσπαστὸν ἐποιήσαντο.
καὶ ἀναλαβόντες παῖδας καὶ γυναῖκας, ἀπεδίδρησκον ἐπὶ θάλασσαν.
οἱ δὲ τινὲς αὐτῶν καὶ κατέμειναν, ἀρρωδήσαντες, αὐτοῦ. ἐπείτε δὲ
οἱ Παίονες ἀπίκοντο ἐπὶ θάλασσαν, ἐνθεῦτεν ἐς Χίον διέβησαν. [4]
ἐόντων δὲ ἤδη ἐν Χίῳ, κατὰ πόδας ἐληλύθεε Περσέων ἵππος πολλή,
διώκουσα τοὺς Παίονας. ὡς δὲ οὐ κατέλαβον, ἐπηγγέλλοντο ἐς τὴν
Χίον τοῖσι Παίοσι ὅκως ἂν ὀπίσω ἀπέλθοιεν. οἱ δὲ Παίονες τοὺς λόγους
οὐκ ἐνεδέκοντο. ἀλλ᾽ ἐκ Χίου μὲν Χῖοι σφέας ἐς Λέσβον ἤγαγον.
Λέσβιοι δὲ ἐς Δορίσκον ἐκόμισαν. ἐνθεῦτεν δὲ πεζῇ κομιζόμενοι
ἀπίκοντο ἐς Παιονίην.

V.98.1 ὠφελίη: Herodotus continues his criticism of Aristagores.   **ἔσεσθαι:**
complementary with ἔμελλε.   **τούτου εἵνεκα:** refers back to Aristagores'
failure to act in the best interests of the Ionians.   **λυπήσειε:** a hypothetical
optative, giving the reason why Aristagores acts as he does; the intent forms part
of Herodotus's analysis.   **ἄνδρα:** the antecedent for the upcoming ὅς.   **ἐπ᾽
ἑωυτῶν:** "by themselves."   **τάδε:** looks forward to what comes next.   **98.2**
τύραννος: in apposition to Ἀρισταγόρης.   **ὑποθησόμενον:** the tense indicates
the reason why Aristagores sent him.   **βούλησθε:** a hypothetical subjunctive
indicative of a possible future outcome.   **πείθεσθαι:** complementary with
βούλησθε.   **ὑμῖν:** to perform the action of σώζεσθαι.   **ἐπὶ τὴν ὑμετέρην**
αὐτῶν: supply an implied γῆν.   **μέχρι μὲν θαλάσσης:** supply an implied τό,
"the journey up to the sea"; subject of an implied μελήσει. It is answered by τὸ δὲ
ἀπὸ τούτου.   **τὸ δὲ ἀπὸ τούτου:** substantive, "the journey from here."   **98.3**
ταῦτα: refers back to what has just been said.   **ἀσπαστόν:** predicate to an
implied εἶναι.   **ἐποιήσαντο:** supply an implied εἶναι.   **αὐτῶν:** partitive
with τινές.   **αὐτοῦ:** adverbial, "there."   **98.4 ἐόντων:** modifies an implied
Παιόνων.   **ὡς:** temporal.   **ἄν...ἀπέλθοιεν:** a hypothetical optative stating the
reason for the Persians' sending the message; in Homer and Herodotus ἄν is present
in purpose clauses.   **ἐκ Χίου μὲν Χῖοι:** is answered by Λέσβιοι δέ.

⁓

V.99.1 Ἀρισταγόρης δέ, ἐπειδὴ οἵ τε Ἀθηναῖοι ἀπίκοντο εἴκοσι νηυσί,
ἅμα ἀγόμενοι Ἐρετριέων πέντε τριήρεας, οἳ οὐ τὴν Ἀθηναίων
χάριν ἐστρατεύοντο ἀλλὰ τὴν αὐτῶν Μιλησίων, ὀφειλόμενά σφι
ἀποδιδόντες· οἱ γὰρ δὴ Μιλήσιοι πρότερον τοῖσι Ἐρετριεῦσι τὸν
πρὸς Χαλκιδέας πόλεμον συνδιήνεικαν, ὅτε περ καὶ Χαλκιδεῦσι

ἀντία Ἐρετριέων καὶ Μιλησίων Σάμιοι ἐβοήθεον. οὗτοι ὦν ἐπείτε
σφι ἀπίκοντο καὶ οἱ ἄλλοι σύμμαχοι παρῆσαν, ἐποιέετο στρατηίην ὁ
Ἀρισταγόρης ἐς Σάρδις. [2] αὐτὸς μὲν δὴ οὐκ ἐστρατεύετο ἀλλ᾽ ἔμενε
ἐν Μιλήτῳ. στρατηγοὺς δὲ ἄλλους ἀπέδεξε Μιλησίων εἶναι, τὸν
ἑωυτοῦ τε ἀδελφεόν, Χαροπῖνον, καὶ τῶν ἀστῶν ἄλλον, Ἑρμόφαντον.

V.99.1 Ἀρισταγόρης δέ: there is no finite verb that Ἀρισταγόρης is the subject of
until ἐποιέετο στρατηίην; so much has intervened that the subject ὁ Ἀρισταγόρης
is repeated. **τήν:** supply an implied χάριν.   **ὀφειλόμενα:** substantive, "a
debt."   **οὗτοι ὦν ἐπείτε σφι ἀπίκοντο:** resumes οἵ τε Ἀθηναῖοι ἀπίκοντο
from above, since so much has intervened.   **99.2 αὐτὸς μέν:** is answered by
στρατηγοὺς δὲ ἄλλους.   **στρατηγούς:** subject of εἶναι.   **εἶναι:** dependent
on ἀπέδεξε.   **ἀδελφεόν:** in apposition to στρατηγούς.   **Χαροπῖνον:** in
apposition with ἀδελφεόν.   **ἄλλον:** partitive with τῶν ἀστῶν; in apposition to
στρατηγούς.   **Ἑρμόφαντον:** in apposition with ἄλλον.

❧

V.100.1 ἀπικόμενοι δὲ τῷ στόλῳ τούτῳ Ἴωνες ἐς Ἔφεσον πλοῖα
μὲν κατέλιπον ἐν Κορησῷ τῆς Ἐφεσίης. αὐτοὶ δὲ ἀνέβαινον χειρὶ
πολλῇ, ποιεύμενοι Ἐφεσίους ἡγεμόνας τῆς ὁδοῦ. πορευόμενοι δὲ
παρὰ ποταμὸν Καΰστριον, ἐνθεῦτεν ἐπείτε ὑπερβάντες τὸν Τμῶλον
ἀπίκοντο, αἱρέουσι Σάρδις, οὐδενός σφι ἀντιωθέντος. αἱρέουσι δὲ
χωρὶς τῆς ἀκροπόλιος τἄλλα πάντα. τὴν δὲ ἀκρόπολιν ἐρρύετο αὐτὸς
Ἀρταφρένης, ἔχων ἀνδρῶν δύναμιν οὐκ ὀλίγην.

V.100.1 πλοῖα μὲν κατέλιπον: is answered by αὐτοὶ δὲ ἀνέβαινον.   **ποιεύμενοι =**
ποιούμενοι.   **ἡγεμόνας:** predicate to Ἐφεσίους.   **τἄλλα = τὰ ἄλλα.**

❧

V.101.1 τὸ δὲ μὴ λεηλατῆσαι ἑλόντας σφέας τὴν πόλιν ἔσχε τόδε. ἦσαν
ἐν τῆσι Σάρδισι οἰκίαι αἱ μὲν πλεῦνες καλάμιναι. ὅσαι δ᾽ αὐτέων καὶ
πλίνθιναι ἦσαν, καλάμου εἶχον τὰς ὀροφάς. τουτέων δὴ μίαν τῶν τις
στρατιωτέων ὡς ἐνέπρησε, αὐτίκα ἀπ᾽ οἰκίης ἐπ᾽ οἰκίην ἰὸν τὸ πῦρ
ἐπενέμετο τὸ ἄστυ πᾶν. [2] καιομένου δὲ τοῦ ἄστεος, οἱ Λυδοί τε καὶ
ὅσοι Περσέων ἐνῆσαν ἐν τῇ πόλι, ἀπολαμφθέντες πάντοθεν ὥστε,
τὰ περιέσχατα νεμομένου τοῦ πυρός, καὶ οὐκ ἔχοντες ἐξήλυσιν ἐκ τοῦ

ἄστεος, συνέρρεον ἔς τε τὴν ἀγορὴν καὶ ἐπὶ τὸν Πακτωλὸν ποταμόν, ὅς,
σφι ψῆγμα χρυσοῦ καταφορέων ἐκ τοῦ Τμώλου, διὰ μέσης τῆς ἀγορῆς
ῥέει. καὶ ἔπειτα ἐς τὸν Ἕρμον ποταμὸν ἐκδιδοῖ· ὁ δὲ ἐς θάλασσαν. ἐπὶ
τοῦτον δὴ τὸν Πακτωλὸν καὶ ἐς τὴν ἀγορὴν ἀθροιζόμενοι, οἵ τε Λυδοὶ
καὶ οἱ Πέρσαι ἠναγκάζοντο ἀμύνεσθαι. [3] οἱ δὲ Ἴωνες, ὁρέοντες
τοὺς μὲν ἀμυνομένους τῶν πολεμίων τοὺς δὲ σὺν πλήθεϊ πολλῷ
προσφερομένους, ἐξανεχώρησαν, δείσαντες, πρὸς τὸ ὄρος τὸν Τμῶλον
καλεόμενον. ἐνθεῦτεν δὲ ὑπὸ νύκτα ἀπαλλάσσοντο ἐπὶ τὰς νέας.

V.101.1 τὸ δέ = ὃ δέ: subject of ἔσχε and an implied ἦν.   **μὴ λεηλατῆσαι:**
translate with σφέας ἔσχε.   **σφέας:** subject of λεηλατῆσαι.   **τόδε:** predicate
to ἦν and looks forward to the next sentence.   **αἱ μὲν πλεῦνες:** is answered by
ὅσαι δ᾽ αὐτέων.   **αὐτέων:** partitive with ὅσαι.   **καλάμου εἶχον:** understand
an implied αὗται.   **τουτέων:** partitive with μίαν.   **μίαν:** modifies an implied
οἰκίαν.   **τῶν ... στρατιωτέων:** partitive with τις.   **ὡς:** temporal, in English
the ὡς would be placed before τουτέων.   **101.2 Περσέων:** partitive with
ὅσοι.   **τὰ περιέσχατα:** substantive, "the outer parts"; object of νεμομένου.   **ὁ
δὲ ἐς θάλασσαν:** supply an implied ἐκδιδοῖ.   **ἀμύνεσθαι:** complementary with
ἠναγκάζοντο.   **101.3 τοὺς μέν ... τοὺς δέ:** "some ... others."   **τῶν πολεμίων:**
partitive with τοὺς μέν and implied with τοὺς δέ.

～

V.102.1 καὶ Σάρδιες μὲν ἐνεπρήσθησαν· ἐν δὲ αὐτῇσι καὶ ἱρὸν ἐπιχωρίης
θεοῦ Κυβήβης, τὸ σκηπτόμενοι οἱ Πέρσαι ὕστερον ἀντενεπίμπρασαν
τὰ ἐν Ἕλλησι ἱρά. τότε δὲ οἱ Πέρσαι οἱ ἐντὸς Ἅλυος ποταμοῦ νομοὺς
ἔχοντες, προπυνθανόμενοι ταῦτα, συνηλίζοντο καὶ ἐβοήθεον τοῖσι
Λυδοῖσι. [2] καὶ κως ἐν μὲν Σάρδισι οὐκέτι ἐόντας τοὺς Ἴωνας
εὑρίσκουσι. ἑπόμενοι δὲ κατὰ στίβον αἱρέουσι αὐτοὺς ἐν Ἐφέσῳ. καὶ
ἀντετάχθησαν μὲν οἱ Ἴωνες· συμβαλόντες δὲ πολλὸν ἑσσώθησαν. [3]
καὶ πολλοὺς αὐτῶν οἱ Πέρσαι φονεύουσι, ἄλλους τε ὀνομαστούς ἐν
δὲ δὴ καὶ Εὐαλκίδην, στρατηγέοντα Ἐρετριέων, στεφανηφόρους τε
ἀγῶνας ἀναραιρηκότα καὶ ὑπὸ Σιμωνίδεω τοῦ Κηίου πολλὰ αἰνεθέντα.
οἳ δὲ αὐτῶν ἀπέφυγον τὴν μάχην, ἐσκεδάσθησαν ἀνὰ τὰς πόλιας.

V.102.1 Σάρδιες μέν: is answered by ἐν δὲ αὐτῇσι; μέν concludes the narrative on
the burning of Sardis, and δέ turns to how the Persians react to the news.   **ἱρόν:**
supply an implied ἐνεπρήσθη.   **τὸ σκηπτόμενοι = ὃ σκηπτόμενοι.**   **ταῦτα:**

refers back to the burning of Sardis.   **102.2 ἐν μὲν Σάρδισι:** is answered by
ἑπόμενοι δέ.   **ἑπόμενοι:** modifies an implied Πέρσαι.   **ἀντετάχθησαν**
μέν: is answered by συμβαλόντες δέ.   **πολλόν = πολύν:** accusative of
respect, "badly."   **102.3 αὐτῶν:** partitive with πολλούς.   **ἄλλους τε…**
καὶ Εὐαλκίδην: τε gives the general and καί the specific.   **ἐν δὲ δὴ καί:**
"including."   **στεφανηφόρους τε ἀγῶνας:** Olympic, Pythian, Nemean, and
Isthmian are the contests for the crown.   **τε … καί:** links the two participles,
ἀναραιρηκότα and αἰνεθέντα.   **πολλά:** accusative of respect, "highly."   **οἳ δέ:**
typically the antecedent, οὗτοι, is present; here it can be implied as the subject of
the main verb ἐσκεδάσθησαν.   **αὐτῶν:** partitive with οἳ δέ.

❧

V.103.1 τότε μὲν δὴ οὕτω ἠγωνίσαντο. μετὰ δὲ Ἀθηναῖοι μέν, τὸ
παράπαν ἀπολιπόντες τοὺς Ἴωνας, ἐπικαλεομένου σφέας πολλὰ δι'
ἀγγέλων Ἀρισταγόρεω, οὐκ ἔφασαν τιμωρήσειν σφι. Ἴωνες δέ, τῆς
Ἀθηναίων συμμαχίης στερηθέντες—οὕτω γάρ σφι ὑπῆρχε πεποιημένα
ἐς Δαρεῖον—οὐδὲν δὴ ἧσσον τὸν πρὸς βασιλέα πόλεμον ἐσκευάζοντο.
[2] πλώσαντες δὲ ἐς τὸν Ἑλλήσποντον, Βυζάντιόν τε καὶ τὰς ἄλλας
πόλιας πάσας τὰς ταύτῃ ὑπ' ἑωυτοῖσι ἐποιήσαντο. ἐκπλώσαντές τε ἔξω
τὸν Ἑλλήσποντον, Καρίης τὴν πολλὴν προσεκτήσαντο σφίσι σύμμαχον
εἶναι καὶ γὰρ τὴν Καῦνον, πρότερον οὐ βουλομένην συμμαχέειν. ὡς
ἐνέπρησαν τὰς Σάρδις, τότε σφι καὶ αὕτη προσεγένετο.

V.103.1 τότε μέν: is answered by μετὰ δέ.   **μετὰ δέ:** adverbial,
"afterward."   **Ἀθηναῖοι μέν:** is answered by Ἴωνες δέ.   **τὸ παράπαν:**
accusative of respect, "wholly" or "completely."   **πολλά:** accusative of respect,
"often."   **τιμωρήσειν:** main verb in indirect statement; the subject is the same
as the subject of ἔφασαν.   **σφι:** agency.   **πεποιημένα:** supplementary with
ὑπῆρχε; πεποιημένα refers to their actions in chapter 100 and 101.   **103.2 ταύτῃ:**
"there."   **ἔξω τὸν Ἑλλήσποντον = ἔξω τοῦ Ἑλλησπόντου.   Καρίης:**
partitive with τὴν πολλήν.   **τὴν πολλήν:** substantive, "the majority";
subject of εἶναι.   **σφίσι:** translate with σύμμαχον.   **εἶναι:** dependent on
προσεκτήσαντο.   **καὶ γάρ:** "including even."   **τὴν Καῦνον:** subject of an
implied εἶναι σύμμαχον.   **συμμαχέειν:** complementary with βουλομένην.   **ὡς:**
temporal and answered by τότε.

❧

V.104.1 Κύπριοι δὲ ἐθελονταί σφι πάντες προσεγένοντο πλὴν
Ἀμαθουσίων· ἀπέστησαν γὰρ καὶ οὗτοι ὧδε ἀπὸ Μήδων. ἦν Ὀνήσιλος

Γόργου μὲν τοῦ Σαλαμινίων βασιλέος ἀδελφεὸς νεώτερος, Χέρσιος
δὲ τοῦ Σιρώμου τοῦ Εὐέλθοντος παῖς. [2] οὗτος ὡνὴρ πολλάκις μὲν καὶ
πρότερον τὸν Γόργον παρηγορέετο ἀπίστασθαι ἀπὸ βασιλέος. τότε
δέ, ὡς καὶ τοὺς Ἴωνας ἐπύθετο ἀπεστάναι, πάγχυ ἐπικείμενος ἐνῆγε.
ὡς δὲ οὐκ ἔπειθε τὸν Γόργον, ἐνθαῦτά μιν φυλάξας ἐξελθόντα τὸ ἄστυ
τὸ Σαλαμινίων, ὁ Ὀνήσιλος ἅμα τοῖσι ἑωυτοῦ στασιώτῃσι ἀπεκλήισε
τῶν πυλέων. [3] Γόργος μὲν δή, στερηθεὶς τῆς πόλιος, ἔφευγε ἐς
Μήδους. Ὀνήσιλος δὲ ἦρχε Σαλαμῖνος καὶ ἀνέπειθε πάντας Κυπρίους
συναπίστασθαι. τοὺς μὲν δὴ ἄλλους ἀνέπεισε· Ἀμαθουσίους δὲ οὐ
βουλομένους οἵ πείθεσθαι ἐπολιόρκεε προσκατήμενος.

V.104.1 ὧδε: looks forward to what comes next.   **Γόργου μέν:** is answered
by Χέρσιος δέ.   **104.2 οὗτος ὡνήρ:** as often οὗτος refers to what was
just mentioned.   **ὡνήρ = ὁ ἀνήρ.   πολλάκις μέν:** is answered by τότε
δέ.   **τὸν Γόργον:** subject of ἀπίστασθαι.   **ἀπίστασθαι:** dependent on
παρηγορέετο.   **τοὺς Ἴωνας:** subject of ἀπεστάναι.   **ἀπεστάναι:** main verb in
indirect statement.   **ὡς:** temporal.   **μιν = αὐτόν = τὸν Γόργον.   ἀπεκλήισε:**
as object understand an implied τὸν Γόργον.   **104.3 Γόργος μέν:** is answered
by Ὀνήσιλος δέ.   **Κυπρίους:** subject of συναπίστασθαι.   **συναπίστασθαι:**
dependent on ἀνέπειθε.   **τοὺς μέν:** is answered by Ἀμαθουσίους δέ.   **οἵ =**
αὐτῷ.   πείθεσθαι: complementary with βουλομένους.

~

V.105.1 Ὀνήσιλος μέν νυν ἐπολιόρκεε Ἀμαθοῦντα. βασιλέϊ δὲ Δαρείῳ
ὡς ἐξαγγέλθη Σάρδις ἁλούσας ἐμπεπρῆσθαι ὑπό τε Ἀθηναίων
καὶ Ἰώνων, τὸν δὲ ἡγεμόνα γενέσθαι τῆς συλλογῆς, ὥστε ταῦτα
συνυφανθῆναι, τὸν Μιλήσιον Ἀρισταγόρην, πρῶτα μὲν λέγεται
αὐτόν, ὡς ἐπύθετο ταῦτα, Ἰώνων οὐδένα λόγον ποιησάμενον, εὖ
εἰδότα ὡς οὗτοί γε οὐ καταπροΐξονται ἀποστάντες, εἰρέσθαι οἵτινες
εἶεν οἱ Ἀθηναῖοι. μετὰ δὲ πυθόμενον αἰτῆσαι τὸ τόξον. λαβόντα δὲ
καὶ ἐπιθέντα δὲ οἰστὸν ἄνω πρὸς τὸν οὐρανὸν ἀπεῖναι. καί μιν ἐς
τὸν ἠέρα βάλλοντα εἰπεῖν· [2] Ὦ Ζεῦ, ἐκγενέσθαι μοι Ἀθηναίους
τίσασθαι. εἴπαντα δὲ ταῦτα προστάξαι ἑνὶ τῶν θεραπόντων, δείπνου
προκειμένου, αὐτῷ ἐς τρὶς ἑκάστοτε εἰπεῖν· Δέσποτα, μέμνεο τῶν
Ἀθηναίων.

V.105.1 Ὀνήσιλος μέν: is answered by βασιλέι δέ.   **βασιλέι δὲ Δαρείῳ ὡς:** in English the subordinating conjunction comes first, ὡς βασιλέι δὲ Δαρείῳ. **ἐξαγγέλθη:** impersonal.   **Σάρδις:** subject of ἐμπεπρῆσθαι.   **ἐμπεπρῆσθαι... γενέσθαι:** main verbs in indirect statement.   **τὸν δὲ ἡγεμόνα:** subject of γενέσθαι.   **ὥστε ταῦτα συνυφανθῆναι:** explains συλλογῆς.   **ταῦτα:** subject of συνυφανθῆναι.   **πρῶτα μέν... μετὰ δέ:** "first of all... second."   **λέγεται:** impersonal and initiating a series of sentences involving participles modifying Dareios and infinitives that Dareios is the subject of. The main things Dareios does are represented by the infinitives; the participles give his subordinate actions. For more see the next note.   **αὐτόν = Δαρεῖον:** subject of εἰρέσθαι, αἰτῆσαι, ἀπεῖναι, εἰπεῖν, προστάξαι and modified by the participles ποιησάμενον, εἰδότα, πυθόμενον, λαβόντα, ἐπιθέντα, βάλλοντα, and εἴπαντα.   **ὡς ἐπύθετο:** temporal.   **εἶεν:** optative standing for an original indicative.   **μιν = αὐτόν = ὀιστόν.**   **105.2 ἐκγενέσθαι:** the infinitive has the force of an imperative.   **μοι:** to perform the action of τίσασθαι.   **ταῦτα:** refers back to what was just said.   **ἐνί:** to perform the action of εἰπεῖν.   **αὐτῷ:** i.e., Dareios.   **τῶν θεραπόντων:** partitive with ἐνί.

~

V.106.1 προστάξας δὲ ταῦτα εἶπε, καλέσας ἐς ὄψιν Ἱστιαῖον τὸν Μιλήσιον, τὸν ὁ Δαρεῖος κατεῖχε χρόνον ἤδη πολλόν· Πυνθάνομαι, Ἱστιαῖε, ἐπίτροπον τὸν σόν, τῷ σὺ Μίλητον ἐπέτρεψας, νεώτερα ἐς ἐμὲ πεποιηκέναι πρήγματα· ἄνδρας γάρ μοι ἐκ τῆς ἑτέρης ἠπείρου ἐπαγαγὼν καὶ Ἴωνας σὺν αὐτοῖσι—τοὺς δώσοντας ἐμοὶ δίκην τῶν ἐποίησαν—τούτους ἀναγνώσας ἅμα ἐκείνοισι ἕπεσθαι, Σαρδίων με ἀπεστέρησε. νῦν ὦν κῶς τοι ταῦτα φαίνεται ἔχειν καλῶς; [2] κῶς δέ, ἄνευ τῶν σῶν βουλευμάτων, τούτων τι ἐπρήχθη; ὅρα μὴ ἐξ ὑστέρης σεωυτὸν ἐν αἰτίῃ σχῇς. [3] εἶπε πρὸς ταῦτα Ἱστιαῖος· Βασιλεῦ, κοῖον ἐφθέγξαο ἔπος, ἐμὲ βουλεῦσαι πρῆγμα ἐκ τοῦ σοί τι ἢ μέγα ἢ σμικρὸν ἔμελλε λυπηρὸν ἀνασχήσειν; τί δ᾽ ἂν ἐπιδιζήμενος ποιέοιμι ταῦτα, τεῦ δὲ ἐνδεὴς ἐών, τῷ πάρα μὲν πάντα, ὅσα περ σοί; πάντων δὲ πρὸς σέο βουλευμάτων ἐπακούειν ἀξιοῦμαι. [4] ἀλλ᾽ εἴπερ τι τοιοῦτον, οἷον σὺ εἴρηκας, πρήσσει ὁ ἐμὸς ἐπίτροπος, ἴσθι αὐτόν, ἐπ᾽ ἑωυτοῦ βαλόμενον, πεποιηκέναι. ἀρχὴν δὲ ἔγωγε οὐδὲ ἐνδέκομαι τὸν λόγον, ὅκως τι Μιλήσιοι καὶ ὁ ἐμὸς ἐπίτροπος νεώτερον πρήσσουσι περὶ πρήγματα τὰ σά. εἰ δ᾽ ἄρα τι τοιοῦτο ποιεῦσι καὶ σὺ τὸ ἐὸν ἀκήκοας, ὦ βασιλεῦ, μάθε οἷον πρῆγμα ἐργάσαο, ἐμὲ ἀπὸ θαλάσσης ἀνάσπαστον ποιήσας. [5] Ἴωνες γὰρ οἴκασι, ἐμεῦ ἐξ ὀφθαλμῶν σφι γενομένου, ποιῆσαι τῶν πάλαι ἵμερον εἶχον. ἐμέο δ᾽ ἂν ἐόντος ἐν Ἰωνίῃ οὐδεμία πόλις ὑπεκίνησε. νῦν ὦν ὡς τάχος ἄπες με πορευθῆναι ἐς Ἰωνίην, ἵνα τοι κεῖνά τε πάντα καταρτίσω ἐς τὠυτὸ καὶ τὸν Μιλήτου ἐπίτροπον τοῦτον, τὸν ταῦτα μηχανησάμενον, ἐγχειρίθετον παραδῶ. [6] ταῦτα δὲ κατὰ νόον τὸν σὸν ποιήσας, θεοὺς ἐπόμνυμι τοὺς βασιληίους μὴ μὲν πρότερον ἐκδύσασθαι τὸν ἔχων κιθῶνα καταβήσομαι ἐς Ἰωνίην, πρὶν ἄν τοι Σαρδὼ νῆσον τὴν μεγίστην δασμοφόρον ποιήσω.

V.106.1 ταῦτα: refers back to Dareios's orders to his servant.   **τόν = ὅν.** **ἐπίτροπον:** subject of πεποιηκέναι.   **τῷ = ᾧ.**   **πεποιηκέναι:** main verb in indirect statement.   **μοι:** object of the prefix ἐπι- of ἐπαγαγών.   **ἐπαγαγών:** the objects are ἄνδρας and Ἴωνας.   **δώσοντας:** the tense indicates what Dareios intends to make happen.   **δίκην τῶν ἐποίησαν = δίκην τούτων ἃ ἐποίησαν:** the antecedent τούτων has dropped out, and τῶν is attracted into its case, serving as an objective genitive with δίκην and as the object of ἐποίησαν.   **τούτους:** subject of ἕπεσθαι; τούτους refers to the noun nearest it, in this case Ἴωνας.   **ἕπεσθαι:** dependent on ἀναγνώσας.   **ἐκείνοισι:** refers to the noun further away, in this case ἄνδρας ἐκ τῆς ἑτέρης ἠπείρου, who are the Athenians.   **τοι = σοι.**   **ἔχειν:** complementary with φαίνεται.   **106.2 τούτων:** partitive with τι.   **ἐξ ὑστέρης:** temporal, "later."   **μή ... σχῇς:** a hypothetical subjunctive indicating a possible future outcome.   **106.3 ταῦτα:** refers back to what Dareios has just said.   **ἐφθέγξαο:** intervocalic sigma has dropped out, and the ending remains uncontracted.   **ἐμέ:** subject of βουλεῦσαι.   **βουλεῦσαι:** main verb in indirect statement.   **ἐκ τοῦ = ἐκ οὗ.**   **ἀνασχήσειν:** complementary with ἔμελλε.   **ἄν ... ποιέοιμι:** potential optative.   **τεῦ δὲ ἐνδεὴς ἐών = τίνος δὲ ἐνδεὴς ὤν.**   **τῷ = ᾧ.**   **πάρα μέν = πάρεστι μέν:** is answered by πάντων δέ.   **ὅσα περ σοί:** supply an implied πάρεστι.   **πρὸς σέο = πρὸς σοῦ.**   **ἐπακούειν:** complementary with ἀξιοῦμαι.   **106.4 αὐτόν:** subject of πεποιηκέναι.   **ἐπ᾽ ἑωυτοῦ βαλόμενον:** "calculating on his own."   **πεποιηκέναι:** main verb in indirect statement.   **ἀρχήν:** accusative of respect, "at all."   **τὸ ἐόν:** substantive, "the truth."   **ἐργάσαο:** intervocalic sigma has dropped out and the ending remains uncontracted.   **ποιήσας:** the participial phrase explains οἷον πρῆγμα ἐργάσαο.   **106.5 ἐμεῦ = ἐμοῦ.**   **σφι:** possesses ὀφθαλμῶν.   **ποιῆσαι:** complementary with οἴκασι.   **τῶν πάλαι ἵμερον εἶχον = ταῦτα ὦν πάλαι ἵμερον εἶχον:** the antecedent ταῦτα has dropped out, and τῶν serves as the object of ποιῆσαι and as an objective genitive with ἵμερον.   **ἐμέο = ἐμοῦ.**   **ἄν ... ὑπεκίνησε:** ἄν renders the indicative counterfactual.   **ὡς τάχος:** "quickly" or "immediately."   **με:** subject of πορευθῆναι.   **πορευθῆναι:** dependent on ἄπες.   **τοι = σοι.**   **καταρτίσω ... παραδῶ:** hypothetical subjunctives indicating Histiaios's reasons for why he wants to go to Ionia.   **ἐς τὠυτό = ἐς τὸ αὐτό.**   **τὸν ταῦτα μηχανησάμενον:** substantive, "the one having devised these matters."   **ἐγχειρίθετον:** predicate to ἐπίτροπον.   **106.6 ταῦτα:** refers back to what was just said.   **μὴ μὲν πρότερον:** looks forward to πρίν.   **ἐκδύσασθαι:** complementary with ἐπόμνυμι.   **τὸν ἔχων κιθῶνα = ὃν ἔχων κιθῶνα:** at times the antecedent, here κιθῶνα, is brought into the relative clause, e.g., εἶδεν ἐν ᾗ οἰκέω χώρᾳ ("he saw in which country I dwell") instead of εἶδεν χώραν ἐν ᾗ οἰκῶ.   **ἄν ... ποιήσω:** a hypothetical subjunctive looking forward to an event that may occur.   **τοι = σοι.**   **δασμοφόρον:** predicate to Σαρδώ.

~

V.107.1 Ἱστιαῖος μέν, λέγων ταῦτα, διέβαλλε· Δαρεῖος δὲ ἐπείθετο καί μιν ἀπίει, ἐντειλάμενος, ἐπεάν, τὰ ὑπέσχετό οἱ, ἐπιτελέα ποιήσῃ, παραγίνεσθαί οἱ ὀπίσω ἐς τὰ Σοῦσα.

V.107.1 Ἱστιαῖος μέν: is answered by Δαρεῖος δέ.   **ταῦτα:** refers back to what Histiaios has just said.   **διέβαλλε:** Herodotus resumes the narrative, indicating that Histiaios has been lying to the king.   **μιν = αὐτόν.**   **ἐντειλάμενος:** understand an implied Ἱστιαῖον as object.   **τὰ ὑπέσχετό οἱ = ταῦτα, ἃ ὑπέσχετό αὐτῷ:** the antecedent ταῦτα has dropped out, and τά serves as the object of ὑπέσχετο and ποιήσῃ.   **ποιήσῃ:** a hypothetical subjunctive looking forward to an event that may occur.   **παραγίνεσθαι:** dependent on ἐντειλάμενος; understand an implied Ἱστιαῖον as subject.

~

V.108.1 ἐν ᾧ δὲ ἡ ἀγγελίη τε περὶ τῶν Σαρδίων παρὰ βασιλέα ἀνήιε καὶ Δαρεῖος, τὰ περὶ τὸ τόξον ποιήσας, Ἱστιαίῳ ἐς λόγους ἦλθε καὶ Ἱστιαῖος, μεμετιμένος ὑπὸ Δαρείου, ἐκομίζετο ἐπὶ θάλασσαν, ἐν τούτῳ παντὶ τῷ χρόνῳ ἐγίνετο τάδε. πολιορκέοντι τῷ Σαλαμινίῳ Ὀνησίλῳ Ἀμαθουσίους, ἐξαγγέλλεται νηυσὶ στρατιὴν πολλὴν ἄγοντα Περσικὴν Ἀρτύβιον, ἄνδρα Πέρσην προσδόκιμον, ἐς τὴν Κύπρον εἶναι. [2] πυθόμενος δὲ ταῦτα, ὁ Ὀνήσιλος κήρυκας διέπεμπε ἐς τὴν Ἰωνίην, ἐπικαλεύμενος σφέας. Ἴωνες δέ, οὐκ ἐς μακρὴν βουλευσάμενοι, ἧκον πολλῷ στόλῳ. Ἴωνές τε δὴ παρῆσαν ἐς τὴν Κύπρον καὶ οἱ Πέρσαι, νηυσὶ διαβάντες ἐκ τῆς Κιλικίης, ἤισαν ἐπὶ τὴν Σαλαμῖνα πεζῇ. τῇσι δὲ νηυσὶ οἱ Φοίνικες περιέπλεον τὴν ἄκρην, αἳ καλεῦνται Κληῖδες τῆς Κύπρου.

V.108.1 ἐν ᾧ ... ἐν τούτῳ παντὶ τῷ χρόνῳ: "during which time ... in this entire time." The relative clause has three verbs in it, ἀνήιε, ἦλθε, and ἐκομίζετο.   **τε ... καί ... καί:** the conjunctions mark the three subjects, ἀγγελίη, Δαρεῖος, and Ἱστιαῖος.   **τὰ περὶ τὸ τόξον:** substantive, "the events concerning the bow."   **τάδε:** looks forward to what comes next.   **ἐξαγγέλλεται:** impersonal.   **Ἀρτύβιον:** subject of εἶναι.   **ἄνδρα Πέρσην προσδόκιμον:** in apposition to Ἀρτύβιον.   **ἐς τὴν Κύπρον:** predicate to Ἀρτύβιον.   **εἶναι:** main verb in indirect statement.   **108.2 ταῦτα:** refers back to the presence of Artybios at Kypros.   **ἐς μακρὴν = ἐς μακρὸν χρόνον.**   **τε ... καί:** links the two subjects, Ἴωνές and Πέρσαι.

⁓

V.109.1 τούτου δὲ τοιούτου γινομένου, ἔλεξαν οἱ τύραννοι τῆς Κύπρου, συγκαλέσαντες τῶν Ἰώνων τοὺς στρατηγούς· Ἄνδρες Ἴωνες, αἵρεσιν ὑμῖν δίδομεν ἡμεῖς, οἱ Κύπριοι, ὁκοτέροισι βούλεσθε προσφέρεσθαι, ἢ Πέρσῃσι ἢ Φοίνιξι. [2] εἰ μὲν γὰρ πεζῇ βούλεσθε, ταχθέντες, Περσέων διαπειρᾶσθαι, ὥρη ἂν εἴη ὑμῖν ἐκβάντας ἐκ τῶν νεῶν τάσσεσθαι πεζῇ, ἡμέας δὲ ἐς τὰς νέας ἐσβαίνειν τὰς ὑμετέρας, Φοίνιξι ἀνταγωνιευμένους. εἰ δὲ Φοινίκων μᾶλλον βούλεσθε διαπειρᾶσθαι, ποιέειν χρεόν ἐστι ὑμέας, ὁκότερα ἂν δὴ τούτων ἕλησθε, ὅκως τὸ κατ᾽ ὑμέας ἔσται ἥ τε Ἰωνίη καὶ ἡ Κύπρος ἐλευθέρη. [3] εἶπαν Ἴωνες πρὸς ταῦτα· Ἡμέας δὲ ἀπέπεμψε τὸ κοινὸν τῶν Ἰώνων φυλάξοντας τὴν θάλασσαν, ἀλλ᾽ οὐκ ἵνα Κυπρίοισι τὰς νέας παραδόντες, αὐτοὶ πεζῇ Πέρσῃσι προσφερώμεθα. ἡμεῖς μέν νυν ἐπ᾽ οὗ ἐτάχθημεν, ταύτῃ πειρησόμεθα εἶναι χρηστοί. ὑμέας δὲ χρεόν ἐστι, ἀναμνησθέντας οἷα ἐπάσχετε δουλεύοντες πρὸς τῶν Μήδων, γίνεσθαι ἄνδρας ἀγαθούς.

V.109.1 οἱ Κύπριοι: in apposition to ἡμεῖς.   **προσφέρεσθαι:** complementary with βούλεσθε.   **109.2 εἰ μὲν γάρ:** is answered by ἡμέας δέ.   **διαπειρᾶσθαι:** complementary with βούλεσθε.   **ἂν εἴη:** a potential optative.   **ὑμῖν:** to perform the action of τάσσεσθαι.   **ἐκβάντας:** the pronoun and the participle refer to the same noun; the participle is in the accusative case when the noun it modifies performs the action of an infinitive.   **τάσσεσθαι:** complementary with ὥρη ἂν εἴη.   **ἡμέας:** subject of ἐσβαίνειν.   **ἐσβαίνειν:** complementary with an implied ὥρη ἂν εἴη.   **ἀνταγωνιευμένους = ἀνταγωνιουμένους:** the tense indicates their reason for boarding the ships.   **διαπειρᾶσθαι:** complementary with βούλεσθε.   **ποιέειν:** epexegetical with χρεόν; looks forward to ὅκως.   **ὑμέας:** subject of ποιέειν.   **ἂν ... ἕλησθε:** a hypothetical subjunctive indicating an event in the future. **τούτων**: partitive with ὁκότερα. **ὅκως**: translate with ποιέειν. **τὸ κατ᾽ ὑμέας**: substantive and accusative of respect, "in so far as you are concerned." **109.3 ταῦτα**: refers back to what has just been said. **τὸ κοινὸν τῶν Ἰώνων**: substantive, "the alliance of the Ionians." **φυλάξοντας**: the tense indicates the reason for the collective's sending them. **προσφερώμεθα**: a hypothetical subjunctive indicating why the alliance did not send them. **ἡμεῖς μέν**: is answered by ὑμέας δέ. **ἐπ᾽ οὗ = ἐπὶ τούτου ᾧ**: the antecedent τούτου has dropped out, and οὗ is attracted into its case, serving as the object of ἐπί and as an instrumental dative with τάχθημεν. **ταύτῃ**: "in this"; though a different gender, ταύτῃ refers back to ἐπὶ τούτου ᾧ. **εἶναι**: complementary with πειρησόμεθα. **ὑμέας**: subject of γίνεσθαι. **οἷα = ταῦτα ἅ**: the antecedent ταῦτα has dropped out, and οἷα serves as the object of ἀναμνησθέντας and ἐπάσχετε. **γίνεσθαι**: epexegetical with χρεόν.

～

V.110.1 Ἴωνες μὲν τούτοισι ἀμείψαντο· μετὰ δὲ ἡκόντων ἐς τὸ πεδίον τὸ Σαλαμινίων τῶν Περσέων, διέτασσον οἱ βασιλέες τῶν Κυπρίων, τοὺς μὲν ἄλλους Κυπρίους κατὰ τοὺς ἄλλους στρατιώτας ἀντιτάσσοντες, Σαλαμινίων δὲ καὶ Σολίων ἀπολέξαντες τὸ ἄριστον ἀντέτασσον Πέρσῃσι. Ἀρτυβίῳ δέ, τῷ στρατηγῷ τῶν Περσέων, ἐθελοντὴς ἀντετάσσετο Ὀνήσιλος.

V.110.1 Ἴωνες μέν: is answered by μετὰ δέ. **τούτοισι**: refers back to what has just been said. **μετὰ δέ**: adverbial, "afterward." **τοὺς μὲν ἄλλους**: is answered by Σαλαμινίων δέ. **Σαλαμινίων … Σολίων**: partitive with τὸ ἄριστον. **τὸ ἄριστον**: substantive, "the best." **Πέρσῃσι**: object of the prefix ἀντι- of ἀντέτασσον. **Ἀρτυβίῳ**: see previous note. **τῷ στρατηγῷ**: in apposition to Ἀρτυβίῳ.

～

V.111.1 ἤλαυνε δὲ ἵππον ὁ Ἀρτύβιος, δεδιδαγμένον πρὸς ὁπλίτην ἵστασθαι ὀρθόν. πυθόμενος ὧν ταῦτα ὁ Ὀνήσιλος—ἦν γάρ οἱ ὑπασπιστὴς γένος μὲν Κὰρ τὰ δὲ πολέμια κάρτα δόκιμος καὶ ἄλλως λήματος πλέος—εἶπε πρὸς τοῦτον· [2] Πυνθάνομαι τὸν Ἀρτυβίου ἵππον, ἱστάμενον ὀρθόν, καὶ ποσὶ καὶ στόματι κατεργάζεσθαι πρὸς τὸν ἂν προσενειχθῇ. σὺ ὧν, βουλευσάμενος, εἰπὲ αὐτίκα ὁκότερον βούλεαι, φυλάξας, πλῆξαι εἴτε τὸν ἵππον εἴτε αὐτὸν Ἀρτύβιον. [3] εἶπε πρὸς ταῦτα ὁ ὀπέων αὐτοῦ· Ὦ βασιλεῦ, ἕτοιμος μὲν ἐγώ εἰμι ποιέειν καὶ ἀμφότερα

καὶ τὸ ἕτερον αὐτῶν καὶ πάντως τὸ ἂν σὺ ἐπιτάσσῃς. ὡς μέντοι
ἔμοιγε δοκέει εἶναι τοῖσι σοῖσι πρήγμασι προσφερέστερον, φράσω. [4]
βασιλέα μὲν καὶ στρατηγὸν χρεὸν εἶναι φημὶ βασιλέι τε καὶ στρατηγῷ
προσφέρεσθαι. ἤν τε γὰρ κατέλῃς ἄνδρα στρατηγόν, μέγα τοι γίνεται.
καὶ δεύτερα, ἢν σὲ ἐκεῖνος—τὸ μὴ γένοιτο—ὑπὸ ἀξιοχρέου καὶ ἀποθανεῖν
ἡμίσεα συμφορή. ἡμέας δέ, τοὺς ὑπηρέτας, ἑτέροισί τε ὑπηρέτῃσι
προσφέρεσθαι καὶ πρὸς ἵππον, τοῦ σὺ τὰς μηχανὰς μηδὲν φοβηθῇς. ἐγὼ
γάρ τοι ὑποδέκομαι μή μιν ἀνδρὸς ἔτι γε μηδενὸς στήσεσθαι ἐναντίον.

V.111.1 ἵστασθαι: complementary with δεδιδαγμένον.   **ὀρθόν:** predicate; i.e., to
stand on his hind legs.   **ταῦτα:** refers back to the horse's fighting prowess.   **οἱ =
αὐτῷ:** possesses ὑπασπιστής.   **γένος μέν:** is answered by τὰ δὲ πολέμια; both are
accusatives of respect.   **τοῦτον:** refers back to the Karian warrior.   **111.2 ἵππον:**
subject of κατεργάζεσθαι.   **καί ... καί:** "both ... and."   **κατεργάζεσθαι:**
main verb in indirect statement.   **πρὸς τόν = τοῦτον πρὸς ὅν:** the antecedent
τοῦτον has dropped out, and τόν serves as the understood object of κατεργάζεσθαι
and as the object of πρός.   **ἂν προσενειχθῇ:** a hypothetical subjunctive
indicating an action that occurs with some frequency.   **πλῆξαι:** complementary
with βούλεαι.   **111.3 ταῦτα:** as often ταῦτα refers back to what has just been
said.   **ἕτοιμος μέν:** is answered by, it seems, ὡς μέντοι ἔμοιγε δοκέει.   **ποιέειν:**
epexegetical with ἕτοιμος.   **καί ... καί ... καί:** indicate the three things the
Karian is willing to do.   **τό = τοῦτο ὅ:** the antecedent τοῦτο has dropped
out, and τό serves as the object of ποιέειν and ἐπιτάσσῃς.   **ἐπιτάσσῃς:**
a hypothetical subjunctive, indicating a possible future event.   **εἶναι:**
complementary with δοκέει.   **φράσω:** a hypothetical subjunctive, indicating
politeness on the part of the Karian.   **111.4 βασιλέα μέν:** is answered by ἡμέας
δέ.   **βασιλέα ... στρατηγόν:** subjects of προσφέρεσθαι.   **χρεόν:** subject of
εἶναι.   **προσφέρεσθαι:** epexegetical with χρεόν.   **κατέλῃς:** a hypothetical
subjunctive, indicating a possible future event.   **τοι = σοι.**   **ἢν σὲ ἐκεῖνος:**
supply an implied κατέλῃ.   **τὸ μὴ γένοιτο = ὃ μὴ γένοιτο:** an optative of
wish, "may this not happen!"   **ὑπὸ ἀξιοχρέου:** substantive, "by a worthy
foe."   **ἀποθανεῖν:** epexegetical with συμφορή.   **συμφορή:** supply an implied
γίνεται.   **ἡμέας:** subject of προσφέρεσθαι.   **τοὺς ὑπηρέτας:** in apposition
to ἡμέας.   **προσφέρεσθαι:** epexegetical with an implied χρεὸν εἶναι.   **καὶ
πρὸς ἵππον:** "even against a horse"; understand an implied χρεὸν εἶναι ἡμέας
προσφέρεσθαι.   **τοῦ = οὗ:** translate with τὰς μηχανάς; the pronoun σύ comes
between the relative pronoun and what it possesses.   **μηδέν:** accusative of
respect.   **φοβηθῇς:** a passive subjunctive.   **τοι = σοι.**   **μή ... μηδενός:** the
negatives are μή because the promise lies in the uncertain future.   **μιν = αὐτόν =
τὸν ἵππον:** subject of στήσεσθαι.   **ἀνδρός:** translate with στήσεσθαι ἐναντίον.

~

V.112.1 ταῦτα εἶπε. καὶ μεταυτίκα συνέμισγε τὰ στρατόπεδα πεζῇ
καὶ νηυσί. νηυσὶ μέν νυν ˮΙωνες ἄκροι γενόμενοι ταύτην τὴν ἡμέρην
ὑπερεβάλοντο τοὺς Φοίνικας καὶ τούτων Σάμιοι ἠρίστευσαν. πεζῇ δέ,
ὡς συνῆλθε τὰ στρατόπεδα, συμπεσόντα ἐμάχοντο. [2] κατὰ δὲ τοὺς
στρατηγοὺς ἀμφοτέρους τάδε ἐγίνετο. ὡς προσεφέρετο πρὸς τὸν
Ὀνήσιλον ὁ Ἀρτύβιος ἐπὶ τοῦ ἵππου κατήμενος, ὁ Ὀνήσιλος, κατὰ τὰ
συνεθήκατο τῷ ὑπασπιστῇ, παίει προσφερόμενον αὐτὸν τὸν Ἀρτύβιον.
ἐπιβαλόντος δὲ τοῦ ἵππου τοὺς πόδας ἐπὶ τὴν Ὀνησίλου ἀσπίδα,
ἐνθαῦτα ὁ Κάρ, δρεπάνῳ πλήξας, ἀπαράσσει τοῦ ἵππου τοὺς πόδας.

V.112.1 **ταῦτα**: refers back to what the Karian just said.   **νηυσί**: dative of
respect.   **νηυσὶ μέν**: is answered by πεζῇ δέ.   **τούτων**: partitive with
ˮΙωνες.   **ὡς**: temporal.   **112.2 τάδε**: looks forward to what comes next.   **ὡς**:
temporal.   **κατὰ τὰ συνεθήκατο = κατὰ ταῦτα ἃ συνεθήκατο**: the antecedent
ταῦτα has dropped out, and τά serves as the object of κατά and συνεθήκατο.   **τῷ**
ὑπασπιστῇ: the object of συν- of συνεθήκατο.

~

V.113.1 Ἀρτύβιος μὲν δή, ὁ στρατηγὸς τῶν Περσέων, ὁμοῦ τῷ ἵππῳ
πίπτει αὐτοῦ ταύτῃ. μαχομένων δὲ καὶ τῶν ἄλλων, Στησήνωρ,
τύραννος ἐὼν Κουρίου, προδιδοῖ, ἔχων δύναμιν ἀνδρῶν περὶ
ἑωυτὸν οὐ σμικρήν. οἱ δὲ Κουριέες οὗτοι λέγονται εἶναι Ἀργείων
ἄποικοι. προδόντων δὲ τῶν Κουριέων, αὐτίκα καὶ τὰ Σαλαμινίων
πολεμιστήρια ἅρματα τὠυτὸ τοῖσι Κουριεῦσι ἐποίεε. γινομένων δὲ
τούτων, κατυπέρτεροι ἦσαν οἱ Πέρσαι τῶν Κυπρίων. [2] τετραμμένου
δὲ τοῦ στρατοπέδου, ἄλλοι τε ἔπεσον πολλοὶ καὶ δὴ καὶ Ὀνήσιλός
τε ὁ Χέρσιος, ὅς περ τὴν Κυπρίων ἀπόστασιν ἔπρηξε, καὶ ὁ Σολίων
βασιλεύς, Ἀριστόκυπρος ὁ Φιλοκύπρου, Φιλοκύπρου δὲ τούτου, τὸν
Σόλων ὁ Ἀθηναῖος, ἀπικόμενος ἐς Κύπρον, ἐν ἔπεσι αἴνεσε τυράννων
μάλιστα.

V.113.1 **Ἀρτύβιος μὲν δή**: is answered by μαχομένων δέ.   **ὁ στρατηγός**: in
apposition with Ἀρτύβιος.   **αὐτοῦ ταύτῃ**: "there on that spot."   **τύραννος**: in
apposition with Στησήνωρ.   **εἶναι**: complementary with λέγονται.   **τὠυτό**
= τὸ αὐτό.   **τοῖσι Κουριεῦσι**: translate with τὠυτό, e.g., τὸ αὐτό σοι ποιέω

("I do the same thing as you do").   **τούτων:** refers back to the events just described.   **τῶν Κυπρίων:** translate with κατυπέρτεροι.   **113.2 τε ... καὶ δὴ καί:** τε introduces the general, πολλοί, and καὶ δὴ καί the specific, Ὀνήσιλός and Ἀριστόκυπρος.   **τόν = ὅν.**   **τυράννων:** partitive with τόν.

V.114.1 Ὀνησίλου μέν νυν Ἀμαθούσιοι, ὅτι σφέας ἐπολιόρκησε, ἀποταμόντες τὴν κεφαλὴν ἐκόμισαν ἐς Ἀμαθοῦντα καί μιν ἀνεκρέμασαν ὑπὲρ τῶν πυλέων. κρεμαμένης δὲ τῆς κεφαλῆς καὶ ἤδη ἐούσης κοίλης, ἑσμὸς μελισσέων, ἐσδὺς ἐς αὐτήν, κηρίων μιν ἐνέπλησε. [2] τούτου δὲ γενομένου τοιούτου—ἐχρέωντο γὰρ περὶ αὐτῆς οἱ Ἀμαθούσιοι—ἐμαντεύθη σφι, τὴν μὲν κεφαλὴν κατελόντας, θάψαι· Ὀνησίλῳ δὲ θύειν ὡς ἥρωϊ ἀνὰ πᾶν ἔτος. καί σφι ποιεῦσι ταῦτα ἄμεινον συνοίσεσθαι.

V.114.1 Ὀνησίλου: translate with τὴν κεφαλήν; separating the genitive noun from what it possesses creates dramatic tension. Consider this similar example, "Queen Anne's—for she had done him many a wrong—head he cut off and placed on a pale."   Ὀνησίλου μέν νυν Ἀμαθούσιοι: is, it seems, answered by Ἴωνες δέ of chapter 115.   μιν = αὐτήν = τὴν κεφαλήν.   μιν: see previous note.   **114.2** ἐμαντεύθη: impersonal.   σφι: to perform the action of θάψαι and θύειν.   τὴν μὲν κεφαλήν: is answered by Ὀνησίλῳ δέ.   κατελόντας: though it should agree with σφι, κατελόντας is accusative because of the upcoming infinitives θάψαι and θύειν.   ποιεῦσι = ποιοῦσι: the dative plural participle and third-person finite verb are look-alike forms; note that the participle in this instance does agree with the pronoun and does not perform the action of the infinitive.   ταῦτα: refers back to what has just been said.   ἄμεινον: impersonal and subject of συνοίσεσθαι.

V.115.1 Ἀμαθούσιοι μέν νυν ἐποίευν ταῦτα καὶ τὸ μέχρι ἐμεῦ· Ἴωνες δέ, οἱ ἐν Κύπρῳ ναυμαχήσαντες, ἐπείτε ἔμαθον τὰ πρήγματα τὰ Ὀνησίλου διεφθαρμένα καὶ τὰς πόλις τῶν Κυπρίων πολιορκευμένας τὰς ἄλλας πλὴν Σαλαμῖνος, ταύτην δὲ Γόργῳ, τῷ προτέρῳ βασιλέι, τοὺς Σαλαμινίους παραδόντας, αὐτίκα μαθόντες οἱ Ἴωνες ταῦτα ἀπέπλεον ἐς τὴν Ἰωνίην. [2] τῶν δὲ ἐν Κύπρῳ πολίων ἀντέσχε χρόνον ἐπὶ πλεῖστον πολιορκευμένη Σόλοι, τὴν πέριξ ὑπορύσσοντες τὸ τεῖχος, πέμπτῳ μηνὶ εἷλον οἱ Πέρσαι.

V.115.1 Ἀμαθούσιοι μέν νυν: resumes Ὀνησίλου μέν νυν Ἀμαθούσιοι from chapter 114.1 and is answered by Ἴωνες δέ.   **ταῦτα**: refers back to the sacrifices to the hero Onesilos.   **καὶ τὸ μέχρι ἐμεῦ**: substantive, "even up to my own day"; it is a temporal marker for Herodotus's audience.   **Ἴωνες**: subject of the upcoming ἀπέπλεον.   **οἱ ἐν Κύπρῳ ναυμαχήσαντες**: substantive, "those in Kypros having fought at sea."   **ἔμαθον**: the three things they realize are expressed by the participles διεφθαρμένα, πολιορκευμένας, παραδόντας, each modifying a different noun.   **οἱ Ἴωνες**: since the main verb has been delayed, the subject is repeated.   **ταῦτα**: refers back to what has just been said.   **115.2 τῶν δὲ ἐν Κύπρῳ πολίων**: partitive with Σόλοι.   **Σόλοι**: a city on Kypros.   **τὴν = ἥν.**   **ὑπορύσσοντες**: for a description of tunneling under a wall during a siege, see Polybius, *Histories* 21.28.

~

V.116.1 Κύπριοι μὲν δή, ἐνιαυτὸν ἐλεύθεροι γενόμενοι, αὖτις ἐκ νέης κατεδεδούλωντο. Δαυρίσης δὲ ἔχων Δαρείου θυγατέρα καὶ Ὑμαίης τε καὶ Ὀτάνης, ἄλλοι Πέρσαι στρατηγοί, ἔχοντες καὶ οὗτοι Δαρείου θυγατέρας, ἐπιδιώξαντες τοὺς ἐς Σάρδις στρατευσαμένους Ἰώνων καὶ ἐσαράξαντες σφέας ἐς τὰς νέας, τῇ μάχῃ ὡς ἐπεκράτησαν, τὸ ἐνθεῦτεν ἐπιδιελόμενοι τὰς πόλις ἐπόρθεον.

V.116.1 Κύπριοι μέν: is answered by Δαυρίσης δέ.   **αὖτις ἐκ νέης**: substantive, "once again."   **ἄλλοι Πέρσαι στρατηγοί**: in apposition to Ὑμαίης and Ὀτάνης.   **Ἰώνων**: partitive with τοὺς ἐς Σάρδις στρατευσαμένους.   **ὡς**: temporal.   **τὸ ἐνθεῦτεν**: substantive, "from that point on."

~

V.117.1 Δαυρίσης μέν, τραπόμενος πρὸς τὰς ἐν Ἑλλησπόντῳ πόλις, εἷλε μὲν Δάρδανον. εἷλε δὲ Ἄβυδόν τε καὶ Περκώτην καὶ Λάμψακον καὶ Παισόν. ταύτας μὲν ἐπ᾽ ἡμέρῃ ἑκάστῃ αἴρεε. ἀπὸ δὲ Παισοῦ ἐλαύνοντί οἱ ἐπὶ Πάριον πόλιν ἦλθε ἀγγελίη τοὺς Κᾶρας, τὠυτὸ Ἴωσι φρονήσαντας, ἀπεστάναι ἀπὸ Περσέων. ἀποστρέψας ὦν ἐκ τοῦ Ἑλλησπόντου, ἤλαυνε τὸν στρατὸν ἐπὶ τὴν Καρίην.

V.117.1 Δαυρίσης μέν: is answered by πυθόμενοι δέ from chapter 118.1.   **εἷλε μὲν Δάρδανον**: is answered by εἷλε δὲ Ἄβυδόν.   **ταύτας μέν**: is answered by ἀπὸ δὲ Παισοῦ.   **ἐπ᾽ ἡμέρῃ ἑκάστῃ**: i.e., he took one city each day.   **οἱ = αὐτῷ.**   **τοὺς Κᾶρας**: subject of ἀπεστάναι.   **τὠυτὸ Ἴωσι φρονήσαντας = τὸ**

αὐτό Ἴωσι φρονήσαντας: consider the similar expression, τὰ αὐτά σοι ποιέω ("I do the same things as you").   ἀπεστάναι: main verb in indirect statement.

~

V.118.1 καί κως ταῦτα τοῖσι Καρσὶ ἐξαγγέλθη πρότερον ἢ τὸν Δαυρίσην ἀπικέσθαι. πυθόμενοι δὲ οἱ Κᾶρες συνελέγοντο ἐπὶ Λευκάς τε Στήλας καλεομένας καὶ ποταμὸν Μαρσύην, ὃς ῥέων ἐκ τῆς Ἰδριάδος χώρης ἐς τὸν Μαίανδρον ἐκδιδοῖ. [2] συλλεχθέντων δὲ τῶν Καρῶν ἐνθαῦτα ἐγίνοντο βουλαὶ ἄλλαι τε πολλαὶ καὶ ἀρίστη γε δοκέουσα εἶναι ἐμοὶ Πιξωδάρου τοῦ Μαυσώλου, ἀνδρὸς Κινδυέος, ὃς τοῦ Κιλίκων βασιλέος, Συεννέσιος, εἶχε θυγατέρα. τούτου τοῦ ἀνδρὸς ἡ γνώμη ἔφερε διαβάντας τὸν Μαίανδρον τοὺς Κᾶρας καὶ κατὰ νώτου ἔχοντας τὸν ποταμὸν οὕτω συμβάλλειν, ἵνα μὴ ἔχοντες ὀπίσω φεύγειν οἱ Κᾶρες, αὐτοῦ τε μένειν ἀναγκαζόμενοι, γινοίατο ἔτι ἀμείνονες τῆς φύσιος. [3] αὕτη μέν νυν οὐκ ἐνίκα ἡ γνώμη. ἀλλὰ τοῖσι Πέρσῃσι κατὰ νώτου γίνεσθαι τὸν Μαίανδρον μᾶλλον ἢ σφίσι. δηλαδή, ἢν φυγὴ τῶν Περσέων γένηται καὶ ἐσσωθέωσι τῇ συμβολῇ, ὡς οὐκ ἀπονοστήσουσι, ἐς τὸν ποταμὸν ἐσπίπτοντες.

V.118.1 ταῦτα: refers back to the conquests of the Persians.   **τὸν Δαυρίσην:** subject of ἀπικέσθαι.   **ἀπικέσθαι:** main verb after πρότερον ἤ.   **118.2 τε … καί:** τε introduces the general, ἄλλαι τε πολλαί, and καί the specific, ἀρίστη. Much of the below offers the perspective of the Karians.   **εἶναι:** complementary with δοκέουσα.   **ἐμοί:** Herodotus inserts himself into the narrative of the Karians.   **ἀνδρὸς Κινδυέος:** in apposition with Πιξωδάρου.   **Συεννέσιος:** in apposition with τοῦ Κιλίκων βασιλέος.   **ἔφερε:** "proposed."   **τοὺς Κᾶρας:** subject of συμβάλλειν.   **συμβάλλειν:** main verb in indirect statement.   **φεύγειν:** complementary with ἔχοντες.   **αὐτοῦ:** "there."   **μένειν:** complementary with ἀναγκαζόμενοι.   **γινοίατο = γίγνοιντο:** a hypothetical optative giving Pixodaros's reason for wanting the river at the Karians' back.   **τῆς φύσιος:** translate with ἀμείνονες; although Herodotus states that the strategy is Pixodaros's, he is nonetheless taken to task for betraying a complete ignorance of military tactics. I am unaware of any data on how well the psychological ploy of "no retreat" works in military affairs. I can note that there is the populist admonition to beware of the trapped animal and that there are at least two military strategists, Sir Basil H. Liddel-Hart (*Strategy*, 1954) and Sun Tzu (*Art of War*), who agree with Pixodaros that a warrior who has no means of escape is a most formidable foe.   **118.3 αὕτη μέν νυν:** is answered by ἀλλὰ τοῖσι Πέρσῃσι.   **τοῖσι**

Πέρσῃσι: possesses νώτου. **γίνεσθαι:** main verb in indirect statement; supply an implied ἐνίκα ἡ γνώμη. **τὸν Μαίανδρον:** subject of γίνεσθαι. **σφίσι:** possesses an implied νώτου. **δηλαδή ... ὡς:** supply an implied ἐστι, "it is clear that." **γένηται ... ἐσσωθέωσι:** hypothetical subjunctives indicating a possible future occurrence. **οὐκ ἀπονοστήσουσι:** understand an implied "home."

V.119.1 μετὰ δὲ παρεόντων καὶ διαβάντων τὸν Μαίανδρον τῶν Περσέων, ἐνθαῦτα ἐπὶ τῷ Μαρσύῃ ποταμῷ συνέβαλόν τε τοῖσι Πέρσῃσι οἱ Κᾶρες καὶ μάχην ἐμαχέσαντο ἰσχυρὴν καὶ ἐπὶ χρόνον πολλόν. τέλος δὲ ἐσσώθησαν διὰ πλῆθος. Περσέων μὲν δὴ ἔπεσον ἄνδρες ἐς δισχιλίους, Καρῶν δὲ ἐς μυρίους. [2] ἐνθεῦτεν δὲ οἱ διαφυγόντες αὐτῶν κατειλήθησαν ἐς Λάβραυνδα ἐς Διὸς στρατίου ἱρόν, μέγα τε καὶ ἅγιον ἄλσος πλατανίστων. μοῦνοι δὲ τῶν ἡμεῖς ἴδμεν Κᾶρες εἰσὶ οἳ Διὶ στρατίῳ θυσίας ἀνάγουσι. κατειληθέντες δὲ ὧν οὗτοι ἐνθαῦτα ἐβουλεύοντο περὶ σωτηρίης, ὁκότερα ἢ παραδόντες σφέας αὐτοὺς Πέρσῃσι ἢ ἐκλιπόντες τὸ παράπαν τὴν Ἀσίην ἄμεινον πρήξουσι.

V.119.1 μετὰ δέ: adverbial, "and so." **τε ... καί:** links συνέβαλον and μάχην ἐμαχέσαντο. **πολλόν = πολύν.** **τέλος:** accusative of respect. **διὰ πλῆθος:** "by superior numbers." **Περσέων μέν:** is answered by Καρῶν δέ; Περσέων is partitive with ἄνδρες. **Καρῶν:** partitive with an implied ἄνδρες. **ἐς μυρίους:** the quantity is believed to be quite a bit too high. **119.2 οἱ διαφυγόντες:** substantive, "those having escaped." **αὐτῶν:** partitive with οἱ διαφυγόντες. **ἄλσος:** in apposition with ἱρόν. **μοῦνοι δὲ τῶν ἡμεῖς ἴδμεν = μοῦνοι δὲ τούτων οὓς ἡμεῖς ἴδμεν:** the antecedent τούτων has dropped out, and τῶν is partitive with μοῦνοι and is also the object of ἴδμεν. **ἄμεινον:** accusative of respect, "better." **πρήξουσι:** instead of the future optative, the future indicative is retained.

V.120.1 βουλευομένοισι δέ σφι ταῦτα παραγίνονται βοηθέοντες Μιλήσιοί τε καὶ οἱ τούτων σύμμαχοι. ἐνθαῦτα δὲ τὰ μὲν πρότερον οἱ Κᾶρες ἐβουλεύοντο μετῆκαν. οἱ δὲ αὖτις πολεμέειν ἐξ ἀρχῆς ἀρτέοντο. καὶ ἐπιοῦσί τε τοῖσι Πέρσῃσι συμβάλλουσι καὶ μαχεσάμενοι ἐπὶ πλέον ἢ πρότερον ἐσσώθησαν. πεσόντων δὲ τῶν πάντων πολλῶν μάλιστα Μιλήσιοι ἐπλήγησαν.

V.120.1 ταῦτα: refers back to the Karians deciding whether to surrender or to flee.   **τὰ μὲν πρότερον = ταῦτα μὲν ἃ πρότερον:** is answered by οἱ δὲ αὖτις; the antecedent ταῦτα has dropped out, and τά serves as the object of ἐβουλεύοντο and μετῆκαν.   **πολεμέειν:** complementary with ἀρτέοντο.   **ἐπὶ πλέον ἢ πρότερον:** "even worse than before."   **πεσόντων δὲ τῶν πάντων πολλῶν:** partitive with μάλιστα Μιλήσιοι.

~

V.121.1 μετὰ δὲ τοῦτο τὸ τρῶμα ἀνέλαβόν τε καὶ ἀνεμαχέσαντο οἱ Κᾶρες· πυθόμενοι γὰρ ὡς στρατεύεσθαι ὁρμέαται οἱ Πέρσαι ἐπὶ τὰς πόλις σφέων, ἐλόχησαν τὴν ἐν Πηδάσῳ ὁδόν, ἐς τὴν ἐμπεσόντες οἱ Πέρσαι νυκτὸς διεφθάρησαν καὶ αὐτοὶ καὶ οἱ στρατηγοὶ αὐτῶν Δαυρίσης καὶ Ἀμόργης καὶ Σισιμάκης. σὺν δέ σφι ἀπέθανε καὶ Μύρσος ὁ Γύγεω. τοῦ δὲ λόχου τούτου ἡγεμὼν ἦν Ἡρακλείδης Ἰβανώλλιος, ἀνὴρ Μυλασσεύς.

V.121.1 στρατεύεσθαι: complementary with ὁρμέαται.   **ἐς τήν =** **ἐς ἥν.**   **Δαυρίσης . . . Ἀμόργης . . . Σισιμάκης:** in apposition with οἱ στρατηγοί.   **ἀνήρ:** in apposition with Ἡρακλείδης.

~

V.122.1 οὗτοι μέν νυν τῶν Περσέων οὕτω διεφθάρησαν. Ὑμαίης δέ, καὶ αὐτὸς ἐὼν τῶν ἐπιδιωξάντων τοὺς ἐς Σάρδις στρατευσαμένους Ἰώνων, τραπόμενος ἐς τὸν Προποντίδα εἷλε Κίον τὴν Μυσίην. [2] ταύτην δὲ ἐξελών, ὡς ἐπύθετο τὸν Ἑλλήσποντον ἐκλελοιπέναι Δαυρίσην καὶ στρατεύεσθαι ἐπὶ Καρίης, καταλιπὼν τὴν Προποντίδα ἐπὶ τὸν Ἑλλήσποντον ἦγε τὸν στρατόν. καὶ εἷλε μὲν Αἰολέας πάντας ὅσοι τὴν Ἰλιάδα νέμονται. εἷλε δὲ Γέργιθας, τοὺς ὑπολειφθέντας τῶν ἀρχαίων Τευκρῶν. αὐτός τε Ὑμαίης, αἱρέων ταῦτα τὰ ἔθνεα, νούσῳ τελευτᾷ ἐν τῇ Τρῳάδι.

V.122.1 οὗτοι μέν νυν: is answered by Ὑμαίης δέ.   **τῶν Περσέων:** partitive with οὗτοι.   **ἐὼν τῶν ἐπιδιωξάντων:** partitive with Ὑμαίης.   **Ἰώνων:** partitive with τοὺς ἐς Σάρδις στρατευσαμένους.   **τράπω =** **τρέπω.**   **122.2 ὡς:** temporal.   **Δαυρίσην:** subject of ἐκλελοιπέναι and στρατεύεσθαι.   **ἐκλελοιπέναι . . . στρατεύεσθαι:** main verbs in indirect statement.   **εἷλε μὲν Αἰολέας:** is answered by εἷλε δὲ Γέργιθας.   **τοὺς**

ὑπολειφθέντας: substantive, "the descendants"; the term is in apposition with Γέργιθας.   τῶν ἀρχαίων Τευκρῶν: partitive with τοὺς ὑπολειφθέντας.

~

V.123.1 οὗτος μὲν δὴ οὕτω ἐτελεύτησε· Ἀρταφρένης δέ, ὁ Σαρδίων ὕπαρχος, καὶ Ὀτάνης, ὁ τρίτος στρατηγός, ἐτάχθησαν ἐπὶ τὴν Ἰωνίην καὶ τὴν προσεχέα Αἰολίδα στρατεύεσθαι. Ἰωνίης μέν νυν Κλαζομενὰς αἱρέουσι, Αἰολέων δὲ Κύμην.

V.123.1 οὗτος μέν: refers back to Hymaies and is answered by Ἀρταφρένης δέ.   ὕπαρχος: in apposition with Ἀρταφρένης.   στρατηγός: in apposition with Ὀτάνης.   στρατεύεσθαι: complementary with ἐτάχθησαν.   Ἰωνίης μέν: is answered by Αἰολέων δέ.   Κύμην: supply an implied αἱρέουσι.

~

V.124.1 ἁλισκομενέων δὲ τῶν πολίων, ἦν γὰρ, ὡς διέδεξε, Ἀρισταγόρης ὁ Μιλήσιος ψυχὴν οὐκ ἄκρος, ὅς, ταράξας τὴν Ἰωνίην καὶ ἐγκερασάμενος πρήγματα μεγάλα, δρησμὸν ἐβούλευε, ὀρέων ταῦτα. πρὸς δέ οἱ καὶ ἀδύνατα ἐφάνη βασιλέα Δαρεῖον ὑπερβαλέσθαι. [2] πρὸς ταῦτα δὴ ὦν, συγκαλέσας τοὺς συστασιώτας, ἐβουλεύετο, λέγων ὡς ἄμεινον σφίσι εἴη κρησφύγετόν τι ὑπάρχον εἶναι, ἢν ἄρα ἐξωθέωνται ἐκ τῆς Μιλήτου. εἴτε δὴ ὦν ἐς Σαρδὼ ἐκ τοῦ τόπου τούτου ἄγοι ἐς ἀποικίην, εἴτε ἐς Μύρκινον τὴν Ἠδωνῶν—τὴν Ἱστιαῖος ἐτείχεε, παρὰ Δαρείου δωρεὴν λαβών—ταῦτα ἐπειρώτα ὁ Ἀρισταγόρης.

V.124.1 ψυχήν: accusative of respect.   οὐκ ἄκρος: a Herodotean evaluation.   ταῦτα: looks back to the captured cities.   πρὸς δέ: adverbial, "and additionally."   οἱ = αὐτῷ.   ὑπερβαλέσθαι: epexegetical with ἀδύνατα.   124.2 ταῦτα: refers back to what has just been said.   εἴη: probably a potential optative without ἄν (Smyth 1821).   κρησφύγετον: subject of εἶναι.   εἶναι: epexegetical with ἄμεινον.   ἐξωθέωνται: a hypothetical subjunctive, indicating a possible future event.   ἄγοι: optative standing for an original deliberative subjunctive.   ἐς Μύρκινον: supply an implied ἄγοι.   τήν = ἥν.   ταῦτα: ταῦτα refers back to the two choices just given by Aristagores.

~

V.125.1 Ἑκαταίου μέν νυν τοῦ Ἡγησάνδρου, ἀνδρὸς λογοποιοῦ, τουτέων μὲν ἐς οὐδετέρην στέλλειν ἔφερε ἡ γνώμη. ἐν Λέρῳ δὲ

τῇ νήσῳ τεῖχος οἰκοδομησάμενον ἡσυχίην ἄγειν, ἢν ἐκπέσῃ ἐκ τῆς
Μιλήτου. ἔπειτα δὲ ἐκ ταύτης ὁρμώμενον κατελεύσεσθαι ἐς τὴν
Μίλητον.

V.125.1 Ἑκαταίου: possesses γνώμη; an historian, c. 500 B.C.E., who wrote
historical and geographical accounts of Asia Minor and the East. Hekataios is
cited by Herodotus in a few passages (II.143; V.36; V.125–26; VI.137).   **μέν νυν:**
is answered by αὐτῷ δὲ Ἀρισταγόρῃ of chapter 126.1.   **τουτέων μέν:** partitive
with οὐδετέρην and is answered by ἐν Λέρῳ δέ.   **στέλλειν:** complementary
with ἔφερε ἡ γνώμη.   **οἰκοδομησάμενον:** modifies an implied Ἀρισταγόρην
and is the subject of ἄγειν.   **ἄγειν:** complementary with an implied ἔφερε
ἡ γνώμη.   **ἐκπέσῃ:** a hypothetical subjunctive, indicating a possible future
event.   **ὁρμώμενον:** modifies an implied Ἀρισταγόρην and is the subject of
κατελεύσεσθαι.   **κατελεύσεσθαι:** complementary with an implied ἔφερε ἡ
γνώμη.

~

V.126.1 ταῦτα μὲν δὴ Ἑκαταῖος συνεβούλευε. αὐτῷ δὲ Ἀρισταγόρῃ
ἡ πλείστη γνώμη ἦν ἐς τὴν Μύρκινον ἀπάγειν. τὴν μὲν δὴ Μίλητον
ἐπιτράπει Πυθαγόρῃ, ἀνδρὶ τῶν ἀστῶν δοκίμῳ. αὐτὸς δέ, παραλαβὼν
πάντα τὸν βουλόμενον, ἔπλεε ἐς τὴν Θρηίκην. καὶ ἔσχε τὴν χώρην
ἐπ᾽ ἣν ἐστάλη. [2] ἐκ δὲ ταύτης ὁρμώμενος, ἀπόλλυται ὑπὸ Θρηίκων
αὐτός τε ὁ Ἀρισταγόρης καὶ ὁ στρατὸς αὐτοῦ, πόλιν περικατήμενος καὶ
βουλομένων τῶν Θρηίκων ὑποσπόνδων ἐξιέναι.

V.126.1 ταῦτα: refers back to what has just been said in chapter 125.   **ταῦτα μὲν
δὴ Ἑκαταῖος:** resumes Ἑκαταίου μέν νυν from chapter 125.1 and is answered by
αὐτῷ δὲ Ἀρισταγόρῃ.   **Ἀρισταγόρῃ:** to perform the action of ἀπάγειν.   **ἡ
πλείστη γνώμη:** "majority opinion."   **ἀπάγειν:** epexegetical with ἡ πλείστη
γνώμη.   **τὴν μὲν δή:** is answered by αὐτὸς δέ.   **ἀνδρί:** in apposition with
Πυθαγόρῃ.   **126.2 ἐξιέναι:** complementary with βουλομένων.

~ APPENDIX A

Case and Function Chart

In making this chart, a primary consideration has been to represent as many different functions as possible with the fewest number of labels. Thus, the genitive of dependence, for example, is used as a catchall for a number of incidences where a genitive noun must be translated with another noun. Likewise, the dative indirect object covers a number of incidences typically found under the dative of reference category. The underlying philosophy is to explain more with less. Should you wish to look at more labels, Smyth's *Greek Grammar* is a good resource to consult.

Case	Function	Supply in English
NOMINATIVE	1. **Subject: he** eats **Καμβύσης** ἐστρατεύετο ("**Kambyses** marched")	none
	2. **Predicate Nominative:** he is a **doctor** οὔνομα αὐτῇ ἦν **Νίτητις** ("her name was **Nitetis**")	none
	3. **Predicate Adjective:** the dog is **brown** τὰ οἰκήια ἦν μέζω **κακά** ("the personal matters were too **terrible**")	none

Case	Function	Supply in English
GENITIVE	1. **Possession:** the car **of John** νεκρὸς **ἀνθρώπου** ("the corpse **of a man**")	*of*
	2. **Partitive:** ἐξ **τῶν ἀνδρῶν** ("six **of the men**")	*of*
	3. **Dependence:** a bag **of gold** τοῦ **χρυσοῦ** θήκη ("chest **of gold**")	*of*
	4. **Object of a Verb or Verb's Prefix:** **χρημάτων** ἐδέοντο ("they were in need **of money**"); **ἐκείνων** ταῦτα προτίθησι ("he places these things **before those**")	
	5. **Absolute:** ἐπιφανοῦς **τούτου γενομένου** ("**this being** clear")	*none*
	6. **Comparison:** ὁ Ὅμηρος δικαιότερος **ἀδελφοῦ** ("Homer is more just than **his brother**")	*than*
	7. **With Certain Adjectives or Adverbs:** **σοῦ** ἄξιος ("worthy **of you**")	
	8. **Value:** αὐτὸν **πολλοῦ** τιμᾷ ("he honors him **a lot**"); ὁ μὲν **λόγου οὐδενός** ("the man **of no account**")	*of*
	9. **Separation:** he frees us **from slavery** τὰ πηδάλια παρέλυσε νεῶν ("he freed the rudders **from the ships**")	*from/away from*
	10. **Time:** δέκα **ἡμερῶν** ("**within ten days**")	*within*
	11. **Object of Preposition:** ὑπὸ **Ὁμήρου** ("**by Homer**")	
DATIVE	1. **Indirect Object:** he gives a book **to Sara** OR he makes a coat **for Jim** **ὑμῖν** ἔχει καλῶς ("it goes well **for you**") δίκην **αὐτῇ** αἱροῦμαι ("I choose justice **for her**")	*to* *for*
	2. **Object of Verb or Verb's Prefix:** ἐπὶ κρήνην **αὐτοῖς** ἡγήσασθαι ("to lead **them** to the spring") τὴν ἐλευθερίαν **ὑμῖν** περιτίθημι ("I place freedom **around you**")	

Case	Function	Supply in English
	3. **Means or Instrument:** he cuts down the tree with **a sword** OR he wins **by his intelligence.** ἔχουσιν αὐτὸ **δόλῳ** ("they held it **by trickery**")	*by/with*
	4. **Possession** typically with verb ("to be"): τῷ **Ὁμήρῳ** ἐστὶ στρατηγός ("there is a general **to Homer**")	*to*
	5. **Dative with an Adjective, Adverb, or Noun:** αὐτῷ ἀσφαλές εἶναι ("to be safe **for him**") πρὸς ἡδονήν **αὐτῷ** ("for pleasure **to him**")	
	6. **Dative with a Verb and Infinitive:** δεῖ **αὐτῷ** ἰέναι ("it is necessary **for him** to go")	
	7. **Dative of Respect:** ἀνὴρ **ἡλικίᾳ** νέος ("a man young **in age**")	*in*
	8. **Time When:** πέμπτῃ **ἡμέρᾳ** ("on the fifth **day**")	*on*
	9. **Dative of Degree of Difference:** πολλῷ ("**by much**")	*by*
	10. **Dative of Accompaniment:** αὐτὸν κτείνει **ἵππῳ** ("he kills him **with his horse**")	none or *σύν*
	11. **Dative of Agent with Perf. and Plup. Pass.:** λέλειμμαι **αὐτῷ** ("I have been left **by him**")	
	12. **Place Where:** ("He sits **on the bench**") ἐν **Αἰγύπτῳ** ("**in** Egypt")	*ἐν (in, on, at)*
	13. **Dative of Possession:** ὁ ἀδελφὸς **αὐτῷ** ("**his** brother") **none**	
	14. **Object of Preposition:** σὺν **Ὁμήρῳ** ("**with** Homer")	
ACCUSATIVE	1. **Direct Object:** he gives me **an apple** ταῦτα αὐτῇ λέγω ("I say **these things** to her")	none
	2. **Accusative Subject of Infinitive or Participle Indirect Statement:** ἔφη **αὐτὴν** βλάπτειν αὐτόν ("he said **she** hit him"); οἰκὸς ἦν τῆς θυγατρὸς ὄντας **παῖδας** ("it was likely that they were **the children** of his daughter")	*that* or none

153

Case	Function	Supply in English
	Result: οὕτω σοφός ἐστι ὥστε τοὺς ἀνθρώπους φιλεῖν αὐτόν ("he is so wise that people love him")	
	Other Instances: δεῖ αὐτὸν ἰέναι ("it is necessary **for him** to go"); συνήνεικε **ὑμᾶς** εἰδέναι ("it happened that **you** knew")	
	3. **Acc. of Respect:** ἀνὴρ ἡλικίαν νέος a man young **in age**	*in*
	4. **Duration of time:** he works **for 3 hours** ὀκτωκαίδεκα **ἔτη** ("for eighteen **years**")	*for*
	5. **Extent of space:** he walks **for 3 miles** ὁδὸν μακράν ("**for a long journey**")	*for*
	6. **Accusative Absolute:** οὕτως **ἔχον** ("**this being so**")	none
	7. **Object of Preposition:** πρὸς Ὅμηρον ("**to Homer**")	
VOCATIVE	1. **Direct Address: John,** come here ὦ βασιλεῦ ("oh king")	none

With the expection of the predicate adjective, the above are all case functions for nouns and pronouns. Remember that adjectives, which include participles, always agree with the nouns or pronouns they modify in gender, number, and case. If no noun or pronoun is present, supply one from the gender and number of the adjective unless it is clear that a noun or pronoun must be supplied from context.

Two grammatical occurrences that happen in all cases are apposition and predicate nouns. Consider the following examples:

Apposition	Predicate Nouns
ὁ Ὅμηρος, **ποιητής**, καλός.	ὁ Ὅμηρος **ποιητής**.
Homer, a **poet**, is good.	Homer is a **poet**.
τὸ βιβλίον τοῦ Ὁμήρου, **ποιητοῦ**, μέγα.	τὸ βιβλίον τοῦ Ὁμήρου ὄντος **ποιητοῦ** μέγα.
The book of Homer, **a poet**, is big.	The book of Homer, being a **poet**, is big.
ταῦτα τῷ Ὁμήρῳ, **ποιητῇ**, δίδωμι.	τὸ βιβλίον τῷ Ὁμήρῳ ὄντι **ποιητῇ**.
I give these things to Homer, a **poet**.	There is a book to Homer being a **poet**.
νομίζει τὸν Ὅμηρον **ποιητὴν** καλόν.	νομίζει τὸν Ὅμηρον **ποιητὴν** εἶναι.
He thinks that Homer, a **poet**, is good.	He thinks Homer is a **poet**.
ὦ βασιλεῦ, **Κῦρε**, ἔλθε.	ὦ παιδία ὄντα **ποιηταί**, ἔλθετε.
King, **Kyros**, come!	Children, being **poets**, come!

~ APPENDIX B

INFINITIVES

An infinitive can be used in conjunction with another adjective, noun, or verb:

1. **Complementary:** προδοῦναι γάρ σὲ θέλει ("he wishes to betray you"); ταῦτα λέγειν δύναμαι ("I am able to say these things").
2. **Dependent:** μὲ ἔρχεσθαι κελεύει ("she orders me to come"); μὲ ἔρχεσθαι θέλει ("he wants me to come").
3. **Epexegetical:** καλὸν πυθεῖν νέα ("it is good to learn new things"); ἐλπὶς ἡμῖν νικᾶν "there is hope for us to win").
4. **Purpose:** σῖτον ἐμοὶ ἐσθίειν δίδωσιν ("he gives food to me to eat"); βιβλίον ἐμοὶ λέγειν δίδωσιν ("he gives a book to me to read").

Used as a noun:

5. **Articular:** τὸ μάχεσθαι κάλλιστον ("fighting is best"); περὶ τοῦ φεύγειν νομίζομεν ("we consider fleeing").

Used as a main verb in indirect statement, after ὥστε and πρίν, or as an imperative:

6. **Main Verb:** ἔφη αὐτοὺς ἐλεύσεσθαι ("he said that they would come"); ἔφη εἶναι μακαρίᾱ ("she said that she is blessed").

7. **Main Verb:** πολλὰ ἔμαθον πρὶν θανεῖν ("I learned much before I died"); λέγει ὥστε ἡμᾶς ἀκοῦσαι ("she speaks and so we listen").

8. **Main Verb:** ἔφη· Φεύγειν ("he said, flee!"); ἔφη· Σπεύδειν ("she said, hurry up!")

~

THE INFINITIVE IN AN
INDIRECT STATEMENT OR QUESTION

The infinitive is used as the main verb in the dependent clause. It stands for an original finite verb of the direct statement.

1. The **present infinitive stands** for an original present indicative, imperfect indicative, present subjunctive, or present optative.

2. The **future infinitive stands** for an original future indicative or a future optative.

3. The **aorist infinitive stands** for an original aorist indicative, aorist subjunctive, or aorist optative.

4. The **perfect infinitive stands** for an original perfect indicative.

THE SUBJUNCTIVE AND OPTATIVE MOODS
IN SUMMARY

The Subjunctive, when considered in the big picture, is the mood that is used to express nonfactual or hypothetical events. These events lie in the unforeseeable or hypothetical future, and the possibility of their occuring is typically uncertain. When encountering the subjunctive, use context to determine whether you should translate it into English with the English indicative or whether you should add in a word like "may" so as to emphasize the mood's uncertainty.

The Hortatory Subjunctive, usually in the first-person plural, expresses a request or a proposal: "let us go"; "let's eat"; "let's dance." The negative is μή: "let us not bow down." Since the action has not yet occurred, it is considered hypothetical. Thus, "let's dance" implies that we may or we may not. Consider the following examples:

νῦν ἀκούωμεν τοῦ ἀνδρός. ("Let us now listen to the man.")

νῦν μὴ ἀκούωμεν τοῦ ἀνδρός. ("Let us now not listen to the man.")

The Deliberative Subjunctive is used when a hypothetical question is asked, such as "Am I to go?" Note the difference between the deliberative subjunctive and an indicative question, such as "Am I going?" Consider the following examples:

νῦν ἀκούωμεν τοῦ ἀνδρός; ("Are we now to listen to the man?")

νῦν μὴ ἀκούωμεν τοῦ ἀνδρός; ("Are we now not to listen to the man?")

The Prohibitive Subjunctive is used with the aorist subjunctive when expressing a negative command. The negative is μή. Note that a command is hypothetical in nature because the event takes place in the unforeseeable future and so there is no certainty as to what actually will happen. If I say "Don't jump," I have no idea whether the command will carry weight or not. Consider the following examples:

μὴ ἀκούσῃς τοῦ ἀνδρός. ("Don't listen to the man.")

μὴ αὐτοὺς θύσῃς. ("Don't sacrifice them.")

The Subjunctive of Doubtful Assertion and Negation is used occasionally when the speaker wishes to make an assertion in a quiet and less assertive manner. This subjunctive is not so common. Consider the following examples:

μὴ καλὸν ταῦτα ᾖ ποιεῖν. ("It may be good to do these things.")

μὴ οὐ κακὸν ταῦτα ᾖ ποιεῖν. ("It may not be bad to do these things.")

The Optative, when considered in the big picture, is either a mood that stands for an original indicative, and thus is factual in nature, or it is a mood used to express nonfactual or hypothetical events. These events lie, relative to the time of the main verb, in the unforeseeable or hypothetical future, and the possibility of their occuring is typically uncertain.

When encountering the optative, use context to determine whether you should translate it into English with the indicative or whether you should add in a word like "may," "might," "would," or "could" so as to emphasize the mood's uncertainty.

The Potential Optative states the possibility of an event occuring: "it could happen" or "we would go." The potential optative is always found with ἄν, and the negative is οὐ. Consider the following examples:

Κῦρος ἂν ἔλθοι. ("Kyros could come.")

ἂν συμφέροι εἶναι τοῦτο. ("This could happen to be.")

οὗτοι ἂν σφάλλοιντο. ("They could be tripped up.")

The Optative of Wish expresses a subject's desire for something to happen: "I hope he comes"; "May he come"; "Would that he comes." Greek uses the optative to express a wish for something to happen at some time in the future. εἴθε or εἰ γάρ may introduce the wish but need not be present. Consider the following examples:

εἴθε Κῦρος ἔλθοι. ("May Kyros come.")

εἰ γὰρ Κῦρος ἔλθοι. ("May Kyros come.")

Κῦρος ἔλθοι. ("May Kyros come.")

The Optative in Indirect Statement and Question:

1. When encountering a **present optative** in indirect statement, consider that it may stand for one of the following:
   a. the present indicative;
   b. the imperfect indicative;
   c. the present subjunctive;
   d. the present optative.

2. When encountering a **future optative** in indirect statement, consider that it may stand for one of the following:
   a. the future indicative;
   b. the future optative.

3. When encountering an **aorist optative** in indirect statement, consider that it may stand for one of the following:
   a. the aorist indicative;
   b. the aorist subjunctive;
   c. the aorist optative.

The Subjunctive and Optative in Purpose and Fear Clauses

When Greek expresses **purpose** with the subjunctive or optative moods, it does so in the following way: introductory finite verb + ἵνα, ὡς, or ὅπως +

a verb in the subjunctive or optative mood. If the introductory finite verb is a primary tense, the verb after ἵνα, ὡς, or ὅπως will be in the subjunctive. If the introductory finite verb is a secondary tense, the verb after ἵνα, ὡς, or ὅπως will be in the optative. The present, future, and perfect tenses of the verb are primary tenses. The imperfect, aorist, and pluperfect tenses of the verb are secondary.

Fear Clauses represent the speaker's fear that something will or will not happen. In primary sequence, a fear that something will happen ("I fear that we will lose") has the following formula: verb of fearing (present, future, or perfect tense) + μή + finite verb in the subjunctive. A fear that something will not happen ("I fear that he will not come") has the following form: verb of fearing (present, future, or perfect tense) + μὴ οὐ + finite verb in the subjunctive. In secondary sequence, a fear that something will occur ("I feared that we might lose") has the following formula: verb of fearing (imperfect, aorist, or pluperfect tense) + μή + finite verb in the optative. A fear that something will not happen ("I feared that he might not come") has the following form: verb of fearing (imperfect, aorist, or pluperfect tense) + μὴ οὐ + finite verb in the optative. The subjunctive and optative moods emphasize the uncertainty of an event, which may or may not come to pass.

THE SUBJUNCTIVE OR OPTATIVE IN THE PROTASIS OF CONDITIONS

One of the functions of the subjunctive and optative moods is to express nonfactual (or hypothetical) situations. Remember that the indicative mood is, in most cases, the mood of fact. In the hypothetical "if-clause" of conditions, the subjunctive or optative may be found. The negative is μή.

Future More Vivid Conditions state a hypothetical situation ("if we win") followed by a factual consequence in the future ("we will receive much praise"). Greek uses the subjunctive (present or aorist) in the "if-clause" or "protasis," and the future indicative in the "then-clause" or "apodosis." Note that there is often a factual implication to this condition: "if he comes, we will be happy," and the implication is that he does come and we are happy.

Future Less Vivid Conditions state a hypothetical situation ("if we should win") followed by a consequence in the future ("we would receive much praise"). Greek uses εἰ + the optative (present or aorist) in the protasis and the optative (present or aorist) + ἄν in the apodosis. The future less vivid condition is similar to the future more vivid condition—they both state a hypothetical condition followed by a future consequence. The difference between them is that in the protasis and apodosis, the future less vivid is more hypothetical than the future more vivid and there is not the implication that the condition is met and comes true.

Present General Conditions state a hypothetical situation ("if we win") followed by a factual consequence in the present ("we receive much praise"). Greek uses the subjunctive (present or aorist) in the protasis, and the present indicative in the apodosis. Note that there is often a factual implication to this condition: "if he comes, we are happy," and the implication is that he does come and we are happy.

Past General Conditions state a general truth about the past. The protasis states the situation under which the apodosis holds true: "if (or whenever) he saw her, he was happy"; "if (or whenever) they heard that song, they started to dance." Greek uses εἰ + the optative (present or aorist) in the protasis and the imperfect indicative in the apodosis. Note that the optative remains suppositional, but the supposition is one that carries with it the implication that it has occurred, often with some frequency. And so in this sense the optative is factual: "whenever he saw her, he was happy." His seeing her and his consequent happiness occurred with some frequency.

In Conditions, the Protasis may be introduced by a relative pronoun (ὅς ἄν; ὅστις ἄν; ὅς; ὅστις: "whoever") or adverb (ὅπου ἄν; ὅπου: "wherever") instead of by ἐάν and εἰ or by a temporal conjunction (such as ἐπειδάν, ὅταν, ἐπεί: "whenever").

Parsing Terms

Adverbial Accusative (or Dative Accusative): an adjective in the accusative or dative case that functions as an adverb. Used adverbially πολύ, for example, means "by far." Similarly used is ταύτῃ, which means "there."

Agency: expresses the person who performs an action. Herodotus uses a variety of prepositions; ὑπό, ἐκ, and πρός are the most common: ταῦτα ὑπὸ αὐτοῦ ποιεῖται ("these things are done by him").

Agreement, Lack of: at times a noun or pronoun may be in a different case from the participle that modifies it. The lack of agreement between the two is typical when the noun or pronoun the participle modifies is also performing the action of an upcoming infinitive. Contrast αὐτῷ ἰέναι δεῖ ("it is necessary for him to go") with αὐτῷ, χρήματα αἱροῦντα, ἰέναι δεῖ ("it is necessary for him, grabbing the money, to go").

Anastrophe of the Disyllabic Preposition: when the accent of a preposition shifts from the ultima to the penult, it indicates that the object comes before instead of after: for example, τῆς χώρης ταύτης πέρι ("concerning this country").

Antecedent Omitted: the antecedent is omitted: ταῦτα ἃ βούλει ποιῶ ("I do the things you want") becomes ἃ βούλει ποιῶ ("I do what you want").

Antecedent in the Relative Clause: at times the antecedent is brought into the relative clause; for example, εἶδεν ἐν ᾗ οἰκέω χώρᾳ ("he saw in which country I dwell") instead of εἶδεν χώραν ἐν ᾗ οἰκῶ ("he saw the country in which I dwell").

Attraction of the Relative Pronoun: when the antecedent is omitted, the pronoun may be attracted into the case of the omitted antecedent: τούτων οὓς εἶδες ἦρξα ("I ruled those whom you saw") becomes ὧν εἶδες ἦρξα ("I ruled whom you saw").

Optative, Hypothetical: the optative refers to something that may or may not happen or to something in a hypothetical way, but context makes clear that it did in fact happen. The past general condition is a good example of this: "whenever he came (optative mood), we were happy." For more see appendix C.

Optative, Standing for an Original Indicative: often the optative stands in for an original indicative. When this is the case, it is noted. For more see appendix C.

Optative, Standing for an Original Subjunctive: though not common, the optative may stand for an original subjunctive. When this occurs, it is noted. For more see appendix C.

Parsing: an analysis of the role each word plays in a sentence.

Proximity, Rule of: words that are to be translated together are typically near each other.

Sense Unit: words that are to be translated together because they logically form a unit: for example, τὴν ἐν τῇ ὁδῷ τὴν παιδίον ἔχουσαν ("the woman in the street the one holding a child").

Subjunctive, Hypothetical: rather than identify a subjunctive as present in a purpose clause in indirect statement, the notes suggest the underlying reason behind the mood's presence. Often this underlying reason is because the subjunctive refers to something that may or may not happen. At other times the mood refers to something in a hypothetical way, but context makes clear that it does in fact happen. The present general condition is a good example of this: "whenever he comes (subjunctive mood), we are happy." For more see appendix C.

Substantive Adjective: an adjective used as a noun: for example, κακά ("bad things; evils; troubles") and σοφά ("wise things").

Substantive Article: the article works in conjunction with another word to create a noun: for example, τὰ τότε ("the things then"), αἱ νῦν ("the women of today"), and οἱ ἐν τῇ ὁδῷ ("the men in the street").

Substantive Participle: the article combines with the participle to create a noun: for example, οἱ φονεύοντες ("the murderers").

～ APPENDIX E

Top 500 Ancient Greek Words

The following list is a combination of searches performed in Logeion by the author and the top 500 core list found at http://dcc.dickinson.edu/greek-core-list.

ἀγαθός, -ή, -όν: good, noble

ἀγορά, -ᾶς ἡ: marketplace

ἄγω, ἄξω, ἤγαγον, ἦχα, ἦγμαι ἤχθην: do, drive, lead; χάριν ἄγω: I give thanks

ἀγών, ἀγῶνος ὁ: contest, struggle

ἀδελφός, -οῦ ὁ: brother

ἀδικέω, ἀδικήσω, ἠδίκησα, ἠδίκηκα, ἠδίκημαι, ἠδικήθην: be unjust, do wrong

ἀδικός, -όν: unjust

ἀδύνατος, -ον: impossible, weak, unable

ἀεί: always

Ἀθῆναι, -ῶν αἱ: Athens

Ἀθηναῖος, -ᾱ, -ον: Athenian, of or from Athens

αἷμα, -ατος τό: blood

αἱρέω, αἱρήσω, εἷλον (ἑλεῖν), ᾕρηκα, ᾕρημαι, ᾑρέθην: seize, grab; capture; ὁ λόγος αἱρεῖ: it makes sense, it is reasonable; choose

αἴρω, ἀρῶ, ἦρα, ἦρκα, ἦρμαι, ἤρθην: take up, lift up; remove

αἰσθάνομαι, αἰσθήσομαι, ᾐσθόμην, ——, ᾔσθημαι, ——: perceive, apprehend, be sensible of + gen. or acc. object

αἰσχρός, -ά, -όν: shameful, disgraceful, base

αἰτέω, αἰτήσω, ᾔτησα, ᾔτηκα, ᾔτημαι, ᾐτήθην: ask, demand, request; ask for + gen.; ask "x" in acc. for "y" in acc.; αἰτεῖ αὐτὸν χρήματα: he asks him for money

αἰτίᾱ, -ᾱς ἡ: reason, cause, responsibility, guilt, blame; αἰτία ἔχει: there is an accusation that

αἴτιος, -ᾱ, -ον: responsible for, the cause of, guilty of + gen.

ἀκούω, ἀκούσομαι, ἤκουσα, ἀκήκοα, ἤκουσμαι, ἠκούσθην: hear, hear of or about, listen, heed + gen. or acc.; have a reputation; κακῶς ἀκούειν: to be spoken ill of

ἀκριβής, -ές: exact, accurate, precise

ἀληθής, -ές: true

ἁλίσκομαι, ἁλώσομαι, ἑάλων (ἥλων), ἑάλωκα (ἥλωκα), ——, ——: be taken, conquered, fall into an enemy's hand

ἀλλά: but, for

ἀλλήλων: (gen. adj.) one another, each other

ἄλλος, ἄλλη, ἄλλο: one, other; ἄλλος ἄλλο λέγει: one man says one thing, another says another; τῇ ἄλλῃ: elsewhere

ἅμα: at once; at the same time as + dat.

ἁμαρτάνω, ἁμαρτήσομαι, ἡμάρτησα or ἥμαρτον, ἡμάρτηκα, ἡμάρτημαι, ἡμαρτήθην: make a mistake; err; fail; miss the mark off + gen

ἀμείνων, ἄμεινον: better, abler, stronger, braver

ἀμύνω, ἀμυνέω, ἤμυνα, ——, ——, ——: ward off, keep off, defend; assist, help + dat.

ἀμφί: about, for the sake of + gen; about, around + dat.; about, around (motion often implied) + acc.

ἀμφότερος, ἀμφοτέρᾱ, ἀμφότερον: both

ἄν: (particle) indicates something hypothetical, nonfactual, or with the indicative something repeated over time

ἀνά: on, upon + gen. or dat.; up, up to, throughout + acc.; (adv.) thereon, thereupon, throughout

ἀναγκάζω, ἀναγκάσω, ἠνάγκασα, ἠνάγκακα, ἠνάγκασμαι,
ἠναγκάσθην: force, constrain, compel

ἀνάγκη, -ης ἡ: force, necessity, fate

ἀναιρέω, ἀναιρήσω, ἀνεῖλον, ἀνήρηκα, ἀνήρημαι, ἀνηρέθην: take
up, pick up, make away with; destroy, kill

ἄνευ: without, away from, from afar + gen.

ἀνήρ, ἀνδρός ὁ: man, husband

ἄνθρωπος, -ου ὁ or ἡ: man, human being

ἀντί: over, against; opposite; for the sake of; instead of; in return for +
gen.

ἄνω: up, upward

ἄξιος, -ᾱ, -ον: worthy, responsible (+ gen.)

ἀξιόω, ἀξιώσω, ἠξίωσα, ἠξίωκα, ἠξίωμαι, ἠξιώθην: deem worthy,
think fit; expect; deem "x" in acc. worthy of "y" in gen.

ἀπαλλάττω, ἀπαλλάξω, ἀπήλλαξα, ἀπήλλαχα, ἀπήλλαγμαι,
ἀπηλλάχθην: set free, release, deliver from; depart

ἅπας, ἅπασα, ἅπαν: all, each, every, whole

ἀπό: from, away from + gen; (adv.) from far away, consequently

ἀποδείκνυμι: point away from, show, display; point out, make known;
appoint; dedicate, consecrate; produce, perform

ἀποδίδωμι: give back; allow, permit; pay; (mid.) sell

ἀποθνήσκω (θνήσκω) , ἀποθανέομαι, ἀπέθανον, τέθνηκα, ——,
——: die, perish

ἀποκρίνω (κρίνω, κρινέω, ἔκρῑνα, κέκρικα, κέκριμαι, ἐκρίθην): pick
out, choose, select; + gen. τοῦ στρατοῦ ἀποκρίνειν: to pick out from
the army

ἀποκτείνω, ἀποκτενέω, ἀπέκτεινα, ἀπέκτονα, ——, ——: kill

ἀπόλλυμι (ὄλλυμι), ἀπολέω, ἀπώλεσα or ἀπωλόμην (intr.),
ἀπολώλεκα or ἀπόλωλα, ——, ——: destroy, slay; die, perish

ἄρα: and so, therefore, then, in that case

ἆρα: indicates a question, often expects the answer "no"; ἆρα οὐ expects
a "yes"

Ἀργεῖος, -ᾱ, -ον: Argive, of or from Argos; Greek

ἀρετή, -ῆς ἡ: virtue, excellence

ἀριθμός, -οῦ ὁ: number

ἄριστος, -η, -ον: best

ἀρχή, -ῆς ἡ: rule, command; beginning

ἄρχω, ἄρξω, ἦρξα, ἦρχα, ἦργμαι, ἤρχθην: rule; begin + gen.; ἄρχειν
    ἀπὸ τῶν πατέρων: to begin with the fathers

ἀτάρ: but, yet

αὖ, αὖθις (αὖτις): again, in turn, hereafter, in the future

αὐτίκα: immediately

αὐτός, -ή, -ό: he, she, it; -self (pred.); same (att.) often + dative; (adv.)
    αὐτοῦ: there

ἀφαιρέω, ἀφαιρήσω, ἀφεῖλον, ἀφῄρηκα, ἀφῄρημαι, ἀφῃρέθην:
    take away from; take "x" in acc. away from "y" in acc.; (pass.) be
    deprived of + "x" in acc.

ἀφίημι: send forth, discharge, let go, call off; suffer, permit; αφῆκε τὸ
    πλοῖον φέρεσθαι: he allowed the boat to be carried away

ἀφικνέομαι, ἀφίξομαι, ἀφικόμην, ——, ἀφῖγμαι, ——: arrive, reach,
    come to

ἀφίστημι: stand, stand off or away, separate; cause to revolt; to revolt

Ἀχαιός, -ά, -όν: Akhaian, one of the four major tribes of Greece (the
    others being the Aiolians, Dorians, and Ionians)

βαίνω, βήσομαι, ἔβην, βέβηκα, βέβαμαι, ἐβάθην: step, walk, go

βάλλω, βαλέω, ἔβαλον, βέβληκα, βέβλημαι, ἐβλήθην: throw, hit;
    (mid.) ἐπ' ἑαυτῶν βαλλόμενοι: acting on their own

βάρβαρος, -ου ὁ: barbarian, foreigner, non–Greek speaker

βαρύς, βαρεῖα, βαρύ: heavy, grievous, tiresome

βασιλεύς, -έως (-έος) ὁ: king, chief

βελτίων, βελτίον: better, more virtuous

βίος, -ου ὁ: life

βλέπω, βλέψω, ἔβλεψα, βέβλεφα, βέβλεμμαι, ἐβλέφθην: see, have
    the power of sight

βοηθέω, βοηθήσω, ἐβοήθησα, βεβοήθηκα, βεβοήθημαι, ——: assist,
    help + dat.

βουλεύω, βουλεύσω, ἐβούλευσα, βεβούλευκα, βεβούλευμαι,
    ἐβουλεύθην: plan, plot, devise; (impers. pass.) be decided that "x" in

acc. + inf.; ἐβεβούλευτο αὐτὸν ταῦτα ποιεῖν: it had been decided that
he was to do these things

βουλή, -ῆς ἡ: council, senate

βούλομαι, βουλήσομαι, ——, ——, βεβούλημαι, ἐβουλήθην: want,
wish, be willing

βοῦς, βοός ὁ or ἡ: bull, ox, cow

βραχύς, βραχεῖα, βραχύ: brief, short

γάρ (postpositive): for

γε (enclitic): indeed, in fact merely, at least

γένος, γένους (γένεος) τό: race, kind, sort; birth, origin

γῆ, γῆς ἡ: land, earth

γίγνομαι (γίνομαι), γενήσομαι, ἐγενόμην, γέγονα, γεγένημαι, ——,
(ἐγενήθην, in late authors): be, be born, happen, become; γεγονός
εὖ: be well-born, be of noble-birth

γιγνώσκω, γνώσομαι, ἔγνων, ἔγνωκα, ἔγνωσμαι, ἐγνώσθην: know

γνώμη, -ης ἡ: judgment, thought, opinion, purpose

γράμμα, -ατος τό: letter, written character; (pl.) piece of writing,
document(s)

γραφή, -ῆς ἡ: a drawing, painting, writing; indictment

γράφω, γράψω, ἔγραψα, γέγραφα, γέγραμμαι, ἐγράφην: write

γυνή, -αικός ἡ: woman, wife

δαίμων, -ονος ὁ or ἡ: spirit, god, demon

δέ: and, but; (sometimes just indicates change of subject)

δεῖ, δεήσει, ἐδέησε(ν), δεδέηκε(ν), ——, ——: it is necessary (+ inf.;
+ subj. dat. + inf.; + subj. acc. + inf.); δεῖ ἐλθεῖν: it is necessary to
come; δεῖ τοῖς στρατιώταις ἐλθεῖν or δεῖ τοὺς στρατιώτας ἐλθεῖν:
it is necessary for the soldiers to come; there is a need of (+ gen. or +
gen. + inf.); δεῖ τινος: there is a need of something; δεῖ στρατηγοῦ
εὑρεθῆναι: there is a need of a general to be found; δεῖ μοί τινος:
I have need of something (literally, "there is a need to me of something")

δείδω, δείσω, ἔδεισα, δέδοικα, ——, ——: fear, be afraid, dread

δείκνυμι, δείξω (δέξω), ἔδειξα (ἔδεξα), δέδειχα, δέδειγμαι,
ἐδείχθην: show, display

δεινός, -ή, -όν: awesome, fearsome, terrible; δεινὸς λέγειν: clever at speaking

δέκα: ten

δεύτερος, -ᾱ, -ον: second; (adv.) next

δέχομαι, δέξομαι, ἐδεξάμην, ——, δέδεγμαι, ἐδέχθην: receive; meet; encounter; accept; undertake + inf.

δέω, δεήσω, ἐδέησα, δεδέηκα, δεδέημαι, ἐδεήθην: want, lack, miss, stand in need of, want + gen.; long or wish for + gen.; ask for "x" in gen. or acc. from "y" in gen.; τοῦτο (or τούτου) ὑμῶν δέομαι: I ask you for this

δέω, δήσω, ἔδησα, δέδεκα, δέδεμαι, ἐδέθην: bind, tie, fetter; bind "x" in acc. by "y" in gen.

δή: in deed, in fact, certainly

δῆλος, -η, -ον: visible, conspicuous, clear

δηλόω, δηλώσω, ἐδήλωσα, δεδήλωκα, δεδήλωμαι, ἐδηλώθην: make clear, show

δῆμος, δήμου ὁ: people

διά: on account of + gen.; through + acc.

διαφέρω, φέρω, οἴσω, ἤνεγκα or ἤνεγκον, ἐνήνοχα, ἐνήνεγμαι, ἠνέχθην: carry over or across; carry different ways; make a difference; be different from, excel + gen.

διαφθείρω, διαφθερέω, διέφθειρα, διέφθαρκα or διέφρορα, διέφθαρμαι, διεφθάρην: destroy, corrupt, kill, ruin; (intrans.) be ruined, perish

διαφορά, -ᾶς ἡ: difference, disagreement

διδάσκω, διδάξω, ἐδίδαξα, δεδίδαχα, δεδίδαγμαι, ἐδιδάχθην: teach, instruct

δίδωμι, δώσω, ἔδωκα, δέδωκα, δέδομαι, ἐδόθην: give; allow "x" in dat. + inf.

δίκαιος, -ᾱ, -ον: just

δικαστής, -οῦ ὁ: judge

δίκη, -ης ἡ: custom, usage; justice; penalty

διώκω, διώξω, ἐδίωξα, δεδίωχα, δεδίωγμαι, ἐδιώχθην: cause to run; set in quick motion; chase

δοκέω, δόξω, ἔδοξα, ——, δέδογμαι, ἐδόχθην: seem, think; seem best, think best; δοκεῖ μόρσιμον τῇ πόλι ἁλίσκεσθαι: it seems fated for the city to be taken; δοκεῖν ἐμοί: it seems to me

δόμος, -ου ὁ: house

δόξᾱ, -ης ἡ: expectation, notion, opinion; reputation

δοῦλος, -ου ὁ: slave

δράω, δράσω, ἔδρᾱσα, δέδρᾱκα, δέδρᾱμαι, ἐδράσθην: do, act

δύναμαι, δυνήσομαι, ——, ——, δεδύνημαι, ἐδυνήθην: be able, be strong enough; be worth

δύναμις, -εως (-ιος) ἡ: power, force, army; κατὰ δύναμιν: as far as possible

δυνατός, -ή, -όν: able, possible; powerful, strong, mighty

δύο: two

ἐάν: if

ἑαυτοῦ, ἑαυτῆς, ἑαυτοῦ: himself, herself, itself

ἐάω (imperfect: εἴων > εἴαον), ἐάσω, εἴασα, εἴακα, εἴαμαι, εἰάθην: suffer, permit, allow, leave, let go

ἐγώ, ἐμοῦ or μου: I

ἐθέλω (θέλω), ἐθελήσω (θελήσω), ἠθέλησα, ἠθέληκα, ——, ——: want, wish, be willing

ἔθνος, -ους (-εος) τό: tribe, people, ethnos

εἰ: if

εἶδος, -ους (-εος) τό: form, shape, figure

εἰκός, -ότος τό: likelihood, probability

εἰμί, ἔσομαι, ——, ——, ——, ——: be, be possible

εἶμι: come, go

εἰρήνη, -ης ἡ: peace

εἷς, μία, ἕν, ἑνός, μιᾶς, ἑνός: one

εἰς: to, toward; about + acc.; ἐς οὗ: until which point

εἶτα: then, next, accordingly

εἴτε: either, whether

ἐκ: from, out of, by (used by H. like ὑπό)

ἕκαστος, -η, -ον: each

ἑκάτερος, -ᾱ, -ον: each

ἐκεῖ: there, in that place

ἐκεῖνος, ἐκείνη, ἐκεῖνο (κεῖνος, κείνη, κεῖνο): that, those; he, she, it, they

ἐλάσσων, ἐλάσσον: less, fewer, smaller

ἐλαύνω, ἐλάω, ἤλασα, ἐλήλακα, ἐλήλαμαι, ἠλάθην or ἠλάσθην: drive, march

Ἑλλάς, -άδος ἡ: Greece, Hellas

Ἕλλην, -ηνος ὁ: Greek

ἐλπίς, -ίδος ἡ: hope, expectation

ἐμός, ἐμή, ἐμόν: my

ἐν: in, on, at, among + dat.

ἐναντίος, -ᾱ, -ον: opposite + gen.

ἕνεκα (εἵνεκα): on account of, for the sake of + gen.

ἔνθα: there, where; then, when

ἐνταῦθα (ἐνθαῦτα): here, there, then

ἔξω: outside; except

ἔοικα (perf. with pres. sense), εἴξω, ——, ——, ——, ——: be likely, be reasonable, seem

ἐπεί (ἐπείτε: ἐπεί + τε): when, since

ἔπειτα: thereupon, thereafter, then

ἐπί: on, upon, in the time of + gen.; toward + gen. (ἐπὶ Ἀθηνέων); on, next to, against + dat.; ἐφ᾽ ᾧ: on condition that; on, to, against + acc.

ἐπίσταμαι: know

ἐπιστήμη, -ης ἡ: knowledge

ἕπομαι (imp. εἱπόμην), ἕψομαι, ἑσπόμην, ——, ——, ——: follow + dat.

ἔπος, ἔπους (ἔπεος) τό: word, speech

ἐργάζομαι (augments εἰ and ἠ), ἐργάσομαι, ἠργασάμην (εἰργασάμην), ——, εἴργασμαι, ἠργάσθην: be busy, work at; do "x" in acc. to "y" in acc.

ἔργον, -ου τό: work, deed, task; building

ἔρομαι (εἴρομαι), ἐρήσομαι (εἰρήσομαι), ἠρόμην, ——, ——, ——: ask, ask "x" in acc. "y" in acc.

ἔρχομαι, ἐλεύσομαι, ἦλθον, ἐλήλυθα, ——, ——: come, go

ἐρωτάω (εἰρωτάω), ἐρωτήσω, ἠρώτησα, ἠρώτηκα, ἠρώτημαι,
   ἠρωτήθην: ask, question

ἕτερος, -ᾱ, -ον: other

ἔτι: yet, still

ἔτος, ἔτους (ἔτεος) τό: year

εὖ: well

εὐθύς, εὐθεῖα, εὐθύ: straight, direct

εὑρίσκω, εὑρήσω, ηὗρον, ηὕρηκα, ηὕρημαι, ηὑρέθην: find out,
   discover

ἐχθρός, -ά, -όν: hated, hostile, inimical + gen. or dat.

ἔχω (imp. εἶχον), ἕξω or σχήσω, ἔσχον, ἔσχηκα, -ἔσχημαι, ——:
   have, hold; (+ adv) be; καλῶς ἔχω: I am well; ὧδε ἔχει: it is like so;
   ἔχειν παρὰ σοί: to keep to oneself; be able + inf. (often impersonal);
   hinder, prevent; ἔχω αὐτὸν ταῦτα μὴ ποιεῖν: I keep him from doing
   these things; (mid.) cleave, cling to + gen.; (mid.) be near or border +
   gen.; ἐχόμενον ἐστι: there belongs + gen.

ἕως: until, till

ζάω (ζῇς, ζῇ), ζήσω, ἔζησα, ἔζηκα, ——, ——: live, breathe, be full of
   life

Ζεύς, Διός ὁ: Zeus

ζητέω, ζητήσω, ἐζήτησα, ἐζήτηκα, ——, ἐζητήθην: seek, seek for

ἦ: in truth, verily

ἤ: or, than

ἡγεμών, -όνος ὁ: leader, commander, guide

ἡγέομαι, ἡγήσομαι, ἡγησάμην, ——, ἥγημαι, ἡγήθην: lead, believe;
   lead, command + dat.; lead "x" in gen. for "y" in dat.; ἡγεῖται ἡμῖν
   χοροῦ: he leads our dance; rule, have dominion + gen.

ἤδη: already, by this time, now

ἡδονή, -ῆς ἡ: pleasure

ἡδύς, ἡδεῖα, ἡδύ: pleasant

ἥκω, ἥξω, ——, ——, ——, ——: come, go

ἥλιος, -ου ὁ: sun

ἡμέρᾱ, -ᾱς ἡ: day

ἥσσων, ἧσσον: less, inferior; ἥσσων αὐτοῦ θηρεύειν: inferior to him at running

θάλασσα, -ης ἡ: sea

θάνατος, -ου ὁ: death

θαυμάζω, θαυμάσω, ἐθαύμασα, τεθαύμακα, τεθαύμασμαι, ἐθαυμάσθην: wonder, be astonished, marvel; admire; wonder at + gen.

θεῖος, -ᾱ, -ον: divine

θεός, -οῦ ὁ or ἡ: god, goddess

Θηβαῖος, -ᾱ, -ον: Theban, of or from Thebes, a Greek city in Boiotia

θυγάτηρ, θυγατέρος or θυγατρός ἡ: daughter

θυμός, -οῦ ὁ: soul, spirit; passion, heart, will, desire

θύω, θύσω, ἔθυσα, τέθυκα, τέθυμαι, ἐτύθην: sacrifice

ἴδιος, -ᾱ, -ον: one's own; one's self; ἰδίῃ: personally, privately, for one's own self

ἱερός, -ά, -όν: holy; (n. s.) temple; (n. pl.) sacrifices

ἵημι, -ἥσω, -ἧκα, -εἷκα, -εἷμαι, -εἵθην: release, hurl, send

ἱκανός, -ή, -όν: befitting; sufficient, enough; able

ἵνα: in order that, so that, where

ἱππεύς, -έως ὁ: knight, cavalryman; one who fights from a chariot, horseman, rider

ἵππος, -ου ὁ or ἡ: horse; (fem.) cavalry

ἴσος, -η, -ον: equal, as many as

ἵστημι, στήσω, ἔστησα or ἔστην, ἔστηκα, ἔσταμαι, ἐστάθην: place, stand, make stand

ἰσχυρός, -ά, -όν: strong

καθίστημι (ἵστημι, στήσω, ἔστησα or ἔστην, ἔστηκα, ἔσταμαι, ἐστάθην): set, place, establish; appoint; settle, settle down

καί: and, even, also, merely, indeed; (after ὅμοιος, ἴσος, ὁ αὐτός) as

καιρός, -οῦ ὁ: opportunity; proper moment; critical time; crisis

καίτοι: and indeed, and yet; though

κακός, -ή, -όν: bad, evil, wicked, evil, cowardly

καλέω, καλέω, ἐκάλεσα, κέκληκα, κέκλημαι, ἐκλήθην: call

καλός, -ή, -όν: beautiful, beauteous, fair

κατά: down from, against + gen.; down, during, by, according to + acc.; **καθ᾽ ἅ:** according, just as; (adv.) as, just as

καταλαμβάνω, καταλήψομαι, κατέλαβον, κατείληφα, κατείλημμαι, κατελήφθην: seize, hold down; catch; check, stop; befall, happen; comprehend; (impers.) καταλαμβάνει ταῦτα αὐτὸν ποιεῖν: it falls to his lot to do these things, it is his fortune to do these things; ἀναγκαία καταλαμβάνει αὐτὸν φεύγειν: necessity falls upon him to flee

κατασκευάζω, κατασκευάσω, κατεσκεύασα, κατεσκεύακα, κατεσκεύασμαι, ——: equip, furnish, supply; construct, build

κατηγορέω, κατηγορήσω, κατηγόρησα, κατηγόρηκα, κατηγόρημαι, κατηγορήθην: speak against, accuse + gen. of person accused; charge "x" in gen. with "y" in acc.

κεῖμαι, κείσομαι, ——, ——, ——, ——: lie

κελεύω, κελεύσω, ἔκελευσα, κεκέλευκα, κεκέλευσμαι, ἐκελεύσθην: order, command; bid, ask; urge, encourage; order "x" in dat. or in acc. + inf.; give the order to; κελεύει σώζειν: he gives the order to save

κεφαλή, -ῆς ἡ: head

κίνδυνος, -ου ὁ: danger

κινέω, κινήσω, ἐκίνησα, κεκίνηκα, κεκίνημαι, ἐκινήθην: move; set in motion; urge on

κοινός, -ή, -όν: shared, common; ἀπὸ τοῦ κοινοῦ: on behalf of the whole; τὸ κοινόν: the state

κομίζω, κομιέω, ἐκόμισα, κεκόμικα, κεκόμισμαι, ἐκομίσθην: take care of, supply, heed; bring; accompany; carry away; convey; journey

κόσμος -ου ὁ: world, universe; order; ornament

κρατέω, κρατήσω, ἐκράτησα, ——, ——, ἐκρατήθην: be strong, powerful, rule + gen.

κρείττων, κρεῖττον: better, stronger, mightier

κρίνω, κρινέω, ἔκρῑνα, κέκρικα, κέκριμαι, ἐκρίθην: judge, decide, pick out, separate

κτάομαι, κτήσομαι, ἐκτησάμην, ——, κέκτημαι, ἐκτήθην: get, gain; have, hold; acquire, possess

κτείνω, κτενέω, ἔκτεινα or ἔκτανον, ἔκτονα, ἔκταμαι, ἐκτάνθην:
kill, slay, slaughter

κύκλος, -ου ὁ: ring, circle, wheel, orb, disc

κύριος, -ᾱ, -ον: with power, able, sovereign; appointed, fixed

Κῦρος, -ου ὁ: Kyros the Great, c. 600–530, Persian king who ruled for
about 30 years

κωλύω, κωλύσω, ἐκώλῡσα, κεκώλῡκα, κεκώλῡμαι, ἐκωλύθην:
hinder, prevent; prevent "x" in acc. from "y" in gen.

λαλέω, λαλήσω, ἐλάλησα, λελάληκα, λελάλημαι, ἐλαλήθην: talk,
chat, prattle, babble

λαμβάνω, λήψομαι, ἔλαβον, εἴληφα, εἴλημμαι, ἐλήφθην: take,
receive; capture

λαμπρός, -ά, -όν: bright, brilliant, well-known

λανθάνω, λήσω, ἔλαθον, λέληθα, ——, ——: escape notice + participle (doing something); do (the action of the participle) + λανθάνω
(without being seen)

λαός, -οῦ ὁ: people

λέγω, ἐρέω or λέξω, εἶπον or ἔλεξα, εἴρηκα, εἴρημαι or λέλεγμαι,
ἐλέχθην or ἐρρήθην: say, tell; (personal) νοῦσον λέγεται ἔχειν ὁ
Καμβύσης: Kambyses is said to have an illness; (impers.) νοῦσον
λέγεται ἔχειν Καμβύσην: it is said that Kambyses has an illness

λείπω, λείψω, ἔλιπον, λέλοιπα, λέλειμμαι, ἐλείφθην: leave, quit

λίθος, -ου ὁ: rock, stone

λόγος, -ου ὁ: account, word; value, esteem, talk, conversation; τῷ
λόγῳ: for the sake of argument, in word, i.e., falsely; ἐν λόγῳ: in the
rank of; κατὰ λόγον: according to the value or esteem

λοιπός, -ή, -όν: left, remaining

λύω (ῡ), λύσω, ἔλῡσα, λέλυκα, λέλυμαι, ἐλύθην: loose, free, destroy;
(mid.) ransom

μάλα: very

μάλιστα: especially, most; (with numbers) about

μᾶλλον: more, rather

μανθάνω, μαθήσομαι, ἔμαθον, μεμάθηκα, ——, ——: learn, understand

μάχη, -ης ἡ: battle

μάχομαι, μαχέομαι, ἐμαχεσάμην, ——, μεμάχημαι, ——: fight, fight with + dat.

μέγας, μεγάλη, μέγα: big, great

μέγεθος (μέγαθος), -ους (-εος) τό: greatness, magnitude

μέλλω, μελλήσω, ἐμέλλησα, ——, ——, ——: be about to, be going to; be likely to

μέν: on the one hand (looks forward to δέ to create contrast or parallelism); οἱ μέν . . . οἱ δέ: some . . . others

μέντοι: indeed, to be sure

μένω, μενέω, ἔμεινα, μεμένηκα, ——, ——: stay, remain, wait, await

μέρος, -ους (-εος) τό: share, portion, part; limb

μέσος, -η, -ον: middle, middle of; ἐς μέσον: in common, altogether

μετά: with + gen; after + acc; (adv.) after, next

μέχρι: up to, until + gen.; μέχρι τούτου: meanwhile

μή: not, lest

μηδέ: and . . . not

μηδείς, μηδεμία, μηδέν: no one, nothing

μήν, μηνός ὁ: month; (adv.) truly, surely

μήτε: neither; μήτε . . . μήτε: neither . . . nor

μήτηρ, μητέρος or μητρός ἡ: mother

μίγνυμι (μίσγω), μίξω, ἔμιξα, ——, μέμιγμαι, ἐμίχθην or ἐμίγην: mix, mix up, mingle

μικρός, μικρά, μικρόν: small, little

μιμνήσκω, μνήσω, ἔμνησα, ——, μέμνημαι, ἐμνήσθην: remember + gen.

μόνος, -η, -ον: alone, sole, solitary; one

ναός, νεώς ὁ: temple, inner shrine of a temple

ναῦς, νεώς (νηί, ναῦν, νῆες, νεῶν, ναυσί, ναῦς) ἡ: ship

νέος, -ᾱ, -ον: new, fresh, young; strange, unexpected

νῆσος, -ου ἡ: island

νῑκάω, νῑκήσω, ἐνίκησα, νενίκηκα, νενίκημαι, ἐνῑκήθην: conquer, prevail

νομίζω, νομιέω, ἐνόμισα, νενόμικα, νενόμισμαι, ἐνομίσθην: think, have the custom of, hold as custom

νόμος, -ου ὁ: law, custom

νόος (νοῦς), -ου ὁ: mind, intellect

νόσος, -ου ὁ: disease, sickness

νῦν: now

νύξ, νυκτός ἡ: night

ξένος (ξεῖνος), -η, -ον: foreign, strange; (n.) guest, stranger

ὁ, ἡ, τό: the; my, your, his, her; our, your, their; used with abstract nouns, with names of famous or important people, and to generalize; οἱ ἄνθρωποι: people in general

ὅδε, ἥδε, τόδε: he, she, it; this, these; the following; τῇδε: here, thus, in the following way

ὁδός, -οῦ ἡ: road

οἶδα, εἴσομαι, ——, ——, ——, ——: know, think

οἰκεῖος, -ᾱ, -ον: domestic, belonging to the house; one's own

οἰκέω, οἰκήσω, ᾤκησα, ᾤκηκα, ᾤκημαι, ᾠκήθην: live, dwell

οἰκία, -ας ἡ: house

οἶκος, -ου ὁ: house

οἴομαι or οἶμαι, οἰήσομαι, ᾠσάμην, ——, ——, ᾠήθην: think, suppose, believe

οἷος, -ᾱ, -ον: such, such a kind; οἷός τε εἰμί: I am able, I am of such a kind to; οἷον or οἷα: how, like, as, because

ὀλίγος, -η, -ον: few, little, small

ὅλος, -η, -ον: whole, entire

ὅμοιος, -ᾱ, -ον: like, resembling + dat.

ὁμολογέω, ὁμολογήσω, ὡμολόγησα, ὡμολόγηκα, ὡμολόγημαι, ὡμολογήθην: speak together; agree; admit

ὅμως: nevertheless, yet, still

ὄνομα, -ατος τό: name

ὀνομάζω, ὀνομάσω, ὠνόμασα, ὠνόμακα, ὠνόμασμαι, ὠνομάσθην: speak of by name, call

ὀξύς, ὀξεῖα, ὀξύ: sharp, keen, shrill, pungent

ὅπλον, -ου τό: weapon

ὅπου: where, wherever

ὅπως: so that, in order that; how; whenever

ὁράω, ὄψομαι, εἶδον (ἰδεῖν), ἑόρακα or ἑώρακα, ἑώραμαι or ὦμμαι, ὤφθην: see

ὀρθός, -ή, -όν: straight, correct, proper

ὁρμάω, ὁρμήσω, ὥρμησα, ὥρμηκα, ὥρμημαι, ὡρμήθην: set in motion, urge on, cheer on; (intr.) go, rush; start, begin, be eager, hasten + inf.

ὄρος, -ους (-εος) τό: mountain

ὅς, ἥ, ὅ: who (whose, whom), which, that; ᾗ: by which way, just as; ἐν ᾧ: while; ἐς ὅ: until

ὅσος, -η, -ον: so many, as many as; ὅσῳ: in so far as; to the degree that; ὅσον: as far as; ἐπ' ὅσον: how far, to how great an extent

ὅστις, ἥτις, ὅ τι: whoever, whatever

ὅταν: whenever

ὅτε: when

ὅτι: that, because

οὐ, οὐκ, οὐχ: not (proclitic—pronounced closely with the word that comes after it). Use οὐκ if the word that comes after starts with a smooth breathing. Use οὐχ if the word that comes after starts with a rough breathing. Otherwise use οὐ.

οὐδέ: and not, but not, nor

οὐδείς, οὐδεμία, οὐδέν; οὐδένος, οὐδεμίας, οὐδένος: no one, nothing

οὐκέτι: no more, no longer, no further

οὔκουν (οὔκων): and so . . . not

οὖν: then, therefore

οὐρανός, -οῦ ὁ: sky, heaven

οὐσία, -ας ἡ: property; being, essence, reality

οὔτε: and not; neither

οὗτος, αὕτη, τοῦτο: he, she, it; this, these; ταύτῃ: here, there, where; in this way

οὕτως (οὕτω): in this way, such, so, thus

ὀφθαλμός, -οῦ ὁ: eye

πάθος, -ους (-εος) τό: suffering; experience; passion; emotion

παιδεύω, παιδεύσω, ἐπαίδευσα, πεπαίδευκα, πεπαίδευμαι,
  ἐπαιδεύθην: educate, teach; (middle) cause "x" in acc. to be educated
  or taught

παῖς, παιδός ὁ or ἡ: child

παλαιός, -ά, -όν: old, ancient; aged

πάλιν: back

πάνυ: perfectly, verily, by all means

παρά: from + gen.; beside + dat.; to, toward, contrary to + acc.

παραδίδωμι (δίδωμι, δώσω, ἔδωκα, δέδωκα, δέδομαι, ἐδόθην):
  give, give over; betray

παρασκευάζω, παρασκευάσω, παρεσκεύασα, παρεσκεύακα,
  παρεσκεύασμαι, ——: prepare, make ready

πάρειμι: be near, be present, be beside

πάρειμι: go in, enter

παρέχω (ἔχω, ἕξω or σχήσω, ἔσχον, ἔσχηκα, -ἔσχημαι, ——):
  hold, supply, hand over; allow, grant; be in one's power, be allowed;
  παρέχει: it is possible

πᾶς, πᾶσα, πᾶν: all, each, whole

πάσχω, πείσομαι, ἔπαθον, πέπονθα, ——, ——: suffer, have done to
  one

πατήρ, πατρός ὁ: father

πατρίς, -ίδος ἡ: fatherland

παύω, παύσω, ἔπαυσα, πέπαυκα, πέπαυμαι, ἐπαύθην: make to end,
  stop

πεδίον, -ου τό: plain

πεζός, -ή, -όν: on foot, on land; πεζῇ: on land

πείθω, πείσω, ἔπεισα, πέπεικα, πέπεισμαι, ἐπείσθην: persuade; (mid.
  or pass.) listen to, obey + dat. or gen.

πειράω, πειράσω, ἐπείρασα, ——, πεπείραμαι, ἐπειράθην: attempt,
  undertake; try one's fortunes, try the chances of war; (mid. and pass)
  try, make an attempt; make trial of, test + gen.

πέμπω, πέμψω, ἔπεμψα, πέπομφα, πέπεμμαι, ἐπέμφθην: send

περ: (enclitic) very, indeed, surely

περί: round about, all round, concerning + gen; about near + acc.

Πέρσης, -ου ὁ: a Persian, believed to be Indo-European in origin and comprised of two major groups, the Persians and the Medes; in the sixth century the Akhaimenid Empire stretched from Greece to India, c. 550–330

πίνω, πίομαι or πιέομαι, ἔπιον, πέπωκα, ——, ἐπόθην: drink

πίπτω, πεσέομαι, ἔπεσον, πέπτωκα, ——, ——: fall

πιστεύω, πιστεύσω, ἐπίστευσα, πεπίστευκα, πεπίστευμαι, ἐπιστεύθην: trust, believe, confide in, rely on + dat.

πλεῖστος, -η, -ον: most, greatest, largest

πλείων, πλεῖον (πλέων, πλέον): more

πλέω (πλώω), πλεύσομαι or πλευσέομαι, ἔπλευσα, πέπλευκα, πέπλευσται, ἐπλεύσθη: sail

πλῆθος, -ους (-εος) τό: great number, multitude; sum

πλήν: except, save + gen.; (adv.) and yet, however

ποιέω, ποιήσω, ἐποίησα, πεποίηκα, πεποίημαι, ἐποιήθην: do, make, consider; περὶ πολλοῦ κάρτα ποιεῖν: consider very important; ἐν ἐλαφρῷ ποιεῖν: make light of; κακὰ ποιεῖν αὐτόν: do harm to him; οὐδένα λόγον ποιεῖ: to consider "x" in gen. of no account; make a poem, compose

ποιητής, -οῦ ὁ: poet

ποῖος, -ᾱ, -ον: of what kind, sort, or quality

πολεμέω, πολεμήσω, ἐπολέμησα, πεπολέμηκα, πεπολέμημαι, ἐπολεμήθην: fight, go to war against + dat.

πολέμιος, -ᾱ, -ον: hostile

πόλεμος, -ου ὁ: war

πόλις, -εως (-ιος) ἡ (acc. pl. = πόλιας or πόλις): city

πολῑτεία, -ας ἡ: government

πολίτης (πολιήτης), -ου ὁ: citizen, freeman

πολλάκις: many times; often

πολύς, πολλή, πολύ: much, many

πονηρός, -ά, -όν: worthless, evil, base

πορεύω, πορεύσω, ἐπόρευσα, ——, πεπόρευμαι, ἐπορεύθην: bring, carry, convey, supply; go ποταμός, -οῦ ὁ: river

ποτε (enclitic): at some time, once, ever

πότερος, -ᾱ, -ον: whether, which

που: anywhere, somewhere, I suppose

πούς, ποδός ὁ: foot; κατὰ πόδας: on the heels

πρᾱγμα, -ατος τό: matter, thing, affair; problem

πρᾶξις, -εως ἡ: doing, affair, action, condition

πράττω (πρήσσω), πράξω, ἔρπαξα, πέπρᾱχα or πέπρᾱγα,
    πέπρᾱγμαι, ἐπράχθην: do, make, fare; pass through; πολλὰ
    πράττειν: to be a busybody, to make trouble; κακῶς πράττειν: to fare
    badly, fail, suffer; exact payment of "x" in acc. from "y" in acc.

πρέσβυς, -εως (-εος) ὁ: old man, elder; ambassador, envoy

πρίν: before; πρὶν (ἢ) αὐτοὺς πέμψαι ταῦτα: before they sent these things

πρό: before, in front of; because of + gen.

πρός: from + gen; toward + gen.; in the direction of + gen.; (with passive
    verb just like ὑπό) by; at, by, near, in addition + dat; toward, against, in
    comparison to + acc.; πρὸς ταῦτα: in regard to these things, for these
    reasons; πρὸς ταύτῃ: additionally; (adv.) additionally, in addition

προσήκω: come to, be near; belong to, be related to + dat.

πρόσωπον, -ου τό: face, mask, person

πρότερος, -ᾱ, -ον: prior, before, sooner

πρῶτος, -η, -ον: first, for the present, just now; τὴν πρώτην: first

πυνθάνομαι, πεύσομαι, ἐπυθόμην, ——, πέπυσμαι, ——: learn, learn
    from inquiry; inquire about; hear or inquire concerning + gen.; find
    out from "x" in gen.

πῦρ, πυρός τό: fire

πῶς: how

πως: somehow, someway

ῥᾴδιος, ῥᾳδίᾱ, ῥᾴδιον: easy

σαφής, -ές: clear, distinct

σημεῖον, -ου τό: sign, mark, token

σκοπέω, σκοπήσω, ἐσκόπησα, ——, ἐσκόπημαι or ἔσκεμμαι, ——:
    look at or after; behold; contemplate; consider

σός, σή, σόν: your

σοφός, -ή, -όν: wise

στάδιον, -ου τό (plural is οἱ or τά): stade; racecourse

στρατεύω, στρατεύσω, ἐστράτευσα, ——, ἐστράτευμαι
ἐστρατεύθην: wage war, launch a campaign

στρατηγός, -οῦ ὁ: general

στρατιά, -ᾶς ἡ: army

στρατιώτης, -ου ὁ: soldier

στρατόπεδον, -ου, τό: camp, encampment

στρατός, -οῦ ὁ: army

σύ, σοῦ or σου: you

συμβαίνω (βαίνω, βήσομαι, ἔβην, βέβηκα, βέβαμαι, ἐβάθην): stand
with feet together; stand beside; come together; come to an agreement; come to terms; assist, meet + dat.; (impers.) happen, come to
pass; agree

σύμμαχος, -ον: allied

συμφέρω: gather, carry, bring together; be useful, be expedient; happen
συμφέρει εἶναι τοῦτο: it happens to be

συμφορά, -ᾶς ἡ: bringing together, collecting; fortune; disaster or
misfortune

σύν: with, with help of + dat.

σφάλλω, σφαλέω, ἔσφηλα, ἔσφαλκα, ἔσφαλμαι, ἐσφάλην: make to
fall, overthrow

σφεῖς, σφέα; σφῶν, σφῶν (σφέων): they

σχῆμα, -ατος τό: form, figure, appearance, character

σῴζω, σώσω, ἔσωσα, σέσωκα, σέσωμαι or σέσωσμαι, ἐσώθην:
save, keep

σῶμα, -ατος τό: body

σωτηρία, -ας ἡ: saving, safety, deliverance

τάξις, -εως ἡ: order, arrangement; military unit

τάττω (τάσσω), τάξω, ἔταξα, τέταχα, τέταγμαι, ἐτάχθην: order,
appoint; arrange, set in order

ταχύς, ταχεῖα, ταχύ: swift

τε (enclitic): and; τε … τε: both … and

τεῖχος, -ους (-εος) τό: wall; (pl.) stronghold

τέκνον, -ου τό: child

τελευτάω, τελευτήσω, ἐτελεύτησα, τετελεύτηκα, τετελεύτημαι,
ἐτελευτήθην: end; die, perish

τέλος, -ους (-εος) τό: end, boundary; power; office; (acc.) finally

τέμνω, τεμέω, ἔτεμον, τέτμηκα, τέτμημαι, ἐτμήθην: cut

τέσσαρες, τέσσαρα: four

τέταρτος, -η, -ον: fourth

τέχνη, -ης ἡ: art, skill, craft

τίθημι, θήσω, ἔθηκα, τέθηκα, τέθειμαι, ἐτέθην: put, place; set, establish

τίκτω, τέξομαι, ἔτεκον, τέτοκα, τέτεγμαι, ἐτέχθην: bear, beget

τιμάω, τιμήσω, ἐτίμησα, τετίμηκα, τετίμημαι, ἐτιμήθην: honor

τιμή, -ῆς ἡ: honor; price, cost; rank; esteem, respect

τις, τι: (pronoun) anyone, anything; someone, something; (adjective)
some, any, a, a certain

τίς, τί: who, what, which

τοίνυν: then, therefore

τοιόσδε, τοιάδε, τοιόνδε: of such a kind

τοιοῦτος, -αύτη, -οῦτο: of such a kind or sort

τολμάω, τολμήσω, ἐτόλμησα, τετόλμηκα, τετόλμημαι, ἐτολμήθην:
undertake, undergo, take courage, venture

τόπος, -ου ὁ: place, spot

τοσοῦτος, -αύτη, -οῦτο: so much, so many

τότε: at that time, then

τρεῖς, οἱ, αἱ; τρία τά: three

τρέπω (τράπω), τρέψω, ἔτρεψα, τέτροφα, τέτραμμαι, ἐτράπην or
ἐτρέφθην: turn, rout

τρέφω, θρέψω, ἔθρεψα or ἔτραφον, τέτροφα or τέτραφα,
τέθραμμαι, ἐτράφην or ἐθρέφθην or ἐθράφθην: rear, nourish;
thicken; cause to grow

τρίτος, -η, -ον: third

τρόπος, -ου ὁ: way, manner, turn, course; (pl.) character

τυγχάνω, τεύξομαι, ἔτυχον, τετύχηκα, ——, ——: happen + suppl.
participle: τυγχάνει βλάπτων: he happens to strike; obtain + gen.; hit
the mark, strike + gen.

τύραννος, -ου ὁ: tyrant

τύχη, -ης ἡ: fortune, luck, fate

ὕδωρ, ὕδατος τό: water

υἱός, -οῦ ὁ: son, child

ὑμέτερος, -ᾱ, -ον: your

ὑπάρχω (ἄρχω, ἄρξω, ἦρξα, ἦρχα, ἦργμαι, ἤρχθην): begin, start +
    gen.; arise; be; belong to; fall to; accrue; be sufficient; be in existence;
    (impers.) be allowed, be possible; happen + part.

ὑπέρ: above, on behalf of + gen; over, exceeding + acc.

ὑπό: by, under + gen; subject to, under + dat.; under (motion implied) +
    acc.

ὑπολαμβάνω, ὑπολήψομαι, ὑπέλαβον, ὑπείληφα, ὑπείλημμαι,
    ὑπελήφθην: take up; catch up, overtake; come next; reply, retort;
    receive; understand

ὕστερος, -ᾱ, -ον: after, later

φαίνω, φανέω, ἔφηνα, πέφαγκα or πέφηνα, πέφασμαι, ἐφάνθην or
    ἐφάνην: bring to light, uncover; show, display, exhibit; seem, appear

φανερός, -ά, -όν: clear, plain

φέρω, οἴσω, ἤνεγκα or ἤνεγκον, ἐνήνοχα, ἐνήνεγμαι, ἠνέχθην:
    bring, bear, carry; endure, suffer; consider; propose; turn out

φεύγω, φεύξομαι, ἔφυγον, πέφευγα, ——, ——: flee; be banished, be
    in exile; be a defendant

φημί, φήσω, ἔφησα, ——, ——, ——: say, tell

φιλίᾱ, -ᾱς ἡ: affectionate regard, friendship

φίλος, -η, -ον: friendly, kind, well-disposed

φοβέω, φοβήσω, ἐφόβησα, ——, πεφόβημαι, ἐφοβήθην: fear

φόβος, -ου ὁ: fear

φράζω, φράσω, ἔφρασα (ἔφρασσα), πέφρακα, πέφρασμαι,
    ἐφράσθην: tell, point out, show; advise; (mid. and pass.) suppose,
    believe; watch, guard, beware of

φρονέω, φρονήσω, ἐφρόνησα, πεφρόνηκα, ——, ——: think,
    consider

φυλάσσω, φυλάξω, ἐφύλαξα, πεφύλαχα, πεφύλαγμαι, ἐφυλάχθην:
    keep watch and ward, keep guard; watchfully await; φυλάσσειν μὴ

ποιεῖν: to take care not to do, to guard against doing; φυλάσσειν τοῦτο μὴ γενέσθαι: to guard that this not happen

φύσις, -εως (-ιος) ἡ: nature

φύω, φύσω, ἔφυσα or ἔφυν, πέφυκα, ——, ἐφύην: bring forth, produce, put forth; grow

χαίρω, χαιρήσω, ——, κεχάρηκα, κεχάρημαι or κεχαρμαι, ἐχάρην: be well; rejoice at, take pleasure in + dat. or + participle; be unpunished, be safe and sound; hail or farewell

χαλεπός, -ή, -όν: hard to bear; sore; difficult; bitter; hostile

χάρις, -ιτος ἡ: charm, grace, favor; gratitude; χάριν εἰδέναι: feel grateful; χάριν: for the sake of + gen.

χείρ, χειρός ἡ: hand; force, army

χράομαι, χρήσομαι, ἐχρησάμην, ——, κέχρημαι, ἐχρήσθην: use, employ, experience + dat.; consult an oracle + dat.

χρή (inf. χρῆναι; imp. ἐχρῆν or χρῆν; fut. χρήσει): it is necessary; it is fated

χρῆμα, -ατος τό: thing (singular), matter, affair; heap, quantity; wealth (plural)

χρόνος, -ου ὁ: time

χώρᾱ, -ᾱς ἡ: land, country

χωρίον, -ου τό: place, spot, district

χωρίς: apart from, separately + gen.

ψυχή, -ῆς ἡ: life, soul

ὦ: oh; marks for the vocative case and is often not translated

ὧδε: in this wise, thus

ὡς: as, how, when, since, because + indicative; in order that + subjunctive or optative; + super.: as "x" as possible; (with numbers) about, nearly

ὥσπερ: just as

ὥστε: and so, such that, with the result that

ᵥ GLOSSARY

Principal parts are provided when the forms occur in the lexicon of Liddell, Scott, and Jones, except for compound verbs. For these look to the root verb. For example, for ἀναβαίνω, see βαίνω.

Ἄβυδος, -ου ἡ: Abydos, a city of Mysia on the Hellespont
ἄγαλμα, -ατος τό: a glory, delight, honor; statue of a deity
ἀγγελία, -ας ἡ: a message
ἄγγελος, -ου ὁ: a messenger
ἄγγος, -ους (-εος) τό: a vessel
ἀγεννής, -ές: low-born
ἀγηλατέω: drive out one accursed
ἅγιος, -α, -ον: holy
ἀγνωμοσύνη, -ης ἡ: want of sense; folly; unkindness; arrogance; (pl.)
   misunderstandings
ἀγοραῖος, -α, -ον: in, of the agora
ἀγορεύω, ἀγορεύσω, ἠγόρευσα, ἠγόρευκα, ἠγορευμαι, ἠγορεύθην:
   speak in the assembly, harangue
Ἀγριᾶναι, -ῶν οἱ: Agrianai, a tribe of Paionia
ἀγρός, -οῦ ὁ: a field
Ἀγχιμόλιος, -ου ὁ: Ankhimolios, a Spartan and son of Aster c. 530 B.C.E.
ἄγχιστος, -ον: nearest + gen.

189

ἀγχοῦ: near + gen. or dat.

ἀγωνίζομαι, ἀγωνιζέομαι, ἠγωνισάμην, ——, ἠγώνισμαι,
  ἠγωνίσθην: contend for a prize

ἀγωνιστής, -οῦ ὁ: a combatant

ἀδαής, -ές: unknowing; be ignorant of

ἀδελφεή = ἀδελφή

ἀδελφή, -ῆς ἡ: a sister

ἀνδάνω, ἀδήσω, ἔαδον or ἦσα, ἄδηκα, ——, ——: please, gratify,
  delight + dat.

ἀδήσεις < ἀνδάνω

ἀδίκιον, -ου τό: a wrongdoing

ἀδικώτερος, -α, -ον: more unjust

Ἄδρηστος, -ου ὁ: Adrastos, a hero

Ἀδρία, -ας ἡ: the Adriatic, west of Greece

ἄδυτον, -ου τό: innermost sanctuary

ἀεθλεύω, ἀεθλεύσω, ἠέθλευσα, ——, ——, ——: contend for a prize

ἄεθλον, -ου τό: a contest, prize

ἀέκων, -ουσα, -ον: unwilling

ἀήρ, ἀέρος ὁ: air

ἀθανατίζω: be immortal, deathless

Ἀθήνη (Ἀθηναίη), -ης ἡ: Athene (Athena)

ἀθροίζω, ἀθροίσω, ἤθροισα, ἤθροικα, ἤθροισμαι, ἠθροίσθην: gather
  together, collect, muster

Αἰακίδης, -ου (-εω) ὁ: of or from Aiakos

Αἰακός, -οῦ ὁ: Aiakos, mythical king of Aigina

Αἴας, Αἴαντος ὁ: Aias, Trojan war hero

αἴγεος, -α, -ον: of a goat's skin

Αἰγιαλεύς, -έως (-έος) ὁ: Aigialeus, son of Adrastos; (pl.) a tribe of
  Sikyonians

Αἰγικόρης, -ους (-εος) ὁ: Aigikores, one of the sons of Ion, founder of
  the Ionians

Αἴγινα, -ας ἡ: Aigina, a nymph

Αἴγινα, -ας ἡ: Aigina, an island off the coast of Athens

Αἰγίναιος, -α, -ον: of or from Aigina an island off the coast of Athens

Αἰγινήτης, -ου (-εω) ὁ: an Aiginetan, from Aigina

αἰετός = ἀετός, -οῦ ὁ: an eagle

αἴνεσε = ἤνεσε < αἰνέω

αἰνέω, αἰνήσω, ἤνησα, ἤνηκα, ἤνημαι, ἠνήθην: tell of, speak of; praise, approve; promise, vow

αἰνίσσομαι, αἰνίξομαι, ᾐνιξάμην, ——, ——, ——: speak darkly

Αἰολεύς, -έως (-έος) ὁ: Aiolean, one of the four major tribes of Greece

Αἰολίδης, -ου (-εω) ὁ: son of Aiolos, founder of the Aiolians

αἰρεθῆναι < αἱρέω

αἵρεσις, -εως (-ιος) ἡ: a choice

αἴτεον = ᾔτεον

αἰτιάομαι, αἰτιάσομαι, ᾐτιᾱσάμην, ——, ᾐτίᾱμαι, ᾐτιάθην: accuse, censure

αἰχμάλωτος, -ον: taken by the spear, captive, prisoner

αἰχμή, -ῆς ἡ: a point of a spear

ἀκέομαι, ἀκέομαι, ἠκεσάμην, ——, ——, ——: heal, cure; make amends for, repair

ἀκήκοας < ἀκούω

ἀκήρυκτος, -ον: without a herald, unannounced

ἀκλεῶς: without fame

ἀκμάζω, ——, ἤκμησα, ——, ——, ——: be in full bloom, be at the prime; flourish, abound

ἀκρομανής, -ές: somewhat mad

ἀκρόπολις, -εως (-ιος) ἡ: an acropolis

ἄκρος, -α, -ον: high, outermost, uppermost; ἡ ἄκρα: headland; ψυχὴν ἄκρος: courageous

ἀλγηδών, -όνος ἡ: a pain, grief

ἄλγος, -ους (-εος) τό: pain

Ἀλέξανδρος, -ου ὁ: Alexandros (Alexander) I of Makedon, king 495–452 B.C.E.

ἀλία, -ας ἡ: an assembly of people

ἀλίζω, ἀλίξω, ἤλῑσα, ——, ἤλισμαι, ἡλίσθην: gather

Ἀλκαῖος, -ου ὁ: Alkaios (Alcaeus) of Mytilene, a Greek lyric poet c. 620 B.C.E.

ἄλκιμος, -η, -ον: stout, brave

Ἀλκμεωνίδης, -ου (-εω) ὁ: Alkmeonid, a family of prominence in Athens

ἄλλοθι: elsewhere, in another way

ἀλλοῖος, -α, -ον: of another sort

ἀλλοφρονέω: be of another mind; think otherwise; be senseless

ἄλλως: otherwise

ἀλούσας < ἁλίσκομαι

ἄλσος, -ους (-εος) τό: a grove

Ἅλυς, Ἅλυος ὁ: Halys, a river of Asia Minor

Ἀλωπεκαί, -ῶν αἱ: Alopekai, a place located in the area of Attika

Ἀμαθοῦς, -οῦντος ἡ: Amathous, a city on the coast of Kypros

Ἀμαθούσιοι, -ων οἱ: Amathousioi, inhabitants of Amathous on Kypros

ἀμαχητί: without battle, without stroke of sword

ἄμαχος, -ον: invincible, without battle

ἀμείβω, ἀμείψω, ἤμειψα, ἤμειπται, ——, ἠμείφθην: answer, respond; change, exchange; pass, cross

ἀμήχανος, -ον: without resource

Ἀμόργης, -ου (-εω) ὁ: Amorges, Persian general c. 500 B.C.E.

Ἀμύντης, -ου (-εω) ὁ: Amyntes, a Makedonian c. 540–498 B.C.E.

ἀμφιβολία, -ας ἡ: a state of being attacked on both sides

ἀμφιδέξιος, -α, -ον: ambidextrous, ambiguous, having a double meaning

Ἀμφικτυόνες, -ων οἱ: Amphiktyones, a "league of nations," devoted to a particular cause and supporting a temple, a sacred place, or athletic games

ἀμφίπολος, -ον: busy; (f. n.) a handmaiden, serving woman

Ἀμφιτρύων, -ονος ὁ: Amphitryon, son of Alkaios and a Theban general

Ἀμφίων, -ονος ὁ: Amphion, one of the Bakkhiadai, a powerful oligarchical faction of Korinth

ἀναβαίνω: go up; mount; make go on board

ἀναβάλλω: throw or toss up; delay

ἀναβλαστέω: shoot up

ἀναγιγνώσκω: know; persuade

ἀνάγω: lead up; raise up, bring up

ἀναδέκομαι: take up, catch, receive; undertake, promise

ἀναδέχομαι: take up, catch, receive; undertake, promise

ἀναισιμόω: use up, use, spend, consume

ἀναισίμωμα, -ατος τό: an expenditure

ἀνακαίω: kindle, fire, rouse

ἀνακλίνω: lean, push back

ἀνακομίζω: carry up; (pass.) return, come back

ἀνακρεμάννυμι: hang up on

ἀνακύπτω: lift up the head, rise

ἀναλαμβάνω: take up or back; resume; undertake; restore, repair, recover

ἀναμάρτητος, -ον: unerring, unfailing

ἀναμάχομαι: renew the fight

ἀναμένω: wait for, await; endure; delay, put off; stand firm against

ἀναμιμνήσκω: remind; recall + gen.

ἀνανεύω: throw the head back, refuse

Ἀναξανδρίδης, -ου (-εω) ὁ: Anaxandrides, king of Sparta

ἀναξυρίδες, -ίδων αἱ: trousers

ἀναπαύω: make cease, stop, rest

ἀναπείθω: persuade

ἀναπίμπλημι: fill up or full; fulfill; accomplish; appease

ἀναπλῆσαι < ἀναπίμπλημι

ἀναποδίζω: make to step back; call back and question, cross-examine

ἀναπυνθάνομαι: search out; inquire

ἀνάρσιος, -α, -ον: incongruous; hostile, strange

ἀνασπαστός, -όν: dragged up or back

ἀνασπάω: draw, pull up

ἀνατίθημι: set up, establish, dedicate, offer

ἀναφύω: make grow; grow; grow again

ἀναχωρέω: go back

ἀνδραγαθία, -ας ἡ: bravery, manly virtue

ἀνδραποδίζω, ἀνδραποδίω, ἠνδραπόδισα, ——, ἠνδραπόδισμαι, ἠνδραποδίσθην: enslave ἀνδράποδον, -ου τό: one taken in war and sold as a slave

Ἄνδρος, -ου ἡ: Andros, an island

ἀνδρόω, ἀνδρώσω, ἤνδρωσα, ἤνδρωκα, ἤνδρωμαι, ἠνδρώθην: change into a man

ἀνέβη < ἀναβαίνω

ἀνέθηκ' = ἀνέθηκε < ἀνατίθημι

ἄνειμι: go up, reach

ἀνέκαθεν: from above; from the first

ἄνεμος, -ου ὁ: a wind

ἄνεσις, -εως (-ιος) ἡ: a relaxing

ἀνεστηκυίῃ < ἀνίστημι

ἀνέχευ = ἀνέχου

ἀνέχω (ἀνίσχω): hold up, lift up; (intrans.) rise up; continue; endure, put up with; wait, pause

ἀνεψιός, -οῦ ὁ: a cousin

ἀνηγέομαι: tell, relate

ἀνήιε = ἀνῆν < ἄνειμι

ἀνήκω: come up to; ἀνήκειν ἐς τὰ πρῶτα: to come to the highest point

Ἀνθεμοῦς, Ἀνθεμοῦντος ὁ: Anthemous, a Makedonian town

ἀνθίστημι: set against

ἀνθρωπέη, -ης ἡ: a person's skin

ἀνθρωπήιος, -α, -ον: mortal, human

ἀνιάω, ἀνιάσω, ἠνίασα, ἠνίακα, ἠνίαμαι, ἠνιάθην: grieve, distress

ἀνίστημι: make to stand up, raise up; be ravaged, be wasted

ἄνοδος, -ου ἡ: a way up

ἀνταγωνιευμένους = ἀνταγωνιουμένους < ἀνταγωνίζομαι

ἀνταγωνίζομαι: struggle against

Ἄντανδρος, -ου ἡ: Antandros, a city

ἀντεμπίμπρημι: burn in return, burn in retaliation

ἀντέχω: hold against; withstand; suffice

ἀντιβαίνω: go against, resist, withstand

ἀντιθέω: run, run against

ἀντικαθίζω: sit opposite

ἀντικατιζόμενοι = ἀντικαθιζόμενοι < ἀντικαθίζω

ἀντιόομαι, ἀντιώσομαι, ——, ——, ——, ἠντιώθην: meet, resist, oppose

ἀντίος, -α, -ον: opposite, set against + gen. or dat.

ἀντισταθείσης = ἀνθισταθείσης < ἀνθίστημι

ἀντιστασιώτης, -ου (-εω) ὁ: a member of the opposite faction

ἀντιτάσσω: line up against or opposite

ἀντιτεχνάομαι: contrive in opposition, counter-plan

Ἀντιχάρης, -ου (-εω) ὁ: Antikhares, from Eleon c. 500 B.C.E.

ἄνω: up, above

ἀξιαπήγητος, -ον: worth telling

ἀξιοχρέος, -ον: worthy, considerable

ἀοίκητος, -ον: not inhabited

ἀπαγγέλλω: report, announce, tell

ἀπάγω: lead away, carry off

ἀπαθής, -ές: without suffering, unharmed

ἄπαις, ἄπαιδος ὁ or ἡ: a childless person

ἀπαιτέω: demand back, demand to have returned

ἀπαίτησις, -εως (-ιος) ἡ: a demanding back

ἀπαμύνω: keep off, ward off

ἀπαράσσω: strike off

ἀπαρτί: completely

ἀπέβησε < ἀποβαίνω

ἀπέδεξ- < ἀποδείκνυμι

ἀπέθανε < ἀποθνῄσκω

ἀπειλόμεθα = ἀφειλόμεθα < ἀφαιρέω

ἄπειμι: go away

ἀπεῖναι = ἀφεῖναι < ἀφίημι

ἀπειπάμενος = ἀπειπόμενος < ἀπολέγω

ἀπείργω: keep away from, debar from; ward off; divide, separate; shut up, confine

ἄπειρος, -ον: without trial, without experience

ἀπεκτόνεε < ἀποκτείνω

ἀπελαύνω: drive away, expel from

ἀπελθ- < ἀπέρχομαι

ἀπελόμενος = ἀφελόμενος < ἀφαιρέω

ἀπενειχθέντα < ἀποφέρω

ἀπέντα = ἀφέντα < ἀφίημι

ἀπεργμένους < ἀπείργω

ἀπέρχομαι: go away, depart

ἄπες = ἄφες < ἀφίημι

ἀπέστη- < ἀφίστημι

ἀπεστήκεε = ἀφεστήκεε < ἀφίημι

ἄπετε = ἄφετε < ἀφίημι

ἀπέχω: keep off or away from; hold oneself from, abstain or desist from
+ gen.; + inf. abstain from; ἀπέχει στρατεύεσθαι: he abstains from
marching; be away from "x" in gen. a distance of "y" in acc.

ἀφηγέομαι: lead the way from; tell

ἀπηγέομαι = ἀφηγέομαι

ἀπήγησις = ἀφήγησις

ἀπήγηται < ἀπηγέομαι

ἀπήιε = ἀπήιει < ἄπειμι

ἀπῆκαν = ἀφῆκαν < ἀφίημι

ἀπιγμένα = ἀφιγμένα < ἀφικνέομαι

ἀπίει = ἀφίει < ἀφίημι

ἀπίεσαν = ἀφίεσαν < ἀφίημι

ἀπικ- = ἀφικ- < ἀφικνέομαι

ἀπίξεται = ἀφίξεται < ἀφικνέομαι

ἄπιξις, -εως (-ιος) ἡ: an arrival

ἀπίστασθαι = ἀφίστασθαι < ἀφίστημι

ἀπίστημι = ἀφίστημι

ἀπιστία, -ας ἡ: distrust

ἀπῖχθαι < ἀφικνέομαι

ἀποβαίνω: step off, dismount; turn out

ἀποβάντας < ἀποβαίνω

ἀπογίγνομαι: be, be from, be away

ἀπόγονος, -ον: born, descended from

ἀπογράφω: write off, copy

ἀποδείρω: skin, flay

ἀποδέξαντας < ἀποδείκνυμι

ἀποδέξω < ἀποδείκνυμι

ἀποδιδράσκω: run away, flee; shun

ἄφοδος, -ου ἡ: a departure, going away

ἄποδος = ἄφοδος

ἀποδράντα < ἀποδιδράσκω

ἀποδύω: strip off, take off

ἀποικία, -ας ἡ: a colony, settlement

ἄποικος, -ον: away; abroad; (n.) colonist

ἀποκλείω: shut off from

ἀποκληίω = ἀποκλείω

ἀποκομίζω: carry away, escort; return

ἀποκορυφόω: bring to a point

ἀπολαγχάνω: obtain a portion of

ἀπολαμβάνω: take off, take away; regain, recover; cut off

ἀπολαμφθέντες < ἀπολαμβάνω

ἀπολέγω: speak out, declare; pick out; forbid

ἀπολείπω: leave off or behind; lose; abandon

ἀπολέσθαι < ἀπόλλυμι

Ἀπόλλων, -ωνος ὁ: Apollo, god of prophecy and music

ἀπολομένους < ἀπόλλυμι

ἀπομνημονεύω: remind, recount, remember; τὸ αὐτὸ ὄνομα
    ἀπεμνημόνευσε αὐτῷ θέσθαι τὸν Μεγάβαζον: he gave in memory
    the same name, Megabazos, to him

ἀπονοστέω: return home

ἀποξυράω: shave clean

ἀποπέμπω: send, send off or away

ἀποπλέω: sail off or away

ἄπορος, -ον: without passage

ἀποσημαίνω: announce by signs

ἀποσταλῆναι < ἀποστέλλω

ἀποστάς < ἀφίστημι

ἀποστάσιος, -α, -ον: standing away, revolting

ἀπόστασις, -εως (-ιος) ἡ: a standing away, revolt

ἀποστέλλω: send off, send away

ἀποστερέω: rob, despoil, defraud

ἀποστῆναι < ἀφίστημι

ἀπόστολος, -ου ὁ: a messenger, ambassador, envoy

ἀποστρέφω: turn back

ἀποσώζω: save

ἀποταμόντες < ἀποτέμνω

ἀποτελέω: bring to an end, complete

ἀποτέμνω: cut off, sever

ἀποτιμάω: fail to honor, slight

ἀποτίνω: avenge; seek vengeance

ἀποφαίνω: show, display, prove

ἀποφέρω: carry off; report; pay back

ἀποφεύγω: flee from; escape

ἀποχράω: suffice, be enough

ἅπτω, ἅψω, ἦψα, ——, ἧμμαι, ἑάφθην or ἥφθην: fasten, grab + gen.

ἀπωθέω: thrust away, push back

ἀπωσμένον < ἀπωθέω

Ἀργάδης, -ου (-εω) ὁ: Argades, one of the sons of Ion, founder of the
    Ionians

Ἀργεῖος, -α, -ον: of or from Argos; Greek

ἀργός, -ή, -όν: not working the ground

Ἄργος, -ους (-εος) τό: Argos, a Greek city

ἀργύρεος, -η, ον: of silver

ἀργύριον, -ου τό: silver

ἄργυρος, -ου ὁ: silver

ἄρδω, ——, ἦρσα, ——, ——, ——: water

Ἄρης, -ους (-εος) ὁ: Ares, god of war

Ἀρισταγόρης, -ου (-εω) ὁ: Aristagores (Aristagoras), governor of
    Miletos

Ἀρισταγόρης, -ου (-εω) ὁ: Aristagores (Aristagoras), tyrant of Kyme c.
    500 B.C.E.

ἀριστερός, -ά, -όν: left

ἀριστεύω, ἀριστεύσω, ἠρίστευσα, ——, ——, ——: be the best, brav-
    est; be the best at + inf.

Ἀριστογείτων, -ονος ὁ: Aristogeiton, Athenian, died 514 B.C.E.

Ἀριστόκυπρος, -ου ὁ: Aristokypros, king of the Solioi c. 500 B.C.E.

Ἀρίστων, -ωνος ὁ: Ariston, Spartan and father of Demaretos c. 550 B.C.E.

Ἀρκάς, -άδος ὁ: Arkadian

ἄρκτος, -ου ὁ or ἡ: a bear; the North

ἅρμα, -ατος τό: a chariot, wagon

ἁρματηλατέω: drive a chariot

Ἀρμενία, -ας ἡ: Armenia, the region south of the Black sea

Ἀρμένιοι, -ων οἱ: Armenians, inhabitants of the region south of the Black sea

Ἁρμόδιος, -ου ὁ: Harmodios, Athenian and killer, along with Aristogeiton, of the tyrant Hipparkhos; died 514 B.C.E.

ἁρμόζω, ἁρμόσω, ἥρμοσα, ἥρμοκα, ἥρμοσμαι, ἡρμόσθην: join, fit together

ἄρουρα, -ας ἡ: arable land, corn-land

ἁρπαγή, -ῆς ἡ: a seizure, theft, rape

ἄρρητος, -η, -ον: unspoken, secret

ἀρρωδέω: dread, fear, shrink from, shudder at + gen. or acc.

Ἀρταφρένης, -ου (-εω) ὁ: Artaphrenes, brother of Dareios I and satrap of Sardis

ἀρτάω, ἀρτήσω, ἤρτησα, ἤρτηκα, ἤρτημαι, ἠρτήθην: fasten to; depend on

Ἄρτεμις, -ιδος ἡ: Artemis, hunter and protector of animals

ἀρτέομαι: be prepared, make ready

ἄρτος, -ου ὁ: a cake

Ἀρτύβιος, -ου ὁ: Artybios, Persian general under Dareios I the Great

ἀρχαῖος, -α, -ον: ancient, from the beginning

Ἀρχέλαοι, -ων οἱ: Arkhelaoi, a tribe of the Sikyonians, named by Kleisthenes, tyrant of Sikyon

ἀρχῆθεν: from the beginning

ἄσημος, -ον: without mark; unintelligible

ἀσθενέης, -ες = ἀσθενής, -ές

ἀσθενής, -ές: weak

Ἀσία, -ας ἡ: Asia

ἀσπαστός, -ή, -όν: welcome

ἀσπίς, -ίδος ἡ: a shield

Ἀστακός, -οῦ ὁ: Astakos, a Theban

ἄσταχυς, -υος ὁ: ear of corn

Ἀστήρ, -έρος ὁ: Aster, a Spartan c. 550 B.C.E.

ἄστικτος, -η, -ον: not marked with

ἀστός, -οῦ ὁ: a townsman, a townsperson

ἄστυ, -ους (-εος) τό: a town

ἀστυγείτων, -ον: bordering a city

ἀσφαλής, -ές: safe, certain, secure

Ἀσωπός, -οῦ ὁ: Asopos River

ἅτε (conj. or adv.): as, just as; since, because; as if

ἀτέκμαρτος, -ον: without distinctive mark, obscure, baffling

ἀτιμότατος, -η, -ον: most unhonored, dishonored

ἄτλητος, -ον: unendurable

ἄτοκος, -ον: childless

ἄτρακτος, -ου ὁ: a spindle

ἀτρεκέως: truly, exactly

ἀτρεκής, -ές: strict, precise, exact

ἀτρέμας: silently

Ἀττική, -ῆς ἡ: Attike (Attika), the region of greater Athens

Ἀττικός, -ή, -όν: Attic, Athenian, of or from Athens

αὐδάζομαι, αὐδάξομαι, ηὐδαξάμην, ——, ——, ηὐδάχθην: cry out,
   speak

αὐλή, -ῆς ἡ: an open court

αὐξάνω (αὔξω), αὐξήσω, ηὔξησα, ηὔξηκα, ηὔξημαι, ηὐξήθην:
   increase, augment, make large

Αὐξησία, -ας ἡ: Auxesia, fertility goddess at Aigina

αὐτίκα: immediately

αὖτις = αὖθις: again, in turn, hereafter, in the future

αὐτόθι: from there, thence

αὐτοῦ: here, there

ἀφανίζω, ἀφανίσω, ἠφάνισα, ἠφάνικα, ——, ἠφανίσθην: make
   unseen, hide

ἄφθονος, -ον: without envy; plentiful

ἀφραστότατος, -η, -ον: most unutterable; very strange; numberless; most unexpected

Ἀχαιμενίδης, -ου (-εω) ὁ: Akhaimenid, a ruling family of Persia

ἀχάριστος, -ον: ungracious, unpleasant

Ἀχέρων, -οντος ὁ: Akheron River

ἄχθη < ἄγω

Αχίλλειος, -α, -ον: of Akhilleus, son of Peleus and Thetis and hero of the Trojan War

Ἀχιλληίος = Αχίλλειος, -α, -ον

ἀχλυόεις, -εσσα, -εν: murky, gloomy

βάθος, -ους τό: a depth

βάθρον, -ου τό: a base, step, stage (something you step on)

βαθύτατος, -η, -ον: deepest; strongest

Βακχιάδαι, -ῶν οἱ: Bakkhiadai, a powerful oligarchical faction of Korinth

βαρύς, -εῖα, -ύ: deep, heavy

βασίλειον, -ου τό: palace; royal treasury; royal tent

βασίλειος, -α, -ον: royal

βασιλεύω, βασιλεύσω, ἐβασίλευσα, ——, ——, ——: be king, rule, reign + gen.

βασιληία, -ας ἡ: a kingdom

βασιλήιον = βασίλειον

βασιλήϊος = βασίλειος

βοηθός, -όν: helping, assisting

Βοιωτία, -ας ἡ: Boiotia, a region of Greece

Βοιωτοί, -ῶν οἱ: Boiotians, of or from Boiotia, a region of Greece

Βορέας, -ου (-εω) ὁ: north wind

Βουβάρης, -ου (-εω) ὁ: Boubares, a Persian and son of Megabazos c. 500 B.C.E.

βούλευμα, -ατος τό: a resolution, purpose, plan

Βουτακίδης, -ου (-εω) ὁ: Boutakides

Βραγχίδαι, -ῶν αἱ: Brankhidai, a promontory and site of the oracle of Apollo Didymeus in Miletos βραχίων, -ονος ὁ: an arm

βραχύς, -εῖα, -ύ: short, brief

βροντή, -ῆς ἡ: thunder

βυβλίον, -ου τό: a book

βύβλος, -ου ἡ: a papyrus; book

Βυζάντιος, -α, -ον: Byzantine

βωμός, -οῦ ὁ: a raised platform, stand, base for a statue; altar

βοάω, βοήσω, ἐβόησα, βεβόηκα, βεβόημαι, ἐβοήθην: shout, roar, proclaim

βώσαντες < βοάω: cry aloud, shout

γαμβρός, -οῦ ὁ: a son, father, or brother-in-law

γαμέω, γαμέω, ἔγημα, γεγάμηκα, γεγάμημαι, ἐγαμήθην: marry

γάμος, -ου ὁ: a wedding

Γελέων, Γελέοντος ὁ: Geleon, one of the sons of Ion, founder of the Ionians

γενεά, -ᾶς ἡ: a race, family

γεραίρω, γερᾰρέω, ἐγέρηρα, ——, ——, ——: honor, reward

Γέργιθαι, -ῶν οἱ: Gergithai, inhabitants of Gergis near Troy on the Skamander

γέρων, γέροντος ὁ: an old man

Γέται, -έων οἱ: Getai, a Thrakian tribe

γέφυρα, -ας ἡ: a bridge

Γεφυραῖοι, -ων οἱ: Gephyraians, an Athenian clan

γῆμ- < γαμέω

γονεύς, -έως ὁ: a begetter, father

γόνος, -ου ὁ or ἡ: a child, offspring; race, birth

γόνυ, γόνατος (γούνατος) τό: a knee

Γόργος, -ου ὁ: Gorgos, king of Salamis c. 500 B.C.E.

Γοργώ, -όνος ἡ: Gorgo, a Spartan

γούνατα = γόνατα < γόνυ

γούνατος = γόνατος < γόνυ

γράμμα, -ατος τό: a word, letter

Γυγαία, -ας ἡ: Gygaia, Makedonian and daughter of Amyntas c. 500 B.C.E.

Γύγης, -ου (-εω) ὁ: Gyges, king of Lydia from 716 to 678 B.C.E., known
for his great wealth

γυμνός, -ή, -όν: naked

γυναικεῖος, -α, -ον: of women

γυναικηίη = γυναικῶν

γυναικήιος = γυναικεῖος

γυναικών, -ῶνος ἡ: a women's chamber

Γύνδης, -ου (-εω) ὁ: Gyndes River

δαίμων, -ονος ὁ or ἡ: god, goddess

δάκτυλος, -ου ὁ: a finger

δαμάω, δαμάσω, ἐδάμασα, δεδάμακα, δέδμημαι, ἐδμήθην: subdue,
tame

Δαμία, -ας ἡ: Damia, fertility goddess at Aigina

δαπάνη, -ης ἡ: a cost, expenditure

Δάρδανος, -ου ἡ: Dardanos, a city of the Troad near the Hellespont

Δαρεῖος, -ου ὁ: Dareios (Darius) I the Great, third king of the Akhaimenids; according to Herodotus and the Behistun inscription he
defeated the Magi to come to power c. 550–486 B.C.E.

δασμοφόρος, -ον: paying tribute

Δαυρίσης, -ου (-εω) ὁ: Daurises, son-in-law of Dareios I and Persian
commander c. 500 B.C.E.

δεδογμένα < δοκέω

δεθέντος < δέω

δείδω, δείσω, ἔδεισα, δέδοικα, ——, ——: fear, be afraid, dread

δειμαίνω: be afraid

δεῖπνον, -ου τό: a meal, food

δέκατος, -η, -ον: tenth; (f.) tenth part

δεκάφυλος, -ον: divided into ten tribes

δέκαχα: in ten parts

δέκομαι = δέχομαι

Δελφός, -ή, -όν: Delphian; (m. pl.) Delphians; (f. pl.) Delphi, site of the
oracle of Apollo

δέρμα, -ατος τό: skin

δεσμός, -οῦ ὁ: a fetter

δεσπότης, -ου (-εω) ὁ: a master

δέω, δήσω, ἔδησα, δέδεκα, δέδεμαι, ἐδέθην: bind, tie, fetter; bind "x" in acc. by "y" in gen.

δηιόω, δηώσω, ἐδηίωσα or ἐδήωσα, δεδήωκα, δεδήωμαι, ἐδηώθην: cut down, slay

δηλαδή: clearly

δηλέομαι, δηλήσομαι, ἐδηλησάμην, ——, δεδήλημαι, ——: hurt, do a mischief to

Δημάρητος, -ου ὁ: Demaretos, son of Ariston and king of Sparta c. 520 B.C.E.

Δημαρμένος, -ου ὁ: Demarmenos, a Spartan c. 570 B.C.E.

Δημήτηρ, -τερος (-τρος) ἡ: Demeter, goddess of the harvest

δημόσιος, -α, -ον: of the people, belonging to the people

δημότης, -ου (-εω) ὁ: a citizen, private citizen

δῆσαι < δέω

διαβαίνω: cross, go through

διαβάλλω: throw over, cross over; slander; deceive

διαβά- < διαβαίνω

διαβεβλημένος < διαβάλλω

διαδείκνυμι: show plainly

διάδοχος, -ου ὁ: succeeding; (n.) a successor

δίαιτα, -ας ἡ: a way of life

διαιτάω, διαιτήσω, ἐδιαίτησα, δεδιήτηκα, δεδιήτημαι, ἐδιῃτήθην: support, maintain, live a certain way

διαιτητής, -οῦ ὁ: an arbiter, umpire

διακόσιοι, -αι, -α: two hundred

διαλαμβάνω: take; separate; intercept

διαλύω: loose, break up, discharge

διανοέομαι: intend

διανοεύμενος = διανοούμενος

διαπειράομαι: make trial or proof of a thing; experience something + gen.

διαπέμπω: send over or across, send in different directions

διαπεραιόω: take across, ferry over

διαπίνω: have a drinking contest
διαπλέκω: weave, plait; finish the web of one's life
διαπορθμεύω: carry over or across
διασημαίνω: mark out, point out clearly
διασκεδάννυμι: scatter
διατάσσω: arrange; set up in order
διατελέω: bring to an end, fulfil; continue doing
διαφεύγω: flee, escape
διάφορος, -ον: different, unlike; at odds
διδασκάλιον, -ου τό: science, art, lesson
διδαχή, -ῆς ἡ: a teaching
διδοῖ = δίδωσι < δίδωμι
διδοῖς = δίδως < δίδωμι
δίδυμος, -η, -ον: double, twofold, twin
διέβη- < διαβαίνω
διεκπεράω: pass through or by
διελθ- < διέρχομαι
διαιρέω: divide; distribute
διελόντας < διαιρέω
διέξειμι: go out through
διεξελ- < διεξελαύνω
διεξελαύνω: drive, ride, march through
διεξελθ- < διεξέρχομαι
διεξέρχομαι: go through, pass through
διεξήιε = διεξήει < διέξειμι
διεξῆλθε < διεξέρχομαι
διεξιοῦσι < διέξειμι
διέπω: manage, conduct
διεργάζομαι: work at; do; cultivate; destroy
διέρχομαι: come, go, go through or across
διεφθάρ- < διαφθείρω
δίζημαι, διζήσομαι, ἐδιζησάμην, ——, ——, ——: seek, search out
διηκόσιοι = διακόσιοι
δικάζω, δικάσω, ἐδίκασα, ——, δεδίκασμαι, ἐδικάσθην: judge

δικαιόω, δικαιώσω, ἐδικαίωσα, δεδικαίωμαι, ——, ἐδικαιώθην: set right; think right; δικαιῶ δρᾶν: I think it right to do; judge; punish; justify, hold guiltless

δίμνεως: worth or costing two minas

διξός, -ή, -όν: twofold, double

Διόνυσος, -ου ὁ: Dionysos, god of wine

Διός < Ζεύς, Διός ὁ

διπλόος, -η, -ον: twofold, double

διπλός = διπλόος

δίς: twice, doubly

δισχίλιοι, -αι, -α: two thousand

διφθέρα, -ας ἡ: a prepared hide, piece of leather

διχοστασία, -ας ἡ: a dissension

διῶρυξ, -υχος ἡ: a ditch, canal

Δόβηραι, -ῶν οἱ: Doberians, a tribe of Paionia

δοθ- < δίδωμι

δόκιμος, -ον (-ος, -α, -ον): worthy, of good repute

δόλος, -ου ὁ: a bait; trick, deceit, craft

Δορίσκος, -ου ἡ: Doriskos, a coastal town of Thrake

δόρυ, -ατος τό: a spear

δορύφορος, -ον: spearbearing

δορυφόρος, -ου ὁ: a spearbearer, guard

δουλεύω, δουλεύσω, ἐδούλευσα, δεδούλευκα, ——, ——: be a slave

δουλοσύνη, -ης ἡ: slavery, slavish work

δούς < δίδωμι

δρέπανον, -ου τό: a sickle

δρησμός, -οῦ ὁ: a running away, flight

Δυμνάται, -ῶν οἱ: Dymnatai, a tribe of Sikyonians

δυναστεύω, δυναστεύσω, ἐδυνάστευσα, ——, ——, ——: hold power

δύσριγος, -ον: unable to endure cold

δυσφορέω: suffer

Δύσωρον, -ου τό: Dysoron Mountain

δύω, δύσω , ἔδῡσα or ἔδῡν, δέδῡκα, δέδυμαι, ἐδύθην: cause to sink; sink, plunge

δωρεά, -ᾶς ἡ: a gift, present
δωρέω, δωρήσω, ἐδώρησα, δεδώρηκα, δεδώρηται, ἐδωρήθην:
give, present, reward
Δωριεύς, -έως (-έος) ὁ: Dorieus, king of Sparta c. 515 B.C.E; a Dorian,
descendant of Dorus
Δωρίς, -ίδος ἡ: Dorian, one of the four major tribes of the Greeks
δῶρον, -ου τό: a gift
δώσειν < δίδωμι
ἔα = ἔαε < ἐάω
ἔαρ, ἔαρος τό: spring
ἔατε = ἦτε < εἰμί
ἐγγίγνομαι: be, be in; arise in; be produced in, happen; intervene
ἐγείρω, ἐγερέω, ἤγειρα, ἐγήγερκα, ἐγήγερμαι, ἠγέρθην: awaken,
rouse
Ἐγεσταίος, -ου ὁ: man of Egesta, one of three major cities of the Elymi
of Sikelia
ἐγκατίζω = ἐγκαθίζω: seat, sit
ἐγκεκολαμμένα < ἐγκολάπτω: cut
ἐγκεράννυμι: mix
ἐγκτίζω: found, build among
ἐγκωμιάζω: praise
ἔγνω- < γιγνώσκω
ἐγχειρίδιος, -ον: in the hand; (n.) dagger
ἐγχειρίζω: put into one's hands, entrust
ἐγχειρίθετος, -ον: put into one's hands
Ἐγχέλεες, -ων οἱ: Enkhelians, a tribe of Illyria
ἐδεδέατο = ἐδέδεντο < δέω
ἐδέδοκτο < δοκέω
ἐδέκετο = ἐδέχετο
ἐδέξαντο < δέχομαι
ἐδέξαο = ἐδέξω < δέχομαι
ἐθελοκακέω: pretend to be bad
ἐθελοντής, -οῦ ὁ: a volunteer
ἔθε- < τίθημι

ἔθω, ——, εἶθον, εἴωθα or ἔωθα, ——, ——: be accustomed, be wont

εἰδ- < ὁράω

εἴδωλον, -ου τό: an image, idol

εἶεν < εἰμί

εἴη < εἰμί

εἴησαν < εἰμί

εἴκοσι(ν): twenty

εἴκω, εἴξω, εἶξα, ἔεικα, ——, ——: give way, retire, yield, withdraw, be inferior

εἴλ- < αἱρέω

εἵνεκα: for the sake of + gen

εἶπαν = εἶπον < λέγω

εἴπας = εἰπών < λέγω

εἰπ- < λέγω

εἴρη- < λέγω

εἴρομαι = ἔρομαι

ἐρωτάω, ἐρωτήσω, ἠρώτησα, ἠρώτηκα, ἠρώτημαι, ἠρωτήθην: ask, question

εἰρωτάω = ἐρωτάω

εἰσαράσσω: drive, drive in on

εἰσβαίνω: go on board, embark

εἰσβάλλω: throw; throw to; attack

εἰσδύνω: get or crawl into

εἴσειμι: go in, enter

εἰσέρχομαι: enter

εἰσφέρω: carry in

ἑκάστοτε: each time, on each occasion

Ἑκαταῖος, -ου ὁ: Hekataios (Hecataeus) of Miletos, a historian c. 500 B.C.E.

ἑκατόν: one hundred

ἐκβαίνω: go out, go out from

ἐκβάλλω: throw out

ἐκγίγνομαι: be born of, emerge, come about; be allowed, be granted

ἐκδέκομαι = ἐκδέχομαι

ἐκδέχομαι: take, receive

ἐκδιδοῖ = ἐκδίδωσι < ἐκδίδωμι

ἐκδίδωμι: give up, give out; exit, empty

ἐκδύω: strip "x" in acc. from "y" in acc.

ἑκηβόλος, -ον: attaining his aim

ἐκλείπω: leave out; omit; abandon

ἐκμανθάνω: learn thoroughly; learn about from "x" in the gen.

ἐκπέμπω: send out

ἐκπέσῃ < ἐκπίπτω

ἐκπίπτω: fall out, lose, be banished

ἐκπλέω (ἐκπλώω): sail out

ἐκποιέω: put out; give in adoption; finish

ἐκπολεμέω: excite to war; make hostile

ἐκστρατεύω: march out, take the field

ἐκτελέω: bring to an end, accomplish, achieve

ἔκτηντο < κτάομαι

ἐκφαίνω: bring to light, reveal

ἐκφέρω: bring, bear; bring, bear out

ἐκφεύγω: flee from; escape

ἐκφήνας < ἐκφαίνω

ἐκχωρέω: go out, depart; give way

ἑκών, -οῦσα, -όν: willing, voluntary

ἐλαία, -ας ἡ: an olive tree

ἐλάσσων, ἐλάσσον: less, fewer

Ἑλένη, -ης ἡ: Helen of Troy

ἐλευθερία, -ας ἡ: freedom, liberty

ἐλεύθερος, -α, -ον: free

ἐλευθερόω, ἐλευθερώσω, ἠλευθέρωσα, ——, ——, ἠλευθερώθην:
    free

Ἐλευσίς, -ῖνος ἡ: Eleusis, a Greek town in west Attika, sacred to Demeter

Ἐλεώνιος, -η, -ον: of Eleon, a village of Tanagra in Boiotia

ἐληλύθεε < ἔρχομαι

ἕλησθε < αἱρέω

ἐλθ- < ἔρχομαι

ἔλιπ- < λείπω

ἕλκω, ἕλξω, ἥλκυσα or εἵλκῡσα, εἵλκῠκα, ἥλκυσμαι, εἱλκύσθην:
  draw, drag, pull at

Ἑλλήνιος, -η, -ον: Greek

Ἑλληνοδίκαι, -ῶν οἱ: chief judges at the Olympic games

Ἑλλήσποντος, -ου ὁ: the Hellespont, the narrow passage between the
  Aegean and Marmara Seas

ἑλομένου < αἱρέω

ἑλ- < αἱρέω

ἐμαντεύθη < μαντεύομαι

ἐμβάλλω: throw in; put in; attack

ἔμπειρος, -ον: experienced in

ἐμπεσόντες < ἐμπίπτω

ἐμπεσοῦσα < ἐμπίπτω

ἐμπικραίνομαι: be bitter against

ἐμπίμπλημι: fill; satisfy acc. of person; fill "x" in acc. with "y" in gen.

ἐμπίμπρημι: burn, set on fire

ἐμπίπλημι = ἐμπίμπλημι

ἐμπίπτω: fall on; burst in

ἐμπόδιος, -α, -ον: in the way; obstructing + dat.

ἔμπροσθε: before; in front of

ἐμφανής, -ές: showing in, visible to the eye, manifest

ἐναγής, -ές: under a curse

ἐνάγω: lead in or on; urge, persuade; propose suggest; promote; bring
  into court, accuse

ἐναργέστατος, -η, -ον: most visible, palpable, in bodily shape

ἐνδεής, -ές: defective, in need of + gen.

ἕνδεκα: eleven

ἐνδέκομαι = ἐνδέχομαι

ἐνδέχομαι: take on oneself; accept; admit; welcome; (impers.) it is possible

ἔνειμι: be in, be within, be among

ἐνενήκοντα: ninety

ἐνέπλησε < ἐμπίμπλημι

ἐνέπρησαν < ἐμπίμπρημι

ἔνερθε: from beneath, below + gen.

ἐνετέταλτο < ἐντέλλω

ἐνετέτμητο < ἐντέμνω

Ἐνετοί, -ῶν οἱ: Enetoi or Venetoi, inhabitants of northeastern Italy

ἐνθεῦτεν (ἐντεῦθεν): thence, hence

ἔνι = ἔνεστι: be in; be possible

ἐνιαυτός, -οῦ ὁ: a year

ἐννέα: nine

ἐνοράω: see, look, look on

ἐντανύω: stretch, strain

ἐντειλάμενος < ἐντέλλω

ἐντείνω: stretch

ἐντέλλω: order, enjoin, command

ἐντέμνω: cut in, engrave

ἐντετμημένην < ἐντέμνω

ἐντεῦθεν (ἐνθεῦτεν): thence, hence

ἐνύπνιον, -ου τό: thing seen in sleep

ἐνύπνιος, -ον: appearing in sleep

ἕξ: six

ἐξαγγέλλω: announce

ἐξάγω: lead out, lead away

ἐξαγωγή, -ῆς ἡ: a leading out

ἐξαίρετος, -ον: taken out, picked out

ἐξαιρέω: take out

ἐξαμέτρος, -ον: of six meters, hexameter

ἐξανασπάω: tear away from

ἐξαναστάντων < ἐξανίστημι

ἐξαναχωρέω: go out of the way, withdraw, retreat

ἐξανιστέαται = ἐξανίστανται < ἐξανίστημι

ἐξανίστημι: cause to stand, raise up; drive out; destroy; be driven out

ἐξαπαλάσσω: free, remove, release

ἔξειμι (only impersonal): it is possible

ἔξειμι: go from; depart

ἐξελασθείς < ἐξελαύνω

ἐξέλασις, -εως (-ιος) ἡ: a driving out

ἐξελαύνω: drive out, expel; march out

ἐξεληλάκεσαν < ἐξελαύνω

ἐξελθ- < ἐξέρχομαι

ἐξελ- < ἐξαιρέω

ἐξενείκαντας < ἐκφέρω

ἔξεο < ἐξίημι

ἐξεπίσταμαι: know thoroughly

ἐξεργάζομαι: finish, complete, bring to perfection; destroy

ἐξέργω: shut out from

ἐξέρχομαι: go, go away, go out

ἔξεσις, -εως (-ιος) ἡ: a dismissal, divorce

ἐξευρίσκω: find out, discover

ἐξευρόντας < ἐξευρίσκω

ἐξηγέομαι: be leader of; manage, direct

ἐξηγητής = ἐσηγητής

ἑξήκοντα οἱ, αἱ, τά: sixty

ἐξηλάσαμεν < ἐξελαύνω

ἐξήλυσις, -εως (-ιος) ἡ: way out, outlet

ἐξιέναι < ἔξειμι

ἐξίημι: send out, let go

ἐξιούσης < ἔξειμι

ἐξίτηλος, -ον: going out

ἐξοικοδομέω: build up; finish a building

ἔξω: outside, without

ἐξωθέω: thrust out

ἐόν = ὄν < εἰμί

ἐόντ- = ὄντ- < εἰμί

ἑορτή, -ῆς ἡ: a festival

ἐοῦσ- = οὖσ- < εἰμί

ἐούσ- = οὖσ- < εἰμί

ἐπαγγέλλω: tell, proclaim; command; denounce

ἐπάγω: bring on

ἐπαερθέντες < ἐπαείρω = ἐπαίρω

ἐπαίρω: raise; excite

ἐπακούω: listen to, obey

ἐπανίστημι: stand up; make rise; revolt

ἐπεάν (ἐπεί + ἄν): when, whenever

ἐπέδρη = ἐφέδρα

ἐπέθηκε < ἐπιτίθημι

ἐπειδή: when, since

ἔπειμι: be on or at

ἔπειμι: come upon; approach; go against, attack

ἐπειρ- < πειράω

ἐπειρωτάω: consult, ask

ἐπείτε (ἐπεί + τε): when, since

ἐπελθ- < ἐπέρχομαι: go forth, go against

ἐπέλκω = ἐφέλκω

ἐπεξῆς: in order

ἐπερωτάω: ask, consult

ἔπεσον < πίπτω

ἐπέτειος, -ον: annual

ἐπεύχομαι: pray

ἐπέχω: have, hold on; intend, purpose; (intrans.) pause

ἐπῆκαν = ἐφῆκαν < ἐφίημι

ἔπηλυς, -υδος ὁ or ἡ: a stranger, foreigner

ἐπιβάλλω: throw or cast on

ἐπιβοάω: call on

ἐπιγίγνομαι: be born; come upon; fall on; ensue

ἐπίγραμμα, -ατος τό: an inscription; epitaph; epigram; mark branded
on slave's forehead

ἐπιγράφω: write, write on; inscribe

Ἐπιδαύριοι, -ων οἱ: Epidaurians, of or from Epidauros, a Greek town

Ἐπίδαυρος, -ου ἡ: Epidauros, a Greek city in the Peloponnesos

ἐπιδαψιλεύω: abound; lavish on

ἐπιδιαιρέω: divide over again; distribute

ἐπιδιελόμενοι < ἐπιδιαιρέω

ἐπιδίζημαι: seek for; demand

ἐπιδιώκω: pursue, chase after

ἐπιζητέω: seek, seek out

ἐπιθαλλάσιος, -α, -ον: of the sea, by the sea

ἐπιθέντα < ἐπιτίθημι

ἐπιθήσεαι < ἐπιτίθημι

ἐπιθυμέω: set one's heart on

ἐπικαλεύμενος = ἐπικαλούμενος < ἐπικαλέω

ἐπικαλέω: summon; bring a charge against

ἐπίκειμαι: be laid on; put to; press on; hang on

ἐπίκλητος, -ον: called upon, summoned

ἐπικουρία, -ας ἡ: aid

ἐπικρατέω: command, rule over + gen.; get possession of + dat.

ἐπιλαμβάνω: take, get hold of + gen.

ἐπιλέγω: say, pick out, choose; think over, consider; (mid) read

ἐπίλοιπος, -η, -ον: still left, remaining

ἐπιμαρτυρέω: bear witness to

ἐπιμελέομαι: take care of, have a concern for + gen.

ἐπιμελής, -ές: careful, attentive; (+ dat.) be a care to

ἐπινέμω: allot, distribute

ἐπινοέω: intend, consider, think on, plan

ἐπιόντ- < ἔπειμι

ἐπιοῦσι < ἔπειμι

ἐπιπεσεῖν < ἐπιπίπτω

ἐπιπίπτω: fall on

ἐπιπλέω: sail, sail for or against

ἐπιποθέω: desire besides

ἐπιστάντα < ἐφίστημι

ἐπιστᾶσι < ἐφίστημι

ἐπίστιος = ἐφέστιος

ἐπιστρατεύω: march against

ἐπισχόντας < ἐπέχω

ἐπίσχω: hold on, out, or back; adjourn; occupy

ἐπιτάσσω: put in command; order

ἐπιτάττω = ἐπιτάσσω

ἐπιτελεῦσι = ἐπιτελοῦσι < ἐπιτελέω

ἐπιτελέω: complete, finish, accomplish

ἐπιτελής, -ές: accomplised, fulfilled

ἐπιτήδειος, -α, -ον: made for an end

ἐπιτίθημι: set on (can take gen.); put to; add; set against, attack; command; apply; aim at + dative

ἐπιτράπω: turn to

ἐπιτρέπω: turn to

ἐπιτροπεύω: be an administrator, guardian

ἐπίτροπος, -ον: being in charge or an overseer

ἐπιφαίνω: show forth, display

ἐπιφανέστατος, -η, -ον: very much coming to light, coming suddenly into view, appearing

ἐπιφέρω: bring on; inflict

ἐπιφράζω: tell, think, consider

ἐπιχειρέω: put one's hand to or on

ἐπιχώριος, -α, -ον: of a place; of or in the country; indigenous

ἐπλήγησαν < πλήσσω

ἐποίευν = ἐποίουν

ἐποιεῦντο = ἐποιοῦντο

ἐπόμνυμι: swear to or on

ἑπτά: seven

ἑπτακόσιοι, -αι, -α: seven hundred

ἐπωνυμία, -ας ἡ: a name given after or because of someone; (acc. as adv.) named after, called after

ἐπώνυμος, -ον: given as a name; giving one's name to something

ἐργάτης, -ου (-εω) ὁ: a workman

ἐργάτις, -ιδος ἡ: a servant, working woman

ἔργμα, -ατος τό: work, deed, business

ἔργω (εἴργω), ἔρξω (εἴρξω), ἔρξα (εἴρξα), ἔργμαι (εἴργμαι), ἔρχθην (εἴρχθην): confine, shut in; bar

ἔργω = ἔρδω

ἔρδω, ἔρξω, ἔρξα, ἔοργα, ——, ——: work, do

Ἐρετρία, -ας ἡ: Eretria, a Greek city on the island of Euboia

Ἐρετριεύς, -έως (-έος) ὁ: Eretrian, of or from Eretria, a Greek city on the island of Euboia

ἐρευνάω, ἐρευνήσω, ἠρευνήσω, ——, ——, ——: seek

Ἐρεχθεύς, -έως (-έος) ὁ: Erekhtheus, an archaic king of Athens

ἐρῆμος, -η, -ον (-ος, -ον): desolate, lonely, solitary

ἐρίζω, ἐρίσω, ἤρισα, ἤρῖκα, ἐρήρισμαι, ——: wrangle, quarrel, strive; strive with + dat.

ἔρις, -ιδος ἡ: strife

Ἑρμῆς, -οῦ (-έω) ὁ: Hermes, a god

Ἕρμος, -ου ὁ: Ermos, a river flowing through Lydia

Ἑρμόφαντος, -ου ὁ: Hermophantos, general of Miletos c. 500 B.C.E.

Ἐρξάνδρος, -ου ὁ: Erxandros, Mytilenean and father of Koës c. 530 B.C.E.

ἐρρύετο < ῥύομαι

Ἐρυκίνος, -η, -ον: Erukine, of Eryx

ἐρύκω, ἐρύξω, ἤρυξα, ——, ——, ——: restrain, hold back, withstand

Ἔρυξ, Ἔρυκος ἡ: Eryx, a city in Sikily, founded by the indigenous hero Eryx

ἔρως, -ωτος ὁ: love, desire

ἐρωτάω, ἐρωτήσω, ἠρώτησα, ἠρώτηκα, ἠρώτημαι, ἠρωτήθην: ask, question

ἐς = εἰς

ἐσάγω: bring to, lead to; lead forth or into

ἐσάξαντο < σάττω

ἐσβάς < εἰσβαίνω

ἔσβεσαν < σβέννυμι

ἐσβολή, -ῆς ἡ: a pouring forth or out; attack

ἐσδύς < εἰσδύνω

ἐσελθών < ἐσέρχομαι

ἐσηγητής, -οῦ ὁ: one who leads on, adviser

ἐσηνείκαντο < ἐσφέρω

ἐσθής, -ῆτος ἡ: clothing, raiment

ἔσιθι < ἔσειμι

ἐσιόντα = εἰσιόντα < εἴσειμι

ἐσκαταβαίνω: go down, enter

ἐσμός, -οῦ ὁ: a swarm; swarm of bees

ἔσοδος, -ου ἡ: an avenue, access

ἐσπαρμένην < σπείρω

ἑσπέρα, -ας ἡ: west

ἐσπίπτω: fall to, fall into

ἐσσωθέωσι = ἐσσωθῶσι < ἡσσάομαι (ἐσσόομαι)

ἐσσώθησαν < ἡσσάομαι (ἐσσόομαι)

ἐστάλη < στέλλω

ἐστεῶ- < ἵστημι

ἑστιάω, ἑστιάσω, εἱστίᾱσα, εἱστίᾱκα, ——, ——: receive at one's
    hearth; entertain, feast

ἐστίχθαι < στίζω

ἐσύστερον: for the future

ἐσφάλη < σφάλλω

ἔσχατος, -η, -ον: farthest, uttermost, extreme

ἔσω: inside, within + gen.

ἑταιρεία, -ας ἡ: an association, brotherhood

ἑταιρηΐη = ἑταιρεία, -ας ἡ

ἑταῖρος, -ου ὁ: a comrade, companion

ἐτάχθ- < τάσσω

ἐτέθη < τίθημι

ἔτεκε < τίκτω

Ἐτεοκλῆς, -οῦς (-έος) ὁ: Eteokles, son of Oidipous and king of Thebes

ἑτοῖμος, -η, -ον: ready, at hand; able, prepared (+ inf.)

Εὐαλκίδης, -ου (-εω) ὁ: Eualkides, general of the Eretrians c. 500 B.C.E.

Εὔβοια, -ας ἡ: Euboia, a Greek island

εὐγενής, -ές: well-born, noble

εὐδαιμονία, -ας ἡ: good fortune

εὐδαίμων, -ον: blessed with a good genius

εὐειδής, -ές: good-looking, well-formed; well-shaped, comely

Εὐέλθων, -οντος ὁ: Euelthon, a Greek and father of Siromos

εὐεπής, -ές: melodious

εὐεργεσία, -ας ἡ: a good deed

εὔμορφος, -ον: good-looking

εὔνοος, -η, -ον (εὔνους = εὔνοος; pl. εὔνοι): well-minded, well-disposed

εὐπετεία, -ας ἡ: an ease

εὐπετέως: easily

εὐπετής, -ές: falling well, easy

Εὔριπος, -ου ὁ: Euripos, the strait between Euboia and the mainland

εὑρόντες < εὑρίσκω

Εὐρυλέων, -ονος ὁ: Euryleon, Spartan c. 520 B.C.E.

Εὐρυσθενής, -οῦς (-έος) ὁ: Eurysthenes, king of Sparta

Εὐρώπη, -ης ἡ: Europe

εὔσκοπος, -ον: keen sighted, watchful

Εὐφρήτης, -ου (-εω) ὁ: Euphretes (Euphrates), a river in Asia Minor

εὐωχέω, εὐωχήσω, εὐώχησα, ——, εὐώχημαι, εὐωχήθην: to entertain sumptuously; feed well; (mid./pass.) feast

ἔφασαν < φημί

ἐφέδρα, -ας ἡ: a sitting by, siege, blockade

ἔφεδρος, -ον: the competitor next in line to fight the victor; sitting, succeeding

ἐφέλκω: drag

Ἐφεσίος, -α, -ον: Ephesian, of or from Ephesos, a Greek city on the coast of Ionia

Ἔφεσος, -ου ἡ: Ephesos, a Greek city on the coast of Ionia

ἐφέστιος (ἐπίστιος), -ον: at one's own fireside, at home

ἐφίημι: send to or against; let go, yield; allow, permit + "x" in dat. + inf.

ἐφίστημι: set or place on

ἔφορος, -ον: overseeing, guarding; (n.) ephor, Spartan magistrate

ἐχειρώθησαν < χειρόω

Ἐχεκράτης, -ους (-εος) ὁ: Ekhekrates, a Lapith and father of Eetion

ἔχθιστος, -η, -ον: most hateful

ἔχθρα, -ας ἡ: a hatred, enmity

ἐώθεσαν < ἔθω

ἐών = ὤν < εἰμί

ἔωσι = ὦσι < εἰμί

ἑωυτ- = ἑαυτ-

ζεύγνυμι, ζεύξω, ἔζευξα, ———, ἔζευγμαι, ἐζεύχθην or ἐζύγην: yoke, join, put to

ζημιόω, ζημιώσω, ἐζημίωσα, ἐζημίωκα, ἐζημίωμαι, ἐζημιώθην: cause loss, punish

ζῆν = ζάειν < ζάω

ζήτησις, -εως (-ιος) ἡ: a seeking, searching

ζωγρέω, ζωγρήσω, ἐζώγρησα, ———, ———, ———: take, take captive

ἦ: in truth, verily

Ἡγησάνδρος, -ου ὁ: Hegesandros, father of Hekataios of Miletos c. 570 B.C.E.

Ἡγησίστρατος, -ου ὁ: Hegesistratos, bastard son of Peisistratos, tyrant of Sigeion

ἥδομαι, ———, ἡσάμην, ———, ———, ἥσθην or ἡδέσθην: delight in; take pleasure, rejoice; be delighted with + dat.

Ἠδωνοί, -ῶν οἱ: Edonoi, inhabitants of Thrakia

Ἠετίδης, -ου (-εω) ὁ: son of Eetion, king of Kilikian Thebe and father of Andromache

Ἠετίων, -ωνος ὁ: Eetion, king of Kilikian Thebe and father of Andromache

ἦθος, -ους (-εος) τό: a custom, usage, habit; haunt

ἤια = ᾖα < εἶμι

ἤιε = ᾖει < εἶμι

ἤισαν = ᾖσαν < εἶμι

ἤλασαν < ἐλαύνω

Ἠλεῖος, -α, -ον: Elean, of or from Elea

ἦλθ- < ἔρχομαι

ἡλικία, -ας ἡ: a time of life, age

ἡλικιώτης, -ου (-εω) ὁ: a man of equal age, comrade

ἡλίκος, -η, -ον: of similar age

ἤλωσαν < ἁλίσκομαι

ἥμερος, -ον (-ος, -α, -ον): tame, cultivated

ἡμερόω: tame

ἡμέτερος, -α, -ον: our

ἡμιόλιος, -α, -ον: half as much again

ἥμισυς, -εια, -υ: half

ἠνείκατο < φέρω

ἠνέσχετο < ἀνέχω

ἤπειρος, -ου ἡ: a mainland, continent, land, terra firma

ἤπιος, -α, -ον: gentle, kind

ἠπιστέατο = ἠπίσταντο < ἔπισταμαι

Ἥραιος, -α, -ον: of Hera; (n. s.) her temple

Ἡρακλείδης, -ου (-εω) ὁ: Herakleides, of Herakles

Ἡράκλειος, -α, -ον: of Herakles; (n. s.) his temple; (n. pl.) his festival

Ἡρακλῆς, -οῦς (-έος) ὁ: Herakles

ἦρσε < ἄρδω

ἡρώιος, -α, -ον: concerning heroes; (n.) hero temple

ἥρως, -ος ὁ or ἡ: a hero

ἡσθείς < ἥδομαι

ἡσσάομαι (ἐσσόομαι): be less or inferior; be defeated; ἡσσᾶται ὑπὸ αὐτῆς: he is smaller than her

ἡσυχία, -ας ἡ: a calmness, peace

ἀφανίζω: make unseen, hide

ἠφάνιστο < ἀφανίζω

ἠώς, ἠοῦς ἡ: dawn

θαλαμία, -ας ἡ: an oar, porthole

θαλασσοκράτωρ, -ορος ὁ: master of the sea

θάπτω, θάψω, ἔθαψα, τέταφα, τέθαμμαι, ἐτάφην: bury, honor with funeral rites

θαρσέω, θαρσήσω, ἐθάρσησα, τέθαρρηκα or τεθάρσηκα, ——, ——: take courage, dare

θαυμάζω, θαυμάσω, ἐθαύμασα, τεθαύμακα, τεθαύμασμαι, ἐθαυμάσθην: wonder, be astonished, marvel; admire; wonder at + gen.

θεμιτός, -ή, -όν: lawful, righteous

θεοπρόπος, -ου ὁ: prophet; one who consults a prophet

θεραπεία, -ας ἡ: a service, attendance

θεραπηίη = θεραπεία

θεράπων, -οντος ὁ: a henchman, servant, attendant

θέσθαι < τίθημι

Θεσπιέες, -ων οἱ: Thespians, inhabitants of Thespia in Boiotia

Θεσπρωτοί, -ῶν οἱ: Thesprotoi, inhabitants of Epiros in northwest Greece

Θεσσαλία, -ας ἡ: Thessaly, south of Makedonia

Θεσσαλοί, -ῶν ὁ: Thessalians, of or from Thessaly

Θεσσαλός, -οῦ ὁ: Thessalos, a Spartan c. 520 B.C.E.

θέω, θεύσομαι, ἔθευσα, ——, ——, ——: run

Θῆβαι, -ῶν αἱ: Thebes, a Greek city in Boiotia

Θήβη, -ης ἡ: Thebe, a nymph

Θηραῖος, -ου ὁ: Theraian, inhabitants of Thera, an island in the Aegean

θησαυρός, -οῦ ὁ: a treasury

Θράκη, -ης: Thrake (Thrace)

Θρᾷξ, Θρᾳκός ὁ: a Thrakian (Thracian), of or from a region to the west of the Black Sea and the north of the Aegean

Θρασύβουλος, -ου ὁ: Thrasyboulos, tyrant of Miletos c. 650 B.C.E.

Θρηΐκη = Θράκη

Θρῆϊξ, Θρηΐκος ὁ = Θρᾷξ, Θρᾳκός ὁ

Θρῆϊξ, Θρηΐκος ὁ: a Thrakian

θρίξ, τριχός ἡ: hair

θρόνος, -ου ὁ: a throne, seat

θυγατριδοῦς (θυγατριδέος), -οῦ ὁ: a daughter's son, grandson

θυμόω, θυμώσω, ἐθύμωσα, τεθύμωκα, τεθύμωμαι, ἐθυμώθην: make angry, provoke; be angry

θύρα, -ας ἡ: a door

θυσία, -ας ἡ: a burnt offering, sacrifice

θῶμα, -ατος τό: a wonder, marvel

θωμάζω = θαυμάζω

Ἰαμιδαί, -ῶν οἱ: Iamids, a tribe from Elea, a Greek city in Thesprotia

Ἰάς, -άδος ἡ: Ionian, of or from Ionia

Ἰβανώλλις, -ιος ὁ: Ibanollis, father of Oliatos, the tyrant of Mylasa

ἰδεῖν < ὁράω

ἴδη, -ης ἡ: a timber tree

ἴδιος, -α, -ον: one's own; one's self

ἴδμεν < οἶδα

ἴδ- < ὁράω

ἰδό- < ὁράω

ἰδοῦσι < ὁράω

Ἰδριάς, Ἰδριάδος ἡ: Idrias, town in Karia

ἰδρύω, ἰδρύσω, ἵδρῡσα, ἵδρῡκα, ἵδρῡμαι, ἱδρύθην: make sit down; fix; settle

ἰέναι < εἶμι

ἱερεία, -ας ἡ: a priestess

ἱερεῖον, -ου τό: a victim, animal for sacrifice

ἵζω, ——, εἷσα or ἵζησα, ἵζηκα, ——, ——: make sit, seat, place, set

ἴη < εἶμι

ἴης < εἶμι

Ἰητραγόρης, -ου (-εω) ὁ: Ietragores (Ietragoras), of Miletos

ἰθέως: directly straight

ἱκετεύω, ἱκετεύσω, ἱκέτευσα, ——, ——, ——: approach as a suppliant

ἱκετηρία, -ας ἡ: an olive branch of a suppliant

ἱκέτης, -ου (-εω) ὁ: one who comes to seek aid

ἴκρια, -ων τά: a halfdeck, platform

ἱλάσκομαι, ἱλάσομαι, ἱλασάμην, ——, ——, ἱλάσθην: appease

Ἰλιάς, -άδος ἡ: Ilium, Troy

ἱμάς, -άντος ὁ: leather, a strap

ἱμάτιον, -ου τό: a piece of dress, cloak

Ἴμβρος, -ου ἡ: Imbros, an island

ἵμερος, -ου ὁ: a longing, desire

Ἰνδοί, -ῶν οἱ: Indoi, Indians

ἰόν < εἶμι

ἰπνός, -οῦ ὁ: an oven, furnace

Ἵππαρχος, -ου ὁ: Hipparkhos, son of Peisistratos and possibly cotyrant of Athens with his brother Hippias c. 520 B.C.E.

ἱππάσιμος, -η, -ον: fit for horses, fit for riding

Ἱππίης, -ου (-εω) ὁ: Hippiës (Hippias), son of Peisistratus and tyrant of Athens c. 520 B.C.E.

ἱπποβότης, -ου (-εω) ὁ: a feeder of horses

Ἱπποκόων, -ωντος ὁ: Hippokoön, a Spartan who deposed his brother

ἱερεῖον, -ου τό: a victim, an animal for sacrifice

Ἱπποκράτης, -ου (-εω) ὁ: Hippokrates, father of Peisistratos c. 580 B.C.E.

ἱρήϊον = ἱερεῖον

ἱροεργία = ἱρουργία

ἱρός = ἱερός

ἱρουργία, -ας ἡ: religious service, sacrifice

ἱρώτατος, -η, -ον: most holy

Ἰσαγόρης, -ου (-εω) ὁ: Isagores (Isagores), Athenian and opponent of Kleisthenes

ἰσηγορία, -ας ἡ: an equal right of speech

ἴσθι < οἶδα

Ἰσμήνιος, -α, -ον: Ismenian, of or belonging to Apollo Ismenios

ἰσοκρατία, -ας ἡ: equal power; equal rights; political equality

ἰσονομία, -ας ἡ: an equal distribution, equilibrium, balance

ἰσοπαλής, -ές: equal in the struggle

ἰσόρροπος, -ον: equal in strength

ἴστε < οἶδα

ἱστία, -ας ἡ: a hearth

Ἱστιαῖος, -ου ὁ: Histiaios (Histiaeus), tyrant of Miletos c. 500 B.C.E.

ἱστιῆσθαι = ἱστιᾶσθαι = ἑστιᾶσθαι < ἑστιάω

Ἴστρος, -ου ὁ: Istros (Ister or Danube), a river running from Germany to the Black Sea

ἴσχω: hold, restrain, have, possess; ἴσχειν αὐτὸν ταῦτα ποιεῖν: to prevent him from doing these things

Ἰταλία, -ας ἡ: Italia (Italy)

ἰχθύς, -ύος ὁ (ἰχθῦς = ἰχθύες or ἰχθύας): fish

Ἰωλκός, -οῦ ὁ: Iolkos, a Greek city of Thessaly

Ἴων, Ἴωνος ὁ: Ion, mythical founder of the Ionians

Ἴωνες, -ων οἱ: Ionians, of or from Ionia, located on the coast of Asia Minor

Ἰωνία, -ας ἡ: Ionia, Greek region on the coast of Asia Minor

Ἰωνικός, -ή, -όν: Ionic, Ionian, of or from Ionia, Greek region located centrally on the coast of Asia Minor

Καδμεῖος, -α, -ον: Kadmean, of Kadmos, from Phoinikia and mythical founder of Thebes

Καδμήϊος = Καδμεῖος, -α, -ον

Κάδμος, -ου ὁ: Kadmos, from Phoinikia and mythical founder of Thebes

Κάειρα, -ας ἡ: Karian, of or from Karia

καθαιρέω: take down; pull down; accomplish

καθηγέομαι: act as guide, lead the way

κάθημαι: be seated; sit

καθίζω: make sit, place, set

καθίημι: let fall, drop

καθοράω: look at, look on

Καινείδης, -ου (-εω) ὁ: of Kaineus, a Lapith hero from Thessaly

καίπερ: although

καίω (κάω), καύσω, ἔκαυσα, κέκαυκα, κέκαυμαι, ἐκαύθην: kindle

κακότης, -ητος ἡ: badness, wickedness

κακόω, κακώσω, ἐκάκωσα, ——, κεκάκωμαι, ——: treat badly, ill-use, maltreat, distress

καλάμινος, -η, -ον: of reed

κάλαμος, -ου ὁ: a reed

καλευμένας = καλουμένας < καλέω

καλεῦνται = καλοῦνται < καλέω

Καλλίης, -ου (-εω): Kallies (Kallias) from Elea and a seer c. 510 B.C.E.

κάλλιστος, -η, -ον: most beautiful

καλλίων, κάλλιον: lovelier, better

κάλλος, -ους (-εος) τό: beauty

καλύβη, -ης ἡ: a hut, cabin

Καλχηδόνιοι, -ων οἱ: Kalkhedonians (Calchedonians), inhabitants of Kalkhedon in Bithynia on the coast of the Propontis

Καμβύσης, -ου (-εω) ὁ: Kambyses (Cambyses), king of Persia

κάπηλος, -ου ὁ: a merchant; thief

Καππαδόκαι, -ῶν οἱ: Kappadokians, from Kappadocia in Asia Minor, north of Kypros

Καππαδοκία, -ας ἡ: Kappadokia, in Asia Minor, north of Kypros

Κάρ, Καρός ὁ: Karian, of or from Karia, a region of Asia Minor, south of Lydia

Καρία, -ας ἡ: Karia, a region of Asia Minor, south of Lydia

Καρίος, -α, -ον: Karian

καρπός, -οῦ ὁ: fruit

κάρτα: even, especially; very, extremely

καρτερός, -ά, -όν: strong, staunch

Καρχηδόνιοι, -ων οἱ: Karkhedonians, (Carthaginians), of or from Karthage (Carthage)

καταβαίνω: go down, go down to

καταγελάω: laugh at, jeer, mock + dat.

κατάγω: lead down, bring down; bring back

καταγωγή, -ῆς ἡ: a bringing down; resting place

καταδαπανάω: squander

καταδέκομαι = καταδέχομαι

καταδέχομαι: receive, admit, take back

καταδέω: bind on

καταδουλόω: enslave

καταθύμιος, -α, -ον: in the mind, at heart; welcoming, pleasing

καταινέω: agree to, consent to

καταιρέω = καθαιρέω

καταιτιάομαι: accuse, arraign + gen.

κατακαίω: burn completely

κατακαυθέντων < κατακαίω

κατακαύσαντες < κατακαίω

κατακρύπτω: hide, conceal

κατακυλίνδω: roll down

καταλαμφθείς < καταλαμβάνω

καταλέγω: say, tell, recount; lay down; pick out, choose; reckon

καταλείπω: leave behind

καταλεύω: stone to death

καταλλάσσω: change, reconcile

κατάλυσις, -εως (-ιος) ἡ: a dissolving, ending, finishing; resting; resting place, inn

καταλύω: dissolve, destroy; unloose

καταμένω: remain, stay behind; continue in a state

κατανέμω: distribute, allot

καταπακτός, -ή, -όν: shutting downwards, trap

κατάπαυσις, -εως (-ιος) ἡ: a stopping

καταπαύω: put an end to, stop

καταπροίξομαι: do a thing without return, i.e., with impunity

καταρτίζω: adjust; put in order; restore, repair

καταρτιστήρ, -ῆρος ὁ: one who restores order, mediator

κατάσκοπος, -ου ὁ: one who reconnoiters, scout, spy

κατάστασις, -εως (-ιος) ἡ: a settling; establishing; state, institution

καταστῆσαι < καθίστημι

καταστήσας < καθίστημι

καταστρέφω: turn down; overturn, subdue, trample on

κατατίθημι: put, place

καταφεύγω: flee for refuge

καταφορέω: carry down

κατέβησαν < καταβαίνω

κατεῖλε = καθεῖλε < καθαιρέω

κατειλέω: force into a narrow space

κατειλήθησαν < κατειλέω

κάτειμι: go or come down; return

κατείργω (κατέργω): drive into, shut in

κατέλαβε < καταλαμβάνω

κατελεύσεσθαι < κατέρχομαι

κατέλῃς = καθέλῃς < καθαιρέω

κατέλθωσι < κατέρχομαι

κατελόντας = καθελόντας < καθαιρέω

κατεργάζομαι: effect, accomplish, achieve; destroy, conquer, overpower

κατερέω < καταλέγω

κατέρχομαι: go down; return

κατεστεῶτος = καθεστῶτος < καθίστημι

κατέχω: hold, keep back, occupy; (int.) check oneself

κατηγέοντο = καθηγέοντο < καθηγέομαι

κατήκειν = καθήκειν < καθήκω

καθήκω: come or go down; suffice; τὰ καθήκοντα: present state of things, circumstances

κατήκοος, -α, -ον: listening to; obeying; subject to + gen.

κατήκω = καθήκω

κατήμενοι = καθήμενοι < κάθημαι

κατήμενος = καθήμενος < κάθημαι

κατιδέσθαι < καθοράω

κατιεῖ = καθιεῖ < καθίημι

κατιέναι < κάτειμι

κατίζων = καθίζων

κατιστάναι = καθιστάναι < καθίστημι

κατίστατο = καθίστατο < καθίστημι

κάτοδος, -ου ἡ: a return

κατοικέω: colonize, settle in, dwell, inhabit

κατοικίζω: settle, establish

κατοικτείρω: have mercy

κατοχή, -ῆς ἡ: a holding back, detention; possession

κατύπερθε: from above, above, before + gen.

κατυπέρτερος, -α, -ον: higher; superior, having the upper hand

κάτω: downward

Καύκασα, -ων τά: Kaukasa, a harbor on the southwest coast of Khios

Καῦνος, -ου ἡ: Kaunos, a city of Karia

Καΰστριος, -ου ὁ: Kayster River in Ephesos of Ionia

κέεται = κεῖται < κεῖμαι

κεινῇσι < κεῖνος, -η, -ον

κεινός, -ή, -όν: empty

κείρω, κερέω, ἔκειρα, κέκαρκα, κέκαρμαι, ἐκέρθην or ἐκάρην: cut, shave; ravage, waste

κέκριται < κρίνω

Κελέης, -ου (-εω) ὁ: Kelees, Spartan c. 520 B.C.E.

κεντέω, κεντήσω, ἐκέντησα, ——, κεκέντημαι, ἐκεντήθην: prick, goad, spur on

κέραμος, -ου ὁ: clay, potter's clay

κερτόμιος, -α, -ον: mocking, taunting, cutting, stinging, reproachful, abusive, satirical

κεχαρηκότες < χαίρω

κῃ = πῃ

Κήιος, -α -ον: Kean, of or from Keos, a Greek island of the Kyklades

κηρίον, -ου τό: a honeycomb

κήρυγμα, -ατος τό: a public notice

κῆρυξ, -υκος ὁ: a herald

κίβδηλος, -ον: adulterated, base

κιθών = κιτών

Κίλικες, -ων οἱ: Kilikian, of or from Kilikia

Κιλικία, -ας ἡ: Kilikia, an area of Asia Minor to the south of Kappadokia

Κινδυής, Κινδυέος ἡ: Kindyes (Kindya), a town in Karia

Κινέης, -ου (-εω) ὁ: Kineës, king of the Thessalians c. 530 B.C.E.

Κίνυψ, -υπος ὁ: Kinyps, a river in Libya

Κίος, -ου ἡ: Kios, a Greek city

Κίσσιος, -η, -ον: Kissian, of or from Kissia, a district in Susiana

κιτών, -ῶνος ὁ: a khiton (chiton), shirt

Κλαζομεναί, -ῶν αἱ: Klazomenai, a Greek city on the coast of Ionia

κλεηδών = κληδών

Κλεισθένης, -ου (-εω) ὁ: Kleisthenes, an Athenian and Alkmaionid, reformer of the constitution, regarded as the father of Athenian democracy c. 540 B.C.E.

κλειτός, -ή, -όν: renowned, famous

Κλεόμβροτος, -ου ὁ: Kleombrotos, Spartan and father of Pausanias c. 500 B.C.E.

Κλεομένης, -ου (-εω) ὁ: Kleomenes, son of Anaxandrides of the Agiad house; king of Sparta c. 520–90 B.C.E.

κλέπτω, κλέψω, ἔκλεψα, κέκλοφα, κέκλεμμαι, ἐκλάπην: steal

κληδών, -όνος ἡ: an omen, presage

Κληῖδες, -ων αἱ: Kleides, a northeast headland of Kypros

κληροῦχος, -ου ὁ: one who holds an allotment of land

κλώθω, κλώσω, ἔκλωσα, ——, κέκλωσμαι, ἐκλώσθην: twist by spinning, spin

Κόδρος, -ου ὁ: Kodros, last of the semimythical kings of Athens

κοῖλος, -η, -ον: hollow

κοίτη, -ης ἡ: a bedstead, bed chamber; a going to bed; intercourse

κολούω, κολούσω, ἐκόλουσα, ——, κεκόλουμαι or κεκόλουσμαι, ἐκολούθην or ἐκολούσθην: cut short, dock, curtail

κομάω (Ion. κομέω): let the hair grow long; plume oneself, give oneself airs, aim at

κομπέω: clash, ring; boast

Κονδαῖος, -α, -ον: Kondaian, a city of Thessaly

Κορησός, -οῦ ἡ: Koresos, part of Ephesos a Greek city on the coast of Ionia

Κορίνθιος, -α, -ον: Korinthian, of or from Korinth, a Greek city

Κόρινθος, -ου ὁ and ἡ: Korinth, a Greek city on the isthmus

Κορωναῖοι, -ων οἱ: inhabitants of Koroneia

κουρίδιος, -α, -ον: wedded; lawfully wedded

Κουριέες, -έων οἱ: Kouriees, of or from Kourion, a Greek city on Kypros

Κουρίον, -ου τό: Kourion, a Greek city on Kypros

Κράθιος, -α, -ον: Krathian, of or from Krathis, a river in southern Italy

Κρᾶθις, -εως (-ιος) ὁ: Krathis, a river in the Sybarite interior in southern Italy

κράτιστος, -η, -ον: strongest

κρεμάννυμι, κρεμάσω or κρεμάω, ἐκρέμασα, κεκρέμᾰκα, κεκρέμασμαι (κέκρημαι), ἐκρεμάσθην: hang up

κρέσσων, -ον: greater, stronger

Κρηστωναῖοι, -ων οἱ: Krestonians, a Thrakian tribe

κρησφύγετον, -ου τό: a place of refuge

κρίσις, -εως (-ιος) ἡ: a decision

Κροῖσος, -ου ὁ: Kroisos (Croesus), Lydian king c. 595–547 B.C.E.

Κρότων, -ωνος ἡ: Kroton, a Greek city in Italy, founded in 733 B.C.E. by Akhaians

Κροτωνιήτης, -ου (-εω) ὁ: of Kroton, a Greek colony in southern Italy

Κροτωνιῆτις, -ιδος ἡ: Krotonian, of Kroton, a Greek colony in southern Italy

κρύπτω, κρύψω, ἔκρυψα, κέκρυφα, κέκρυμμαι, ἐκρύφθην: hide, cover; bend, stoop

κτάομαι, κτήσομαι, ἐκτησάμην, ——, κέκτημαι, ἐκτήθην: get, gain; have, hold; acquire, possess

κτῆμα, -ατος τό: a possession, thing

κτίζω, κτίσω, ἔκτισα, ἔκτῐκα, ἔκτισμαι, ἐκτίσθην: found

Κυβήβη, -ης ἡ: Kybebe, earth mother goddess

κυέω, κυήσω, ἐκύησα, ——, ——, ——: be pregnant with; conceive

Κυκλάδες, -ων αἱ: Kyklades, a group of islands in the Aegean

Κύλων, -ονος ὁ: Kylon, an Athenian and Olympic victor

Κυμαῖος, -α, -ον: of or from Kyme, an Aiolian city close to Lydia

Κύμη, -ης ἡ: Kyme, an Aiolian city close to Lydia

Κυνόσαργες, -ους (-εος) τό: Kynosarges, a public gymnasium just outside the walls of Athens

Κύπριοι, -ων οἱ: Kyprians, of or from Kypros, an island in the Mediterranean

Κύπρος, -ου ἡ: Kypros, an island in the Mediterranean

κυρβασία, -ας ἡ: a Persian bonnet

Κυρήνη, -ης ἡ: Kyrene, a Greek settlement in eastern Libya

κύριος, -α, -ον: having power, appointed, fixed

κυψέλη, -ης ἡ: a chest, box

Κύψελος, -ου ὁ: Kypselos, first tyrant of Korinth 657–627 B.C.E.

κύων, κυνός ὁ or ἡ: a dog

Κώης, -ου (-εω) ὁ: Koës, from Mytilene and made tyrant of it by Dareios I c. 500 B.C.E.

κώμη, -ης ἡ: an unwalled village

κωπεύς, -έως (-έος) ὁ (always in pl.): pieces of wood fit for making oars, spars

Λάβδα, -ας ἡ: Labda, a Korinthian and daughter of Amphion

Λαβδάκος, -ου ὁ: Labdakos, king of Thebes and father of Laios

Λάβραυνδα τό: Labraunda, a town in Karia

λαθεῖν < λανθάνω

Λάϊος, -ου ὁ: Laïos, king of Thebes

Λακεδαιμόνιος, -α, -ον: Lakedaimonian

Λακεδαίμων, -ονος ἡ: Lakedaimon, the official name of Sparta

Λαμπώνιον, -ου τό: Lamponion, an Aiolian town in southwest of the Troad

Λάμψακος, -ου ἡ: Lampsakos, a city of Mysia on the Hellespont

Λαοδάμας, -αντος ὁ: Laodamas, son of Eteokles and king of Thebes

Λαπίθης, -ου (-εω) ὁ: Lapith, a legendary people inhabiting Thessaly

λάσιος, -α, -ον: hairy, hirsute

λεηλατέω: drive away booty

λειογένειος, -α, ον: smooth-chinned, beardless

Λειψύδριον, -ου τό: Leipsydrion, a fort on Mount Parnes in Paionia

Λέρος, -ου ἡ: Leros, a Greek island in the south of the Aegean off the coast of Asia Minor

Λέσβιος, -α, -ον: Lesbian, of Lesbos

Λέσβος, -ου ἡ: Lesbos, a Greek island off the coast of Asia Minor

Λευκαί Στήλαι αἱ: the White Pillars

λευστήρ, -ῆρος ὁ: a stone thrower

λέων, -οντος ὁ: a lion

Λέων, -οντος ὁ: Leon, a Spartan

Λεωνίδας, Λεωνίδου (-εω) ὁ: Leonidas, famous Spartan king, who died fighting at Thermopylae in 480 B.C.E.

λέως, -ω (acc.: λέων) ὁ: people

λήιον, -ου τό: a crop; crop of corn, field of corn

ληϊστύς, -ύος ἡ: a plundering

λῆμα, -ατος τό: a will, desire, purpose

Λήμνιος, -α, -ον: a Lemnian, of or from Lemnos

Λῆμνος, -ου ἡ: Lemnos, a Greek island in the northeast of the Aegean

Λιβύη, -ης ἡ: Libya, in Africa adjacent to Egypt

Λίβυς, -υος ὁ: a Libyan, of or from the area in north Africa

Λίγυες, -ων οἱ: Ligues, inhabitants of Liguria of northern Italy

λίμνη, -ης ἡ: a pool of standing water, lake

λίνεος, -α, -ον: of flax, linen

λίνον, -ου τό: anything made of flax

λιπαρέω, λιπαρήσω, ἐλιπάρησα, ——, ——, ——: persist, persevere; λιπαρεῖ ποιῶν: he continues doing; persist in + dat.

λιποστρατία, -ας ἡ: a desertion from the army, refusal to serve

λιπών < λείπω

λογίζομαι, λογίσομαι λογιεομαι, ἐλογισάμην, ——, λελόγισμαι, ἐλογίσθην: think, consider, calculate

λογοποιός, -όν: word making

λούω, λούσω, ἔλουσα, ——, λέλουμαι, ἐλούθην: wash, bathe

λοχάω, λοχήσω, ἐλόχησα, ——, λελόχημαι, ——: lie in waiting; waylay, ambush

λόχος, -ου ὁ: an ambush

Λυδία, -ας ἡ: Lydia

Λύδιος, -α, -ον: of Lydia, Lydian

Λυδός, -ή, -όν: Lydian, of or from Lydia, centrally located in Asia Minor

Λυκάρητος, -ου ὁ: Lykaretos, governor

λῡμαίνομαι, λῡμαίνέομαι, ἐλῡμηνάμην, ——, λελυμάσμαι, ἐλῡμάνθην: outrage, maim, mutilate; be maltreated; be destroyed; inflict outrages or indignities on + dat.

λυπέω, λυπήσω, ἐλύπησα, λελύπηκα, λελύπημαι, ἐλυπήθην: give pain to, distress, grieve, annoy

λυπηρός, -ή, -όν: painful

Λυσαγόρης, -ου ὁ: Lysagores, father of Histiaios c. 520 B.C.E.

λύτρον, -ου τό: price of release

μάθητε < μανθάνω

Μαιανδρίος, -ου ὁ: Maiandrios, king of Samos c. 500 B.C.E.

Μαίανδρος, -ου ὁ: Maiandros River

Μακέαι, -ῶν οἱ: Makeai, inhabitants of Libya

Μακεδονία, -ας ἡ: Makedonia (Macedonia), a region north of Greece

Μακεδών, -ῶνος ὁ: Makedonian (Macedonian), of or from Makedonia

μακρός, -ά, -όν: long

μαντεῖον, -ου τό: an oracular response, oracle

μαντεῖος, -α, -ον: oracular

μαντεύομαι, μαντεύσομαι, ἐμαντευσάμην, ——, μεμάντευμαι, ἐμαντεύθην: divine, prophesy; presage, forbode, surmise; consult an oracle

μαντήιον = μαντεῖον

μαντήιος = μαντεῖος

Μαντινή, -ῆς ἡ: Mantiene, a city on the mainland to the east of Kypros

μάντις, -εως (-ιος) ὁ: a diviner, seer, prophet

Μαντύης, -ου (-εω) ὁ: Mantyes, a Paionian

Μαρσύης, -ου ὁ: Marsyas River in Phrygia

μαρτυρέω, μαρτυρήσω, ἐμαρτύρησα, ——, μεμαρτύρημαι,
    ἐμαρτυρήθην: witness, give witness, testify

μαρτύριον, -ου τό: proof; testimony; (pl.) evidence

Μασσαλίη, -ης ἡ: Massalie, Italy

μαστός, -οῦ ὁ: a breast; hill

Ματιηνοί, -ῶν οἱ: Matienoi, inhabitants of the mainland to the east of
    Kypros

Μαυσῶλος, -ου ὁ: Mausolos, father of Pixodaros, a Karian from Kindya
    c. 510 B.C.E.

Μεγάβαζος, -ου ὁ: Megabazos, Persian general serving under Dareios I
    c. 500 B.C.E.

Μεγαβάτης, -ου (-εω) ὁ: Megabates, Persian general and admiral c. 500
    B.C.E.

μέγαθος = μέγεθος

μεγαλοπρεπής, -ές: splendid, magnificent

μεγαλωστί: far and wide

Μέγαρα, -ων τά: Megara, a Greek city

μέγαρον, -ου τό: a megaron, great hall

μέγιστος, -η, -ον: biggest, greatest

μεζόνως: in a greater degree

μέζων = μείζων

μέθη, -ης ἡ: a strong drink

μεθίημι: set loose, let go, let fall; give up, abandon; (mid. and intrans.)
    let oneself go; be allowed to go

μείζων (μέζων), μεῖζον: greater, bigger

Μελάνθιος, -ου ὁ: Melanthios, an Athenian admiral c. 500 B.C.E.

Μέλανθος, -ου ὁ: Melanthos, a descendant of Neleus, king of Messenia,
    and later king of Athens

Μελάνιππος, -ου ὁ: Melanippos, one of seven defenders of Thebes μέλισσα, -ης ἡ: a bee

Μέλισσα, -ης ἡ: Melissa of Korinth

μέλος, -ους (-εος) τό: a limb; song; melody

μέλω, μελήσω, ἐμέλησα, μεμέληκα, ——, ——: be an object of care
to + dat.; πᾶσι μέλω: I am a care to all; care for, attend to + gen.;
(impers.) be a care to + dat.; "x" in gen. is a care to "y" in dat.; μέλει
μοι τοῦδε: I care for this

μεμετιμένος = μεμεθιμένος < μεθίημι

μέμνεο < μιμνήσκω

μεμνῆσθαι < μιμνήσκω

Μεμνόνειος, -α, -ον: of Memnon

Μεμνόνιος, -α, -ον: of Memnon

Μενέλαος, -εως (-εω) ὁ: Menelaos, king of Sparta, husband of Helen,
hero of the Trojan War

μεσόγαιος, -α, -ον: inland, in the heart of a country

Μεσσηνίοι, -ων οἱ: Messenians, of or from Messenia of the Peloponnesos

μέτα = μέτεστι: be among, have a share of, belong to

μεταβαίνω: pass over

μεταβάλλω: turn, alter, change

μεταδοκέω: change one's opinion; (impers.) be a change of heart + dat.

μέταλλον, -ου τό: a mine, quarry

μεταπέμπω: send, send after, summon

μεταρρυθμίζω: change the form

μετατίθημι: place among; change, alter

μεταυτίκα: forthwith, thereupon

μέτειμι: be among, be to, have a share of "x" in gen.

μετείς = μεθείς < μεθίημι

μετεόν < μέτειμι

μετέπειτα: afterward, thereafter

μετέχω: partake of, have a share of + gen.

μετέωρος, -ον: in mid air

μετῆκαν = μεθῆκαν < μεθίημι

μετήσεσθαι = μεθήσεσθαι < μεθίημι

μετίσχω = μετέχω

μετρέω, μετρήσω, ἐμέτρησα, ——, ——, ——: measure

μέτρον, -ου τό: size; moderation

μετωνομάζω: call by a new name

μέχρι: up to, until + gen.

Μηδία, -ας ἡ: Media

Μηδικός, -ή, -όν: Median

Μῆδος, -ου ὁ: a Mede, Persian

μηκέτι: no more, no longer, no further

Μηκιστεύς, -έως ὁ: Mekisteus, one of the attackers of Thebes in the
    seven against Thebes

μηκύνω, μηκῡνέω, ἐμήκῡνα, ——, μεμήκυσμαι, ἐμηκύνθην:
    lengthen, prolong, delay

μηνίω, μηνίσω or μηνιέω, ἐμήνῑσα, ——, ——, ——: cherish wrath,
    be angry with + dat.

μητροπάτωρ, -ορος ὁ: a mother's father

μηχανάομαι, μηχανήσομαι, ἐμηχανησάμην, ——, μεμηχάνημαι,
    ——: devise, construct, build; bring about

μηχανή, -ῆς ἡ: a machine, contrivance

μιαιφονώτερος, -α, -ον: more blood stained, bloody

Μιλήσιος, -α, -ον: Milesian, of Miletos, a Greek city on the coast of Karia

Μίλητος, -ου ἡ: Miletos, a Greek city

μιμέομαι, μιμήσομαι, ἐμιμησάμην, ——, μεμίμημαι, ——: imitate,
    represent, portray, make exactly like

Μινώη, -ης ἡ: Minoë, a city of Sikelia

μίσγω = μίγνυμι

μισθός, -οῦ ὁ: wages, pay, hire

μισθόω, μισθώσομαι, ἐμίσθωσα, μεμίσθωκα, μεμίσθωμαι,
    ἐμισθώθην: hire, engage, hire "x" in acc. for the amount of "y" in
    gen.; (mid.) be hired + inf.

μνήμη, -ης ἡ: a remembrance, memory; μνήμην ποιήσεσθαι αὐτῶν: to
    deal with them later

μοῖρα, -ας ἡ: a lot; portion; fate

Μολπαγόρης, -ου (-εω) ὁ: Molpagores, father of Aristagoras, deputy
    governor of Miletos c. 520

μοναρχέω: be monarch

μόναρχος, -ου ὁ: a monarch, sole ruler

μονομαχία, -ας ἡ: a single combat

μόρος, -ου ὁ: fate, destiny

μουναρχέω = μοναρχέω

μουναρχέω: rule alone; be monarch

μούναρχος = μόναρχος

μούναρχος, -ου ὁ: a monarch, sole ruler

μουνομαχίη, -ης ἡ: a single combat

μοῦνος = μόνος

Μυλασσεύς, -έως (-έος) ὁ: of or from Mylasa, a Karian city of Asia Minor

Μύνδιος, -α, -ον: Myndian, of or from Myndos, a Lelegian town of Asia Minor

Μυόεις, Μυοῦντος ἡ: Myous, an Ionian city about 15 kilometers from Miletos

μυριάς, -άδος ἡ: number of ten thousand; myriad

μυρίος, -α, ον: numberless, infinite

Μύρκινος, -ου ἡ: Myrkinos, a city in Makedonia near Prasiad Lake

Μύρσος, -ου ὁ: Myrsos, Lydian and son of Gyges c. 500 B.C.E.

Μυσίος, -η, -ον: Mysian, of or from Mysia in northwest Asia Minor

Μυτιλήναιος, -α, -ον: Mytilenian, of or from Mytilene, a city on Lesbos

Μυτιλήνη, -ης ἡ: Mytilene, a city

Νάξιος, -α, -ον: Naxian, of or from Naxos

Νάξος, -ου ἡ: Naxos, a Greek island

ναός, νεώς ὁ: temple, inner shrine of a temple

ναύκραρος, -ου ὁ: the chief official of a division

ναυκρατής, -ές: ruling the sea

ναυμαχέω: battle on the sea

ναυμαχία, -ας ἡ: a sea battle

ναυπηγήσιμος, -η, -ον: useful in shipbuilding

νεηνίσκος = νεανίσκος, -ου ὁ: a youth

νεκρός, -οῦ ὁ: a corpse

νεκυομαντήιον, -ου τό: an oracle

νέμω, νεμέω, ἔνειμα, νενέμηκα, νενέμημαι, ἐνημήθην: deal out, distribute; inhabit; pasture; graze; manage, control; spread

νεόκτιστος, -η, -ον: newly built

νεοχμόω: make new; innovate politically

Νέστωρ, -ορος ὁ: Nestor, king of Pylos

νεώτερος, -α, -ον: younger, earlier, newer (implying a revolt); (n.) stranger

Νηλεῖδαι, -ῶν οἱ: Neleidai, of the house of Neleus, born from Neleus

νηός = ναός

νήπιος, -η, -ον: infant, child

νησιώτης, -ου (-εω) ὁ: an islander

νηυσιπέρητος, -ον: crossed by ship

νόθος, -η, -ον: bastard, base-born

νοσέω, νοσήσω, ἐνόσησα, νενόσηκα, ——, ——: be sick, ail

νοστέω, νοστήσω, ἐνόστησα, ——, ——, ——: go home, return

νῶτον, -ου τό: a back

ξεινία = ξενία

ξεινία, -ας ἡ: guest friendship

ξεινίζω, ξενίσω, ἐξένισα, ——, ——, ἐξενίσθην: host, entertain

ξεινίζω = ξενίζω

ξεινικός, -ή, -όν: of a foreigner, stranger

ξείνιος = ξένιος

ξείνιος, -α, -ον: hospitable; of or pertaining to hospitality

ξεῖνος = ξένος

ξενία, -ας ἡ: guest friendship

ξένιος, -α, -ον: hospitable; of or pertaining to hospitality

ξηρός, -ά, -όν: dry

ξύλον, -ου τό: wood, log, beam, post; bench, table

ξυρέω (ξυράω), ξυρήσω, ἐξύρησα, ——, ἐξύρημαι, ἐξυρήθην: (also άω): shave; shave + double acc.: ξυρεῖν αὐτὸν τὰς τρίχας: to shave his hair

Ὀδομάντοι, -ων οἱ: Odomantoi, a tribe from Paionia, a region of Thrake

ὅθεν: from where; whence; where

Οἴα, -ας ἡ: Oia, a Greek city of Aigina

οἷα: seeing that, because

Οἰδίπους, -εω ὁ: Oedipus, son of Laios and king of Thebes

οἴεος, -α, -ον: of a sheep's skin

οἴκατε = ἐοίκατε < ἔοικα

οἰκεῖος, -α, -ον: belonging to the house

οἰκήιος, -α, -ον = οἰκεῖος, -α, -ον

οἰκήιος, -α, -ον: belonging to the house

οἰκηιότατος, -η, -ον: most domestic; belonging most to the house; most
    of all one's own

οἴκημα, -ατος τό: a dwelling place

οἰκίζω, οἰκιέω, ᾤκισα, ᾤκικα, ᾤκισμαι, ᾠκίσθην: found as a colony

οἰκίον, ου τό: a house, palace

οἰκοδομέω: build, construct

οἰκό- = ἐοικό- < ἔοικα

οἰκοφθορέω: squander one's substance

οἶκτος, -ου ὁ: pity, compassion

Οἰνόη, -ης ἡ: Oinoë, a deme on the border of Attika

οἰνόω, οἰνώσω, ——, ——, ᾤνωμαι, ᾠνώθην: intoxicate

ὀϊστός = οἰστός, -οῦ ὁ: an arrow

οἴχομαι, οἰχήσομαι, ——, οἴχωκα or ᾤχηκα, ᾤχημαι or οἴχημαι,
    ——: go, be gone, have gone

οἰχώκεε < οἴχομαι

ὀκόσος = ὁπόσος

ὀκτακισχιλίος, -α, -ον: eight thousand

ὀκτώ: eight

ὄλβιος, -α, -ον: happy, blest

Ὀλίατος, -ου ὁ: Oliatos, son of Ibanollis and tyrant of Mylasa c. 500
    B.C.E.

ὀλιγαρχία, -ας ἡ: an oligarchy

ὀλοοίτροχος, -ου ὁ: a rolling stone, round rock, millstone

ὀλοφύρομαι, ὀλοφυρέομαι, ὠλοφυράμην, ——, ——, ὠλοφύρθην:
    lament, wail; pity "x" in acc. for "y" in the accusative

Ὀλυμπία, -ας ἡ: Olympia, Greek city in the Peloponnesos

Ὀλυμπιονίκης, -ου (-εω) ὁ: a victor in the Olympic games

ὁμαίμων, -οντος ὁ: of the same blood

Ὁμήρειος, -ον: Homeric

ὁμιλέω, ὁμιλήσω, ὡμίλησα, ——, ——, ——: (+ dat.) be in company
   with, consort with; join battle with; be friends with; address, speak
   to; visit

ὅμιλος, -ου ὁ: a crowd, throng

ὄμνυμι, ὀμέομαι, ὤμοσα, ὀμώμοκα, ὀμώμομαι or ὀμώμοσμαι,
   ὠμόθην or ὠμόσθην: swear

ὁμοπάτριος, -α, -ον: of the same father

ὁμοῦ: together; along with; near by + dat.

ὁμώνυμος, -ον: having the same name

Ὀνεᾶται, -ῶν οἱ: Oneatai, Asses

ὄνειδος, -ους (-εος) τό: a report; reproach, rebuke, censure, blame

ὀνειρόπολος, -ου ὁ: a dream interpreter

Ὀνήσιλος, -ου ὁ: Onesilos, brother of Gorgos, king of Salamis c. 500
   B.C.E.

ὀνομαστί: by name

ὀνομαστός, -ή, -όν: named; be named

ὄνος, -ου ὁ or ἡ: an ass

ὀξύτατος, -η, -ον: most swift, sharp

ὀπάων, -ονος ὁ: companion, comrade

ὀπέων = ὀπάων

ὄπισθε: after, behind

ὀπίσω: back, behind

Ὅπλης, Ὅπλητος ὁ: Hoples, one of the sons of Ion, founder of the
   Ionians

ὁπλίτης, -ου (-εω) ὁ: hoplite

ὁποδαπός, -ή, -όν: of what country, what countryman

ὁπόσος, -η, -ον: as many, as many as; how many

ὁπότερος, -α, -ον: which

ὀπώπεε < ὁράω

Ὄρβηλος, -ου ὁ: Orbelos Mountain

ὄργια, -ίων τά: secret rites

ὀρέοντες = ὀράοντες < ὀράω

ὀρέω = ὀράω

ὀρέων = ὀράων

ὀρμέαται = ὥρμηνται < ὀρμάω

ὅρος, -ου ὁ: a boundary

ὀροφή, -ῆς ἡ: roof of a house

ὀρρωδέω: dread, fear, shrink from, shudder at + gen. or acc.

ὀρτή = ἑορτή

ὀρτή, -ῆς ἡ: a festival

ὄρυγμα, -ατος τό: a pit, ditch

Ὀτάνης, -ου (-εω) ὁ: Otanes, Persian nobleman and leader of the
    conspirators

οὐδαμά: never, in no way

οὐδαμός, -ή, -όν: not any one, no one; οὐδαμῇ: nowhere

οὐδαμοῦ: nowhere, in no way

οὐδαμῶς: in no way, never

οὐδέτερος, -α, -ον: neither of two, none

οὔνομα = ὄνομα

οὔπω: not yet

οὖρον, -ου τό: a boundary

οὖρος = ὅρος

οὖρος, -ου ὁ: a boundary

οὔτις, οὔτι: no one

ὀφείλω, ὀφειλήσω, ὠφείλησα or ὤφελον, ὠφείληκα, ——,
    ὠφειλήθην: owe, be in debt

ὄφελος, -ου ὁ: help, profit

ὀφρυόεις, -εσσα, -εν: on the brow or edge of a rock; towering

ὄχημα, -ατος τό: a cart, wagon; ship

ὀχλέω, ὀχλήσω, ὤχλησα, ——, ——, ὠχλήθην: disturb, trouble

ὄψις, -εως (-ιος) ἡ: a sight, appearance, vision

Πάγγαιον, -ου τό: Pangaion Mountain in Makedonia

πάγχυ: quite, wholly, entirely, altogether

παθόντας < πάσχω

παιδίον, -ου τό: a child

παίζω, παίξομαι or παιξέομαι, ἔπαισα or πέπαικα, πέπαισμαι or
  πέπαιγμαι, ἐπαίχθην: play, sport, dance
Παίονες, -ων οἱ: Paionians, of or from Paionia, a region of Thrake
Παιονία, -ας ἡ: Paionia, a region of Thrake
Παιόπλαι, -ῶν οἱ: Paioplai, a people of Paionia on the Strymon River
Παισός, -οῦ ἡ: Paisos, a city of Mysia on the Hellespont
παίω, παίσω or παιήσω, ἔπαισα, πέπαικα, πέπληγμαι or πέπαισμαι,
  ἐπλήγην or ἐπαίσθην: strike, smite, drive away
παιωνίζω, παιωνίσω, ἐπαιώνισα, ——, πεπαιώνισμαι, ——: chant
  the paean
Πακτωλός, -οῦ ὁ: Paktolos, a small river of Lydia
πάλαι: long ago
παλλακή, -ῆς ἡ: a concubine
Παλλάς, -άδος ἡ: Athene (Pallas Athene)
Παμφύλοι, -ων οἱ: Pamphyloi, a tribe of the Sikyonians
Παναθήναια, -ων τά: the Panathenaia, festivals in honor of Athene
πανδαισία, -ας ἡ: a complete banquet at which no one and nothing fails
πανταχῇ: everywhere
παντελέως: completely, absolutely
πάντοθεν: from all quarters, from every side
παντοῖος, -η, -ον: of all sorts, manifold; take all shapes, i.e., try every
  expedient
πάπραξ, -ακος ὁ: paprax, a type of fish
παραγίγμομαι: be present at
παραγορέω: address, exhort
παράγω: lead by
παράδειγμα, -ατος τό: a pattern, model, example
παραθαλάσσιος, -α, -ον (-ος, -ον): by the sea; coastal
Παραιβάτης, -ου (-εω) ὁ: Paraibates, a Spartan c. 520 B.C.E.
παραίνεσις, -εως (-ιος) ἡ: advice, counsel
παραινέω: exhort, recommend, advise
παραιτέομαι: obtain by prayer; entreat
παρακαταθήκη, -ης ἡ: a deposit, trust
παραλαμβάνω: take; receive; receive "x" in acc. from "y" in gen.

παραλία, -ας ἡ: a seacoast

παραλύω: loose and take off, detach; release from

παραμείβω: alter; excel; pass by

παράπας, -πασα, -παν: altogether, absolutely

παραπλήξ, -ῆγος ὁ or ἡ: struck sideways; mad; (n.) a beach struck sideways by waves

παραπλήσιος, -α, -ον: resembling, similar, same

παραπρήσσω: do, do in addition

παρασάγγης, -ου (-εω) ὁ: parasang (unit of measure = 30 stadia)

παρασκευή, -ῆς ἡ: a preparation, apparatus, equipment

παράσχοι < παρέχω

παραχράομαι: abuse, misuse, disregard, slight; act wrongly

πάρεδρος, -ον: sitting beside

πάρειμι: be present, be beside

παρελθόντες < παρέρχομαι

παρέξ: outside + gen; beyond + acc.

παρέξειμι: go out, pass, overstep, transgress

παρεξήιε = παρεξήει < παρέξειμι

παρεόντα = παρόντα < πάρειμι

παρεόντων = παρόντων < πάρειμι

παρέρχομαι: go beside, go past

παρεσομένου < πάρειμι

παρεών = παρών < πάρειμι

παρῆν < πάρειμι

παρῆσαν < πάρειμι

παρθένος, -ου ἡ: a maiden, girl

παριέναι < πάρειμι

παρίζω: sit, sit beside

Πάριος, -α, -ον: Parian, of or from Paros, a Greek isle in the central Aegean

παρίστημι: place beside; set beside; dispose; cause to stand aside, depose; bring over by force, bring to terms; (intrans.) come to terms, submit

Πάρος, -ου ἡ: Paros, a Greek island

Παυσανίης, (-εω) -ου ὁ: Pausaniës (Pausanias), a Spartan παχύς, -εῖα, -ύ: thick, stout, wealthy

πέδη, -ης ἡ: a fetter

Πειθαγόρης, -ου (-εω) ὁ: Peithagores (Peithagoras) tyrant of Selinous of Sikelia

πειθαρχέω: obey one in authority

Πειρήνη, -ης ἡ: Peirene, a fountain or spring in Korinth

πείσεσθαι < πάσχω

Πεισιστρατίδαι, -ῶν οἱ: followers of Peisistratos

Πεισίστρατος, -ου ὁ: Peisistratos (Pisistratos), tyrant of Athens

Πελασγικός, -ή, -όν: Pelasgian, an indigenous inhabitant of Greece

Πελασγός, -οῦ ὁ: a Pelasgian, an indigenous inhabitant of Greece

Πελοποννήσιος, -α, -ον: Peloponnesian, of or from the southern part of Greece

Πελοπόννησος, -ου ἡ: Peloponnesos, the southern part of Greece

πέμπτος, -η, -ον: fifth

πεντακόσιοι, -αι, -α: five hundred

πέντε: (indecl.) five

πεντεκαίδεκα: fifteen

πεντήκοντα: fifty

περαιόω, περαιώσω, ἐπεραίωσα, ——, πεπεραίωμαι, ἐπεραιώθην: convey, carry, cross

περαιωθείς < περαιόω

Περδίκκης, -ου (-εω) ὁ: Perdikkes, king of Makedon c. 680 B.C.E.

πέρην: beyond, on the other side, across

Περίανδρος, -ου ὁ: Periandros (Periander), second tyrant of Korinth, considered one of the seven sages of Greece c. 625–585 B.C.E.

περιβάλλω: throw around; throw "x" in acc. around "y" in dat.

περιγίγνομαι: be over or superior; survive + gen.

περιδεής, -ές: very timid

περίειμι: be around, exist, survive

περίειμι: go around

περιεοῦσαι = περιοῦσαι < περίειμι

περιεοῦσι = περιοῦσι < περίειμι

περιέπω: treat, handle; tend, take care of

περιέσχατα, -ων τά: extremities, edges

περιεφθέντων < περιέπω

περιέχω: hold around, embrace; hold on to + gen.

περιεών = περιών < περίειμι

περιίζομαι: sit round

περιιόντος < περίειμι

περικάθημαι: sit round, beseige

περικαλλής, -ές: very beautiful

περικατήμενος = περικάθημαι

περιλαμβάνω: embrace, grasp

Περινθίος, -α, -ον: a Perinithian, of or from Perinthos on the north
    coast of the Propontis

Πέρινθος, -ου ἡ: Perinthos, a city on the north coast of the Propontis
    and a colony of the Samians

πέριξ: round, round about + gen. or acc.; (adv) accordingly

περίοδος, -ου ἡ: a going round; a patrol

περιοικέω: dwell around

περίοικος, -ον: dwelling around

περιοπτέος, -α, -ον: must be overlooked

περιπεφλευσμένων < περιφλεύω

περιπλέω: sail around

περιυβρίζω: insult wantonly

περιφλεύω: scorch, singe

περιχαρής, -ές: exceedingly glad

Περκώτη, -ης ἡ: Perkote, a town of Mysia on the Hellespont

περόνη, -ης ἡ: a pin

Περσικός, -ή, -όν: Persian

πεσ- < πίπτω

πέτρα, -ας ἡ: a rock

Πέτρα, -ας ἡ: Petra, a town of Boiotia

πεφραγμένους < φράσσω

πῃ: someway, somehow

πήγνυμι, πήξω, ἔπηξα, πέπηχα or πέπηγα, πέπηγμαι, ἐπήχθην,
    ἐπάγην: stick, fix in

Πηδάσος, -ου ὁ: Pedasos, a town of Karia

Πίγρης, -εως ὁ: Pigres from Paionia

πιέζω, πιέσω, ἐπίεσα or ἐπίεξα, πεπίεκα, πεπίεσμαι, ἐπιέσθην or
ἐπιέχθην: press, squeeze, weigh down

πίναξ, -ακος ὁ: a board, plank

Πιξωδάρος, -ου ὁ: Pixodaros, a Karian from Kindya c. 490 B.C.E.

πιστός, -ή, -όν: trusty, trustworthy + dat.

πίσυνος, -ον: trusting on, relying on

πλατάνιστος, -ου ἡ: a plane tree

πλεῖστος, -η, -ον: most

πλέον = πλεῖον

πλεόνως: too much

πλέος, -α, -ον: full

πλεῦνας = πλείονας < πλείων, πλεῖον

πλεῦνες = πλείονες < πλείων, πλεῖον

πλήρης, -ες: full of + gen.

πλήσσω, πλήξω, ἔπληξα, πέπληγα, πέπληγμαι, ἐπλήγην or
ἐπλάγην: strike, smite; confound, stun

πλέω (πλώω), πλεύσομαι or πλευσέομαι, ἔπλευσα, πέπλευκα,
πέπλευσται, ἐπλεύσθη: sail

πλίνθινος, -η, -ον: made of brick

πλοῖον, -ου τό: a ship

πλοῦτος, -ου ὁ: wealth

πλώσαντα < πλέω

ποιευ- = ποιου- < ποιέω

ποιεύμενοι = ποιούμενοι

ποικίλος, -η, -ον: many colored

πολεμιστήριος, -α, -ον: of or for a warrior

Πολιάς, -άδος ἡ: Athene Polias

πολίζω, πολίσω, ἐπόλισα, ——, πεπόλισμαι, ——: settle, build, found

πολιορκευμένας = πολιορκουμένας

πολιορκέω, πολιορκήσω, ἐπολιόρκησα, πεπολιόρκηκα,
πεπολιόρκημαι, ἐπελιορκήθην: besiege

πολιορκία, -ας ἡ: a seige

πολίων = πόλεων

πολλαπλήσιος, -α, -ον: many times as many; many times more

πολλόν = πολύν or πολύ

πολλός = πολύς

πολυαργυρώτατος, -η, -ον: very rich in silver

Πόλυβος, -ου ὁ: Polybus, king of Sikyon

Πολυδώρος, -ου ὁ: Polydorus, king of Thebes and father of Labdakos

πολυκαρπότατος, -η, -ον: very rich in fruit

πολυπρόβατος, -η, -ον: rich in sheep or cattle

πολύτιτος, -ον: worthy of high honor

πολύφημος, -ον: abounding in songs

πομπή, -ῆς ἡ: a sending; procession

πορθέω, πορθήσω, ἐπόρθησα, ——, πεπόρθημαι, ——: destroy, plunder

πόσις, -εως (-ιος) ἡ: a drinking, drink

ποτόν, -οῦ τό: a drink

που: anywhere, somewhere, I suppose

ποῦ: where

Πρασιάδα, -άδος ἡ: Prasiad Lake

πρεσβεύω, πρεσβεύσω, ἐπρέσβευσα, πεπρέσβευκα, πεπρέσβευμαι, ——: be the elder

πρεσβύτατος, -η, -ον: eldest, honored

πρεσβύτερος, -α, -ον: older

προακούω: hear beforehand

Πρινητάδης, -ου (-εω) ὁ: Prinetades, a Spartan c. 540 B.C.E.

προακηκοόσι < προακούω

προάστειον, -ου τό: the space immediately in front of

προβαίνω: go on, advance

προδιδοῖ = προδίδωσιν < προδίδωμι

προδίδωμι: give beforehand; pay in advance; betray, forsake, abandon, desert; surrender, give up

προέστατε < προίστημι

προθυμέομαι: be willing, eager

προθυμία, -ας ἡ: an eagerness

πρόθυμος, -ον: ready, willing, eager

προθύμως: eagerly, earnestly

προίστημι: set before; honor; stand in front of; be in charge of + gen.

προκαθίζω: sit before

προκατίζω = προκαθίζω

πρόκειμαι: be set before one

προκλαίω: weep beforehand

προκλαύσαντες < προκλαίω

πρόκλησις, -εως (-ιος) ἡ: a calling forth, challenge

προοράω: see before, look forward to; look out for + gen.

προοφείλω: owe beforehand

προπλώω = προπλέω: sail before

Προποντίς, -ίδος ἡ: Propontis, a sea connecting the Aegean and the Black sea

προπύλαιος, -α, -ον: before the gate

προπυνθάνομαι: learn by inquiring before, hear beforehand

προσαγορεύω: address, greet

προσαναισιμόομαι: be spent besides

προσγελάω: gladden

προσγίγνομαι: come or go to; attack; be added + dat.

προσδέκομαι = προσδέχομαι

προσδέκομαι: receive favorably, accept

προσδέομαι: want, need; beg, ask; ask "x" in gen. for "y" in gen.

προσδέχομαι: receive favorably, accept

προσδόκιμος, -ον: expected, looked for

προσενειχθῇ < προσφέρω

προσεπιλαμβάνομαι: take part with + gen.

προσερέων (fut.) < προσαγορεύω

προσέρχομαι: come

προσεταιρίζομαι: take as a friend

προσεχής, -ές: next to

προσέχω: hold to, offer; hold against; bring a ship to port, put into port; devote oneself to + dat.; have in addition

πρόσθε: before, prior

προσίστημι: set against, stand by

προσκάθημαι: be seated, sit, besiege

προσκάτημαι = προσκάθημαι

προσκτάομαι: gain; get

προσλογίζομαι: reckon; count also

προσμένω: bide, wait

προσμίγνυμι: meet with; go against

προσουδίζω: dash against

πρόσουρος, -ον: adjoining, bordering

προσποιέω: make over to, add

προσπταίω: strike against; fail

προσσχών < προσέχω

προστάσσω: place; prescribe, command

προστάτης, -ου (-εω) ὁ: one who stands before, front-rank man

προστίθημι: put to, add to; place beside; hand over, deliver; impose on; add; side with, agree + dat.

προσφερέστερος, -α, -ον: closer, nearer

προσφέρω: bring, bring to, apply to; offer, propose; contribute, pay; resemble + acc. of resp.; (pass.) attack, assualt; approach

πρόσχημα, -ατος τό: that which is held before; ornament; outward appearance; costume, uniform

προσχρηίζω: require; desire (+ gen.), προσχρήζω σου ἐλθεῖν: I desire you to come

προσχωρέω: go to; surrender; concur

πρόσω: forward, onward, further + gen.

προσωτέρω: beyond, further

προτείνω: stretch, stretch forth, extend

προτιθεῖσι = προτιθέασι < προτίθημι

προτίθημι: place before; set before; display; offer

πρόφαντος, -ον: appearing at a distance; foreshown

πρόφασις, -εως (-ιος) ἡ: a pretext, excuse, cause, reason; (acc.) as pretext

προφέρω: bring forth; produce; propose, surpass + gen.

προχωρέω: go forward, advance, come forth; go well, succeed

πρυτανεῖον, -ου τό: the magistrates' hall, town hall

πρυτανηίον, -ου τό: the magistrates' hall, town hall

πρύτανις, -εως (-ιος) ὁ: ruler, lord

πυγμαχέω: practise boxing, be a boxer

Πυθαγόρης, -ου (-εω) ὁ: Pythagores, a citizen of Miletos c. 500 B.C.E.

πυθέσθαι < πυνθάνομαι

Πυθία, -ας ἡ: Pythia, the priestess of Apollo at Delphi

πύλη, -ης ἡ: a gate

Πύλιοι, -ων οἱ: Pylians

πω: up to this time, yet

πωλεῦσι = πωλοῦσι < πωλέω

πωλέω, πωλήσω, ἐπώλησα, ——, ——, ἐπωλήθην: sell

πώρινος, -η, -ον: made of tufa or porous limestone

ῥαψῳδός, -οῦ ὁ: a reciter of epic poems

ῥέω, ῥυήσομαι or ῥεύσομαι, ——, ἐρρύηκα, ——, ἐρρύην: flow

ῥήγνῡμι, ῥήξω, ἔρρηξα, ἔρρωγα, ἔρρηγμαι, ἐρρήχθην or ἐρράγην:
    break asunder, rend, shatter

ῥήξας < ῥήγνυμι

ῥητός, -ή, -όν: said, spoken; settled

ῥῑγέω, ῥῑγήσω, ἐρρίγησα, ἔρρῑγα, ——, ——: shudder

ῥίπτω, ῥίψω, ἔρριψα, ἔρριφα, ἔρριμμαι, ἐρρίφθην or ἐρρίφην:
    throw, cast, hurl

ῥυθμός, -οῦ ὁ: rhythm; form, shape

ῥύομαι, ῥύσομαι, ἐρρυσάμην, ——, ——, ——: draw to oneself, save;
    αὐτὸν θανεῖν ῥύομαι: I save him from dying

Σαλαμίνιος, -α, -ον: Salaminian, of or from Salamis, a city on Kypros

Σαλαμίς, -ῖνος ἡ: Salamis, a city of Kypros

Σάμιοι, -ων οἱ: Samians

Σάμος, -ου ἡ: Samos, a Greek island

Σάρδεις, -εων (-ιων) αἱ (Σάρδις (acc.)): Sardis, capital of Lydia and
    principal city of Persia, located near the coast of Asia Minor

Σαρδώ, -όος ἡ (acc. Σαρδώ): Sardo, Sardinia, an island off the coast of
    Italy

σάττω, σάξω, ἔσαξα, ——, σέσαγμαι, ἐσάχθην: fill quite full, pack,
    stuff; load with armor; (mid.) strengthen

σαυτός, -ή, -όν: yourself

σβέννυμι, σβέσω, ἔσβεσα, ἔσβηκα, ἔσβεσμαι, ἐσβέσθην: quench,
  put out

σέβομαι, σεβήσομαι, ——, ——, ——, ἐσέφθην: feel awe or fear; feel
  shame; be afraid; worship, honor

σεισμός, -οῦ ὁ: a shaking, shock

Σελινοῦς, -οῦντος ἡ: Selinous, a Greek colony on the southwest coast
  of Sikelia

Σελινούσιοι, -ων οἱ: Selinousioi, of or from Selinous, a Greek colony on
  the southwest coast of Sikelia

σεωυτός = σαυτός

σεωυτοῦ = σαυτοῦ < σαυτός, -ή, -όν

σημαίνω, σημανέω, ἐσήμηνα, σεσήμαγκα, σεσήμασμαι,
  ἐσημάνθην: point out, show, give a signal

σημανέω = σημαίνω

σημανέω: point out, show, give a signal

σημῆναι < σημαίνω

σιγάω, σιγήσομαι, ἐσίγησα, σεσίγηκα, σεσίγημαι, ἐσιγήθην: be
  silent

Σίγειον, -ου τό: Sigeion, a Greek town

Σιγύνναι, -ῶν οἱ: the Sigynnai, a people dwelling to the north of the
  Danube

σιγύννης, -ου (-εω) ὁ: a spear; merchant; huckster

σιδήρεος, -α, -ον: of iron

Σικελία, -ας ἡ: Sikelia (Sicily), an island off the boot of Italy

Σικυών, -ῶνος ἡ: Sikyon, a city in the north of the Peloponnesos

Σικυωνίος, -α, -ον: Sikyonian, of or from Sikyon

σιμός, -ή, -όν: flat-nosed, steep

Σιμωνίδης, -ου (-εω) ὁ: Simonides, a Greek lyric poet from Keos

σινάμωρος, -ον: mischievous, hurtful; destroying + gen.

σίνομαι, σινήσομαι, ἐσινάμην, ——, ——, ——: hurt, harm, damage;
  plunder

Σιριοπαίονες, -ων οἱ: Siriopaionians, of or from Siris on the Strymon
  in Makedonia

Σίρωμος, -ου ὁ: Siromos, a Greek

Σισάμνης, -ου (-εω) ὁ: Sisamnes, father of Otanes and royal Persian
judge

Σισιμάκης, -ου (-εω) ὁ: Sisimakes, a Persian general

σῖτος, -ου ὁ (pl.: -α τά): grain, food

Σκαῖος, -ου ὁ: Skaios, boxer and son of Hippokoon

Σκάμανδρος, -ου ὁ: Skamandros River

σκεδάννυμι, σκεδάσω or σκεδάω, ἐσκέδασα, ——, ἐσκέδασμαι,
ἐσκεδάσθην: scatter, disperse

σκευάζω, σκευάσω, ἐσκεύασα, ἐσκεύακα, ἐσκεύασμαι,
ἐσκευάσθην: prepare, make ready

σκήπτω, σκήψω, ἔσκηψα, ἔσκηφα, ἔσκημμαι, ἐσκήφθην: prop,
stay; allege by way of excuse

σκῆψις, -εως (-ιος) ἡ: an excuse, pretext

σκοπιά, -ᾶς ἡ: a lookout place, watch

Σκύθης, -ου (-εω) ὁ: Skythian

Σκύλαξ, -ακος ὁ: Skylax, a naval captain

σμικρός = μικρός

σμικρός, -ή, -όν: small

Σολίοι, -ων οἱ: Solioi, inhabitants of Soloi, a town on Kypros

Σόλοι, -ων ἡ: Soloi, a town on Kypros

Σόλων, -ονος ὁ: Solon from Athens, a statesman, politician, and poet
known for his wisdom c. 638–558 B.C.E.

σόος, -η, -ον: safe; whole; unhurt

Σοῦσα, -ων τά: Sousa, a Persian city, north of the Persian Gulf

Σοῦσοι, -ων οἱ: Sousoi, of or from Sousa, a city north of the Persian
Gulf

σοφία, -ας ἡ: wisdom

σπαδίζω, σπαδίξω, ἐσπάδιξα, ——, ——, ——: draw off

σπάνιος, -α, -ον: rare, scarce, scanty

σπάνις, -εως (-ιος) ἡ: a scarcity, dearth, lack

Σπάρτη, -ης ἡ: Sparte (Sparta)

Σπαρτιήτης, -ου (-εω) ὁ: Spartan

Σπαρτιητικός, -ή, -όν: Spartan

σπάρτον, -ου τό: a rope, cable

σπείρω, σπερέω, ἔσπειρα, ἔσπαρκα, ἔσπαρμαι, ἐσπάρην: sow

σπέρχω, σπέρξομαι, ἐσπερξάμην, ——, ——, ἐσπέρχθην: set in rapid motion; to be hasty or hot

σπουδαῖος, -α, -ον: in haste, quick; serious, earnest; excellent

σπουδή, -ῆς ἡ: an eagerness, earnestness

σπυρίς, -ίδος ἡ: a large basket

σταθμός, -οῦ ὁ: a stable; post; balance

στασιάζω: rebel, revolt, quarrel

στάσις, -εως (-ιος) ἡ: a placing, setting; faction

στασιώτης, -ου (-εω) ὁ: a member of a party

σταυρός, -οῦ ὁ: a pale, stake, pole

στεινός, -ή, -όν: narrow, confined

στέλλω, στελέω, ἔστειλα, ἔσταλκα, ἔσταλμαι, ἐστάλην or ἐστάλθην: make ready; provide, equip; start, set forth

στερέω, στερήσω, ἐστέρησα, ἐστέρηκα, ἐστέρημαι, ἐστερήθην: deprive, rob

στεφανήφορος, -ον: wearing a crown

Στησήνωρ, -ορος ὁ: Stesenor, a tyrant of Kourion, an Argive settlement on Kypros c. 500 B.C.E.

στίβος, -ου ὁ: a trodden way, track, path

στίγμα, -ατος τό: prick, puncture, mark, spot

στίζω, στίξω, ἔστιξα, ——, ἔστιγμαι, ἐστίχθην: mark, tattoo

στόλος, -ου ὁ: an expedition; equipment

στόμα, -ατος τό: a mouth

στρατεία, -ας ἡ: an expedition, campaign

στρατηγέω, στρατηγήσω, ἐστρατήγησα, ἐστρατήγηκα, ἐστρατήγημαι, ἐστρατηγήθην: be general, command

στρατηγία, -ας ἡ: an office of general, command, generalship

στρατηίη = στρατεία

στρατηίη, -ας ἡ: an expedition, campaign

στρατηλατέω: lead an army into the field

στράτιος, -α, -ον: of an army

στρέφω, στρέψω, ἔστρεψα, ἔστροφα, ἔστραμμαι, ἐστρέφθην or ἐστράφην: twist, turn; turn about or aside

Στρυμών, -όνος ὁ: Strymon River in northern Greece

Σύβαρις, -εως (-ιος) ἡ: Sybaris, a Greek town in southern Italy noted for its luxury

Συβαρίτης, -ου (-εω) ὁ: a Sybarite, of or from Sybaris, a Greek town in southern Italy

Συβαριτικός, -ή, -όν: of or from Sybaris, a Greek town in southern Italy

συγγενής, -ές: related

συγγιγνώσκω: think with; agree with; yield; allow + dat.

συγκαλέω: call together

συγκαταθάπτω: bury along with

σύγκειμαι: lie together; agree; (impers.) it is agreed on

συγκίστης, -ου ὁ: a joint cofounder

Συεννέσις, -εως (-ιος) ὁ: Syennesis, king of Kilikia c. 510 B.C.E.

συλάω, συλήσω, ἐσύλησα, ——, σεσύλημαι, ἐσυλήθην: strip off, despoil, plunder

συλλαμβάνω: take, bring together; collect, arrest; understand; engage in + gen.

συλλέγω: gather, collect; call together

συλλογή, -ῆς ἡ: a gathering, collecting, meeting, conspiracy

συμβάλλω: throw together, dash together; attack + dat.

συμβόλαιον, -ου τό: a mark, sign, token

συμβολή, -ῆς ἡ: a coming together, meeting, joining

συμβουλεύω: plot, plan, advise

σύμβουλος, -ου ὁ: an adviser

συμμαχέω: be an ally, help, aid

συμμαχία, -ας ἡ: an alliance

συμμίγνυμι: mix, mingle

συμπέμπω: send together

συμπεσόντα < συμπίπτω

συμπίπτω: fall, fall with or together; (impers.) happen, come to pass

συμπλευσασέων < συμπλέω

συμπλέω: sail with

συμπράττω: do with; help, assist

συμφορέω: bring together, gather

συναινέω: consent; agree with + dat.; grant "x" in acc. to "y" in dat.

συναιρέω: take with; seize together; comprehend

συναλίζω: gather

συνάπας, -ασα, -αν: all, every; altogether

συναπίστασθαι = συναφίστασθαι < συναφίστημι

συναποθνῄσκω: die together with

συνάπτω: join together

συναφίστημι: draw into revolt together

συνδιαφέρω: bear along with one, wage along with

συνδιήνεικαν < συνδιαφέρω

συνέθεντο < συντίθημι

συνειδώς < σύνοιδα

συνεκπίπτω: fall out; run equal to

συνελεῖν < συναιρέω

συνελευθερόω: join in freeing

συνελθόντα < συνέρχομαι

συνελόντα < συναιρέω

συνέντες < συνίημι

συνεξάγω: lead out together

συνεξέρχομαι: come out together

συνέπαινος, -ον: assenting to, consenting to + dat.

συνεπιλαμβάνομαι: take part in; have a share in + gen.

συνέπομαι: follow, accompany + dat.

συνέρχομαι: come, go; come, go with or together

συνετετάρακτο < συνταράσσω

συνετός, -ή, -όν: intelligent

συνέχω: hold, keep together; constrain, engage

συνῆκαν < συνίημι

συνῆλθε < συνέρχομαι

συνηνείχθη < συμφέρω

συνθάπτω: bury together, join in burying

σύνθημα, -ατος τό: a thing put together; an agreement; signal

συνιείς < συνίημι

συνιέναι < συνίημι

συνίημι: send together; perceive; understand

σύνοιδα: know, understand

συνοίσεσθαι < συμφέρω

συντάμνω: cut, cut down

συνταράσσω: throw into confusion

συντίθημι: put or place together; contrive, devise; comprehend; (mid.) make an agreement with + dat.

σύντομος, -ον: cut short, abridged

συντυχία, -ας ἡ: an incident; good fortune; bad fortune

συνυφαίνω: weave together

συνχωρέω: go with, go along

συνῳδός, -όν: singing; according with, in harmony with

Σύριοι, -ων οἱ: Syrians, from Syria

συρρέω: flow together

σύρω, σῡρέω, ἔσῡρα, σέσῡρκα, σέσυρμαι, ἐσύρην: draw, drag along; sweep away

σύσσιτος, -ον: eating together

συστασιώτης, -ου (-εω) ὁ: a member of the same faction, partisan

συστρατεύω: join a campaign

συχνός, -ή, -όν: long, many

σφάζω, σφάξω, ἔσφαξα, ἔσφᾰκα, ἔσφαγμαι, ἐσφάγην or ἐσφάχθην: slay, cut the throat, slaughter

σφέτερος, -α, -ον: their, of them

σχεδία, -ας ἡ: a raft, float, craft, light bridge

σχεδόν: near, roughly speaking, about, almost

σχήσων < ἔχω

σχοινίον, -ου τό: a rope, cord

σχοῖνος, -ου ὁ: a rush, reed; cord

σχών < ἔχω

Σωκλέης, -έος ὁ: Soklees, Korinthian ambassador c. 500 B.C.E.

Σωσικλέης, -ους (-εος) ὁ: Sosiklees, Korinthian ambassador c. 500 B.C.E.

τάλαντον, -ου τό: a talent (unit of money)

Ταλαός, -οῦ ὁ: Talaos, king of Argos

ταμέσθαι < τέμνω

τάμνω = τέμνω

Ταναγραῖοι, -ων οἱ: Tanagraioi, inhabitants of Tanagra, a town of Boiotia

Ταναγρικός, -ή, -όν: from Tanagra, a town of Boiotia

τάξις, -εως (-ιος) ἡ: an arranging, arrangement

ταράσσω, ταράξω, ἐτάραξα, ——, τετάραγμαι, ἐταράχθην: stir trouble

τάσσω: order, appoint; arrange, set in order

τάττω (τάσσω), τάξω, ἔταξα, τέταχα, τέταγμαι, ἐτάχθην: order, appoint; arrange, set in order

ταύτῃ: there

ταφή, -ῆς ἡ: a burial, tomb

τάφος, -ου ὁ: a burial, tomb

ταχθέντες < τάσσω

τάχιστα: most swiftly

τάχος, -ους (-εος) τό: swiftness, speed

τεθνεῶτος < θνήσκω

τέθριππος, -ον: with four horses abreast

τείνω, τενέω, ἔτεινα, τέτακα, τέταμαι, ἐτάθην: stretch, extend

τειχέω, τειχήσω, ἐτείχησα, ——, ——, ——: build a wall; construct

τειχίζω, τειχίσω τειχιέω, ἐτείχισα, τετείχικα, τετείχισμαι, ἐτειχίσθην: build a wall

τεκνοποιός, -όν: child producing

τεκούσῃ < τίκτω

τέλειος (τέλεος), -α, -ον: perfect

τελευταῖος, -α, -ον: last

τελέω, τελέω or **τελέσω, ἐτέλεσα, τετέλεκα, τετέλεσμαι, ἐτελέσθην:** accomplish, complete

τέλλω, τελέω, ἔτειλα, τέταλκα, τέταλμαι, ἐτάλθην: accomplish, arise

τέμενος, -ου τό: a holy parcel of land

Τερμερής, -οῦς (-έος) ὁ: of Termera, on the west coast of Asia Minor

τεσσαράκοντα: forty

τέσσερες: four

τέταρτος, -η, -ον: fourth

τετρακισχίλιοι, -αι, -α: four-thousand

τετρακόσιοι, -αι, -α: four hundred

τετραμμένου < τρέπω

τετράφυλος, -ον: divided into four tribes

Τευκροί, -ῶν οἱ: Teukrians, inhabiting the Troad of Asia Minor

τεῳ = τῳ < τις, τι

τέως: so long, in the meantime

τῇ: where

Τηλεβόαι, -ῶν οἱ: Teleboaai, a tribe from Akarnania in west central
  Greece

Τῆλυς, -υος ὁ: Telys, tyrant of Sybaris

Τίγρης, -ου (-εω) ὁ: Tigris River

τιθεῖσι = τιθέασι < τίθημι

τίλων, -ωνος ὁ: a tilon, a type of fish

Τιμησίθεος, -ου ὁ: Timesitheos, a Delphian, known for his prowess in
  the arena and on the battlefield c. 500 B.C.E.

τιμιώτατος, -η, -ον: most valued

τιμωρέω, τιμωρήσω, ἐτιμώρησα, ——, τετῑμώρημαι, ἐτῑμωρήθην:
  help, avenge + dat.; seek vengeance for "x" in dat. for "y" in gen.;
  avenge "x" in acc. for "y" in dat.; seek vengeance + dat.; punish "x" in
  dat. or acc. for "y" in gen.

τιμωρητήρ, -ῆρος ὁ: an avenger

τιμωρία, -ας ἡ: retribution, revenge

τίνυμαι: punish, chastise

τίνω, τείσω, ἔτεισα or ἔτισα, τέτεικα, τέτεισμαι, ἐτείσθην: pay a
  price or debt; pay a penalty; to get revenge for + gen.; punish, take
  retribution on "x" in acc. for "y" in gen.

τίσις, -εως (-ιος) ἡ: revenge, vengeance, punishment; payment

τλάω, τλήσομαι, ἔτλην or ἐτάλασα, τέτληκα, ——, ——: endure;
  dare

τίω, τίσω, ἔτισα, ——, τέτιμαι, ——: honor, revere

τλῆθι < τλάω

Τμῶλος, -ου ὁ: Tmolos, king of Lydia; mountain in Lydia; mountain god

τοιόσδε, τοιήδε, τοιόνδε: such as this

τόνος, -ου ὁ: a rope, chord; tone

τόξον, -ου τό: a bow

τόσος, -η, -ον: so much, so great; ἐκ τόσου: ever since that time

τραγικός, -ή, -όν: tragic

τράπεζα, -ης ἡ: a table

τράπω = τρέπω

τράπω (τρέπω), τρέψω, ἔτρεψα, τέτροφα, τέτραμμαι, ἐτράπην or
   ἐτρέφθην: turn, rout

Τραυσοί, -ῶν οἱ: Trausoi, a Thrakian people

τρέπω (τράπω), τρέψω, ἔτρεψα, τέτροφα, τέτραμμαι, ἐτράπην or
   ἐτρέφθην: turn, rout

τρηχέως: roughly, harshly

τριάκοντα: thirty

τριήκοντα = τριάκοντα

τριήκοντα: thirty

τριηκοσίοι, -αι, -α: three hundred

τριηκοστός, -ή, -όν: thirtieth

τριήρης, -ους (-εος) ἡ: a trireme

τριηρίτης, -ου (-εω) ὁ: one who goes in a trireme

τρίμηνος, -ον: of three months

τρίπους, -ποδος ὁ or ἡ: a tripod, three footed, three legged

τρίς: thrice, three times

τριφάσιος, -η, -ον: triple

τρίχας < θρίξ

Τροία, -ας ἡ: Troy

Τρωάς, -άδος ἡ: Trojan

τρῶμα = τραῦμα, -ατος τό: a wound

Τυδεύς, -έως (-εος) ὁ: Tydeus, Aeolian hero and one of the attackers in
   the seven against Thebes

Τύμνης, -ου (-εω) ὁ: Tymnes, father of Histiaios and from Termera, on
   the west coast of Asia Minor c. 530 B.C.E.

Τυνδαρίδης, -ου (-εω) ὁ: Tyndarides, son of Tyndareos, Spartan king
   and father of Kastor, Helen, Klytemnestra, and Polydeukes; (pl.) Kastor and Polydeukes, the Dioskouri

τυραννεύω, τυραννεύσω, ἐτυράννευσα, τετυράννευκα, ——,
  ἐτυραννεύθην: be tyrant, rule

τυραννίς, -ίδος ἡ: a tyranny

τυχεῖν < τυγχάνω

τὠυτό = τὸ αὐτό

Ὑᾶται, -ῶν οἱ: Hyatai, Swinites

ὕβρις, -εως (-ιος) ἡ: hubris

Ὑλλέαι, -ῶν οἱ: Hylleai, a name of one of the tribes of the Sikyonians

Ὑμαίης, -ου (-εω) ὁ: Hymaies, a Persian

ὑμνέαται = ὕμνηνται < ὑμνέω

ὑμνέω, ὑμνήσω, ὕμνησα, ὕμνηκα, ——, ——: sing of

ὑπαιρέονται = ὑφαιρέονται < ὑφαιρέω

ὑπαρπάζω = ὑφαρπάζω

ὕπαρχος, -ου ὁ: a lieutenant, commander under another

ὑπάρχω: begin; arise; be

ὑπασπιστής, -οῦ ὁ: a shield bearer

ὑπέγγυος, -ον: under surety, subject to penalty

ὑπείροχος, -ον: prominent, distinguished

ὑπεξέχω: withdraw

ὑπερβαίνω: go over, go beyond

ὑπερβάλλω: throw over; exceed, go beyond + dat. of resp.; ὑπερβαλεῖν
  τόλμῃ: to exceed in daring; πλήθεϊ ὑπερβαλλόμενος: with over-
  whelming force; put off, delay

ὑπερδειμαίνω: be afraid, fear, be really afraid

ὑπερέχω: hold over; (intrans.) be above

ὑπερθέντι < ὑπερτίθημι

ὑπερθέωμαι < ὑπερτίθημι

ὑπεριδών < ὑπεροράω

ὑπεροράω: look over; overlook, disregard; disdain + gen. or acc.

ὑπερτίθημι: put or set over; erect; commit, entrust, disclose; hand over,
  communicate

ὑπεστεῶτας = ὑφεστῶτας < ὑφίστημι

ὑπήκοος, -ον: hearkening, being obedient, subject to + gen.

ὑπηρέτης, -ου (-εω) ὁ: a rower

ὑπίστημι = ὑφίστημι

ὑπισχνέομαι: take on oneself, promise

ὑποβάλλω: throw, lay under; substitute

ὑποδέκομαι: receive under; harken; listen; admit, allow; promise

ὑποδέχομαι: receive under; harken; listen; admit, allow; promise

ὑποζύγιον, -ου τό: a beast for the yoke

ὑποθέμενος < ὑποτίθημι

ὑποθήκη, -ης ἡ: a suggestion, counsel, warning

ὑποκινέω: move, stir; move gently

ὑποκρίνομαι: reply, make answer, answer

ὑπόκρισις, εως (-ιος) ἡ: a reply, answer

ὑπολείπω: leave remaining

ὑπολειφθέντας < ὑπολείπω

ὑπολειφθέντες < ὑπολείπω

ὑπορύσσω: dig; dig under; undermine

ὑπόσπονδος, -ον: under a truce

ὑποστρέφω: turn round; turn and flee; elude

ὑπόσχεσις, -εως (-ιος) ἡ: an undertaking, engagement, promise

ὑποταμομένους < ὑποτέμνω: cut away under

ὑποτίθημι: place under; put under; propose, suggest

ὑποχείριος, -α, -ον (-ος, -ον): under the hand, in hand; subject to

ὗς, ὑός ἡ: a sow, pig

Ὑσιαί, -ῶν αἱ: Hysiai, a region on the border of Attika

Ὑστάσπης, -ους (-εος) ὁ: Hystaspes, a Persian and father of Artaphrenes and Darius 1 c. 580 B.C.E.

ὑφαιρέω: draw, take away from under

ὑφαρπάζω: snatch away from under

ὑφίστημι: place under

ὑψηλός, -ή, -όν: high, lofty

Φάληρον, -ου τό: Phaleron, a port of Attika

φάμενοι < φημί

φάς < φημί

φᾶσα < φημί

φασί < φημί

φατίζω, φατίσω or φατίξω, ἐφάτισα, ——, πεφάτισμαι, ἐφατίσθην: tell of, report; promise, betroth; name, call

φερέγγυος, -ον: giving surety, trusty, competent

φήμη, -ης ἡ: a report, rumor, prophecy

φθέγγομαι, φθέγξομαι, ἐφθεγξάμην, ——, ἔφθεγμαι, ——: utter a sound

φιλέω, φιλήσω, ἐφίλησα, πεφίληκα, πεφίλημαι, ἐφιλήθην: love, kiss

Φίλιππος, -ου ὁ: Philip, son of Butakides

Φιλοκύπρος, -ου ὁ: Philokypros, tyrant of the Soli c. 530 B.C.E.

φιλοφρόνως: kindly

φιλοφροσύνη, -ης ἡ: a friendliness, kindliness

Φοίνικες, -ων οἱ: Phoinikians, of or from Phoinikia, an area on the coast of the Mediterranean to the east of the island of Kypros

Φοινικήιος, -η, -ον: Phoinikian, of or from Phoinikia, an area on the coast of the Mediterranean to the east of the island of Kypros

Φοῖνιξ, Φοίνικος ὁ: Phoinikian, of Phoinikia, on the Mediterranean coast

φοιτάω, φοιτήσω, ἐφοίτησα, ——, ——, ——: go to and fro; roam; come; go

φονεύς, -έως (-έος) ὁ: a murderer

φονεύω, φονεύσω, ἐφόνευσα, ——, ——, ἐφονεύθην: murder

φόνος, -ου ὁ: murder, slaughter

φορέω, φορήσω, ἐφόρησα, ——, πεφόρημαι, ——: bear, carry

φόρος, -ου ὁ: tribute

φράσοντας < φράζω

φράσσω, φράξω, ἔφραξα, πέφρᾰκα or πέφρᾰγα, πέφραγμαι, ἐφράχθην or ἐφράγην: fence in; fortify

φρενήρης, -ες: of sound mind

φροντίζω, φροντιέω, ἐφρόντισα, πεφρόντικα, πεφρόντισμαι, ——: consider, reflect, take thought; take thought for, give heed to + gen.

Φρύγες, -ῶν οἱ: Phrygians, of or from Phrygia, a region in central Asia Minor

Φρυγία, -ας ἡ: Phrygia, in Asia Minor

φυγάς, -άδος ὁ or ἡ: an exile, deserter

φυγή, -ῆς ἡ: flight

φυλακή, -ῆς ἡ: a guard, watch, garrison

φυλακτήριον, -ου τό: a guardhouse, garrison, outpost

φύλαρχος, -ου ὁ: a chief

φυλή, -ῆς ἡ: a race, tribe

φωνή, -ῆς ἡ: a sound

χάλκεος, -α, -ον: of copper, bronze, brass

Χαλκιδέες, -έων οἱ: Khalkideans, of or from Khalkis, a town on Euboia

χαλκός, -οῦ ὁ: brass, copper, bronze

Χαροπῖνος, -ου ὁ: Kharopinos, a Milesian and brother of Aristagoras c. 500 B.C.E.

χειρόω, χειρώσω, ἐχείρωσα, ——, κεχείρωμαι, ——: handle, worst, master, subdue

Χέρσις, -εως (-ιος) ὁ: Khersis, a Greek and father of Onesilos c. 520 B.C.E.

χέω, χέω, ἔχεα, κέχυκα, κέχυμαι, ἐχύθην: pour

χίλιοι, -αι, -α: thousand

Χίος, -ου ἡ: Khios (Chios), a Greek island famous for its wine

Χοάσπης, -ου (-εω) ὁ: Khoaspes River, passes by Susa and flows into the Tigris

Χοιρεᾶται, -ῶν οἱ: Khoireatai, Porkies

χορηγός, -οῦ ὁ: a chorusleader

χορός, -οῦ ὁ: a dance; chorus

χόρτος, -ου ὁ: feeding place; fodder

χρεών (χρεόν), -οῦ τό: a necessity

χράω, χρήσω, ἔχρησα, κέχρηκα, κέχρησμαι, ἐχρήσθην: proclaim, announce; furnish, lend

χρήζω, χρήσω, ἔχρησα, ——, ——, ἐχρήσθην: desire, need, lack + gen.; desire, ask "x" in gen. or acc. + infinitive

χρησμός, -οῦ ὁ: an oracular response, oracle

χρηστηριάζω: give oracles, prophesy

χρηστήριον, -ου τό: an oracle

χρηστός, -ή, -όν: useful; good; favorable

χρήσω < χράω

χρυσός, -οῦ ὁ: gold

χυτρίς, -ίδος ἡ: a small pot

χωλός, -ή, -όν: lame, limping

χῶμα, -ατος τό: earth thrown up; a bank, mound; breakwater

χωρέω, χωρήσω, ἐχώρησα, κεχώρηκα, κεχώρημαι, ἐχωρήθην: make room, make room for + dat.; retire, withdraw; advance, proceed; κακῶς χωρεῖν: to turn out poorly

χωρίζω, χωριέω χωρίσω, ἐχώρισα, ——, κεχώρισμαι, ——: separate

χωρίς: apart from, separately + gen.

χῶρος, -ου ὁ: a place

ψαύω, ψαύσω, ἔψαυσα, ——, ἔψαυσμαι, ἐψαύσθην: touch + gen.

ψεύδω, ψεύσω, ἔψευσα, ——, ἔψευσμαι, ἐψεύσθην: cheat by lies, beguile; (pass.) be deceived or mistaken

ψῆγμα, -ατος τό: that which is rubbed, scrapings, chips

ψηφίζω, ψηφίσω or ψηφιέω, ἐψηφισάμην, ——, ἐψήφισμαι, ἐψηφίσθην: vote

ψῦχος, -ους (-εος) τό: cold, frigidity

ψυχρός, -ά, -όν: cold

ὠμηστής, -οῦ ὁ: eating raw flesh, savage, cruel, brutal

ὠνέομαι, ὠνήσομαι, ἐωνησάμην, ——, ἐώνημαι, ἐωνήθην: buy, purchase

ὠνήρ = ὁ ἀνήρ

ὥρα = ὥραε < ὁράω

ὥρα, -ας ἡ: a season, hour, time

ὥρων = ὥραον < ὁράω

ὥς: and so, thus, in this way

ὡυτός = ὁ αὐτός

ὠφέλεια, -ας ἡ: help, aid, succour; profit, advantage

∿ INDEX

Abydos, 145
Adrastos, 95–97
Adriatic, 41
Aegean, 86
Aeschylus, 10
Agamemnon, 96
Agrianai, 46–47
Aiakos, 108–9, 116–17
Aias, 95
Aigialeus, 97–98
Aigikores, 95
Aigina, 108–17
Aiolis, 101, 105, 128, 148–49
Akhaian, 90, 101, 105
Akhaimenid, 37, 58, 63, 84
Akheron, 126
Akhilleus, 39, 128–29
Alexandros, 37, 48, 50–54
Alkaios, 129
Alkmaion, 91
Alkmeonid, 90–92, 95, 99–101, 117–18
Alopekai, 92
Amathous, 135–36, 139, 144–45

ambiguity, oracle, 124
Amorges, 148
Amphiktyones, 90–91
Amphion, 121
Amphitryon, 89
Amyntes, 48–51, 128
Anaxandrides, 70–73, 93
Anaximander, 58
Anaximenes, 58
Andros, 62
Ankhimolios, 92
Antandros, 57
Antartica, 42
Anthemous, 128
Antikhares, 75, 195
Apollo, 89–90
Aramaic, 37
Ares, 40
Argades, 95
Argos, 53–54, 71, 80, 87, 90, 95–97, 113–16, 128, 143
Aristagores, 58, 60–70, 79–82, 85–86, 94, 119, 130–33, 135–36, 149–50

Aristogeiton, 86

Aristokypros, 143–44

Ariston, 103

Aristophanes, 103

Aristotle, 99, 107

Arkadian, 80

Arkhelaoi, 97

Armenia, 80, 83–84

Artaphrenes, 19, 56, 60–66, 102, 129–30, 133, 149

Artemis, 40

Artybios, 139–41, 143

Asia, 43, 46, 48, 60, 68, 80–81, 128–30, 147, 150

Asopos River, 107–8

Astakos, 96

Aster, 92

Astyages, 14

Athena, 87, 91, 105, 109–10

Athens and Athenians, 58, 76–78, 80, 86, 87, 90–119, 127–38, 143

audience, 40–41, 51, 54, 57, 61, 82, 84, 104, 145

Auge, 113

author, 68, 75

autopsy, 89

Auxie, 113

Babylonian, 37

backstory, 59–61, 67, 108, 130

Bakis, 74

Bakkhiadai, 121, 122, 124

bias, 54, 100

Boiotia, 87–90, 96, 103, 105–8, 116, 118–19

Boutakides, 78

Brankhidai, 68

Butkova, 46

Byzantion, 57, 135

Christians, 82

Colonus, 39

commentary, 73, 82

context, 54, 65, 75, 88, 94, 97, 101, 103

contrast, 52, 56, 87

counterfactual, 77, 79, 94, 121, 138

Croton, 33

custom, 37, 39–40, 43–50, 71–74, 103–4, 115–16, 120, 126–27, 131, 134

Damia, 109–10, 113

Dardanos, 145

Dareios, 35–37, 42–45, 48–49, 54–57, 60–61, 63, 67, 69, 84, 94, 102, 129, 131, 135–40, 145, 149

Daurises, 145–46, 148

Delphi, 73–75, 90–91, 95, 101, 109, 116–17, 119, 121, 124

Demaretos, 71, 103, 104

Demarmenos, 73

Deme, 98, 131

Demeter, 90

Diodorus, 111

Dionysos, 40, 96–97

Diyarbakır, 84

Doberians, 46–47

Doïran, 46

Dorian, 73–79, 96–101, 104–5, 110, 114–16

Dorieus, 71, 74–75, 79

Doriskos, 132

dream, 45, 49, 86–87, 90–91, 137

Dymnatai, 97

Dysoron Mountain, 48

earth and water, 48–49, 102

earthquakes, 112–14

Edonia, 32–33, 43, 149

Eetion, 121–24

Eetion, son of, 124

Egesta, 77–78
Ekhekrates, 121
Elea, 74–76
Eleusis, 71, 103–4
Elymi, 78
Enetoi, 41
Enkhelians, 90
Entella, 78
Ephesos, 85–86, 133–34
Epidauros, 109–11, 113
Erekhtheus, 109–10
Eretria, 87, 132–34
Ermos River, 134
Erukine, 76
Erxandros, 69
Eteokles, 90
ethnicities, 47, 95
Eualkides, 134–35
Euboia, 62–63, 105
Euelthon, 136
Euphrates, 83
Euripos Strait, 105
Europe, 35, 43
Euryleon, 77–78
Eurysthenes, 70
Eusebius, 111
expectation, 65, 71, 74, 115, 130
eye, 43–44, 50

focalization, 42, 119, 124
foreknowledge, 66

Geleon, 95
Gephyraians, 86–88, 90–91
Gergithai, 148–49
Getai, 37–38
Gorgo, 78, 82, 136, 144
Gygaia, 53
Gyges, 148

Gyndes River, 84

Halys River, 83, 134
Harmodios, 86
Hegesandros, 149
Hegesistratos, 128–29, 219
Hekataios, 67–69, 149–50
Helen, 128
Hellenodikai, 53
Heraion, 126
Herakleides, 69, 74–75, 148
Herakles, 54, 74–75, 92
Hermes, 40
Hermophantos, 133
Hipparkhos, 86–87, 90–91
Hippias, 86, 90–91, 118–20, 126–31
Hippokoon, 89
Hippokrates, 94
Histiaios, 42–44, 54–56, 60, 66–69, 137,
    139–40, 149
historicity, 36, 50, 74
Homer, 39, 70, 95, 129, 132
Hoples, 95
Hornblower, S., 50, 69, 71, 75, 81, 98, 108
hubris, 102–3, 105, 118
Hyatai, 97
Hylleai, 97
Hymaies, 145, 148–49
hyperbole, 131
hyperinflation, 15
Hysiai, 103
Hystaspes, 60–61, 102

Iamids, 75
Ibanollis, 69, 148
Idrias, 146
Ietragores, 69
Iliad (Homer), 106
Ilium, 33

Imbros, 57
India, 37
influence: divine, 35–36, 86–87, 114–15, 121–22; ghost, 126–27
inscription, 88
intentions, 63, 74, 124, 132, 138
intrusion, 37, 41–42, 51, 53, 61, 73, 79, 81–82, 88–89, 95–96, 98, 107
Iolkos, 128
Ionian revolt, 58, 62, 80, 94, 135–39
Isagores, 95, 99–100, 102–3
isegoria, 37, 106
Ismenian, 89
isokratia, 120
isonomia, 23, 69–70
Isthmian, 135
Istros River, 41–42
Italia, 74, 76

Kadmos, 87–90
Kaineus, child of, 121
Kalkhedon, 57
Kallies, 75–77
Kambyses, 37, 56
Kappadokia, 79, 83
Karia, 95, 115, 135, 141–48
Karkhedon, 32, 74, 77
Kastor, 104
Kaukasa, 64
Kaunos, 135
Kayster River, 133
Kelees, 77
Keos, 134
Khalkedon, 106
Khalkis, 103, 105–6, 118–19, 132
Kharopinos, 133
Khersis, 136, 143
Khios, 64–65, 132
Khoaspes River, 80, 84

Khoireatai, 97
Kilikia, 79–80, 83, 139, 146
Kindyes, 146
Kinees, 92
Kinyps River, 74
Kios, 148
Kissia, 80, 84
Klazomenai, 149
Kleides, 139
Kleisthenes, 95–102, 106
Kleombrotos, 63, 73
Kleomenes, 70–74, 78–85, 93, 99–104, 117–18, 130–31
Kodros, 94, 104
Koes, 43, 44, 69, 70
Kondaian, 92
Koresos, 133
Korinth, 101, 103–4, 110, 113–14, 120–28
Koroneia, residents of, 107
Kourion, 143
Krathis River, 76–77
Krestonian, 37–39
Kroisos, 68
Kroton, 75–78
Kybebe, 134
Kyklades, 60–62
Kylon, 91, 99–100
Kyme, 69–70, 149
Kynosarges, 92
Kypros, 41, 62, 80, 135–36, 139–45
Kypselos, 124–26, 129
Kyrenaians, 74, 78
Kyros, 37, 58, 84, 87, 109

Labda, 121–24
Labdakos, 89
Labraunda, 147
Laios, 74, 89
Lamponion, 57

Lampsakos, 145
Laodamas, 90
Lapith, 121
Leipsydrion, 90
Lemnos, 57, 64
Leon, 70
Leonidas, 73
Leros, 149–50
Lesbos, 57, 64, 132
Libya, 73–74
Ligues, 41
Lukania, 76
Lydia, 37, 43, 68, 79, 81, 83–84, 133–34
Lykaretos, 57–58
Lysagores, 60
Lysistrata (Aristophanes), 103

Maiandros River, 57, 146–47
Makeai, 74
Makedon, 48–53, 128
Mantyes, 43–44
Marsyas River, 146–47
Massalie, 41
Matiene, 80–81, 84
Mausolos, 146
Meandros, 58
Media, 37, 41, 105–6, 135–36, 140
Mediterranean, 87
medize, 102, 104, 108
Megabates, 63–67
Megabazos, 35–37, 42–48, 54–57, 131
Megakles, 91
Megara, 104–5
Mekisteus, 96–97
Melanippos, 96–97, 129
Melanthios, 130–31
Melanthos, 94
Melissa, 126–27
Memnon, 85

Menelaos, 128–29
Messenia, 80
Miletos, 42–43, 54–81, 85, 94, 125, 130–33,
    136–38, 147–50
Minoe, 77–78
Molpagores, 60
Mylasa, 69, 148
Myndos, 64
Myous, 68–69
Myrkinos, 43, 54–55, 149–50
Myrsos, 148
Mysia, 148
Mytilene, 43, 69–70, 128–29

Naxos, 58, 60–69, 89, 119
Neleidai, 94
Nemean, 135
Nestor, 91, 94
Nitetis, 151

Odomantoi, 46–47
Odyssey (Homer), 39
Oedipus at Colonus (Sophocles), 39
Oia, 110–11
Oidipous, 89
Oinoe, 103
Oliatos, 69
Olympia, 53, 100–101, 135
Oneatai, 97
Onesilos, 135–37, 139, 141, 143–45
oracle, 73–77, 91, 95, 107–8, 116–19, 121–22,
    124, 127, 134, 144
Orbelos, 47
Orthagoras, 96
Otanes, 56–58, 145, 149

paian, 36
Paionia, 35–36, 43–46, 48, 54, 90, 131–32
Paioplai, 46

Paisos, 145
Paktolos, 134
Pamphyloi, 97
Panathenaia, 86–87
Pangaion Mountain, 46–47
Paraibates, 77
Paros, 58–60, 62, 90–91, 145
Pausanias, 63, 101, 110, 113
Pedasos, 148
Peirene, 121
Peisistratids, 90–94, 99, 104, 106, 117–18, 127
Peisistratos, 86, 91, 94, 99–100, 118, 128
Peithagores, 77–78
Pelasgian, 57, 93
Peleus, 108
Peloponnesos, 74, 102–4, 119
Pelops, 100
Pentathlon, 87
Pentekontaetia, 119
Perdikkes, 53
Periandros, 125, 126, 129
Perinthos, 35–37
Perkote, 145
Persia, 35–37, 42–43, 46, 48–58, 61, 63–67, 69, 82, 87, 91, 102, 104, 106, 108, 128, 129–35, 139–41, 143–48
Petra, 121–22
Phaleron, 92, 108–9, 112
Philippos, 78
Philokypros, 143
Phoinikia, 74, 77–78, 87–88, 95, 139–40, 143
Phrygia, 79, 83, 131
Phrynikhos, 10, 58
Pigres, 43, 44
Pixodaros, 146
Plataia, 104
Plato, 107

Plutarch, 95, 100
Polias, 110
Pollux, 36
Polybius, 145
Polybos, 96
Polydeukes, 104
Polydoros, 89
Polykrates, 109
Prasiad Lake, 46, 48
Prinetades, 73
Propontis, 148
Pylian, 94
Pythagores, 150
Pythia, 71, 74, 91–92, 95, 107, 109, 117–18, 121, 135

royal road, 83–86

sacred precinct, 76, 96, 116–17
Salamis, 136, 139, 141, 143–44
Samos, 57, 64, 133, 143
Sardis, 54–56, 62, 85, 86, 101–2, 129, 133–39
Sardo, 138–39, 149
Selinous, 77
Sigeion, 93, 118, 128–30
Sigynnai, 41–42
Sikelia, 74–75, 77–78
Sikyon, 95–98
Simonides, 134
Siriopaionian, 46
Siromos, 136
Sisamnes, 56
Sisimakes, 148
Skaios, 89
Skamandros River, 93
Skylax, 64–65
Skythia, 55, 57, 71, 105
Soklees, 122–25, 127–28
Solioi, 141, 143

Soloi, 143–45
Solon, 100
Sophocles, 39
Sosiklees, 120
Sousa, 55–56, 60, 63, 66–67, 80, 84–85, 139
Sparta, 63, 70–74, 78–82, 85–86, 91–93, 96, 99–104, 117–20, 126–31
Spartiates, 71–73, 77, 81, 91–92, 103, 118
stasis, 58, 59, 95
Stesenor, 143
Strymon River, 35, 44–45, 54, 131
Sun Tzu, *Art of War*, 146
Sybaris, 75–78
Syennesis, 146
Syria, 79, 81

Talaos, 95
talent, 48, 80–82
Tanagra, 87, 107
tattoo, 40, 67
Teisandros, 95
Telamon, 108
Teleboaai, 89
Telys, 75, 78
Temenos, 54
Termera, 69
Teukrians, 44, 148–49
Thales, 58

Thebe, 89, 96, 106–9, 116
Thera, 73–74
Thespia, 107
Thesprotia, 126
Thessalia, 77, 92–93, 128
Thoukydides, 54, 63, 80, 91, 100, 107, 109, 119
Thrakia, 36–40, 42, 45–46, 54–55, 150
Thrasyboulos, 125, 126
thunder, 112–14
Tigris, 84
Timesitheos, 101
Tmolos, 133–34
Trausians, 37–38
Troad, 57, 148
Troy, 44, 96, 128, 148
Turkey, 84
Tydeus, 96–97
Tymnes, 69
Tyndareos, 104
Tyndarides, 103–4

White Pillars, 146

Xerxes, 63

Zeus, 77, 80, 95, 100, 136, 147